TREASURY
OF
PRESIDENTIAL
QUOTATIONS

TREASURY
OF
PRESIDENTIAL
QUOTATIONS

Compiled and edited by
CAROLINE THOMAS HARNSBERGER

FOLLETT PUBLISHING COMPANY
CHICAGO

*To those presidents
whose greatness has emerged
from the impartial pen
of history*

Preface

"There shall be a President," says the Constitution of the United States. Beyond that it prudently does not go, except to give the method of his election and to specify that he must be at least thirty-five years of age. The President, in the minds of the framers of the Constitution, was to be as Olympian as George Washington, as aloof, as majestic and as nonpolitical; that is, above parties and prejudices.

However, General Washington was followed in office by John Adams and Thomas Jefferson, both able and skilled but highly partisan men, and, later, by James Madison, James Monroe, John Quincy Adams, Martin Van Buren and Andrew Jackson—not one of whom could be a Washington but who could be, and were, excellent statesmen and political leaders. Vigorous action was required of them and bold maneuvering in the national arena to advance their programs. They had to speak out, sometimes to cry out, to exhort and to demand, to deliver addresses and pronouncements. And as the republic grew, the Presidents, from time to time, had to assume the different mantles that the Constitution had apportioned to the executive wardrobe, not the least of these that of the Commander-in-Chief. The clash of arms, the framing of treaties, and the acquisition of territories required new dimensions in the chiefs of this state.

With the quadriennial elections, political destiny conferred the nation's highest laurels upon men of very different stripes and of very different qualities. Always the Presidents appeared to reflect, in remarkable measure, the posture of this expanding nation with its flexing muscles and the deep conviction of its righteousness. A list of the Presidents will reveal, as could be expected, valleys as well as peaks in human stature. A few may not have been representative of the full intellectual, or even political, power of the country. But, in the main, the nation was unusually fortunate. For it had a Jefferson as well as a Jackson, a Lincoln as well as a Theodore Roosevelt, a Woodrow Wilson as well as a Franklin D. Roosevelt, a Harry S. Truman and a Dwight D. Eisenhower as well as a John Fitzgerald Kennedy. History quickly counts these blessings and passes over the lesser men; even the least of them left something of a heritage that cannot easily be forgotten.

As each President responded to the needs of his hour, he voiced his feelings, his requirements, even his demands upon party, legislature, industry, labor, commerce, and foreign neighbors. Some Presidents expressed very well personal articles of faith; some expounded wisely indeed on the issues of the day; others merely echoed the rhetoric of the hustings. A few went into even this office as into a hasty marriage, and departed as if relieved to be freed from the overpowering burdens. Some conducted themselves in the White House with such marked dedication and zeal that they re-shaped the office and broadened its influence—and thrilled the nation and caused the rest of the civilized world to take notice, in envy if not always in admiration, that the American Presidency had become the most powerful position of state on the globe.

Men have dreamed of reaching this high place as they secretly yearn for immortality. Many have striven boldly to attain it and some, once elected, have been able to move the whole country as if it were their own family. Some of the Presidents have written plainly enough in workaday prose, a few as if they have known that what they were saying would become imperishable. Whether before, during, or after, their tenures of office, the Presidents have spoken and written upon thousands of topics, often significantly and sometimes memorably, reflecting their convictions regarding the country, its people, its government and its ideals. Generally, the Presidential words, whether in speech or in state paper, in tabletalk or in correspondence, have borne the stamp of the man, thus providing not only an image of the individual personality but, *in toto,* a gallery of figures representative of the Republic since its birth 175 years ago.

Taking it all in all, history has been as kind to this nation as geography. To have so many great men in a list of only thirty-five! No dynasty of ancient, medieval, or even later times can boast as much. What the dynasts of earlier ages said has been largely forgotten; much of what these men said is still recalled and sometimes cited, especially because the late John Fitzgerald Kennedy,

with his remarkable sense of history, quoted liberally from his predecessors in office. Largely because of him the public has taken an
increasingly vital interest in the utterances of all the Chief Executives.

However, anyone who goes hunting for any random quotation will
find that the writings and speeches of the Presidents have become
so voluminous that the complete collected works can be found only
in the largest libraries. Even at the Library of Congress, where all
such documents are assembled, the quest for specific Presidential
quotations or for quotable statements by a President on a particular
topic can be long and arduous and, upon occasion, even fruitless.
Some Presidents, for example, Thomas Jefferson, preserved every
scrap of their writings; others saved little. Some Presidents wrote so
extensively that their works literally fill dozens of volumes; Fitzpatrick's *Collected Works of George Washington,* to name one important collection, is in thirty-nine volumes. Furthermore, through
the years the authorship of some quotations has become so ob-
scured that a number have been attributed to a President who did not
say or write them. *Treasury of Presidential Quotations* is a compilation which places within convenient reach of everyone the exact
meaningful statements by the Presidents on topics of significance or
of *some* interest to present-day readers and students. (No attempt
has been made to include what the Presidents have said about each
other, such a compilation having been reserved for another time.)

In undertaking even a modest collection of quotations from the
Presidents the editor was confronted by the natural hazards of any
task of compilation: what to include, what to leave out. In each
instance an included quotation meets one of three criteria; that it is of
historic interest, that it has some meaningful application to our
times, or that it adds a dimension to the image of the man who
said or wrote it. Inevitably, every such anthology will reflect in
some degree, and in spite of every effort to be objective, the com-
piler's own taste. I am thus aware that quotations have been included which another might gladly have left out; and it may be that
I have omitted some very trenchant and useful quotations that I
could not locate, or that did not, in my opinion, meet the criteria
aforementioned. Therefore, I invite both laymen and scholars who
have favorite Presidential quotations neglected here to submit them
for consideration in future revisions of this work.

In the vast majority of instances the following information has
been given after each quotation: the occasion when it was uttered

or written, the date and, in italics, the published source where the quotation may be found. Despite the difficulties attending this search few of the quotations are without full sources. For information to supply this lack, I should be grateful.

While this work was in galleys the present incumbent in the White House was sworn into office. With the cooperation of the Publisher the work was revised to include important statements made by President Lyndon B. Johnson up to his State of the Union Address on January 8, 1964. In future editions, additional quotations from later addresses, correspondence and interviews will be included.

Caroline Thomas Harnsberger

A Note to the Reader

The source of all inaugural addresses is *Inaugural Addresses of Presidents of the United States, House Document No. 28.*

Common identifications such as "Speech *at*" and "Letter *to*" have been shortened to "At" and "To" when the title of the source indicates letter or speech, for example, *The Speeches of Ulysses S. Grant* and *Letters of Theodore Roosevelt.*

In most instances, the titles of the sources in the text are abbreviated forms using keywords from the complete title, for example, *Familiar Letters* is the abbreviation of *Familiar Letters of John Adams to His Wife Abigail. During the Revolution.* All the complete titles appear in the Bibliography.

In the Bibliography, sources of quotations of only one President's work are listed under that President's name. Sources containing the works of more than one Chief Executive are listed under "Presidents."

For the convenience of those readers who may want the full text from which a quotation has been taken, I have supplied page number and, where applicable, volume number of each given source. However, *Messages and Papers of the Presidents,* a source I relied upon heavily, confronted me, in some instances, with a special problem because of a confusion in the volume numbers as they were published. Volume numbers, therefore have been omitted with *Messages and Papers;* the page number given is the most useful guide to help locate the actual quotation.

Contents

The Succession of the Presidents

1. George Washington
   Born 1732, died 1799. Trained as a surveyor, lived as a gentleman farmer. Became Commander-in-Chief of the Continental Army. President from 1789 to 1797. State: Virginia; party: Federalist; religion: Episcopalian.

2. John Adams
   Born 1735, died 1826. A Harvard graduate and lawyer. President from 1797 to 1801. State: Massachusetts; party: Federalist; religion: Unitarian.

3. Thomas Jefferson
   Born 1743, died 1826. A William and Mary graduate, politician, inventor, Governor of Virginia, Minister to France, Vice-President, founder of the University of Virginia. President from 1801 to 1809. State: Virginia; party: Democratic Republican; no specific religion.

4. James Madison
   Born 1751, died 1836. A Princeton graduate and politician. President from 1809 to 1817. State: Virginia; party: Democratic Republican; religion: Episcopalian.

5. James Monroe
   Born 1758, died 1831. A William and Mary graduate, politician, diplomat. President from 1817 to 1825. State: Virginia; party: Democratic Republican; religion: Episcopalian.

6. John Quincy Adams
   Born 1767, died 1848. A Harvard graduate, lawyer, diplomat, Secre-

tary of State. President from 1825 to 1829. State: Massachusetts; party: Democratic Republican; religion: Unitarian.

7. Andrew Jackson
   Born 1767, died 1845. Lawyer, country gentleman, Army general. President from 1829 to 1837. State: Tennessee; party: Democratic; religion: Presbyterian.

8. Martin Van Buren
   Born 1782, died 1862. Politician, Senator, Vice-President. President from 1837 to 1841. State: New York; party: Democratic; religion: Dutch Reformed.

9. William Henry Harrison
   Born 1773, died 1841. Soldier in the Indian Wars, Secretary of Northwest Territory, Governor of Indiana Territory. President in 1841; served one month; died in office. State: Ohio; party: Whig; religion: Episcopalian.

10. John Tyler
    Born 1790, died 1862. A William and Mary graduate, lawyer, Representative, Governor of Virginia, Vice-President. President from 1841 to 1845. State: Virginia; party: Whig; religion: Episcopalian.

11. James K. Polk
    Born 1795, died 1849. A University of North Carolina graduate, Representative, Speaker of the House, Governor of Tennessee. President from 1845 to 1849. State: Tennessee; party: Whig; religion: Presbyterian.

12. Zachary Taylor
    Born 1784, died 1850. Soldier in War of 1812, Black Hawk and Seminole Wars. President from 1849 to 1850; died in office. State: Virginia; party: Whig; religion: Episcopalian.

13. Millard Fillmore
    Born 1800, died 1874. Lawyer, Politician, Representative, Vice-President. President from 1850 to 1853. State: New York; party: Whig; religion: Unitarian.

14. Franklin Pierce
    Born 1804, died 1869. A Bowdoin College graduate, lawyer, Representative. President from 1853 to 1857. State: New Hampshire; party: Democratic; religion: Episcopalian.

15. James Buchanan
    Born 1791, died 1868. A Dickinson College graduate, Representative, Senator, Minister to Russia, Secretary of State. President from 1857 to 1861. State: Pennsylvania; party: Democratic; religion: Presbyterian.

16. Abraham Lincoln
    Born 1809, died 1865. Rail-splitter, lawyer. President from 1861 to 1865; assassinated. State: Illinois; party: Republican; no specific religion.

17. Andrew Johnson
    Born 1808, died 1875. Tailor, Representative, Senator, Governor of Tennessee, Vice-President. President from 1865 to 1869. State: Tennessee; party: Democratic; no specific religion.

18. Ulysses S. Grant
    Born 1822, died 1885. A West Point Military Academy graduate, Army general. President from 1869 to 1877. State: Ohio; party: Republican; religion: Methodist.

19. Rutherford B. Hayes
    Born 1822, died 1893. A Kenyon College and Harvard Law School graduate. Lawyer, Army general, Representative, Governor of Ohio. President from 1877 to 1881. State: Ohio; party: Republican; religion: Methodist.

20. James A. Garfield
    Born 1831, died 1881. A Williams College graduate, teacher, Army general, Representative. President in 1881; served six months; assassinated. State: Ohio; party: Republican; religion: Disciples of Christ.

21. Chester A. Arthur
    Born 1830, died 1886. A Union College graduate, lawyer, Army general, Representative, Vice-President. President from 1881 to 1885. State: New York; party: Republican; religion: Episcopalian.

22. Grover Cleveland
and Born 1837, died 1908. Clerk, teacher, sheriff, mayor. President from
24. 1885 to 1889 and from 1893 to 1897. State: New York; party: Democratic; religion: Presbyterian.

23. Benjamin Harrison
    Born 1833, died 1901. A Miami University graduate, lawyer, Senator.

President from 1889 to 1893. State: Indiana; party: Republican; religion: Presbyterian.

25. William McKinley
Born 1843, died 1901. Attended Allegheny College; Army officer, lawyer, Representative, Governor of Ohio. President from 1897 to 1901; assassinated. State: Ohio; party: Republican; religion: Methodist.

26. Theodore Roosevelt
Born 1858, died 1919. A Harvard graduate, state Assemblyman, Secretary of the Navy, Governor of New York, Vice-President. President from 1901 to 1909. State: New York; party: Republican; religion: Dutch Reformed.

27. William Howard Taft
Born 1857, died 1930. A Yale graduate, U. S. Solicitor-General, Governor-General of Philippines, Secretary of War, Chief Justice of Supreme Court. President from 1909 to 1913. State: Ohio; party: Republican; religion: Unitarian.

28. Woodrow Wilson
Born 1856, died 1924. A Princeton and Johns Hopkins graduate, teacher, President of Princeton University, Governor of New Jersey. President from 1913 to 1921. State: New Jersey; party: Democratic; religion: Presbyterian.

29. Warren G. Harding
Born 1865, died 1923. Attended Ohio Central College, newspaper publisher, Lieutenant-Governor of Ohio, State Senator, U. S. Senator. President from 1921 to 1923; died in office. State: Ohio; party: Republican; religion: Baptist.

30. Calvin Coolidge
Born 1872, died 1933. An Amherst College graduate, lawyer, mayor, state senator, Governor of Massachusetts. President from 1923 to 1929. Vice-President. State: Massachusetts; party: Republican; religion: Congregationalist.

31. Herbert Hoover
Born 1874. A Stanford University graduate, mining engineer, United States Food Administrator, Secretary of Commerce. President from 1929 to 1933. State: California; party: Republican; religion: Quaker.

32. Franklin Delano Roosevelt
Born 1882, died 1945. A Harvard and Columbia Law School gradu-

ate, lawyer, state senator, Assistant Secretary of War, Governor of New York. President from 1933 to 1945; died in office. State: New York; party: Democratic; religion: Episcopalian.

33. Harry S. Truman
Born 1884. Farmer, Army officer, haberdasher, Senator, Vice-President. President from 1945 to 1953. State: Missouri; party: Democratic; religion: Baptist.

34. Dwight D. Eisenhower
Born 1890. A West Point Military Academy graduate, Army Chief of Staff, Supreme Allied Commander, President of Columbia University. President of the United States from 1953 to 1961. State: New York; party: Republican; religion: Presbyterian.

35. John F. Kennedy
Born 1917, died 1963. Harvard University, naval officer, Representative, Senator. President from 1961 to 1963; assassinated. State: Massachusetts; party: Democratic; religion: Catholic.

36. Lyndon B. Johnson
Born 1908. A Georgetown University graduate, teacher, naval officer, Congressman, Senator, Vice-President. Became President in 1963. State: Texas; party: Democratic; religion: Christian Church.

TREASURY
OF
PRESIDENTIAL
QUOTATIONS

The President's Oath of Office

I do solemnly swear (or affirm) that I will faithfully execute the office of President of the United States, and will, to the best of my ability, preserve, protect, and defend the Constitution of the United States.

Achievement

1. Unswerving loyalty to duty, constant devotion to truth, and a clear conscience will overcome every discouragement and surely lead the way to usefulness and high achievement.

GROVER CLEVELAND
1901; *Man and Statesman, II,* 301

2. Satisfaction does not come from indulgence or satiety; it comes from achievement.

CALVIN COOLIDGE
Address at University of Vermont, June 28, 1920;
Citizenship, p. 285

3. Happiness lies not in the mere possession of money; it lies in the joy of achievement, in the thrill of creative effort. The joy and moral stimulation of work no longer must be forgotten in the mad chase of evanescent profits. These dark days will be worth all they cost us if they teach us that our true destiny is not to be ministered unto but to minister to ourselves and to our fellow men.

FRANKLIN DELANO ROOSEVELT
First Inaugural Address, Mar. 4, 1933

See also Education 30, Effort, Life 7, 10, Negroes 8

Action

1. Get action. Do things; be sane, don't fritter away your time; create, act, take a place wherever you are and be somebody; get action.

THEODORE ROOSEVELT
1900; *Many-Sided Roosevelt,* p. 83

2. Life does not consist in thinking, it consists in acting.

WOODROW WILSON
Speech in New York, N.Y., Sept. 28, 1912; *Crossroads,* p. 300

3. Words are not of any great importance in times of economic disturbance. It is action that counts.

HERBERT HOOVER
To business, industrial and labor leaders, Nov. 15, 1929; *Administration,* p. 25

2 AGGRESSION

See also Authors, Declaration of Independence 7, 8, Foreign Relations 27, Friendship 1, History 14, Liberty 37, Life 10, Neutrality 9, Paternalism 4, Patriotism 2, Politics 23, Responsibility 2, Success 2, Unity 2, 7

Aggression

1. The only excuse that America can ever have for the assertion of her physical force is that she asserts it in behalf of the interest of humanity.

WOODROW WILSON
Speech, Apr. 17, 1916; *Ideals*, p. 7

2. We will never be an aggressor. We want adequate security. We want no more than adequacy. But we will accept nothing less.

DWIGHT D. EISENHOWER
Radio and television address, Nov. 13, 1957; *Public Papers . . .
Eisenhower, 1957*, p. 816

See also Defense, Freedom, Life 10, Peace 17, 88, Preparedness 4, 9, Security 8, Terror, War 44, 71, 75, Wealth 5

Agreements
See Principles 7

Agriculture

1. The more I am acquainted with agricultural affairs the better I am pleased with them. Insomuch that I can no where find so great satisfaction, as in those innocent and useful pursuits. In indulging these feelings, I am led to reflect how much more delightful to an undebauched mind is the task of making improvements on the earth, than all the vain glory which can be acquired from ravaging it, by the most uninterrupted career of conquests.

GEORGE WASHINGTON
To Arthur Young, Dec. 4, 1788;
Writings (Fitzpatrick), XXX, 150

2. Agriculture is the most useful of the occupations of man.

THOMAS JEFFERSON
To M. Silvestre, May 29, 1807; *Writings, XI*, 212

3. American agricultural abundance can be forged into both a significant instrument of foreign policy and a weapon against domestic hardship and hunger.

JOHN F. KENNEDY
Message to Congress, Mar. 16, 1961; *Tide*, p. 117

See also Farmers, Foreign Relations 34, Prosperity 2

Aid, Government
See Brotherhood 2, Education 22, 24, Foreign Relations 54, 55, 56, Subsidy

Alliances

1. History tells us that disunity and relaxation are the great internal dangers of an alliance. . . .

Lofty words cannot construct an alliance or maintain it—only concrete deeds can do that. . . .

Let us take heart from the certainty that we are united not only by danger and necessity, but by hope and purpose as well.

For we know now that freedom is more than the rejection of tyranny—that prosperity is more than an escape from want—that partnership is more than a sharing of power. These are, above all, great human adventures. They must have meaning and conviction and purpose—and because they do . . . in all nations of the alliance, we are called to a great new mission.

JOHN F. KENNEDY
At Frankfurt, West Germany, June 25, 1963; *Vital Speeches, July 15, 1963,* p. 580

See also Foreign Relations 3, 6, 15, 32, Friendship 4, Peace 15

Ambassadors

1. An ambassador has no need of spies; his character is always sacred.

GEORGE WASHINGTON
To Gov. Robert Dinwiddie, May 29, 1754;
Writings (Fitzpatrick), II, 34

See also Diplomacy

Ambition

1. To all our means of culture is added the powerful incentive to personal ambition. . . . No post of honor is so high but the poorest may hope to reach it.

JAMES A. GARFIELD

2. Ambition is a commendable attribute, without which no man succeeds. Only inconsiderate ambition imperils.

WARREN G. HARDING
Address in Washington, D.C., May 30, 1922;
Messages and Papers, p. 9130

See also Politicians 4, Politics 11, Presidency (The) 22, Prosperity 10

Amendments

See Constitution 4, 13, 16, 24, Government 41, Prohibition

America

1. There is an option still left to the United States of America, that it

is in their choice and depends upon their conduct, whether they will be respectable and prosperous or contemptible and miserable as a Nation.

GEORGE WASHINGTON
To the Governors, June 8, 1783;
Writings (Fitzpatrick), XXVI, 486

2. The preservation of the sacred fire of liberty, and the destiny of the republican model of government are justly considered, perhaps as *deeply,* as *finally,* staked on the experiment entrusted to the hands of the American people.

GEORGE WASHINGTON
First Inaugural Address, Apr. 30, 1789

3. The name of America . . . must always exalt the just pride of patriotism. . . . The independence and liberty you possess are the work of joint councils and joint efforts, of common dangers, sufferings and successes.

GEORGE WASHINGTON
Farewell Address, Sept. 19, 1796;
Writings (Fitzpatrick), XXXV, 219

4. America is a great, unwieldy body. Its progress must be slow. It is like a large fleet sailing under convoy. The fleetest sailers [*sic*] must wait for the dullest and slowest.

JOHN ADAMS
To Abigail Adams, June 17, 1775; *Familiar Letters,* p. 66

5. The first object of my heart is my own country. In that is embarked my family, my fortune, and my own existence.

THOMAS JEFFERSON
Letter to Elbridge Gerry, Jan. 26, 1799; *Works, IV, 269*

6. America, in the assembly of nations, since her admission among them, has invariably, though often fruitlessly, held forth to them the hand of honest friendship, of equal freedom, of generous reciprocity. She has uniformly spoken among them, though often to heedless and often to disdainful ears, the language of equal liberty, equal justice, and equal rights.

JOHN QUINCY ADAMS
Address in Washington, D.C., July 4, 1821; *Pamphlet,* p. 10

7. The things that will destroy America are prosperity-at-any-price, peace-at-any-price, safety-first instead of duty-first, the love of soft living and the get-rich-quick theory of life.

THEODORE ROOSEVELT
Letter to S. S. Menken, Jan. 10, 1917; *Cyclopedia,* p. 13

8. The only thing that has ever distinguished America among the nations

is that she has shown that all men are entitled to the benefits of the law.

WOODROW WILSON
Address in New York, N.Y., Dec. 14, 1906;
Closed MS, Princeton University Library

9. America lives in the heart of every man everywhere who wishes to find a region where he will be free to work out his destiny as he chooses.

WOODROW WILSON
Speech in Chicago, Ill., Apr. 6, 1912; *Chicago Record Herald,*
Apr. 7, 1912

10. The vision of America will never change. America once, when she was a little people, sat upon a hill of privilege and had a vision of the future. She saw men happy because they were free. She saw them free because they were equal. She saw them banded together because they had the spirit of brothers. She saw them safe because they did not wish to impose upon one another. And the vision is not changed. The multitude has grown, that welcome multitude that comes from all parts of the world to seek a safe place of life and of hope in America. And so America will move forward, if she moves forward at all, only with her face to that same sun of promise.

WOODROW WILSON
Speech at Scranton, Pa., Sept. 23, 1912; *Crossroads,* p. 242

11. This is not America because it is rich. This is not America because it has set up for a great population great opportunities for material prosperity. America is a name which sounds in the ears of men everywhere as a synonym with individual opportunity because it is a synonym of individual liberty.

WOODROW WILSON
Speech at Mobile, Ala., Oct. 27, 1913; *State Papers,* p. 36

12. No man who thinks first of himself, and afterwards of his country can call himself an American. America must be enriched by us. We must not live upon her; she must live by means of us.

WOODROW WILSON
Speech in Washington, D.C., May 16, 1914; *Foreign Policy,* p. 47

13. The day of our country's life is still but in its fresh morning. Let us lift our eyes to the great tracts of life yet to be conquered in the interests of righteous peace. Come, let us renew our allegiance to America, conserve her strength in its purity, make her chief among those who serve mankind, self-reverenced, self-commanded, mistress of all forces of quiet counsel, strong above all others in good will and the might of invincible justice and right.

WOODROW WILSON
Address in New York, N.Y., Nov. 4, 1915; *Ibid.,* p. 124

14.   Just what is it that America stands for? If she stands for one thing more than another, it is for the sovereignty of self-governing people. . . . She stands as an example of free institutions, and as an example of disinterested international action in the main tenets of justice.

WOODROW WILSON
Speech at Pittsburgh, Pa., Jan. 29, 1916; *Public Papers, IV,* 18

15.   America consists . . . of all of us only as our spirits are banded together in a common enterprise. That common enterprise is . . . liberty and justice and right.

WOODROW WILSON
Ibid., p. 19

16.   The thing I . . . count upon . . . is the unity of America—an America united in feeling, in purpose, and in its vision of duty, of opportunity, and of service. . . . Beware that no faction or disloyal intrigue break the harmony or embarrass the spirit of our people.

WOODROW WILSON
Second Inaugural Address, Mar. 5, 1917

17.   America's present need is not heroics but healing; not nostrums but normalcy; not revolution but restoration; . . . not surgery but serenity.

WARREN G. HARDING
Speech in Boston, Mass., May 14, 1920

18.   The meaning of America is not to be found in a life without toil. Freedom is not only bought with a great price; it is maintained by unremitting effort.

CALVIN COOLIDGE
Address at Johns Hopkins University, Feb. 22, 1922;
Citizenship, p. 24

19.   The meaning of our word *America* flows from one pure source. Within the soul of America is the freedom of mind and spirit of man. Here alone are the open windows through which pours the sunlight of the human spirit. Here alone human dignity is not a dream but a major accomplishment.

HERBERT HOOVER
"The Miracle of America," 1948; *American Road,* p. 6

20.   America is great because America is good—and if America ever ceases to be good—America will cease to be great.

DWIGHT D. EISENHOWER
Speech in Boston, Mass., Sept. 21, 1953; *Index,* p. 5

21. America believes in and practices fair play, and decency and justice.

DWIGHT D. EISENHOWER
Radio speech, Apr. 5, 1954; *Public Papers . . . Eisenhower, 1954,*
p. 378

22. America is the greatest force that God has ever allowed to exist on His footstool.

DWIGHT D. EISENHOWER
Radio speech, Apr. 5, 1954; *Ibid.,* p. 381

23. America is best described by one word, freedom.

DWIGHT D. EISENHOWER
Sixth Annual Message to Congress, Jan. 9, 1959; *Public Papers
. . . Eisenhower, 1959,* p. 16

24. My country like all the countries of the Americas is the possessor of a profound revolutionary tradition which has helped shape the modern world. . . .

The history of the Americas . . . is a tribute to the capacity of free men to call upon the deepest reservoirs of human mind and spirit. And if the task of progress with freedom is more complex, subtle and difficult than the promise of progress without freedom, we are unafraid of the challenge. We are prepared to follow that path which advances man's welfare without destroying his dignity. And we know that lessons of our past promise success for our future.

JOHN F. KENNEDY
At San José, Costa Rica, Mar. 21, 1963; *Vital Speeches,
Apr. 15, 1963,* p. 388.

See also Americans, Civil Rights 1, Debts 5, Declaration of Independence, Democracy 7, Duty 9, Foreign Relations 55, Goals 3, God 7, Government, Health 5, History 15, Hope 2, Humanity 2, 3, Ideals 1, 5, 7, Isolationism 2, 4, 6, Labor 14, Leadership 4, Liberty 4, Neutrality 7, Patriotism 10, Peace 32, 73, People (The) 34, Political Parties 16, Preparedness 14, Presidency (The) 46, Principles 10, Prosperity 10, Rights 5, Security 8, 9, Self-Sacrifice, Statesmanship 3, States' Rights 17, Union, United States, War 6, Youth 3

American Revolution

1. The American Revolution was a beginning, not a consummation. . . . The American Revolution was the birth of a nation; it was the creation of a great free republic based upon traditions of personal liberty which heretofore had been confined to a single little island, but which it was purposed should spread to all mankind.

WOODROW WILSON
Address in Washington, D.C., Oct. 11, 1915;
Messages and Papers (Shaw), I, 122

2. The American Revolution was fought for an ideal. We would have been as prosperous under the British Crown, but we should not have been as happy, and we should not have respected ourselves as much. Therefore what America is bound to fight for when the time comes is nothing more than her self-respect.

WOODROW WILSON
Speech in Chicago, Ill., Jan. 31, 1916; *Public Papers, IV*, 68

3. We dare not forget that we are the heirs of that first revolution.

JOHN F. KENNEDY
1961

See also America 24, American System 6, Nationality 1, Revolutions 2, 8

Americans

1. It was my object to make Americans hold up their heads, and look down upon any nation that refused to do them justice; . . . in my opinion, Americans had nothing to fear but from the meekness of their own hearts; as Christians, I wished them meek; as statesmen, I wished them proud; and I thought the pride and the meekness very consistent.

JOHN ADAMS
Diary, Apr. 30, 1783; *Works, III*, 365

2. The American people are slow to wrath, but when their wrath is once kindled it burns like a consuming flame.

THEODORE ROOSEVELT
First Annual Message to Congress, Dec. 3, 1901;
Messages and Papers, p. 6643

3. We can have no "fifty-fifty" allegiance in this country. Either a man is an American and nothing else, or he is not an American at all. We are akin by blood and descent to most of the nations of Europe; but we are separate from all of them; we are a new and distinct nation, and we are bound always to give our wholehearted and undivided loyalty to our own flag, and in any international crisis to treat each and every foreign nation purely according to its conduct in that crisis.

THEODORE ROOSEVELT
Sept. 10, 1917; *Works, XIX*, 33

4. Like all Americans, I like big things: big prairies, big forests and mountains, big wheatfields, railroads . . . and everything else. But no people ever yet benefited by riches if their prosperity corrupted their virtue.

THEODORE ROOSEVELT
Speech at Dickinson, N.D., July 4, 1886; *Bad Lands*, p. 409

5. We have taken millions of foreigners into our civilization, but we have amalgamated them, and . . . we have made them all Americans. We have bred to a type.

WILLIAM HOWARD TAFT

6. A man who thinks of himself as belonging to a particular national group in America has not yet become an American.

WOODROW WILSON
Address in Philadelphia, Pa., May 10, 1915;
Messages and Papers (*Shaw*), I, 115

7. We [Americans] are the predestined mediators of mankind.

WOODROW WILSON
Speech at St. Paul, Minn., Sept. 9, 1919; *Public Papers, VI,* 82

8. American citizenship is a high estate. He who holds it is the peer of kings. It has been secured only by untold toil and effort. It will be maintained by no other method. . . . To attempt to turn it into a thing of ease and inaction would be only to debase it. To cease to struggle and toil and sacrifice for it is not only to cease to be worthy of it but is to start a retreat toward barbarism. . . . This is the stand that those must maintain who are worthy to be called Americans.

CALVIN COOLIDGE
Speech at Arlington National Cemetery, May 30, 1924;
Foundations, p. 23

9. We believe that we can best serve our own country and most successfully discharge our obligations to humanity by continuing to be openly and candidly, intensely and scrupulously, American. If we have any heritage, it has been that.

But if we wish to continue to be distinctively American, we must continue to make that term comprehensive enough to embrace the legitimate desires of a civilized and enlightened people determined in all their relations to pursue a conscientious and religious life. We cannot permit ourselves to be narrowed and dwarfed by slogans and phrases.

CALVIN COOLIDGE
Inaugural Address, Mar. 4, 1925

10. The success and character of a nation are to be judged by the ideals and the spirit of its people. Time and again the American people have demonstrated a spiritual quality, a capacity for unity of action, of generosity, a certainty of results in time of emergency that have made them great in the annals of the history of all nations.

HERBERT HOOVER
Address, Oct. 18, 1931; *Memoirs, III,* 151

11. The American people have solved many great difficulties in the development of national life. The qualities of self-restraint, of integrity, of conscience and courage still live in our people. It is not too late to summon these qualities into action.

HERBERT HOOVER
Address at Stanford University, Aug. 10, 1949;
American Road, p. 21

12. The overwhelming majority of Americans are possessed of two great qualities—a sense of humor and a sense of proportion.

FRANKLIN DELANO ROOSEVELT
Address at Savannah, Ga., Nov. 18, 1933; *Public Papers, II,* 491

13. Only Americans can hurt America.

DWIGHT D. EISENHOWER
Speech in Abilene, Kan., June, 1945;
What Eisenhower Thinks, p. 39

14. The American people . . . have been complacent, self-contented, easy-going. Franklin Roosevelt said in 1928, after two terms of Harding and Coolidge: "The soul of our country, lulled by material prosperity, has passed through eight gray years." These years of drift, of falling behind, of postponing decisions and crises, are "years that the locusts have eaten."

We must put an end to this depression of our national spirit—we must put these dull, gray years behind us and take on the rendezvous with destiny that is assigned us. We must regain the American purpose and promise and become again the creative and purposeful people which, except when we have doped ourselves, we really are. Let us, then, with full production and full employment at home, begin to play our full part in the development of a world of peace and freedom—let us join the human race.

JOHN F. KENNEDY
Address at Milwaukee, Wis., Nov. 13, 1959; *Strategy,* p. 240

15. The American, by nature, is optimistic. He is experimental, an inventor and a builder who builds best when called upon to build greatly. Arouse his will to believe in himself, give him a great goal to believe in, and he will create the means to reach it. This trait of the American character is our greatest single national asset. It is time once more that we rescue it from the sea of fat in which it has been drowning.

JOHN F. KENNEDY
Address in Washington, D.C., Jan. 1, 1960; *Ibid.,* p. 32

See also America, Army 13, Character 13, Depression 2, Duty 10, Flattery 1, Foreign Relations 42, Freedom 34, Liberty 44, Majorities 5, Negroes 4, Patriotism 7, 9, People (The) 22, Physical Fitness 1, Political Parties 21, 23, Politics 13, 15, Republics 17, War 51, Youth 2

American System

1. After the close of the war with Great Britain in 1815 . . . there was . . . a departure from our earlier policy. The enlargement of the powers of the Federal Government by construction, which obtained, was not warranted by any just interpretation of the Constitution. [But] a series of

measures was adopted which, united and combined, constituted what was termed by their authors and advocates the "American System."

JAMES K. POLK
Fourth Annual Message to Congress, Dec. 5, 1848;
Messages and Papers, p. 250

2. The American system rests on the assertion of the equal right of every man to life, liberty, and the pursuit of happiness, to freedom of conscience, to the culture and exercise of all his faculties. As a consequence the State government is limited—as to the General Government in the interest of union, as to the individual citizen in the interest of freedom.

ANDREW JOHNSON
First Annual Message to Congress, Dec. 4, 1865; *Ibid.,* p. 3553

3. In the centuries of our separation from the Old World we had developed something which, for lack of a better term, I called the American System, which was alone the promise of human progress and the force which had led our nation to greatness.

HERBERT HOOVER
1922; *Memoirs, II,* 27

4. At the heart of our American System is embedded a great ideal unique in the world. That is the ideal that there shall be an opportunity in life, and equal opportunity, for every boy and girl, every man and woman. It holds that they have the chance to rise to any position to which their character and ability may entitle them. That ideal is limited or ended if this nation is to be goose-stepped from Washington.

HERBERT HOOVER
At Colorado Springs, Colo., Mar. 7, 1936;
Addresses (1933–38), p. 130

5. If we are going to continue to be proud that we are Americans there must be no weakening of the codes by which we have lived; by the right to meet your accuser face to face, if you have one; by your right to go to church or the synagogue or even the mosque of your own choosing; by your right to speak your mind and be protected in it.

DWIGHT D. EISENHOWER
Address, Nov. 23, 1953; *Public Papers . . . Eisenhower,*
1953, p. 798

6. The revolution which began here in 1776 still runs—throughout the world. The worldwide drive for independence, the aspirations for development, the explosion of expectations for better health, housing, education and opportunity—all the forces which move and shake our times—have the

power they do because of the example of success offered by our American System.

LYNDON B. JOHNSON
Address at Georgetown University, Oct. 12, 1963;
Vital Speeches, Nov. 1, 1963, p. 36

See also Business 11, Character 11, Declaration of Independence 10, Democracy 21, Equality, Liberty 46, Opportunity

Anarchy

See Freedom 10, Government 35, Liberty 23, Peace 38, 89, States' Rights 10, Unity 8

Ancestry

1. A man's rootage is more important than his leafage.

WOODROW WILSON
Speech at Baltimore, Md., Apr. 29, 1912

Anger

1. When angry, count ten before you speak; if very angry, an hundred.

THOMAS JEFFERSON
To Thomas Jefferson Smith, Feb. 21, 1825; *Writings, XVI,* 111

Anxiety

1. We have not men fit for the times. We are deficient in genius, in education, in travel, in fortune, in every thing. I feel inutterable anxiety. God grant us wisdom and fortitude.

JOHN ADAMS
Diary, June 25, 1774; *Works, II,* 338

Appointments

1. In the appointments to the great offices of the government, my aim has been to combine geographical situation, and sometimes other considerations, with abilities and fitness of known characters.

GEORGE WASHINGTON
To Edward Carrington, Oct. 9, 1795; *Writings (Fitzpatrick), II,* 78

2. A fellow once came to me to ask for an appointment as a minister abroad. Finding he could not get that, he came down to some more modest position. Finally, he asked to be made a tidewaiter. When he saw he could not get that, he asked me for an old pair of trousers. It is sometimes well to be humble.

ABRAHAM LINCOLN
Washington, D.C., 1865; *Everyday Life,* p. 690

3. Let appointments and removals be made on business principles, and

by fixed rules. . . . Let no man be put . . . out or in merely because he is our friend.

RUTHERFORD B. HAYES
To Gen. E. A. Merritt, Feb. 4, 1879; *Letters and Messages*, p. 151

4. What we need in appointive positions is men of knowledge and experience who have sufficient character to resist temptations.

CALVIN COOLIDGE
Autobiography, p. 226

See also Congress 4, Office Seekers, Patronage, Public Office

Arbitration
See Foreign Relations 18, 30, Isolationism 1, Peace 48, War 33

Aristocracy
1. There is a natural aristocracy among men. The grounds of this are virtue and talents.

THOMAS JEFFERSON
To John Adams, Oct. 28, 1813; *Writings, XIII,* 396

2. There is something to be said for government by a great aristocracy which has furnished leaders to the nations in peace and war for generations; even a democrat like myself must admit this.

THEODORE ROOSEVELT
Letter to Edward Grey, Nov. 15, 1913; *His Time, II,* 347

See also Government 15, People 24, Republics 12, Slavery 25

Army
1. Had we formed a permanent army in the beginning, which, by the continuance of the same men in service, had been capable of discipline, we never should have had to retreat with a handful of men across the Delaware in Seventy-six; trembling for the fate of America, which nothing but the infatuation of the enemy could have saved. . . .

GEORGE WASHINGTON
To the President of Congress, Aug. 20, 1780;
Writings (Fitzpatrick), XIX, 408

2. Keeping an army in America has been nothing but a public nuisance.

JOHN ADAMS
"Novanglus," in Boston *Gazette,* Feb. 13, 1775; *Works, IV,* 47

3. None but an armed nation can dispense with a standing army.

THOMAS JEFFERSON
Letter, Feb. 25, 1803; *Works, IV,* 469

4. For a people who are free, and who mean to remain so, a well-organized and armed militia is their best security.

THOMAS JEFFERSON
Eighth Annual Message to Congress, Nov. 8, 1808;
Writings, III, 482

5. A standing army is one of the greatest mischiefs that can possibly happen.

JAMES MADISON
Debates, Virginia Convention, 1787; *Complete Madison,* p. 341

6. The Government ought to command for a longer period [than five years from the time of enlistment at West Point] the services of those who are educated at the public expense. I recommend that the time of enlistment be extended to seven years.

MARTIN VAN BUREN
First Annual Message to Congress, Dec. 4, 1837;
Addresses and Messages, p. 641

7. Our standing army is to be found in the bosom of society. It is composed of free citizens, who are ever ready to take up arms in the service of their country when an emergency requires it. . . .

Sound policy requires that we should avoid the creation of a large standing army in a period of peace. . . . Such armies are not only expensive and unnecessary, but may become dangerous to liberty.

JAMES K. POLK
Message to Congress, July 6, 1848; *Messages and Papers,* p. 2441

8. It has been said that one bad general is better than two good ones, and the saying is true if taken to mean no more than that an army is better directed by a single mind, though inferior, than by two superior ones at variance and cross-purposes with each other.

ABRAHAM LINCOLN
First Annual Message to Congress, Dec. 3, 1861; *Ibid.,* p. 3257

9. I like the feeling of the American people that we ought not to have a large standing army; but it has been demonstrated in the last few months that we need the standing army large enough to do all the work required while we are at peace, and can rely upon the great body of the people in an emergency to help us fight our battles.

WILLIAM MCKINLEY
At Montgomery, Ala., Dec. 16, 1898;
Speeches and Addresses, p. 172

10. The army and navy are the sword and the shield which this nation must carry if she is to do her duty among the nations of the earth. . . .

THEODORE ROOSEVELT
Address in Chicago, Ill., Apr. 10, 1899; *Works, XIII,* 328

11. There is a popular feeling that an army in time of peace is not maintained and administered to be used for war, and that the army exists
merely for show. . . . This impression has led a usually practical and
hard-headed people like the Americans to the most absurd military policy.
An Army is for war. If there were no possibility of war . . . and we could
be guaranteed a continuous peace, we should disband the army; but we
have not yet arrived at this happy condition.

WILLIAM HOWARD TAFT
Address at Columbus, Ohio, Apr. 2, 1908; *Problems,* p. 82

12. I am not one of those who believe that a great standing army is the
means of maintaining peace, because if you build up a great profession
those who form parts of it want to exercise their profession.

WOODROW WILSON
Speech at Pittsburgh, Pa., Jan. 29, 1916; *Public Papers, IV,* 33

13. I tell you, fellow citizens, that the war was won by the American
spirit. . . . You know what one of our American wits said, that it took
only half as long to train an American army as any other, because you
had only to train them to go one way.

WOODROW WILSON
Speech at Kansas City, Mo., Sept. 6, 1919; *Ibid., VI,* 12

14. I believe in a small army, but the best in the world, with a mindful-
ness for preparedness which will avoid the unutterable cost of our previous
neglect.

WARREN G. HARDING
At Marion, Ohio, July 22, 1920;
Speeches of Warren G. Harding, p. 33

15. No nation ever had an army large enough to guarantee it against
attack in time of peace, or insure it victory in time of war.

CALVIN COOLIDGE
An address, 1925

See also Defense, Discipline, Duty 3, Military Matters, Navy, Neutrality 2,
People (The) 7, Preparedness, Republics 16, Soldiers, Union 8, 22,
War 44

Arts, The

1. The science of government, it is my duty to study, more than all the
other sciences; the arts of legislation and administration and negotiation,
ought to take place of, indeed to exclude, in a manner, all other arts. I
must study politics and war that my sons may have liberty to study mathematics and philosophy. My sons ought to study mathematics and philosophy, geography, natural history and naval architecture, navigation,

commerce and agriculture, in order to give their children a right to study painting, poetry, music, architecture, statuary, tapestry and porcelain.

JOHN ADAMS
1780; *Family*, p. 67

2. Every time an artist dies part of the vision of mankind passes with him.

FRANKLIN DELANO ROOSEVELT
1941; *As FDR Said*, p. 161

See also Culture, Education, Public Opinion 1, War 16

Assassination

1. If it is [God's] will that I must die by the hand of an assassin, I must be resigned. I must do my duty as I see it, and leave the rest with God.

ABRAHAM LINCOLN
Statement in Washington, D.C., 1864; *War Years, III*, 559

2. If I am killed, I can die but once; but to live in constant dread of it, is to die over and over again.

ABRAHAM LINCOLN
Washington, D.C., 1864; *Abraham Lincoln (Morse)*, II, 345

3. Men may talk about beheading and about usurpation, but when I am beheaded I want the American people to be witnesses. I do not want it, by innuendoes and indirect remarks in high places, to be suggested to men who have assassination brooding in their bosoms. . . .

ANDREW JOHNSON
Speech in Washington, D.C., Feb. 22, 1866; *Document*, p. 6

4. I'd rather have a bullet inside of me than to be living in constant dread of one.

BENJAMIN HARRISON
Upon dismissing the White House detectives, 1889;
As I Knew Them, p. 149

5. No man will ever be restrained from becoming President by any fear as to his personal safety. If the risk to the President's life became great, it would mean that the office would more and more come to be filled by men of a spirit which would make them resolute and merciless in dealing with every friend of disorder.

THEODORE ROOSEVELT
First Annual Message to Congress, Dec. 3, 1901;
Works (Mem. Ed.), XVII, 99

6. One of the noblest sentences ever uttered was uttered by Mr. Garfield before he became President. . . . He said this beautiful thing: "My fellow citizens, the President is dead, but the Government lives and God Omnipo-

tent reigns." America is the place where you cannot kill your government by killing the men who conduct it.

WOODROW WILSON
Address at Helena, Mont., Sept. 11, 1919; *Public Papers, VI,* 137

7. I am a fatalist on the subject of assassination. No vigilance can wholly protect the President, although every possible precaution is exerted.

FRANKLIN DELANO ROOSEVELT
1933; *Omnibus,* p. 60

8. A President has to expect those things. The only thing you have to worry about is bad luck. I never have bad luck.

HARRY S. TRUMAN
After an attempt to assassinate him at Blair House;
Time (magazine), Nov. 13, 1950

See also Declaration of Independence 6

Athletics

1. The athletic spirit is essentially democratic. Athletics are good . . . because they tend to develop . . . courage. Athletics are good; study is even better.

THEODORE ROOSEVELT
Address at Harvard Union, Feb. 23, 1907;
Addresses and Papers, p. 350

2. Competition in play teaches the love of the free spirit to excel by its own merit. A nation that has not forgotten how to play, a nation that fosters athletics is a nation that is always holding up the high ideal of equal opportunity for all. Go back through history and find the nations that did not play and had no outdoor sports and you will find the nations of oppressed peoples.

WARREN G. HARDING
At Galion, Ohio, Aug. 27, 1920;
Speeches by Warren G. Harding, p. 81

See also Exercise, Health, Physical Fitness

Authors

1. The men who act stand nearer to the mass of men than do the men who write; and it is at their hands that new thought gets its translation into the crude language of deeds. The very crudity of that language of deeds exasperates the sensibilities of the authors. . . .

The men who write love proportion, the men who act must strike out practical lines of action and neglect proportion. . . . The great stream of freedom which "broadens down from precedent to precedent" is not a clear mountain current such as the fastidious men of chastened thought like to drink from: it is polluted with not a few of the coarse elements of the gross world on its banks; it is heavy with the drainage of a very material universe.

WOODROW WILSON
New York Times, Nov. 29, 1963

Avarice

1.   Is the paltry consideration of a little pelf to individuals to be placed in competition with the essential rights and liberties of the present generation, and of millions yet unborn? Shall a few designing men, for their own aggrandizement, and to gratify their own avarice, overset the goodly fabric we have been rearing at the expense of so much time, blood, and treasure? And shall we at last become the victims of our own lust of gain? Forbid it Heaven!

GEORGE WASHINGTON
To James Warren, Mar. 31, 1779; *Writings (Fitzpatrick), VI,* 211

Ballots

1.   The ballot box is the surest arbiter of disputes among freemen.

JAMES BUCHANAN
Fourth Annual Message to Congress, Dec. 3, 1860;
Messages and Papers, p. 3177

2.   The ballot is stronger than the bullet.

ABRAHAM LINCOLN
1856; *Life (Tarbell), I,* 298

3.   The purity of the ballot box, the wise provisions and careful guardianship that shall always make the expression of the will of the peoples fair, pure and true, is the essential thing in American life.

BENJAMIN HARRISON
At Salt Lake City, Utah, May 9, 1891; *Speeches,* p. 432

4.   The instrument of all reform in America is the ballot.

WOODROW WILSON
Seventh Annual Message to Congress, Dec. 2, 1919;
Public Papers, VI, 442

5.   The whole system of American Government rests on the ballot box. Unless citizens do their duties there, such a system of government is doomed to failure.

CALVIN COOLIDGE
Address to D.A.R., Washington, D.C., Apr. 19, 1926;
Foundations, p. 386

See also Elections, Suffrage, Voters

Banks

1.   I sincerely believe that banking establishments are more dangerous

than standing armies, and that the principle of spending money to be paid by posterity, under the name of funding, is but swindling futurity on a large scale.

THOMAS JEFFERSON
To John Taylor, May 28, 1816; *Writings, XV,* 23

2.   You are a den of vipers and thieves. I intend to rout you out, and by the eternal God, I will rout you out.

ANDREW JACKSON
Words to a delegation of bankers, 1832

3.   Events have satisfied my mind, and I think the minds of the American people, that the mischiefs and dangers which flow from a national bank far overbalance its advantages.

ANDREW JACKSON
Sixth Annual Message to Congress, Dec. 1, 1834;
Messages and Papers, p. 1330

4.   The re-establishment of a national bank . . . in any form . . . would impair the rightful supremacy of the popular will.

MARTIN VAN BUREN
Special Session Message, Sept. 4, 1837;
Addresses and Messages, p. 613

5.   We need no national banks or other extraneous institutions planted around the Government to control or strengthen it in opposition to the will of its authors.

JAMES K. POLK
Inaugural Address, Mar. 4, 1845

6.   Every man has a right to his own property; which means a right to be assured, to the fullest extent attainable, in the safety of his savings.

FRANKLIN DELANO ROOSEVELT
Campaign address in San Francisco, Cal., Sept. 23, 1932;
Public Papers, I, 754

7.   You can rest assured that, as long as I am President, the gentlemen in Wall Street are not to control the operations of the International Bank.

HARRY S. TRUMAN
Letter, 1947; *Mr. President,* p. 217

See also Capitalists, Prosperity 5

Behavior

1.   Black care rarely sits behind a rider whose pace is fast enough.

THEODORE ROOSEVELT
1887; *Works, I,* 329

2.   I am inclined to follow the course suggested by a friend . . . who says

that he has always followed the rule never to murder a man who is committing suicide.

WOODROW WILSON
To Bernard Baruch, Aug. 19, 1916; *Public Years,* p. 14

3.   People who've had a hanging in the family don't like to talk about a rope.

CALVIN COOLIDGE
1932; *Public Years (Baruch),* p. 194

See also Wrong 2, 3

Beliefs

1.   The beliefs for which men have been willing to suffer martyrdom come from religion.

CALVIN COOLIDGE
Address at Springfield, Mass., Oct. 11, 1921; *Citizenship,* p. 248

2.   I am proud of the revolutionary beliefs for which our forebears fought . . . the belief that the rights of man come not from the generosity of the state but the hands of God.

JOHN F. KENNEDY
Inaugural Address, Jan. 20, 1961

See also Failure 1, Faith, Ideals 4, Morality 8, Principles, Religion 25

Benevolence

1.   Benevolence never developed a man or a nation. We do not want a benevolent government. We want a free and a just government.

WOODROW WILSON
1912; *New Freedom (Hale),* p. 218

See also Brotherhood 2, Charity, Pensions, Philanthropy, Power 3, Relief, Subsidy, War 15

Bible

1.   The Bible is the best book in the world. It contains more of my little philosophy than all the libraries I have seen; and such parts of it as I cannot reconcile to my little philosophy, I postpone for future investigation.

JOHN ADAMS
To Thomas Jefferson, Dec. 25, 1813; *Correspondence, II,* 412

2.   If American democracy is to remain the greatest hope of humanity, it must continue abundantly in the faith of the Bible.

CALVIN COOLIDGE
Speech in Washington, D.C., May 3, 1925; *Foundations,* p. 209

See also Materialism 1, Morality 7, Principles 14, Religion 5, 25, 26, Rights 18, Union 24, United States 6, War 72

Books

1. Books constitute capital. A library book lasts as long as a house, for hundreds of years. It is not, then, an article of mere consumption but fairly of capital, and often in the case of professional men, setting out in life, it is their only capital.

THOMAS JEFFERSON
To James Madison, Sept. 16, 1821; *Writings (Ford)*, X, 195

See also Bible, Censors 3, 4, Knowledge, Letters, Libraries, Public Office 14

Boondoggling

1. Some people in this country have called it "boondoggling" for us to build stadiums and parks and forests to improve the recreational facilities of the Nation. . . .

I am looking forward to a continuation . . . of the policy that will work for the good of the average citizen in the United States, that will not forget the forgotten man.

FRANKLIN DELANO ROOSEVELT
Remarks at Detroit, Mich., Oct. 15, 1936; *Public Papers*, V, 495

Bossism

1. The man we call boss is the agent of those who wish to control politics. . . . A boss is not merely a man who . . . determines and shapes a State for office and what the legislature shall be permitted to do. . . . He is the agent of great selfish interests in seeing that no man gets into office who won't obey their behests and that no law gets on the statute book which is hostile to their interests.

WOODROW WILSON
Speech at Kalamazoo, Mich., Sept. 19, 1912; *Typescript,*
Swen Collection, Princeton University

2. A "boss" is a gum-shoe political manager.

WOODROW WILSON
Epigram

Brains

1. Dollars and guns are no substitutes for brains and will power.

DWIGHT D. EISENHOWER
Radio panel, June 3, 1953; *Index*, p. 31

2. What we need now in this nation, more than atomic power, or airpower, or financial, industrial, or even manpower, is brain power. The dinosaur was bigger and stronger than anyone else—he may even have been more pious—but he was also dumber. And look what happened to him.

JOHN F. KENNEDY
Address in Washington, D.C., Apr. 16, 1959; *Strategy*, p. 203

See also Mind

Bravery

1. There is something better, if possible, that a man can give than his life. That is his living spirit to a service that is not easy, to resist counsels that are hard to resist, to stand against purposes that are difficult to stand against.

WOODROW WILSON
Speech at Suresnes Cemetery, France, May 30, 1919;
Public Papers, V, 507

2. Any dangerous spot is tenable if brave men will make it so.

JOHN F. KENNEDY
Radio and Television address, July 26, 1961; *Tide*, p. 191

See also Valor

Bribery
See Corruption 3

Brotherhood

1. I . . . make it my earnest prayer that God would . . . incline the hearts of the citizens . . . to entertain a brotherly affection and love for one another and for their fellow citizens of the United States at large.

GEORGE WASHINGTON
To the Governor, June 8, 1783; *Writings (Fitzpatrick)*, *XXVI*, 496

2. The rule of brotherhood remains as the indispensable prerequisite to success in the kind of national life for which we strive. Each man must work for himself, and unless he so works no outside help can avail him. . . . To be permanently effective, aid must always take the form of helping a man to help himself.

THEODORE ROOSEVELT
First Annual Message to Congress, Dec. 3, 1901;
Works (Mem. Ed.), *XVII*, 110

3. Hawaii cries insistently to a divided world that all our differences of race and origin are less than the grand and indestructible unity of our common brotherhood. The world should take time to listen with attentive ear to Hawaii.

DWIGHT D. EISENHOWER
Address at New Delhi, India, Dec. 10, 1959;
Public Papers . . . Eisenhower, 1959, p. 831

See also Character 3, Charity 2, Democracy 14, Foreign Relations 15, Justice 14, Peace 46, 58, Politics 16, Responsibility 2, Union 19

Budget
See Debts, Economy, Prosperity 15

Bureaucracy

1. I am accused of usurping power, when my whole life has been one continual battle against the tendency of bureaucracy or aristocracy—the concentration of power in the hands of the few. . . . I am for holding all possible power in the hands of the people permanently. . . .

ANDREW JOHNSON
Interview, Feb. 20, 1867; *Presidents and the Press*, p. 415

2. Bureaucracy is ever desirous of spreading its influence and its power. You cannot extend the mastery of the government over the daily working life of a people without at the same time making it the master of the people's souls and thoughts.

HERBERT HOOVER
1928; *New Day*, p. 162

Business

1. The business of the country is like the level of the ocean, from which all measurements are made of heights and depths.

JAMES A. GARFIELD
Speech to the House of Representatives, Jan. 7, 1870; *Lives*, p. 24

2. Business success, whether for the individual or for the Nation, is a good thing only so far as it is accompanied by and develops a high standard of conduct—honor, integrity, civic courage. . . . This Government stands for manhood first and for business only as an adjunct of manhood.

THEODORE ROOSEVELT
Fifth Annual Message to Congress, Dec. 5, 1905;
Messages and Papers, p. 7360

3. I hold it to be our duty to see that the wage-worker, the small producer, the ordinary consumer, shall get their fair share of the benefit of business prosperity. But it either is or ought to be evident to everyone that business has to prosper before anybody can get any benefit from it.

THEODORE ROOSEVELT
Address to the Ohio Constitutional Convention, Feb. 21, 1912;
Charter, p. 6

4. I hate that old maxim "Business is business," for I understand by it that business is not moral. The man who says, "I am not in business for my health," means that he is not in business for his moral health, and I am an enemy of every business of this kind. But if business is regarded as an object for serving and obtaining private profit by means of service, then I am with that business.

WOODROW WILSON
Speech to Free Synagogue meeting, New York, N.Y., Apr. 24,
1911; *New York Times, Apr. 25, 1911*

5.   Business underlies everything in our national life, including our spiritual life. Witness the fact that in the Lord's prayer, the first petition is for daily bread. No one can worship God or love his neighbor on an empty stomach.

WOODROW WILSON
Speech in New York, N.Y., May 23, 1912; *Public Papers, II,* 432

6.   I have said to the people we mean to have less of Government in business as well as more business in Government.

WARREN G. HARDING
Special Address to Congress, Apr. 12, 1921;
Messages and Papers, p. 8940

7.   The chief business of America is business.

CALVIN COOLIDGE
Address to Society of American Newspaper Editors, Jan. 17, 1925,
Foundations, p. 187

8.   When legislation penetrates the business world it is because there is abuse somewhere. A great deal of this legislation is due rather to the inability of business hitherto to so organize as to correct abuses. . . . Sometimes the abuses are more apparent than real, but anything is a handle for demagoguery. In the main, however, the public acts only when it has lost confidence in the ability or willingness of business to correct its own abuses.

HERBERT HOOVER
Address, May 7, 1924; *Memoirs, II,* 171

9.   American business needs a lifting purpose greater than the struggle of materialism.

HERBERT HOOVER
Address, May 7, 1925; *Ibid.*

10.   It is just as important that business keep out of government as that government keep out of business.

HERBERT HOOVER
Speech in New York, N.Y., Oct. 22, 1928; *Policies,* p. 21

11.   Out of this modern civilization economic royalists carved new dynasties. New kingdoms were built upon concentration of control over material things. Through new uses of corporations, banks and securities, new machinery of industry and agriculture, of labor and capital—all undreamed of by the fathers—the whole structure of modern life was impressed into this royal service.

There was no place among this royalty for our many thousands of small business men and merchants who sought to make a worthy use of the American system of initiative and profit. . . .

The royalists of the economic order have conceded that political freedom was the business of the Government, but they have maintained that economic slavery was nobody's business. . . .

These economic royalists complain that we seek to overthrow the institutions of America. What they really complain of is that we seek to take away their power. Our allegiance to American institutions requires the overthrow of this kind of power.

> FRANKLIN DELANO ROOSEVELT
> Acceptance of Renomination for Presidency, Philadelphia, Pa.,
> June 27, 1936; *Public Papers, V,* 232–34

12. It is easy to charge an Administration is anti-business, but it is more difficult to show how an Administration, composed, we hope, of rational men, can possibly feel they can survive without business, or how the nation can survive without business, or how the nation can survive unless the Government and business and all other groups in our country are exerting their best efforts in an atmosphere of understanding and, I hope, cooperation.

> JOHN F. KENNEDY
> In Washington, D.C., Apr. 30, 1962;
> *Vital Speeches, June 1, 1962,* p. 483

See also Character 9, Privileges 2, Security 5, Square Deal 2, Taxation 15

Capital
See Labor

Capitalists
1. These capitalists generally act harmoniously and in concert, to fleece the people.

> ABRAHAM LINCOLN
> Speech to Illinois Legislature, January, 1837

See also Banks, Labor

Causes
See Beliefs, Convictions, Enthusiasm, Failure 1, Foreign Relations 48, Freedom 25, Greatness 6, Laws 13, Purposes, Russia 1, Tolerance 3, War 50

Censors
1. The people are the only censors of their governors, and even their errors will tend to keep these to the true principles of their institution.

> THOMAS JEFFERSON
> To Edward Carrington, Jan. 16, 1787; *Writings, VI,* 57

2. No government ought to be without censors; and where the press is free, no one ever will.

> THOMAS JEFFERSON
> To George Washington, Sept. 9, 1792; *Ibid., VIII,* 394

3. I am . . . mortified to be told that, in the *United States of America* . . . a question about the sale of a book can be carried before the civil magistrate. . . . Are we to have a censor whose imprimatur shall say what books may be sold, and what we may buy? . . . Whose foot is to be the measure to which ours are all to be cut or stretched? . . . Shall a layman, simple as ourselves, set up his reason as the rule for what we are to read? . . . It is an insult to our citizens to question whether they are rational beings or not.

THOMAS JEFFERSON
To N. G. DuFief, Apr. 19, 1814; *Ibid., XIV*, 127

4. Don't join the book burners. Don't think you're going to conceal faults by concealing evidence that they ever existed. Don't be afraid to go in your library and read every book, as long as any document does not offend our own ideas of decency. That should be our only censorship.

DWIGHT D. EISENHOWER
Remarks at Dartmouth College commencement, June 14, 1953;
American Treasury, p. 290

5. Freedom cannot be censored into existence. A democracy smugly disdainful of new ideas would be a sick democracy. A democracy chronically fearful of new ideas would be a dying democracy.

DWIGHT D. EISENHOWER
Letter to the American Library Association, June 24, 1953;
Ibid., p. 163

See also Power 4, Public Opinion 1

Challenges
See Peace 89

Chance
1. Experience has proved, that chance is often as much concerned in deciding . . . matters as bravery; and always more, than the justice of the cause.

GEORGE WASHINGTON
To the Marquis de Lafayette, Oct. 4, 1778;
Writings (Fitzpatrick), VI, 79

2. I think that any man who has had what is regarded . . . as a great success must realize that the element of chance has played a great part in it. . . . If there is not the war, you don't get the great general; if there is not a great occasion, you don't get the great statesman; if Lincoln had lived in times of peace, no one would have known his name now. The great crisis must come, or no man has the chance to develop great qualities.

THEODORE ROOSEVELT
Address at Cambridge, England, May 26, 1910;
Works (Mem. Ed.), XV, 508

See also Progress

Change

1. I am not one of those who wish for change for the mere sake of variety. The only men who do that are the men who want to forget something. . . . Change is not worth while unless it is improvement.

WOODROW WILSON
1912; *New Freedom (Hale)*, p. 39

2. If you want to make enemies, try to change something.

WOODROW WILSON
Speech at Detroit, Mich., July 10, 1916; *Selections*, p. 68

See also Government 37, Liberalism 2, Libraries 4, Principles 8, 13, Progress

Character

1. I had laid it down as a law to myself, to take no notice of the thousand calumnies issued against me, but to trust my character to my own conduct, and the good sense and candor of my fellow citizens.

THOMAS JEFFERSON
To Wilson Cary Nicholas, June 13, 1809; *Writings, IX,* 253

2. Respect for character, though often a salutary restraint, is but too often overruled by other motives. When numbers of men act in a body, respect for character is often lost, just in proportion as it is necessary to control what is not right.

JAMES MADISON
Speech to Virginia State Convention, Dec. 2, 1829; *Letters, IV,* 52

3. Friends, I am a thorough believer in the American test of character. He will not build high who does not build for himself.

BENJAMIN HARRISON
At Indianapolis, Ind., July 4, 1888; *Speeches,* p. 39

4. In acquiring knowledge there is one thing equally important, and that is character. Nothing in the . . . world is worth so much, will last so long, and serve its possessor so well as good character.

WILLIAM McKINLEY
At Savannah, Ga., Dec. 18, 1898; *Speeches and Addresses,* p. 177

5. It is character that counts in a nation as in a man. It is a good thing to have a keen, fine intellectual development in a nation, to produce orators, artists, successful business men; but it is an infinitely greater thing to have those solid qualities which we group together under the name of character —sobriety, steadfastness, the sense of obligation toward one's neighbor and one's God, hard common sense, and, combined with it, the lift of generous

enthusiasm toward whatever is right. These are the qualities which go to make up true national greatness.

THEODORE ROOSEVELT
Address at Galena, Ill., Apr. 27, 1900; *Works, XIII,* 437

6.   A sound body is good; a sound mind is better; but a strong and clean character is better than either.

THEODORE ROOSEVELT
At Groton, Mass., May 24, 1904; *Presidential Addresses, III,* 14

7.   No man can lead a public career really worth leading, no man can act with rugged independence in serious crises, nor strike at great abuses, nor afford to make powerful and unscrupulous foes, if he is himself vulnerable in his private character.

THEODORE ROOSEVELT
Autobiography, p. 84

8.   Character is a by-product; it is produced in the great manufacture of daily duty.

WOODROW WILSON
Address at Arlington, Va., May 31, 1915; *Public Papers, III,* 337

9.   The one continuing, unchanging and unchangeable thing is character. A business built with conscience as its architect and character as its cornerstone, is destined to stand foursquare and firm.

WARREN G. HARDING

10.   Character is the only secure foundation of the State.

CALVIN COOLIDGE
Address in New York, N.Y., Feb. 12, 1924;
Messages and Papers, p. 9378

11.   National character cannot be built by law. It is the sum of the moral fiber of its individuals. When abuses which rise from our growing system are cured by live individual conscience, by initiative in the creation of voluntary standards, then is the growth of moral perception fertilized in every individual character. . . .

HERBERT HOOVER
Address, May 7, 1924; *Memoirs, II,* 171

12.   Character is the most precious asset of our country.

HERBERT HOOVER
Remarks, Nov. 11, 1948; *Addresses,* p. 171

13.   It is not our nature to shirk our obligations. We have a heritage that constitutes the greatest resource of this nation. I call it the spirit and character of the American people.

HARRY S. TRUMAN
1947; *Memoirs, II,* 108

See also Americans, Democracy 13, Flag (The) 4, Individualism, Liberty 40, Progress 4, Rights 10, Self-Government 5, War 1, 5, 15, 18

Charity

1. I deem it the duty of every man to devote a certain portion of his income for charitable purposes; and that it is his further duty to see it so applied as to do the most good of which it is capable.

THOMAS JEFFERSON
To Drs. Rogers and Slaughter, Mar. 2, 1806; *Writings, XI,* 92

2. Charity literally translated from the original means love, the love that understands, that does not merely share the wealth of the giver, but in true sympathy and wisdom helps men to help themselves.

FRANKLIN DELANO ROOSEVELT
Acceptance of Renomination for Presidency, Philadelphia, Pa.,
June 27, 1936; *Public Papers, V,* 235

3. Better the occasional faults of a Government that lives in a spirit of charity than the consistent omissions of a Government frozen in the ice of its own indifference.

FRANKLIN DELANO ROOSEVELT
Ibid.

See also Benevolence, Government 74, 86, Peace 21, Philanthropy, Relief, Russia 4, States' Rights 15, Subsidy, Unemployment, Wealth

Church

1. The loathsome combination of Church and State.

THOMAS JEFFERSON
To Charles Clay, Jan. 29, 1815; *Writings, XIV,* 232

2. When once more I am clear of politics I will join the church.

ANDREW JACKSON
To Rachel Jackson, *ca.* 1826; *Life (Parton), III,* 101

3. Partisanship should be kept out of the pulpit. . . . It makes saints of sinners and sinners of saints. The balance wheel of free institutions is free discussion. The pulpit allows no free discussion.

RUTHERFORD B. HAYES
Diary, Jan. 3, 1892; *Diary and Letters, V,* 44

See also Religion

Citizenship

1. Every citizen owes to the country a vigilant watch and close scrutiny of its public servants and a fair and reasonable estimate of their fidelity and usefulness. Thus is the people's will impressed upon the whole frame-

work of our civil polity . . . and this is the price of our liberty and the inspiration of our faith in the Republic.

GROVER CLEVELAND
First Inaugural Address, Mar. 4, 1885

2.   Cultivate the highest and best citizenship; for upon it rests the destiny of our government.

WILLIAM MCKINLEY
At G.A.R. Campfire, Buffalo, N.Y., Aug. 24, 1897;
Speeches and Addresses, p. 42

3.   The first requisite of a good citizen in this Republic of ours is that he shall be able and willing to pull his weight—that he shall not be a mere passenger, but shall do his share in the work that each generation of us finds ready to hand; and, furthermore, that in doing his work he shall show not only the capacity for sturdy self-help but also self-respecting regard for the rights of others.

THEODORE ROOSEVELT
To New York State Chamber of Commerce, Nov. 11, 1902;
Presidential Addresses, I, 200

4.   The good citizen is the man who, whatever his wealth or his poverty, strives manfully to do his duty to himself, to his family, to his neighbor, to the State; who is incapable of the baseness which manifests itself either in arrogance or in envy, but who while demanding justice for himself is no less scrupulous to do justice to others.

THEODORE ROOSEVELT
At Syracuse, N.Y., Sept. 7, 1903; *Ibid., II,* 473

5.   Nothing is more important to America than citizenship; there is more assurance of our future in the individual character of our citizens than in any proposal I, and all the wise advisers I can gather, can ever put into effect in Washington.

WARREN G. HARDING
At Galion, Ohio, Aug. 27, 1920;
Speeches of Warren G. Harding, p. 81

6.   Patriotism means equipped forces and a prepared citizenry. Moral stamina means more energy and more productivity, on the farm and in the factory. Love of liberty means the guarding of every resource that makes freedom possible—from the sanctity of our families and the wealth of our soil to the genius of our scientists.

And so each citizen plays an indispensable role.

DWIGHT D. EISENHOWER
First Inaugural Address, Jan. 20, 1953

See also Americans, Homes 2, Rights 11, Suffrage 6

Civilization

1. To correct the evils, great and small, which spring from want of sympathy and from positive enmity among strangers, as nations or as individuals, is one of the highest functions of civilization.

ABRAHAM LINCOLN
Address at Milwaukee, Wis., Sept. 30, 1859;
Complete Works, V, 236

2. An Englishman who was wrecked on a strange shore and wandering along the coast . . . came to a gallows with a victim hanging on it, and fell down on his knees and thanked God that he at last beheld a sign of civilization.

JAMES A. GARFIELD
Speech to House of Representatives, June 15, 1870; *Orator,* p. 15

3. The worth of a civilization is the worth of the man at its center.

THEODORE ROOSEVELT
Outlook (magazine), Sept. 13, 1902

4. No people is wholly civilized where a distinction is drawn between stealing an office and stealing a purse.

THEODORE ROOSEVELT
Speech in Chicago, Ill., June 22, 1912; *Dictionary,* p. 1188

5. The cornerstone of modern civilization must continue to be religion and morality.

WILLIAM HOWARD TAFT
At Portland, Ore., Oct. 3, 1909; *Presidential Addresses, I,* 322

6. Civilization can never be entrenched, it must battle in the open, ever ready to march on. Entrench it and it dies. Its defense must be progressively offensive.

WARREN G. HARDING
Memorial Day address, 1923; *Messages and Papers,* p. 9230

7. Civilization and profits go hand in hand. . . .
The process of civilization consists of the discovery by men of the laws of the universe and of living in harmony with those laws. The most important of them to men are the laws of their own nature.
It is not necessary to suppose that our civilization is perfect.

CALVIN COOLIDGE
Address in New York, N.Y., Nov. 27, 1920; *Freedom,* p. 3

8. Our civilization is much like a garden. It is to be appraised by the quality of its blooms. In degree as we fertilize its soil with liberty, as we maintain diligence in cultivation and guardianship against destructive forces, do we then produce those blossoms, the fragrance of whose lives

stimulate renewed endeavor, give to us the courage to renewed effort and confidence of the future.

HERBERT HOOVER
Speech at Detroit, Mich., Oct. 21, 1929; *State Papers, I,* 112

See also Education 28, Foreign Relations 30, 35, History 13, Jews 1, Knowledge 9, Liberty 42, Pacifists 2, Peace 52, Property 10, Statesmanship 3, War 50, Work 4

Civil Liberty
See Liberty, Union 20

Civil Rights
1. America stands for progress in human rights as well as economic affairs, and a strong America requires the assurance of full and equal rights to all its citizens, of any race of any color. . . .

As we approach the 100th anniversary . . . of the Emancipation Proclamation, let the acts of every branch of Government—and every citizen—portray that "righteousness does exalt a nation."

JOHN F. KENNEDY
To Congress, Jan. 11, 1962; *Vital Speeches,*
Feb. 1, 1962, p. 231

2. We have talked long enough in this country about equal rights. We talked for 100 years or more. Yet, it is time now to write the next chapter—and to write it in books of law.

I urge you . . . to enact a civil rights law so that we can move forward to eliminate from this nation every trace of discrimination and oppression based upon race or color. There could be no greater source of strength to this nation both at home and abroad.

LYNDON B. JOHNSON
Address to Congress, Nov. 27, 1963; *Chicago Daily News,*
Nov. 27, 1963

See also Equality, Negroes, Opportunity, Segregation

Civil Servants
See Confidence 2, Conscience 8, Corruption 4, Debts 2, Public Office

Civil War
See Nationality 1, Union 28, War 23, 29, 42

Class
1. The only kinds of courage and honesty which are permanently useful to good institutions anywhere are those shown by men who decide all

cases with impartial justice on grounds of conduct and not on grounds of class.

THEODORE ROOSEVELT
Autobiography, p. 78

See also Prosperity 10

Cliches

1. We cannot understand and attack our contemporary problems . . . if we are bound by traditional labels and worn-out slogans of an earlier era. . . .

What we need is not labels and *clichés* but more basic discussion of the sophisticated and technical questions involved in keeping a great economic machinery moving ahead.

As every generation has had to disenthrall itself from an inheritance of truisms and stereotypes, so in our time we must move on from the reassuring repetition of stale phrases to a new, difficult but essential confrontation with reality. . . .

Too often, we hold fast to the *clichés* of our forebears. We enjoy the comfort of opinion without the discomfort of thought. . . .

If there is any current trend toward meeting present problems with old *clichés*, this is the moment to stop it—before it lands us all in the bog of sterile acrimony.

JOHN F. KENNEDY
Speech at Yale University, June 11, 1962; *Public Papers . . .
Kennedy, 1962*, p. 473

See also Slogans

Coercion

1. Experience has taught us that men will not adopt and carry into execution measures the best calculated for their own good without the intervention of a coercive power.

GEORGE WASHINGTON
To John Jay, Aug. 1, 1786; *Writings (Ford)*, *XI*, 53

2. When a faction in a state attempts to nullify a constitutional law of congress, or to destroy the union, the balance of the people composing this union have a perfect right to coerce them to obedience. This is my creed.

ANDREW JACKSON
To Gen. John Coffee, Dec. 14, 1832; *Life (Bassett)*, p. 570

3. Coercion is the basis of every law in the universe—Human or Divine. A law is no law without coercion behind it.

JAMES A. GARFIELD
Maxims, p. 23

See also Congress 1, Opinion 2

Colleges

1.   I had not the advantage of a classical education, and no man should, in my judgment, accept a degree he cannot read.

MILLARD FILLMORE
Declining a degree offered by the University of Oxford, 1855;
Millard Fillmore (Rayback), p. 398

2.   Business colleges . . . originated in this country as a protest against the failure, the absolute failure, of our American schools and colleges to fit young men and women for the business of life.

JAMES A. GARFIELD
Speech in Washington, D.C., June 29, 1869; *Lives*, p. 27

3.   A grave charge against our system of higher education [is] that it is disconnected from the active business of life. It is a charge to which our colleges cannot plead guilty, and live. . . . There is scarcely a more pitiable sight than to see . . . learned men so called who have graduated in our . . . universities . . . who know the whole gamut of classical learning . . . and yet could not make out a bill of sale if the world depended upon it.

JAMES A. GARFIELD
Address in Washington, D.C., June 29, 1869;
Garfield and Education, p. 319

4.   Glory we owe in no small part to the all-embracing influence of our colleges and universities. They have wrought mightily in the making of America. They stand like mighty fortresses within whose protection the truth is secure. Against them no enemy shall prevail.

CALVIN COOLIDGE
Address at Amherst College alumni dinner, New York, N.Y.,
Nov. 27, 1920; *Freedom*, p. 3

See also Conservatism 2, Education 7, Knowledge, Libraries 3, Military Matters 5, Universities

Colonialism

1.   The American continents, by the free and independent condition which they have assumed and maintain, are henceforth not to be considered as subjects for future colonialization by any European powers.

We owe it . . . to candor, and to the amicable relations existing between the United States and those powers to declare that we should consider any attempt on their part to extend their system to any portion of this hemisphere as dangerous to our peace and safety. With the existing colonies or dependencies of any European power we . . . shall not interfere. But with the governments . . . whose independence we have . . . acknowledged, we could not view any interposition for the purpose of oppressing them or controlling, in any other manner, their destiny, by any European power, in any other light than as a manifestation of an unfriendly disposition towards the United States.

JAMES MONROE
Seventh Annual Message to Congress, Dec. 2, 1823, *Messages and Papers,* p. 778

See also Conquest, Monroe Doctrine, Territorial Acquisition, Tyranny 4

Commerce
See Foreign Relations 5, 6, Freedom 18, Trade, War 6

Common Man
See Boondoggling 1, Business 3, Fighting 7, Government 47, Ignorance 3, Labor, Opportunity, People (The) 24, Prosperity 10

Common Sense
1.   It has always seemed to me that common sense is the real solvent for the nation's problems at all times—common sense and hard work.

CALVIN COOLIDGE
To Henry Stoddard, 1930; *Meet Calvin Coolidge,* p. 214

See also Nullification

Communism
1.   Communism is a hateful thing and a menace to peace and organized government; but the communism of combined wealth and capital, the outgrowth of overweening cupidity and selfishness, which insidiously undermines the justice and integrity of free institutions, is not less dangerous than the communism of oppressed poverty and toil, which, exasperated by injustice and discontent, attacks with wild disorder the citadel of rule.

GROVER CLEVELAND
Fourth Annual Message to Congress, Dec. 3, 1888; *Messages and Papers,* p. 5361

2.   Communism is merely the imposition of Socialism all at once by violence. . . . It is difficult to find positive definition of Communism among its friends. They are mostly involved in polemics against other systems.

HERBERT HOOVER
1934; *Challenge,* p. 61

3.   The Marshall Plan will go down in history as one of America's greatest contributions to the peace of the world. I think the world now realizes that without the Marshall Plan it would have been difficult for western Europe to remain free from the tyranny of Communism.

HARRY S. TRUMAN
1949; *Memoirs, II,* 119

4. Communism is a system that has no regard for human dignity or human freedom, and no right-thinking government can give its consent to the forcible return [via exchange of prisoners of war] to such a system of men or women who would rather remain free. . . .

We will not buy an armistice by turning over human beings for slaughter or slavery.

HARRY S. TRUMAN
A public statement to the Russians, May 7, 1952; *Ibid.*, p. 460

5. The Communist goal of conquering the world has never changed. For our nation alone to undertake to withstand and turn back Communist imperialism would impose colossal defense spending on our people. It would ultimately cost us our freedom. . . .

We in our own interest, and other free nations in their own interest, have therefore joined in the building and maintenance of a system of collective security in which the effort of each nation strengthens all. Today that system has become the keystone of our own and their security in a tense and uncertain world.

DWIGHT D. EISENHOWER
Special Message to Congress, May 21, 1957; *Public Papers . . . Eisenhower, 1957*, p. 373

6. We in the United States must not fall into the error of blaming ourselves for what the Communists do; after all, Communists will act like Communists. . . .

We must recognize their tactics as a deliberate attempt to split the Free World, causing friction between allies and friends. We must not fall into this trap; all of us must remain firm and steadfast in our united dedication to freedom, and to peace with justice.

Above all, we must bear in mind that successful implementation of any policy against Communist imperialism requires that we never be bluffed, cajoled, blinded or frightened. We cannot win out against the Communist purpose to dominate the world by being timid, passive, or apologetic. . . . We must accept the risks of bold action with coolness and courage. . . . We will always extend friendship wherever friendship is offered honestly to us.

DWIGHT D. EISENHOWER
Radio and television report, June 27, 1960; *Public Papers . . . Eisenhower, 1960–61*, p. 533

7. There is no point in speaking out against the spread of Communism if we are unwilling to recognize which weapons are most needed in that struggle. There is no point in calling for vigorous action to protect our

security if we are unwilling to pay the price and carry the burdens which are necessary to maintain that security.

JOHN F. KENNEDY
Remarks at National Conference on International Economic and
Social Development, June 16, 1961; *Tide,* p. 155

8.   Strike down ignorance, poverty, and disease, and Communism without its allies will wither and die.

LYNDON B. JOHNSON
Address at Medical Journalism luncheon, New York, N.Y.,
May 4, 1961

See also Fear 5, Foreign Relations 46, Ignorance 8, Peace 86, Poverty 2, United Nations 1

Conduct

1.   Observe good faith and justice toward all nations. Cultivate peace and harmony with all. Religion and morality enjoin this conduct.

GEORGE WASHINGTON
Farewell Address, Sept. 19, 1796;
Writings (Fitzpatrick), XXXV, 231

2.   Some person of more advanc'd life and longer standing publick trust sho'd be selected. . . . A person who had marked a line of conduct so decisively that you might tell what he would be hereafter by what he had been heretofore.

JAMES MONROE
To James Madison, Oct. 9, 1792; *Writings, I,* 243

3.   I feel it is not less due to myself and principle than to the American people [who have] sanctioned my political creed, to steer clear of every conduct out of which the idea might arise that I was maneuvering for my own aggrandisement.

ANDREW JACKSON
July, 1826; *Life (Parton), III,* 100

See also Class, Foreign Relations 35, Public Office 21, Religion 18, 25

Confederation

1.   A confederation is not a country.

JOHN QUINCY ADAMS
Eulogy on James Madison; *Chips,* p. 170

Confidence

1.   Industry and economy are the only resources. . . . It is vain to wait for money, or temporise. The great desiderata are public and private confidence. No country in the world can do without them. . . . The circulation of confidence is better than the circulation of money. . . . Confi-

dence produces the best effects. . . . The establishment of confidence will raise the value of property, and relieve those who are so unhappy as to be involved in debts.

JAMES MADISON
Speech to the Virginia Convention, June 20, 1788; *Writings*
(Hunt), *V*, 225

2. The basis of effective government is public confidence, and that confidence is endangered when ethical standards falter or appear to falter.

I have firm confidence in the integrity and dedication of those who work for our government.

JOHN F. KENNEDY
Special Message to Congress, Apr. 27, 1961; *Tide,* p. 107

See also Fear 6, Foreign Relations 39, 49, Politics 3, 5, Religion 15, Revolutions 1

Congress

1. There is no calamity within the compass of my foresight, which is more to be dreaded, than a necessity of coercion on the part of Congress. . . . It must involve the ruin of that State against which the resentment of the others is pointed.

GEORGE WASHINGTON
To Thomas Chittenden, Jan. 1, 1782;
Writings (Fitzpatrick), *XXIII*, 421

2. *Referring to Congress:*
That 150 lawyers should do business together is not to be expected.

THOMAS JEFFERSON
Autobiography, Jan. 6, 1821; *Writings, I,* 87

3. All the public business in Congress now connects itself with intrigues, and there is great danger that the whole government will degenerate into a struggle of cabals.

JOHN QUINCY ADAMS
Diary, January, 1819; *John Quincy Adams (Morse),* p. 154

4. The passion for office among members of Congress is very great, if not absolutely disreputable, and greatly embarrasses the operations of the Government. They create offices by their own votes and then seek to fill them themselves. I shall refuse to appoint them . . . because their appointment would be most corrupting in its tendency. . . . I will not countenance such selfishness, but will do my duty, and rely on the country for an honest support of my administration.

JAMES K. POLK
June 22, 1846; *Diary (Quaife), I,* 483

5.   I begin, more than . . . ever . . . to distrust the disinterestedness and honesty of all mankind. . . . There is more selfishness and less principle among members of Congress, as well as others, than I had any conception of, before I became President of the U.S.

JAMES K. POLK
Dec. 16, 1846; *Ibid., II,* 279

See also Courts, Filibustering, Government 15, Panama Canal 2, Political Philosophy 1, Power 11, Presidency (The) 18, 62, Secrecy 1, States' Rights 13, Veto Power 4

Conquest

1.   Conquest is not in our principles; it is inconsistent with our government.

THOMAS JEFFERSON
To William Carmichael, Aug. 22, 1790; *Writings (Ford), V,* 230

2.   If there be one principle more deeply rooted than any other in the mind of every American, it is, that we should have nothing to do with conquest.

THOMAS JEFFERSON
To William Short, July 28, 1791; *Ibid., VIII,* 219

3.   The United States will never again seek one additional foot of territory by conquest. She will devote herself to showing that she knows how to make honorable and fruitful use of the territory she has, and she must regard it as one of the duties of friendship to see that from no quarter are material interests made superior to human liberty and national opportunity.

WOODROW WILSON
Address at Mobile, Ala., Oct. 27, 1913; *State Papers,* p. 36

4.   We have no selfish ends to serve. We desire no conquest, no dominion. . . . We are but one of the champions of the rights of mankind.

WOODROW WILSON
Address to Congress, asking for war, Apr. 2, 1917; *Ibid.,* p. 381

5.   The day of conquest and aggrandizement has gone by.

WOODROW WILSON
Jan. 8, 1918; *Lasting Peace,* p. 100

6.   The whole world now knows that the United States cherishes no predatory ambitions. We are strong; but less powerful nations know that they need not fear our strength. We seek no conquest; we stand for peace.

FRANKLIN DELANO ROOSEVELT
Address at Chautauqua, N.Y., Aug. 14, 1936;
Public Papers, V, 286

See also War 44

Conscience

1. Labor to keep alive in your breast that little spark of celestial fire called conscience.

GEORGE WASHINGTON
Early copybook, 1746; *Writings (Sparks), II, 415*

2. While we are contending for our own *liberty,* we should be very cautious not to violate the rights of conscience in others, ever considering that God alone is the judge of the hearts of men, and to Him only in this case they are answerable.

GEORGE WASHINGTON
To Benedict Arnold, Sept. 14, 1775;
Writings (Fitzpatrick), III, 91

3. It behooves every man who values liberty of conscience for himself, to resist invasions of it in the case of others.

THOMAS JEFFERSON
To Benjamin Rush, Apr. 21, 1803; *Writings, IX, 457*

4. Conscience is the most sacred of all property; other property depending in part on positive law, the exercise of that, being a natural and inalienable right. To guard a man's house as his castle, to pay public and enforce private debts with the most exact faith, can give no title to invade a man's conscience which is more sacred than his castle. . . .

JAMES MADISON
National Gazette, Mar. 29, 1792; *Complete Madison,* p. 267

5. *My* conscience stands void of offense, and will go quietly with me, regardless of the insinuations of those who, through management, may seek an influence not sanctioned by integrity and merit.

ANDREW JACKSON
To Samuel Swartwout, Feb. 22, 1824; *Life (Parton), III, 76*

6. Let it, then, be henceforth proclaimed to the world, that man's conscience was created free; that he is no longer accountable to his fellow man for his religious opinions, being responsible therefore only to his God.

JOHN TYLER

7. No client ever had money enough to bribe my conscience or to stop its utterance against wrong, and oppression. My conscience is my own— my creator's—not man's. I shall never sink the rights of mankind to the malice—wrong or avarice of another's wishes, though those wishes come to me in relation of client and attorney.

ABRAHAM LINCOLN
Springfield, Ill., *ca.* 1856; *Abraham Lincoln Quarterly,*
Dec. 1941, p. 431

8. I hold that a man cannot serve the people well unless he serves his conscience; but I hold also that where his conscience bids him refuse to do what the people desire, he should not try to continue in office against their will. Our government system should be so shaped that the public servant, when he cannot conscientiously carry out the wishes of the people, shall at their desire leave his office and not misrepresent them in office; and I hold that the public servant can by so doing, better than in any other way, serve both them and his conscience.

THEODORE ROOSEVELT
To Progressive National Convention, Chicago, Ill., Aug. 6, 1912;
Works, XVII, 298

See also Character 9, Government 88, Public Office 23, Religion 2, 16

Conservation

1. Conservation means development as much as it does protection.

THEODORE ROOSEVELT
Speech at Osawatomie, Kan., Aug. 31, 1910;
Works (Natl. Ed.), XVII, 15

2. The Nation behaves well if it treats the natural resources as assets which it must turn over to the next generation increased, and not impaired, in value.

THEODORE ROOSEVELT
Public Papers (of F.D.R.), V, 61

3. The fundamental question of conservation in America is the conservation of energy, the elasticity, the hope of the American people.

WOODROW WILSON
Address in Richmond, Va., Feb. 1, 1912; *Pamphlet,* 1912

4. The history of every nation is eventually written in the way in which it cares for its soil.

FRANKLIN DELANO ROOSEVELT
Statement, Mar. 1, 1936; *Ibid., V,* 99

Conservatism

1. What is conservatism? Is it not adherence to the old and tried, against the new and untried?

ABRAHAM LINCOLN
Speech at Cooper Institute, New York, N.Y., Feb. 27, 1860;
Complete Works, V, 313

2. Generally young men are regarded as radicals. This is a popular misconception. The most conservative persons I ever met are college undergraduates.

WOODROW WILSON
Address in New York, N.Y., Nov. 19, 1905

3.   Conservatism is the policy of "make no change and consult your grandmother when in doubt."

WOODROW WILSON
1918; *Philosophy*, p. 39

4.   A conservative is a man who just sits and thinks, mostly sits.

WOODROW WILSON
Wit and Wisdom, p. 57

See also Liberalism, Political Philosophy 4, Standpatism

Constitution

1.   To every description of citizens, indeed, let praise be given. But let them persevere in their affectionate vigilance over that precious depository of American happiness, the Constitution of the United States.

GEORGE WASHINGTON
Sixth Annual Message to Congress, Nov. 19, 1794; *Messages and Papers*, p. 158

2.   The Constitution is the guide which I never will abandon.

GEORGE WASHINGTON
Speech to Boston Selectmen, July 28, 1795;
Writings (Fitzpatrick), *XXXIV*, 253

3.   The Constitution of the United States is the result of the collected wisdom of our country.

THOMAS JEFFERSON
Letter to Amos Marsh, Nov. 20, 1801; *Works, IV*, 418

4.   Some men look at constitutions with sanctimonious reverence, and deem them like the ark of the covenant, too sacred to be touched. They ascribe to the men of the preceding age a wisdom more than human, and suppose what they did to be beyond amendment. . . . I am certainly not an advocate for frequent and untried changes in laws and constitutions. . . . But I know also, that laws and institutions must go hand in hand with the progress of the human mind. . . . We might as well require a man to wear still the coat which fitted him when a boy, as civilized society to remain ever under the regimen of their barbarous ancestors.

THOMAS JEFFERSON
To Samuel Kercheval, July 12, 1816; *Writings, XV*, 40

5.   Our Constitution professedly rests upon the good sense and attachment of the people. This basis, weak as it may appear, has not yet been found to fail.

JOHN QUINCY ADAMS
To William Vans Murray, Jan. 27, 1801;
Writings (Ford), *II*, 495

6. We have received [the Constitution] as the work of the assembled wisdom of the nation; we have trusted to it as to the sheet anchor of our safety in the stormy times of conflict with a foreign or domestic foe; we have looked to it with sacred awe as the palladium of our liberties.

ANDREW JACKSON
Proclamation, Dec. 10, 1832; *Messages and Papers*, p. 1207

7. The Constitution is still the object of our reverence, the bond of our Union, our defense in danger, the source of our prosperity in peace. [It] forms a *government*, not a league.

ANDREW JACKSON
Proclamation, Dec. 10, 1832; *Ibid.*, p. 1208

8. I believe . . . that constitutions are the work of time and not the invention of ingenuity; and that to frame a complete system of government, depending on the habits of reverence and experience, was an attempt as absurd as to build a tree or manufacture an opinion.

MARTIN VAN BUREN
1820; *Epoch*, p. 226

9. I am determined to uphold the Constitution . . . to the utmost of my ability and in defiance of all personal consequences. What may happen to an individual is of little importance, but the Constitution of the country, or any of its great and clear principles and provisions, is too sacred to be surrendered under any circumstances whatever by those who are charged with its protection and defense.

JOHN TYLER
Protest, Aug. 30, 1842; *Messages and Papers*, p. 2046

10. The usefulness and permanency of this Government and the happiness of the millions over whom it spreads its protection will be best promoted by carefully abstaining from the exercise of all powers not clearly granted by the Constitution.

JAMES K. POLK
Veto Message, Dec. 15, 1847; *Ibid.*, p. 2476

11. Like the Christian faith . . . when it is genuine, good results will inevitably flow from a sincere belief in a strict construction of the Constitution.

JAMES BUCHANAN
To Central Southern Rights Association of Virginia, Apr. 10, 1851;
Life, II, 24

12. There is nothing stable but Heaven and the Constitution.

JAMES BUCHANAN
May 13, 1856; *President*, p. 253

13. Don't interfere with anything in the Constitution. That must be maintained, for it is the only safeguard of our liberties.

ABRAHAM LINCOLN

Speech at Kalamazoo, Mich., Aug. 27, 1856; *Speeches and Writings*, p. 345

14. I will stand by the Constitution of the country as it is, and by all its guaranties. . . . I intend to stand by it as the sheet-anchor of the Government; and I trust and hope, though it seems to be now in the very vortex of ruin, though it seems to be running between Charybdis and Scylla, the rock on the one hand and the whirlpool on the other, that it will be preserved, and will remain a beacon to guide, and an example to be imitated by all the nations of the earth. Yes, I intend to hold on to it as the chief ark of our safety, as the palladium of our civil and our religious liberty.

ANDREW JOHNSON

To the Senate, Dec. 19, 1860; *September*, p. 162

15. Honest conviction is my courage; the Constitution is my guide.

ANDREW JOHNSON

Speech in Washington, D.C., Feb. 22, 1866; *Document*, p. 5

16. Amendments to the Constitution ought not too frequently to be made. . . . If continually tinkered with it will lose all its prestige and dignity, and the old instrument will be lost sight of altogether in a short time.

ANDREW JOHNSON

Speech in Washington, D.C., Feb. 22, 1866; *Ibid.*

17. The time has come to take the Constitution down, to unroll it, to reread it, and to understand its provisions thoroughly.

ANDREW JOHNSON

Speech in Washington, D.C., Feb. 22, 1866; *Ibid.*, p. 7

18. The national Constitution and the Constitutions of most of the States were formed before the locomotive existed. . . .

A government made for the kingdom of Lilliput might fail to handle the forces of Brobdignag.

JAMES A. GARFIELD

Address at Hudson College, July 2, 1873; *Future*, p. 19

19. When the experiment of our Government was undertaken, the chart adopted for our guidance was the Constitution. Departure from the lines there laid down is failure. It is only by strict adherence to the direction they indicate and by restraint within the limitations they fix that we can furnish proof to the world of the fitness of the American people for self-government.

GROVER CLEVELAND

Fourth Annual Message to Congress, Dec. 3, 1888; *Messages and Papers*, p. 5358

20. The Constitution was not made to fit us like a strait jacket. In its elasticity lies its chief greatness.

WOODROW WILSON
Address in New York, N.Y., Nov. 19, 1904; *New York Times, Nov. 20, 1904*

21. The Constitution of the United States is not a mere lawyers' document: it is a vehicle of life, and its spirit is always the spirit of the age.

WOODROW WILSON
1908; *Constitutional Government*, p. 69

22. The Constitution was not meant to hold the government back to the time of horses and wagons.

WOODROW WILSON
1908; *Constitutional Government*, p. 169

23. The Constitution is what the justices say it is rather than what its framers or you might hope it is.

FRANKLIN DELANO ROOSEVELT
1937

24. I just don't believe we should amend . . . the Constitution every time we think a new law ought to be passed.

DWIGHT D. EISENHOWER
Press conference, May 13, 1959; *Public Papers . . . Eisenhower, 1959*, p. 387

25. The Constitution, of course, is still in force—but it is a solemn contract made in the name of "We the People"—and it is an agreement that should be renewed by each generation.

JOHN F. KENNEDY
Address in Washington, D.C., Apr. 16, 1959; *Strategy*, p. 201

26. The Constitution makes us not rivals for power but partners for progress.

JOHN F. KENNEDY
To Congress, Jan. 11, 1962; *Vital Speeches, Feb. 1, 1962*, p. 229

See also Equality 3, Justice 3, Liberty 22, 43, Negroes 10, Power 2, 12, Presidency (The) 17, 18, Republics 8, Revenue, States' Rights 4, 5, 14, Union 12, War 42

Controversy

1. Let it be clear that this Administration recognizes the value of dissent and daring, that we greet healthy controversy as the hallmark of healthy change.

JOHN F. KENNEDY
State of the Union Message, Jan. 29, 1961; *Tide*, p. 32

See also Differences

Convictions

1. The one thing that the world can not permanently resist is the moral force of great and triumphant convictions.

WOODROW WILSON
Address to D.A.R., Washington, D.C., Oct. 11, 1915;
Foreign Policy, p. 114

See also Beliefs, Causes, Peace 59, Principles 4, Purposes, Religion 16, War 37, 42

Cooperation

1. A government can punish specific acts of spoliation; but no government can conscript co-operation.

FRANKLIN DELANO ROOSEVELT
Sixth Annual Message to Congress, Jan. 3, 1938;
Public Papers, VII, 13

See also Democracy 28, Foreign Relations 39, Goals 2, Government 82, 96, Knowledge 10, Labor 13, Liberty 40, Peace 65, 69, Politics 17, Power 28, Progress 6, Space 5

Corporations

1. Corporations, which should be the carefully restrained creatures of the law and the servants of the people, are fast becoming the people's masters.

GROVER CLEVELAND
Fourth Annual Message to Congress, Dec. 3, 1888; *Messages and Papers*, p. 5359

2. There is a widespread conviction in the minds of the American people that the great corporations known as trusts are in certain of their features and tendencies hurtful to the general welfare. . . . It is based upon sincere conviction that combination and concentration should be, not prohibited, but supervised and within reasonable limits controlled; and in my judgment this conviction is right. . . . Great corporations exist only because they are created and safeguarded by our institutions; and it is therefore our right and our duty to see that they work in harmony with these institutions.

THEODORE ROOSEVELT
First Annual Message to Congress, Dec. 3, 1901; *Ibid.*, p. 6645

3. Great corporations are necessary, and only men of great and singular mental power can manage such corporations successfully, and such men must have great rewards. But these corporations should be managed with due regard to the interest of the public as a whole.

THEODORE ROOSEVELT
Fourth Annual Message to Congress, Dec. 6, 1904;
Works, XV, 258

4. One of the most alarming phenomena of the time . . . is the degree to which government has become associated with business. . . . Our government has been for the past few years under the control of heads of great allied corporations with special interests. It has not controlled these interests and assigned them a proper place in the whole system of business. . . . As a result, there have grown up vicious systems and schemes of governmental favoritism . . . far-reaching in effect upon the whole fabric of life . . . stifling everywhere the free spirit of American enterprise.

WOODROW WILSON
1912; *New Freedom (Hale)*, p. 24

See also People 32, Trusts 2

Corruption

1. The time to guard against corruption and tyranny is before they shall have gotten hold of us. It is better to keep the wolf out of the fold than to trust to drawing his teeth and talons after he shall have entered.

THOMAS JEFFERSON
Notes on Virginia, 1782; *Writings, II*, 222

2. Next in importance to the maintenance of the Constitution and the union is the duty of preserving the government free from the taint or even the suspicion of corruption.

JAMES BUCHANAN
Inaugural Address, Mar. 4, 1857

3. There can be no crime more serious than bribery. Other offenses violate one law while corruption strikes at the foundation of all law. . . . The shame lies in toleration, not in correction.

THEODORE ROOSEVELT
Third Annual Message to Congress, Dec. 7, 1903; *Works, XIII*, 52

4. There would be no corruption if it were not for the corrupters. There are always weak people in every human setup. . . . We must find a way to make the corrupter as guilty legally as the one who is corrupted. . . . I have always felt deeply about this subject of corruption. There is nothing I detest so much as a crooked politician or corrupt government official. But the type of businessman who is a fixer is even lower in my estimation.

These are the termites that undermine respect for government and confidence in government and cast doubt on the vast majority of honest and hardworking federal officials.

One of the most important steps to be taken in dealing with the whole problem of corruption in public life is to put key government officials under civil service.

HARRY S. TRUMAN
Interview, *ca.* 1948; *Mr. President*, p. 61

See also Foreign Relations 26

Courage

1. Without belittling the courage with which men have died, we should not forget those acts of courage with which men . . . have lived. The courage of life is often a less dramatic spectacle than the courage of a final moment; but it is no less a magnificent mixture of triumph and tragedy. A man does what he must—in spite of personal consequences, in spite of obstacles and dangers and pressures—and that is the basis of all human morality. . . . In whatever arena of life one may meet the challenge of courage, whatever may be the sacrifices he faces if he follows his conscience—the loss of his friends, his fortune, his contentment, even the esteem of his fellow men—each man must decide for himself the courage he will follow. The stories of past courage can define that ingredient—they can teach, they can offer hope, they can provide inspiration. But they cannot supply courage itself. For this each man must look into his own soul.

JOHN F. KENNEDY
1956; *Profiles,* p. 209

See also Class, Majorities 6, Peace 59, People 25, Political Parties 9, Preparedness 19, Presidency (The) 76, Revolutions 8, Space 2, Success 9, War 3

Courts

1. The national courts are for the most part in the power of Congress. Even the Supreme Court is not beyond its control; for it is the legislative privilege to increase, whenever the legislative will so pleases, the number of the judges upon the supreme bench—to "dilute the Constitution," as Webster once put it, "by creating a court which shall construe away its provisions."

WOODROW WILSON
1885; *Congressional Government,* p. 38

Cowardice

See Fear 3

Creeds

1. My creed had been formed on unsheathing the sword at Lexington.

THOMAS JEFFERSON
To Virginia delegates to Congress, August, 1774; *Writings, I,* 183

2. Our political creed is . . . that the will of the people is the source, and the happiness of the people the end of all legitimate government upon earth.

JOHN QUINCY ADAMS
Inaugural Address, Mar. 4, 1825

See also Conduct 3, Faith 6, Political Philosophy 1, Religion 12, 20, 25, Tolerance 1

Crime

1. Lynchings are a reproach to any community; they impeach the adequacy of our institutions for the punishment of crime.

BENJAMIN HARRISON
Laying the cornerstone of Grant's Tomb, New York, N.Y.,
Apr. 27, 1892; *Public Papers and Addresses*, p. 294

2. We must not allow our interest in criminals to go to the point of making effective prosecution of crime . . . subordinate to schemes for reform of criminals, however admirable they may be.

WILLIAM HOWARD TAFT
To National Crime Commission, Washington, D.C., Nov. 3, 1927

3. Crime and disobedience cannot be permitted to break down the Constitution and laws of the United States.

HERBERT HOOVER
Acceptance of Nomination for Presidency, at Stanford University,
Aug. 11, 1928; *New Day*, p. 29

Crises

1. The man who can look upon a crisis without being willing to offer himself upon the altar of his country is not fit for public trust.

MILLARD FILLMORE
July 10, 1850; *Millard Fillmore (Rayback)*, p. 241

2. There is always another crisis around the corner.

HARRY S. TRUMAN
1945; *Sayings*, p. 233

3. In our uneasy postwar world, crises are a recurrent international diet. . . . By their effect on human action, the peril within them is either magnified or diminished.

A crisis may be fatal when, by it, unstable men are stampeded into headlong panic. Then, bereft of common sense and wise judgment, they hastily resort to armed force in the hope of crushing a threatening foe, although thereby they impoverish the world and may forfeit the hope for enduring peace.

But a crisis may likewise be deadly when inert men, unsure of themselves and their cause, are smothered in despair. Then, grasping at any straw of appeasement, they sell a thousand tomorrows for the pottage of a brief escape from reality.

But a crisis is also the sharpest goad to the creative energies of men, particularly when they recognize it as a challenge to their very resource, and move to meet it in faith, in thought, in courage. Then, greatly aroused—yet realizing that beyond the immediate danger lie vast horizons —they can act for today in the light of generations still to come.

DWIGHT D. EISENHOWER
Address to the Associated Press, New York, N.Y., Apr. 25, 1955;
Peace, p. 82

4. We move from crisis to crisis for two reasons; first, because we have not yet developed a strategy for peace that is relevant to the new world in which we live; and secondly, because we have not been paying the price which that strategy demands—a price measured not merely in money and military preparedness, but in social inventiveness, in moral stamina, in physical courage.

JOHN F. KENNEDY
Washington, D.C., Jan. 1, 1960; *Strategy,* p. 28

See also Americans 3, Freedom 32

Criticism

1. To persevere in one's duty, and be silent is the best answer to calumny.

GEORGE WASHINGTON
Maxims

2. Attacks on me will do no harm, and silent contempt is the best answer to them.

JAMES MONROE
To George Hay, Apr. 29, 1808; *Bulletin, IX,* 56

3. It has been my poor fortune to be much harassed and calumniated let me serve under whom I may. It seems as if I can never get home after the discharge of important trusts abroad, and most faithfully, in peace. My head must be pelted by the storm if ever I expose myself to it.

JAMES MONROE
To David Gelston, Feb. 7, 1809; *Writings, V,* 101

4. As a general rule, I abstain from reading the reports of attacks upon myself, wishing not to be provoked by that to which I cannot properly offer an answer.

ABRAHAM LINCOLN
Address at Washington, D.C., Apr. 11, 1865;
Complete Works, XI, 85

5. It is just as hard to do your duty when men are sneering at you as when they are shooting at you. When they are shooting at you, they can only take your natural life; when they sneer at you, they can wound your heart.

WOODROW WILSON

6. I don't believe that criticism that is honest and fair hurts anybody. . . . Criticism of public figures is a good thing.

DWIGHT D. EISENHOWER
News conference, Apr. 10, 1957; *Public Papers . . . Eisenhower, 1957*, p. 272

See also Character 1, Errors 2, Liberty 45, Power 29, Slander

Crowds

See Nations 13

Cuba

1. Our dealings with Cuba . . . should forever be a subject of just national pride. . . . We freed the island from the Spanish yoke. We then earnestly did our best to help Cubans in the establishment of free education, of law and order, of material prosperity. . . . We did all this at a great expense of treasure, at some expense of life . . . and have asked in return nothing . . . save at no time shall [the Cubans'] independence be prostituted to the advantage of some foreign rival of ours, or so as to menace our well-being.

THEODORE ROOSEVELT
Speech at Minneapolis, Minn., Sept. 2, 1901; *Works, XIII,* 476

2. Just when it was hoped that Cuba was about to enter upon a new era of democracy and social justice, the Soviet Union through its Cuban puppets absorbed the Cuban nation into its despotic empire and it now seeks to extend its rule to shores of the continent itself. . . .

We will build a wall around Cuba—not a wall of mortar or brick or barbed wire, but a wall of dedicated men determined to protect their own freedom and sovereignty.

JOHN F. KENNEDY
At San José, Costa Rica, Mar. 18, 1963; *Vital Speeches, Apr. 15, 1963,* p. 387

See also Territorial Acquisition

Culture

1. Culture is not a thing produced in classrooms, but by the subtler influences of life and association among men of the finer sort of taste and the higher kind of learning.

WOODROW WILSON
Letter in the New York *Evening Post,* Apr. 23, 1910; *The Princeton Alumni, Apr. 27, 1910*

2. The Federal government cannot order that culture exist, but the government can and should provide the climate of freedom, deeper and wider education, and intellectual curiosity in which culture flourishes.

JOHN F. KENNEDY
Saturday Review; Oct. 29, 1960

3. To further the appreciation of culture among all the people, to increase respect for the creative individual, to widen participation by all the processes and fulfillments of art—this is one of the fascinating challenges of these days.

JOHN F. KENNEDY
"Arts in America," Dec. 18, 1962; *Public Papers . . . Kennedy,*
1962, p. 907

4. When power leads man toward arrogance, poetry reminds him of his limitations. When power narrows the areas of man's concern, poetry reminds him of the richness and diversity of his existence. When power corrupts, poetry cleanses. . . . I look forward to an America which will not be afraid of grace and beauty . . . which will steadily enlarge cultural opportunities for all of our citizens . . . which commands respect not only for its strength but for its civilization as well.

JOHN F. KENNEDY
Speech at Amherst College, October, 1963; *Life (magazine),*
Nov. 29, 1963

See also Arts (The), Education, War 16

Dangers

1. It may be well that circumstances have occurred to arouse us from our lethargy . . . to the nearness and magnitude of impending calamities. It is comparatively safe to look dangers in the face, and meet them on the advance, but fatal to be appalled by them.

FRANKLIN PIERCE
Letter, Dec. 7, 1859; *Record,* p. 6

See also Preparedness 17

Death

1. There is a ripeness of time for death . . . when it is reasonable we should drop off, and make room for another growth. When we have lived our generation out, we should not wish to encroach on another.

THOMAS JEFFERSON
To John Adams, Aug. 1, 1816; *Writings, XV,* 57

See also Life 4, Power 31

Debts

1. Avoiding likewise the accumulation of debt, not only by shunning occasions of expense, but by vigorous exertions in time of peace to discharge the debts which unavoidable wars have occasioned, not ungenerously throwing upon posterity the burthen which we ourselves ought to bear.

GEORGE WASHINGTON
Farewell Address, Sept. 19, 1796;
Writings (Fitzpatrick), XXXV, 230

2. I am for a government rigorously frugal and simple, applying all the possible savings of the public revenue to the discharge of the national debt . . . and not for increasing by every device, the public debt, on the principle of its being a public blessing . . . [or] a multiplication of officers and salaries merely to make partisans.

THOMAS JEFFERSON
Letter to Elbridge Gerry, Jan. 26, 1799; *Works, IV,* 268

3. I go on the principle that a public debt is a public curse, and in a Republican Government a greater curse than in any other.

JAMES MADISON
To Henry Lee, Apr. 13, 1790; *Complete Madison,* p. 336

4. I am one of those who do not believe that a national debt is a national blessing, but rather a curse to a republic; inasmuch as it is calculated to raise around the administration a moneyed aristocracy dangerous to the liberties of the country.

ANDREW JACKSON
To Dr. L. H. Colman, Apr. 26, 1824; *Life (Bassett),* p. 346

5. Our country, which exhibits to the world the benefits of self-government, in developing all the sources of national prosperity owes to mankind the permanent example of a nation free from the blighting influence of a public debt.

JAMES K. POLK
First Annual Message to Congress, Dec. 2, 1845;
Messages and Papers, p. 2253

6. It is against sound policy and the genius of our institutions that a public debt should be permitted to exist a day longer than the means of the Treasury will enable the Government to pay it off.

JAMES K. POLK
Message to Congress, July 6, 1848; *Ibid.,* p. 2441

7. The great advantage of citizens being creditors as well as debtors, with relation to the public debt, is obvious. Men readily perceive that they cannot be much oppressed by a debt which they owe to themselves.

ABRAHAM LINCOLN
Fourth Annual Message to Congress, Dec. 6, 1864;
Complete Works, X, 294

8. We should look at the national debt just as it is—not as a national blessing, but as a heavy burden on the industry of the country, to be discharged without unnecessary delay.

ANDREW JOHNSON
First Annual Message to Congress, Dec. 4, 1865;
Messages and Papers, p. 3564

9. I do not favor the cancellation of [foreign] debt. . . . Our country would not wish to assume the role of an oppressive creditor, but would maintain the principle that financial obligations between nations are likewise moral obligations which international faith and honor require should be discharged.

CALVIN COOLIDGE
Message to Congress, Dec. 6, 1923; *Message*, p. 2

10. Borrowed money, even when owing to a nation by another nation, should be repaid.
They hired the money, didn't they? Let them pay it.

CALVIN COOLIDGE
1925; *Public Years (Baruch)*, p. 108

11. Government borrowing . . . is a device to load our extravagance and waste on to the next generation. But increasing government debts can carry immediate punishment, for that is the road to inflation. There is far more courage in reducing our gigantic national debt than in increasing it. And that is a duty to our children.

HERBERT HOOVER
Address at Stanford University, Aug. 10, 1949;
American Road, p. 17

12. The consoling answer of the [deficit spending] inebriate is that there is really no such thing as Government debt. They say, "We owe it to ourselves." Any government which follows this will-o'-the-wisp will sometime break its neck over the precipice of inflation. Some have already done so.

HERBERT HOOVER
Address in Chicago, Ill., June 16, 1950; *Ibid.*, p. 23

See also Economic Matters, Economy, Loans, Money 11, Peace 22, Prosperity 5, 15, Secession, Work 6

Declaration of Independence

1. *After deciding to cast his vote for the adoption of the Declaration of Independence:*
The die was now cast; I had passed the Rubicon. Sink or swim, live or die, survive or perish with my country, was my unalterable determination.

JOHN ADAMS
To Jonathan Sewell, 1774; *Works, IV*, 8

2. The second day of July, 1776, will be the most memorable Epocha, in the history of America. I am apt to believe that it will be celebrated, by succeeding generations, as the great anniversary festival. It ought to be commemorated as the day of deliverance, by solemn acts of devotion to God Almighty. It ought to be solemnized with pomp and parade, with

shews, games, sports, guns, bells, bonfires, and illuminations from one end of this continent to the other from this time forward forever more.

JOHN ADAMS
To Abigail Adams, July 3, 1776; *Familiar Letters,* p. 193

3. When, in the course of human events, it becomes necessary for one people to dissolve the political bands which have connected them with another, and to assume among the powers of the earth the separate and equal station to which the Laws of Nature and of Nature's God entitle them, a decent respect to the opinions of mankind requires that they should declare the causes which impel them to the separation. . . .

For the support of this Declaration, with a firm reliance on the protection of Divine Providence, we mutually pledge to each other our Lives, our Fortunes, and our sacred Honour.

THOMAS JEFFERSON
Preamble, Declaration of Independence, July 4, 1776

4. With respect to our rights, and the acts of the British government contravening those rights, there was but one opinion on this side of the water. . . . When forced, therefore, to resort to arms for redress, an appeal to the tribunal of the world was deemed proper for our justification. This was the object of the Declaration of Independence.

THOMAS JEFFERSON
Letter to Henry Lee, May 8, 1825; *Works, VII,* 407

5. [The Declaration's] authors meant it to be—as, thank God, it is now proving itself—a stumbling block to all those who in after times might seek to turn a free people back into the hateful paths of despotism. They knew the proneness of prosperity to breed tyrants, and they meant when such should reappear in this fair land and commence their vocation, they should find left for them at least one hard nut to crack.

ABRAHAM LINCOLN
Speech in Springfield, Ill., June 27, 1857; *Complete Works, II,* 331

6. If this country cannot be saved without giving up the principle . . . [of the Declaration of Independence], I would rather be assassinated on this spot than surrender it.

ABRAHAM LINCOLN
Speech in Philadelphia, Pa., Feb. 22, 1861; *Ibid., VI,* 156

7. Jefferson's Declaration of Independence is a practical document for the use of practical men. It is not a thesis for philosophers, but a whip for tyrants; it is not a theory of government, but a program of action.

WOODROW WILSON
Speech at Indianapolis, Ind., April 13, 1911;
Indianapolis News, Apr. 14, 1911

8.   The Declaration of Independence was a document preliminary to war. It was a vital piece of practical business, not a piece of rhetoric. . . . Liberty does not consist in mere general declarations of the rights of man. It consists in the translation of those declarations into definite action.

WOODROW WILSON
Speech in Philadelphia, Pa., July 4, 1914; *Public Papers, III,* 139

9.   In its main features the Declaration of Independence is a great spiritual document. It is a declaration not of material but of spiritual conceptions. Equality, liberty, popular sovereignty, the rights of man—these are the elements which we can see and touch. They are ideals. They have their source and their roots in the religious convictions. . . . Unless the faith of the American people in these religious convictions is to endure, the principles of our Declaration will perish.

CALVIN COOLIDGE
Speech in Philadelphia, Pa., July 5, 1926; *Foundations,* p. 451

10.   [The Declaration] acknowledges that man has a soul, and for that reason is equal to every other man, and that . . . is the cornerstone of what we call the American System.

DWIGHT D. EISENHOWER
Remarks to the D.A.R., Apr. 22, 1954; *Public Papers . . .*
Eisenhower, 1954, p. 86

See also Equality 5, Liberty 25, Nationality 1, Nations 1

Defense

1.   We must take care always to keep ourselves, by suitable establishments, in a respectable defensive posture.

GEORGE WASHINGTON
Farewell Address, Sept. 19, 1796; *Writings (Fitzpatrick),*
XXXV, 235

2.   The national defense is one of the cardinal duties of a statesman.

JOHN ADAMS
To James Lloyd, January, 1815; *Works, X,* 111

3.   I am for relying on internal defence on our militia solely, till actual invasion . . . and not for a standing army in time of peace, which may overawe the public sentiment.

THOMAS JEFFERSON
To Elbridge Gerry, Jan. 26, 1799; *Writings, X,* 77

4.   In the wars of the European powers in matters relating to themselves we have never taken any part, nor does it comport with our policy so to

do. It is only when our rights are invaded or seriously menaced that we resent injuries or make preparation for our defence.

JAMES MONROE
Seventh Annual Message to Congress, Dec. 2, 1823;
Messages and Papers, p. 787

5. It is only by an effective militia that we can at once enjoy the repose of peace and bid defiance to foreign aggression; it is by the militia that we are constituted an armed nation, standing in perpetual panoply of defense in the presence of all the other nations of the earth.

JOHN QUINCY ADAMS
First Annual Message to Congress, Dec. 6, 1825; *Ibid.,* p. 869

6. It is not . . . compatible with the interest of the people to maintain, in time of peace, a regular force to the defence of our extensive frontiers.

MARTIN VAN BUREN
First Annual Message to Congress, Dec. 4, 1837;
Addresses and Messages, p. 641

7. Proper armament is of vastly more importance than fortifications. The latter can be supplied very speedily for temporary purposes when needed; the former can not.

ULYSSES S. GRANT
Fifth Annual Message to Congress, Dec. 1, 1873;
Messages and Papers, p. 4202

8. No nation is defenseless with such resources as we possess. . . . We have demonstrated in every war . . . our readiness and adaptation for any emergency—our inherent and almost resistless strength, founded upon a sincere affection for our country.

WILLIAM MCKINLEY
Speech at Canton, Ohio, May 30, 1891; *Life and Speeches,* p. 175

9. The only defensive that is worth anything is the offensive.

THEODORE ROOSEVELT
Campaign speech in New York, N.Y., Oct. 5, 1898;
Works, XIV, 293

10. The American plan is a great body of citizens who are ready to rally to the national defense and adequately serve the national defense when it is necessary to do so.

WOODROW WILSON
Speech at Pittsburgh, Pa., Jan. 29, 1916; *Public Papers, IV,* 32

11. Human nature is a very constant quality. While there is justification for hoping and believing that we are moving toward perfection, it would be idle and absurd to assume that we have already reached it. We cannot disregard history. There have been and will be domestic disorders. There

have been and will be tendencies of one nation to encroach on another. I believe in the maintenance of an Army and Navy, not for aggression but for defense. Security and order are our most valuable possessions. They are cheap at any price. But I am opposed to every kind of military aggrandizement and to all forms of competitive armament. The ideal would be for nations to become parties to mutual covenants limiting their military establishments, and making it obvious that they are not maintained to menace each other.

CALVIN COOLIDGE
Speech at Arlington National Cemetery, May 30, 1924;
Foundations, p. 24

12. My policies in national defense and world disarmament had one simple objective . . . to insure freedom from war to the American people.

The size of naval and military forces required to insure our country against aggression rests partly upon our foreign policies and partly upon the relative strength of possible enemies. The American concept had always been arms for defense, not for aggression.

HERBERT HOOVER
1929; *Memoirs, II,* 338

13. It is to our interest to see that we are strong. . . . Weakness cannot co-operate with anything. Only strength can co-operate. . . . I believe we should be strong, but we should be tolerant. We should be ready to defend our rights but we should be considerate and recognize the rights of the other man.

DWIGHT D. EISENHOWER
Speech in New York, N.Y., June 19, 1945;
Eisenhower Speaks, p. 44

14. Our nuclear weapons and our ability to employ them constitute the most effective deterrent to an attack on the free nations.

We shall continue to expand our nuclear arsenal until an agreement has been reached for reduction and regulation of armaments under safeguarded inspection guaranties.

DWIGHT D. EISENHOWER
Annual Budget Message to Congress, Jan. 16, 1957;
Public Papers . . . Eisenhower, 1957, p. 47

15. Good defense is not cheap defense.

DWIGHT D. EISENHOWER
Radio and television report, May 14, 1957; *Ibid.,* p. 348

16. We must guard against feverish building of vast armaments to meet glibly predicted moments of so-called "maximum peril." The threat we face is not sporadic or dated: It is continuous. Hence we must not be swayed in our calculations either by groundless fear or by complacency.

We must avoid extremes, for vacillation between extremes is inefficient, costly, and destructive of morale.

DWIGHT D. EISENHOWER
Sixth Annual Message to Congress, Jan. 9, 1959;
Public Papers . . . Eisenhower, 1959, p. 8

See also Army, Democracy 7, Disarmament, Experience 1, Freedom 26, Goals 2, Isolationism 10, Military Matters, Navy, Patriotism, Preparedness, Security, Unity 6

Delay

See Errors 6, Foreign Relations 27, Negroes 10, 12

Demagogues

1. Should the people suffer themselves to be dictated to by designing demagogues, who carry on everything by intrigue and management, they can not expect to see their present happy government perpetuated.

ANDREW JACKSON
To John Donelson, Feb. 9, 1824; *Life (Parton), III,* 40

2. Demagogues, I am persuaded, have in times past, done more injury to the cause of freedom and the rights of man than ever did a military chieftain, and in our country at least in times of peace, should be more feared.

ANDREW JACKSON
To Samuel Swartwout, Feb. 22, 1825; *Ibid.,* p. 77

3. To play the demagogue for purposes of self-interest is a cardinal sin against the people in a democracy, exactly as to play the courtier for such purposes is a cardinal sin against the people in other forms of government.

THEODORE ROOSEVELT
Autobiography, p. 91

4. Half-truth, hypocrisy and hate are departments in the art of demagogues. The polite phrase for all this is intellectual dishonesty.

HERBERT HOOVER
Speech at Kansas City, Mo.; *American Quaker,* p. 41

Democracy

1. A democracy is as really a republic as an oak a tree, or a temple a building.

JOHN ADAMS
To J. H. Tiffany, Mar. 31, 1819; *Works, X,* 378

2. One of the worst forms of government is a pure democracy, that is, one in which the citizens enact and administer the laws directly. Such a government is helpless against the mischiefs of faction.

JAMES MADISON
"Publius," 1787; *Federalist, No. 10*

3.   As I would not be a *slave*, so I would not be a *master*. This expresses my idea of democracy. Whatever differs from this, to the extent of the difference, is no democracy.

ABRAHAM LINCOLN
Springfield, Ill., *ca.* 1858; *Wisdom,* p. 60

4.   The Ship of Democracy, which has weathered all storms, may sink through the mutiny of those on board.

GROVER CLEVELAND
To Wilson S. Bissell, Feb. 15, 1894; *Letters,* p. 347

5.   My attachment to true Democracy is so strong that I consider its success as identical with the promotion of the country's good.

GROVER CLEVELAND
To Democratic voters, June 16, 1896; *Ibid.,* p. 441

6.   A great democracy must be progressive or it will soon cease to be great or a democracy.

THEODORE ROOSEVELT
Speech at Cleveland, Ohio, Nov. 5, 1910;
Works (Mem. Ed.), XIX, 69

7.   We in America claim that a democracy can be as efficient for defense as an autocracy, as a despotism. It is idle to make this claim, it is idle to utter windy eloquence in Fourth of July speeches, and to prate in public documents about our greatness and our adherence to democratic principles and the mission we have to do good on the earth by spineless peacefulness, if we are not able, if we are not willing, to make our words count by means of our deeds.

THEODORE ROOSEVELT
Metropolitan Magazine, November, 1915; *Works, XVIII,* 330

8.   Democratic institutions are never done—they are, like the living tissue, always a-making. It is a strenuous thing this of living the life of a free people: and we cannot escape the burden of our inheritance.

WOODROW WILSON
Address at Middletown, Conn., Apr. 30, 1889;
Life and Letters, V, 77

9.   Democracy is not so much a form of government as a set of principles.

WOODROW WILSON
Atlantic Monthly, Mar. 1901; *Public Papers, I,* 414

10.   Democracy is the most difficult form of government, because it is

the form under which you have to persuade the largest number of persons to do anything in particular.

WOODROW WILSON
Address in Washington, D.C., Sept. 28, 1915;
Life and Letters, VI, 1

11. Only governments and not people initiate wars. . . . Democracy, therefore, is the best preventive of such jealousies and suspicions and secret intrigues as produce wars among nations where small groups control rather than the great body of public opinion.

WOODROW WILSON
Interview, Nov. 5, 1916; *Ibid.,* p. 397

12. The world must be made safe for democracy. Its peace must be planted upon the trusted foundations of political liberty.

WOODROW WILSON
Address to Congress, asking for War, Apr. 2, 1917;
Messages and Papers (Shaw), I, 381

13. Democracy is more than a form of government. It is a form of character. It follows upon the long discipline which gives a people self-possession, self-mastery, the habit of order, and peace and common counsel and a reverence for law.

WOODROW WILSON
Public Years (Baruch), p. 147

14. Democracy is not a tearing-down; it is a building-up. It is not a denial of the divine right of kings; it supplements that claim with the assertion of the divine right of men. It does not destroy; it fulfills. . . . It is the alpha and omega of man's relation to man. . . . Its foundation lays hold upon eternity.

CALVIN COOLIDGE
Address at Springfield, Mass., July 4, 1916; *Faith,* p. 23

15. It was the bitter experience of all public men from George Washington down that democracies are at least contemporarily fickle and heartless.

HERBERT HOOVER
1919; *Memoirs, II,* 4

16. Democracy is more than a form of political organization; it is a human faith. True democracy is not and cannot be imperialistic. The brotherhood of this faith is the guarantee of good will.

HERBERT HOOVER
1928; *Ibid.,* p. 214

17. Democracy . . . is a quest, a never-ending seeking for better things,

and in the seeking . . . and the striving for them there are many roads to follow.

FRANKLIN DELANO ROOSEVELT
Address in San Francisco, Cal., Sept. 23, 1932;
Public Papers, I, 727

18.   A democracy, the right kind of democracy, is bound together by the ties of neighborliness.

FRANKLIN DELANO ROOSEVELT
Address to Conference of Catholic Charities, Oct. 4, 1933;
Ibid., II, 380

19.   Democracy is not a static thing. It is an everlasting march.

FRANKLIN DELANO ROOSEVELT
Address at Los Angeles, Cal., Oct. 1, 1935; *Ibid., IV,* 403

20.   We believe in democracy; we believe in freedom; we believe in peace. We offer to every Nation of the world the handclasp of the good neighbor. Let those who wish our friendship look us in the eye and take our hand.

FRANKLIN DELANO ROOSEVELT
Address at Chautauqua, N.Y., Aug. 14, 1936; *Ibid., V,* 292

21.   The deeper purpose of democratic government is to assist as many of its citizens as possible . . . to improve their conditions of life, to retain all personal liberty which does not adversely affect their neighbors, and to pursue the happiness which comes with security and an opportunity for recreation and culture.

FRANKLIN DELANO ROOSEVELT
Annual Message to Congress, Jan. 6, 1937; *Ibid.,* p. 636

22.   As intricacies of human relationships increase, so power to govern them also must increase—power to stop evil; power to do good. The essential democracy of our Nation and the safety of our people depend not upon the absence of power, but upon lodging it with those whom the people can change or continue at stated intervals through an honest and free system of elections.

FRANKLIN DELANO ROOSEVELT
Second Inaugural Address, Jan. 20, 1937

23.   My anchor is democracy—and more democracy.

FRANKLIN DELANO ROOSEVELT
Speech at Roanoke Island, N.C., Aug. 18, 1937;
Public Papers, VI, 331

24.   Democracy is not just a word, to be shouted at political rallies and then put back into the dictionary after election day.

FRANKLIN DELANO ROOSEVELT
Presidential campaign speech, Nov. 4, 1940; *Ibid., IX,* 554

25. We must be the great arsenal of democracy.

FRANKLIN DELANO ROOSEVELT
Fireside Chat, Dec. 29, 1940; *Ibid.,* p. 643

26. There is no indispensable man in a democracy. When a republic comes to a point where a man is indispensable, then we have a Caesar.

HARRY S. TRUMAN
Interview, *ca.* 1946; *Mr. President,* p. 13

27. Democracy is based on the conviction that man has the moral and intellectual capacity, as well as the inalienable right, to govern himself with reason and justice. . . .

Democracy maintains that government is established for the benefit of the individual, and is charged with the responsibility of protecting the rights of the individual and his freedom in the exercise of his abilities. . . .

Democracy has proved that social justice can be achieved through peaceful change. . . .

Democracy holds that free nations can settle differences justly and maintain lasting peace.

HARRY S. TRUMAN
Inaugural Address, Jan. 20, 1949

28. To define democracy in one word, we must use the word "cooperation."

DWIGHT D. EISENHOWER
Speech in Abilene, Kan., June, 1945;
What Eisenhower Thinks, p. 39

29. The constant danger to democracy lies in the tendency of the individual to hide himself in the crowd—to defend his own failure to act forthrightly according to conviction under the false excuse that the effort of one in one hundred forty million has no significance.

DWIGHT D. EISENHOWER
Speech at Northfield, Vt., June 9, 1946; *Eisenhower Speaks,* p. 109

30. Human dignity, economic freedom, individual responsibility, these are the characteristics that distinguish democracy from all other forms devised by man. . . . This democratic system . . . has given to our people the highest standard of living this world has ever known and has made of this nation a force for justice and peace.

DWIGHT D. EISENHOWER
Speech at the University of West Virginia, Sept. 24, 1947;
What Eisenhower Thinks, p. 49

31. "I believe in democracy," said Woodrow Wilson, "because it releases the energy of every human being." The dynamic of democracy is the power and the purpose of the individual; and the policy of this ad-

ministration is to give to the individual the opportunity to realize his own highest possibilities.

JOHN F. KENNEDY

To Congress, Jan. 11, 1962; *Vital Speeches, Feb. 1, 1962,* p. 231

See also Censors 5, Dictatorships, Discrimination 4, Faith 4, Government, Health 5, Libraries 3, Minorities 2, Monopolies 6, Peace 56, Power 23, Press (The) 20, 24, Public Opinion 15, Religion 32, Republics, Rulers, Success 6, Suffrage 1, Unity 3, War 44

Depression

1.   Booms are times of speculation, overexpansion, wasteful expenditures in industry and commerce, with consequent destruction of capital. . . . It is the wastes, the miscalculations and maladjustments, grown rampant during the booms, that make unavoidable the painful processes of liquidation. The obvious way to lessen the losses and miseries of depression is first to check the destructive extremes of booms. Mitigation of depression is a further task of relief and reconstruction.

HERBERT HOOVER

Report to Committee on Business Cycles, Sept. 12, 1921;
Memoirs, II, 174

2.   When Andrew Jackson, "Old Hickory," died, someone asked, "Will he go to Heaven?" and the answer was, "He will if he wants to." If I am asked whether the American people will pull themselves out of this depression, I answer, "They will if they want to." The essence of the plan [National Recovery] is a universal limitation of hours of work per week for any individual by common consent, and a universal payment of wages above a minimum, also by common consent.

FRANKLIN DELANO ROOSEVELT

Fireside Chat, July 24, 1933; *Public Papers, II,* 302

See also Debts 11, 12, Inflation

Desegregation

1.   The military establishment—particularly the Navy—had been strongly opposed to my policy of integration in the armed services, but I had forced it into practice. Then they discovered that no difficulty resulted from integration after all. Integration is the best way to create an effective combat organization in which the men will stand together and fight.

HARRY S. TRUMAN

1948; *Memoirs, II,* 182

2.   It is my position that all students should be given the opportunity to attend public schools regardless of their race, and that is in accordance with the Constitution.

JOHN F. KENNEDY

News conference, Feb. 8, 1961; *Public Papers . . .
Kennedy, 1961,* p. 69

3. I want to congratulate Governor Vandiver of Georgia . . . and citizens of Atlanta, Georgia, for the responsible law-abiding manner in which four high schools were desegregated today. . . . Too often in the past, such steps in other cities have been marred by violence and disrespect for law.

I strongly urge the officials and citizens of all communities . . . to look closely at what Atlanta has done, and to meet their responsibilities . . . with courage, tolerance, and above all, respect for the law.

JOHN F. KENNEDY
News conference, Aug. 30, 1961; *Ibid.*, p. 572

See also Civil Rights, Equality, Negroes, Segregation

Despotism

1. When the white man governs himself, that is self-government; but when he governs himself and also governs another man, that is more than self-government—that is despotism.

ABRAHAM LINCOLN
Speech at Peoria, Ill., Oct. 16, 1854; *Complete Works, II,* 227

See also Force 3, Freedom 10, Government 83, Knowledge 8, Liberty 11, 12, 23, Majorities 5, Power 2, Press (The) 3, 13, States' Rights 10, Supreme Court 1, Union 22

Destiny

1. To be forsaken by all mankind seems to be the destiny that awaits my last days.

JOHN QUINCY ADAMS
Dec. 14, 1833; *John Quincy Adams (Morse),* p. 302

2. It is a familiar matter of history that it is [our] westward expansion . . . [the] never ceasing spread and adaptation of our institutions and our modes of life, that has been the chief instrumentality in giving us national feeling, that has kept our eyes lifted to tasks which had manifest destiny in them.

WOODROW WILSON
1908: *Constitutional Government,* p. 48

3. This generation of Americans has a rendezvous with destiny.

FRANKLIN DELANO ROOSEVELT
Acceptance of Renomination for Presidency, Philadelphia, Pa.,
June 27, 1936; *Public Papers, V,* 235

See also Duty 7, Time 4, Union 27, War 60

Dictatorships

1. I have heard . . . that both the Army and the government needed a

dictator. Only those generals who gain successes can set up dictators. What I now ask . . . is military success, and I will risk the dictatorship.

ABRAHAM LINCOLN
To Gen. Joseph Hooker, Jan. 26, 1863;
Complete Works, VIII, 207

2. History proves that dictatorships do not grow out of strong and successful governments, but out of weak and helpless ones. If by democratic methods people get a government strong enough to protect them from fear and starvation, their democracy succeeds; but if they do not, they grow impatient.

FRANKLIN DELANO ROOSEVELT
Fireside Chat, Apr. 14, 1938; *Public Papers, VII,* 236

3. People who are hungry and out of a job are the stuff of which dictatorships are made.

FRANKLIN DELANO ROOSEVELT
Message to Congress, Jan. 11, 1944; *Ibid., XIII,* 41

4. A dictatorship is the hardest thing in God's world to hold together because it is made up entirely of conspiracies from the inside.

HARRY S. TRUMAN
1945; *Independence,* p. 285

Differences

1. Differences between men and between nations will always remain. In fact, if held within reasonable limits, such disagreements are actually wholesome. All progress begins with differences of opinion and moves onward as the differences are adjusted through reason and mutual understanding.

HARRY S. TRUMAN
Address in San Francisco, Cal., Apr. 25, 1945;
Public Papers . . . Truman, 1945, p. 23

See also Controversy, Principles 7, Progress 4, Religion 8, 9, 10, Security 8, Union 2, 8, War 33

Dignity
See Rights 17, Security 7

Diplomacy

1. The diplomacy of the United States has always been a sentimental diplomacy.

BENJAMIN HARRISON
Speech at Rochester, N.Y., May 30, 1892;
Public Papers and Addresses, p. 294

2. Diplomacy is utterly useless where there is no force behind it; the diplomat is the servant, not the master of the soldier.

THEODORE ROOSEVELT
Address to Naval War College, June 2, 1897; *Biography*, p. 172

3. The peace of the world must henceforth depend upon a new and more wholesome diplomacy.

WOODROW WILSON
Address in Washington, D.C., May 27, 1916; *Life, VI*, 177

See also Foreign Relations 5, 20, Treaties

Disarmament

1. Disarmament can never be of prime importance; there is more need to get rid of the causes of war than of the implements of war.

THEODORE ROOSEVELT
Fifth Annual Message to Congress, Dec. 5, 1905;
Messages and Papers, p. 7374

2. You may be sure that our government will continue its efforts in behalf of effective control and reduction of all armaments. It will be my never-ending purpose to seek a stable foundation for a just and durable peace in the mutual interest of all nations.

DWIGHT D. EISENHOWER
To Nikolai Bulganin, Jan. 2, 1957; *Public Papers . . .
Eisenhower, 1957*, p. 4

3. Men no longer debate whether armaments are a symptom or cause of tension. The mere existence of modern weapons—ten million times more destructive than anything the world has ever known, and only minutes away from any target on earth—is a source of horror, of discord, and distrust. Men no longer maintain that disarmament must await the settlement of all disputes—for disarmament must be a part of any permanent settlement. And men no longer pretend that the quest for disarmament is a sign of weakness—for in the spiraling arms race, a nation's security may well be shrinking even as its arms increase. . . . The risks inherent in disarmament pale in comparison to the risks inherent in an unlimited arms race.

It is therefore our intention to challenge the Soviet Union, not to an arms race, but to a peace race—to advance with us step by step, stage by stage, until general and complete disarmament has actually been achieved. . . .

To destroy arms, however, is not enough. We must create even as we destroy—creating world-wide law and law enforcement as we outlaw world-wide war and weapons.

JOHN F. KENNEDY
Address to the United Nations General Assembly, Sept. 25, 1961;
Public Papers . . . Kennedy, 1961, p. 620

4. If we don't get the atomic test ban now, I would think perhaps the genie is out of the bottle and we'll never get it back again.

JOHN F. KENNEDY
June, 1963

5. The fact remains that the United States, as a major nuclear power, does have a special responsibility to the world.

We believe the Soviet Union also has special responsibilities—and that those responsibilities require our two nations to concentrate less on our differences and more on the means of resolving them peacefully. . . .

Let us move up the steep and difficult path toward comprehensive disarmament, securing mutual confidence through mutual verification, and building the institutions of peace as we dismantle the engines of war.

JOHN F. KENNEDY

To the United Nations General Assembly, Sept. 19, 1963;
Vital Speeches, Oct. 15, 1963, p. 3

See also Army, Defense, Freedom 21, Military Matters, Navy, Peace, Preparedness, Unity 4, War

Discipline

1. It was an observation founded in undoubted facts, that the prosperity of nations had been in proportion to the discipline of their forces by sea and land. . . . Discipline, discipline, had become my constant topic of discourse and even declamation in and out of Congress, and especially in the board of war. I saw very clearly that the ruin of our cause and country must be the consequence, if a thorough reformation and strict discipline could not be introduced. My zeal on this occasion was no doubt represented by my faithful enemies, in great secrecy, however, to their friends in the army; and although it might recommend me to the esteem of a very few, yet . . . it contributed nothing to my popularity among the many.

JOHN ADAMS
Autobiography, Aug. 19, Sept. 19, 1776; *Works, III*, 68, 83

2. Discipline in an army is like the laws in civil society. There can be no liberty in a commonwealth where the laws are not revered, and most sacredly observed, nor can there be happiness or safety in an army for a single hour where the discipline is not observed.

Obedience is the only thing wanting now for our salvation. Obedience to the laws in the States, and obedience to officers in the army.

JOHN ADAMS
To Abigail Adams, Aug. 24, 1777; *Addressed, I*, 255

3. The article of discipline is the most difficult in American education. Premature ideas of independence, too little repressed by parents, beget a spirit of insubordination, which is the great obstacle to science with us and a principle cause of its decay since the revolution. I look to it with dismay

in our institution, as a breaker ahead, which I am far from being confident we shall be able to weather.

THOMAS JEFFERSON
Letter to Thomas Cooper, Nov. 2, 1822; *Works, VII,* 268

See also Education 17, Freedom 1, Greatness 12, Military Matters 2

Discrimination

1. We feel . . . that all legal distinction between individuals of the same community, founded in any such circumstances as color, origin, and the like, are hostile to the genius of our institutions, and incompatible with the true history of American liberty.

ABRAHAM LINCOLN
Speech at Cincinnati, Ohio, May 31, 1842; *Portrait, II,* 531

2. Laws are enacted for the benefit of the whole people, and can not and must not be construed as permitting discrimination against some of the people. I am President of all the people of the United States, without regard to creed, color, birthplace, occupation or social condition.

THEODORE ROOSEVELT
Public statement, Sept. 29, 1903; *Americanism,* p. 169

3. Our Government cannot countenance continued discrimination against American citizens in defense production. Industry must take the initiative in opening the doors of employment to all loyal and qualified workers regardless of race, national origin, religion or color.

FRANKLIN DELANO ROOSEVELT
Memorandum, Washington, D.C., June 12, 1941;
Public Papers, X, 216

4. Those who sincerely desire to see the fullest expression of our democracy can never rest until the opportunity for an education, at all levels, has been given to all qualified Americans, regardless of race, creed, color, national origin, sex or economic status. . . .

We have only recently completed a long and bitter war against intolerance and hatred in other lands. . . . Yet, in this country today there exists disturbing evidence of intolerance and prejudice similar in kind. . . .

Discrimination, like a disease, must be attacked wherever it appears.

HARRY S. TRUMAN
To American Veterans committee, Sept. 4, 1946;
Public Papers . . . Truman, 1946, p. 423

5. Discrimination . . . is but the outward testimony to the persistence of distrust and of fears in the hearts of men.

DWIGHT D. EISENHOWER
State of the Union Address, February, 1953; *Mandate,* p. 235

6. All members of the public should have equal access to facilities open to the public.

All members of the public should be equally eligible for Federal benefits that are financed by the public.

All members of the public should have an equal chance to vote for public officials and to send their children to good schools, and to contribute their talents to the public good.

Today all Americans of all races stand side by side in Berlin and in Vietnam. They died side by side in Korea. Surely they can work and eat and travel side by side in their own country.

. . . we must abolish not some, but all, racial discrimination. For this is not merely an economic issue, or a social, political or international issue. It is a moral issue. . . .

LYNDON B. JOHNSON
State of the Union Address, Jan. 8, 1964;
Vital Speeches, Jan. 15, 1964, p. 196

See also Civil Rights, Class, Foreign Relations 26, Government 94, Jews 2, 4, Minorities 2, Negroes, Segregation

Dogmas
See Past (The) 1, Religion 13

Duty
1. Only aim to do your duty, and mankind will give you credit where you fail.

THOMAS JEFFERSON
To Virginia delegates to Congress, August, 1774; *Writings, I,* 209

2. My great wish is to go on in a strict but silent performance of my duty; to avoid attracting notice, and to keep my name out of newspapers.

THOMAS JEFFERSON
Letter to Francis Hopkinson, Jan. 11, 1789;
Life and Selected, p. 461

3. The first duty of a soldier or good citizen is to attend to the safety and interest of his country; the next, to attend to his own feelings whenever they are rudely or wantonly assailed.

ANDREW JACKSON
To Henry Dearborn, Jan. 8, 1807; *Life (Bassett),* p. 50

4. The public have no idea of the constant accumulation of business requiring the President's attention. No President who performs his duty faithfully and conscientiously can have any leisure. If he entrusts the details and smaller matters to subordinates constant errors will occur. I prefer to supervise the whole operations of the Government myself rather than

entrust the public business to subordinates, and this makes my duties very great.

JAMES K. POLK
Dec. 29, 1848; *Diary* (*Quaife*), *IV*, 261

5.   I hold that while man exists it is his duty to improve not only his own condition, but to assist in ameliorating mankind. . . . I am for those means which will give the greatest good to the greatest number.

ABRAHAM LINCOLN
Address at Cincinnati, Ohio, Feb. 12, 1861;
Complete Works, VI, 120

6.   Toil and a hearty advocacy of the principles of free government have been my lot. . . . The duties have been mine, the consequences are God's.

ANDREW JOHNSON
Upon taking the Oath, Apr. 15, 1861; *Speeches*, p. xlviii

7.   Duty determines destiny. Destiny which results from duty performed may bring anxiety and perils, but never failure and dishonor.

WILLIAM McKINLEY
Speech in Chicago, Ill., Oct. 19, 1898; *Eloquence, II*, 816

8.   The prime requisite is to arouse among our people . . . an understanding that the full performance of duty is not only right in itself but also the source of the profoundest satisfaction.

THEODORE ROOSEVELT
Outlook, Apr. 8, 1911; *Works, XII*, 192

9.   Our whole duty, for the present, at any rate, is summed up in the motto: "America first."

WOODROW WILSON
Speech in New York, N.Y., Apr. 20, 1915;
Messages and Papers (*Shaw*), *I*, 109

10.   My fellow Americans, ask not what your country can do for you; ask what you can do for your country. My fellow citizens of the world, ask not what America will do for you, but what together we can do for the freedom of man.

JOHN F. KENNEDY
Inaugural Address, Jan. 20, 1961

See also Character 8, Citizenship 1, 3, 4, Debts 11, Friendship 5, Government 5, 31, Happiness 13, Homes 4, Laws 29, Liberty 30, Life 7, 8, Nations 8, Negroes 4, Patriotism 5, 7, Peace 33, 40, Political Parties 9, Politicians 6, Principles 13, Public Office 20, Republics 13, Responsibility, Right 6, Russia 4, Strife, Success 5, Taxation 6, Trusts 2, Veto Power 3, War 23, 43

Economic Matters

1. Spiritual and intellectual freedom can not continue to exist without economic freedom. If one dies, all will die.

> HERBERT HOOVER
> 1922; *Memoirs, II*, 28

2. Our economic system is but an instrument of the social advancement of the American People. It is an instrument by which we add to the security and richness of life of every individual. It by no means comprises the whole purpose of life, but it is the foundation upon which can be built the finer things of the spirit.

> HERBERT HOOVER
> Address at Cleveland, Ohio, Oct. 2, 1930; *Administration*, p. 47

3. These unhappy times call for the building of plans that rest upon the forgotten, the unorganized but the indispensable units of economic power, for plans . . . that build from the bottom up and not from the top down, that put their faith once more in the forgotten man at the bottom of the economic pyramid.

> FRANKLIN DELANO ROOSEVELT
> Radio address, Apr. 7, 1932; *Public Papers, I*, 625

4. I will always believe in private enterprise as the backbone of economic well-being in the United States. . . . It was this Administration which saved the system of private profit and free enterprise after it had been dragged to the brink of ruin.

> FRANKLIN DELANO ROOSEVELT
> Address in Chicago, Ill., Oct. 14, 1936; *Ibid., V*, 487

5. There is no question in my mind that the Government, acting on behalf of all the people, must assume the ultimate responsibility for the economic health of the Nation.

> HARRY S. TRUMAN
> Message to Congress, Jan. 21, 1946;
> *Public Papers . . . Truman, 1946*, p. 51

See also Debts, Education 35, Faith 3, Foreign Relations 54, Freedom 18, Money 10, 11, Security 2, 8, War 16

Economy

1. We ought never to forget that true public economy consists not in withholding the means necessary to accomplish important national objects confided to us by the Constitution, but in taking care that the money appropriated for these purposes shall be faithfully and frugally expended.

> JAMES BUCHANAN
> Third Annual Message to Congress, Dec. 19, 1859;
> *Messages and Papers*, p. 3104

2. Under our scheme of government the waste of public money is a crime against the citizen, and the contempt of our people for economy and frugality in the personal affairs deplorably saps the strength and sturdiness of our national character.

GROVER CLEVELAND
Second Inaugural Address, Mar. 4, 1893

3. The duty of economy is not debatable. It is manifest and imperative. In the appropriations we pass we are spending the money of the great people whose servants we are—not our own. We are trustees and responsible stewards in the spending. The only thing debatable and upon which we should be careful to make our thought and purpose clear is the kind of economy demanded of us. I assert with the greatest confidence that the people of the United States are not jealous of the amount their Government costs if they are sure that they get what they need and desire for the outlay, that the money is being spent for objects of which they approve, and that it is being applied with good business sense and management.

WOODROW WILSON
Second Annual Message to Congress, Dec. 8, 1914;
Messages and Papers (Shaw), I, 74

4. After order and liberty, economy is one of the highest essentials of a free government. . . . Economy is always a guarantee of peace.

CALVIN COOLIDGE
Speech at Northampton, Mass., May 30, 1923;
Freedom, p. 350

5. With us economy is imperative. It is a full test of our national character. . . . I am for economy. After that I am for more economy.

CALVIN COOLIDGE
Speech in Washington, D.C., June 30, 1924;
Foundations, pp. 41, 47

6. I favor the policy of economy, not because I wish to save money, but because I wish to save people. The men and women of this country who toil are the ones who bear the cost of the Government. Every dollar that we carelessly waste means that their life will be so much the more meager. . . . Economy is idealism in its most practical form.

The wisest and soundest method of solving our tax problem is through economy.

The result of economic dissipation to a nation is always moral decay.

CALVIN COOLIDGE
Inaugural Address, Mar. 4, 1925

7. Economy is the method by which we prepare today to afford the improvements of tomorrow.

CALVIN COOLIDGE
Message to Congress, 1925; *Message,* p. 3

8.   Any government, like any family, can for a year spend a little more than it earns. But you and I know that a continuance of that habit means the poorhouse.

FRANKLIN DELANO ROOSEVELT
Radio speech, July 30, 1932; *Ibid.*, p. 663

9.   My interest is in an economy which will be strong enough to absorb the potential of a rapidly expanding population, steady enough to avert the wide swings which bring grief to so many of our people, and non-inflationary enough to persuade investors that this country holds a steady promise of growth and stability.

JOHN F. KENNEDY
In Washington, D.C., Apr. 30, 1962; *Vital Speeches,
June 1, 1962*, p. 482

See also Business 10, Government 27, Loans, Money 9, Peace 22, Property 10, Security 5, Wealth 8

Education

1.   Promote, then, as an object of primary importance, institutions for the general diffusion of knowledge. In proportion as the structure of government gives force to public opinion, it is essential that public opinion should be enlightened.

GEORGE WASHINGTON
Farewell Address, Sept. 19, 1796; *Writings
(Fitzpatrick), XXXV*, 230

2.   The preservation of the means of knowledge among the lowest ranks is of more importance to the public than all the property of all the rich men in the country.

JOHN ADAMS
Dissertation on the Canon and the Feudal Law, August, 1765;
Works, III, 457

3.   Education makes a greater difference between man and man, than nature has made between man and brute.

JOHN ADAMS
To Abigail Adams, Oct. 29, 1775; *Familiar Letters*, p. 119

4.   The tax which will be paid for the purpose of education is not more than the thousandth part of what will be paid to kings, priests and nobles who will rise up among us if we leave the people in ignorance.

THOMAS JEFFERSON
To George Wythe, Aug. 13, 1786; *Works, II*, 6

5.   [Academies] commit their pupils to the theatre of the world, with

just taste enough of learning to be alienated from industrial pursuits, and not enough to do service in the ranks of science.

THOMAS JEFFERSON
To John Adams, July 5, 1841; *Writings, XIV,* 151

6. A well-instructed people alone can be permanently a free people.

JAMES MADISON
Second Annual Message to Congress, Dec. 5, 1810;
Messages and Papers, p. 470

7. Learned institutions ought to be favorite objects with every free people. They throw that light over the public mind which is the best security against crafty and dangerous encroachments on the public liberty.

JAMES MADISON
To W. T. Barry, Aug. 4, 1822; *Complete Madison,* p. 337

8. Upon the subject of education, not presuming to dictate any plan or system respecting it, I can only say that I view it as the most important subject which we as a people can be engaged in. . . . I desire to see the time when education—and by its means, morality, sobriety, enterprise and industry—shall become much more general than at present. . . .

ABRAHAM LINCOLN
Political announcement, Sangamon County, Ill., Mar. 9, 1832;
Complete Works, I, 7

9. The true prosperity and greatness of a nation is to be found in the elevation and education of its laborers.

ULYSSES S. GRANT
Third Annual Message to Congress, Dec. 4, 1871;
Messages and Papers, p. 4100

10. Aid to education in the States by the Nation . . . seems to be our best chance to bring up the neglected elements in our population.

RUTHERFORD B. HAYES
To Hon. Guy M. Bryan, Nov. 13, 1884; *Diary and Letters, IV,* 176

11. Learn to know yourself to the end that you may improve your powers, your conduct, your character. This is the true aim of education and the best of all educations is self-education.

RUTHERFORD B. HAYES
Diary, Oct. 4, 1892; *Ibid., V,* 112

12. Next in importance to freedom and justice is popular education, without which neither freedom nor justice can be permanently maintained.

JAMES A. GARFIELD
Letter Accepting Nomination for Presidency, July 12, 1880;
Works, II, 783

13. A more constant and active participation in political affairs on the part of our men of education would be of the greatest possible value to our country.

GROVER CLEVELAND
Address at Princeton University, 1896; *Eloquence, VII,* 253

14. How priceless is a liberal education! In itself what a rich endowment! It is not impaired by age, but its value increases with use. No one can employ it but its rightful owner. He alone can illustrate its worth and enjoy its rewards. It cannot be inherited or purchased. It must be acquired by individual effort. It can be secured only by perseverance and self-denial. But it is as free as the air we breathe. . . . A liberal education is the prize of individual industry. It is the greatest blessing that a man or woman can enjoy, when supported by virtue, morality, and noble aims.

WILLIAM MCKINLEY
In Philadelphia, Pa., Feb. 22, 1898; *Speeches and Addresses,* p. 74

15. Education should not confine itself to books. It must train executive power, and try to create that right public opinion which is the most potent factor in the proper solution of all political and social questions. Book-learning is very important, but it is by no means everything.

THEODORE ROOSEVELT
Address at Lansing, Mich., May 31, 1907; *Works, VI,* 1288

16. The higher education is well for those who can use it to advantage, but it too often fits a man to do things for which there is no demand, and unfits him for work which there are too few to do.

WILLIAM HOWARD TAFT
Inauguration of the Philippine Assembly, Oct. 16, 1907;
Problems, p. 22

17. The object of a liberal training is not learning, but discipline and the enlightenment of the mind.

WOODROW WILSON
Speech at Cambridge, Mass., July 1, 1909; *Ideals,* p. 22

18. The strength and security of the nation will always rest in the intelligent body of its people. Our education should implant conceptions of public duty and private obligation broad enough to envisage the problems of a greatly distraught world.

WARREN G. HARDING
Message for American Education Week, 1922;
Messages and Papers, p. 9157

19. Education is for the purpose of bringing to bear the experiences of the past in finding the solutions of the problems of the present.

CALVIN COOLIDGE
Speech at College of the Holy Cross, June, 1920;
Citizenship, p. 330

20. Education is the result of contact. A great people is produced by contact with great minds.

CALVIN COOLIDGE
Speech at Evanston, Ill., Jan. 21, 1923; *Freedom,* p. 243

21. Upon our educational system must largely depend the perpetuity of those institutions upon which our freedom and our security rest.

FRANKLIN DELANO ROOSEVELT
Message for American Education Week, Sept. 27, 1938;
Public Papers, VII, 538

22. One of the difficulties with all our institutions is the fact that we've emphasized the reward instead of the service. . . .

I've been trying to work out a federal system of help to education, particularly along material lines—that is, improved buildings and increased salaries for teachers, but I think the fundamental purpose of our educational system is to instill a moral code in the rising generation and create a citizenship which will be responsible for the welfare of the Nation.

HARRY S. TRUMAN
To Mr. Moore, Sept. 27, 1949; *Mr. President,* p. 45

23. The educator must teach that tolerance is better than a bullet; that understanding is something worthwhile and of far greater value to us than is prejudice; that international differences in the realm of trade and finance and national pride are not so great as to avoid the establishment of . . . the regimented clusters of white crosses that now stand along the roads of Europe.

I see no hope for the world except through education, but I am most optimistic for the world because I believe in education. . . .

DWIGHT D. EISENHOWER
Address at Boston University, Jan. 31, 1946;
Eisenhower Speaks, p. 72

24. The Federal role should be merely to facilitate—never to control—education.

DWIGHT D. EISENHOWER
Special Message to Congress, Jan. 28, 1957; *Public Papers . . .
Eisenhower, 1957,* p. 90

25. In a Nation which holds sacred the dignity and worth of the individual, education is first and foremost an instrument for serving the aspirations of each person. It is not only the means for earning a living,

but for enlarging life—for maintaining and improving liberty of the mind, for exercising both the rights and obligations of freedom, for understanding the world in which we live.

Collectively, the educational equipment of the whole population contributes to our national character—our freedom as a Nation, our national security, our expanding economy, our cultural attainments, our unremitting efforts for a durable peace.

DWIGHT D. EISENHOWER
Special Message to Congress, Jan. 28, 1957; *Ibid.,* p. 95

26.   I believe with Franklin that freedom and free government depend upon an educated citizenry.

DWIGHT D. EISENHOWER
News conference, Apr. 3, 1957; *Ibid.,* p. 243

27.   It is unwise to make education too cheap. If everything is provided freely, there is a tendency to put no value on anything. Education must always have a certain price on it; even as the very process of learning itself must always require individual effort and initiative. Education is a matter of . . . self-discipline. . . . Prejudice and unreasoning opposition will more and more give way before the clean flood of knowledge.

DWIGHT D. EISENHOWER
Address in Washington, D.C., Apr. 4, 1957; *Ibid.,* p. 266

28.   It is within your power to see that schools no longer produce mathematical illiterates—or students who can identify all the wives of Henry the Eighth, but not the countries bordering Afghanistan—or scholars whose education has been so specialized as to exclude them from participation in current events—men like Lord John Russell, of whom Queen Victoria once remarked that he would be a better man if he knew a third subject, but he was interested in nothing but the Constitution of 1688 and himself. Civilization, according to the old saying, "is a race between education and catastrophe." It is up to you to determine the winner.

JOHN F. KENNEDY
Address at University of Denver, Feb. 24, 1958; *Strategy,* p. 208

29.   I ask only that you offer to the political arena, and to the critical problems of our society which are decided therein, the benefit of the talents which society has helped to develop in you. I ask you to decide, as Goethe put it, whether you will be an anvil—or a hammer. The formal phases of the "anvil" stage are completed for many of you, though hopefully you will continue to absorb still more in the years ahead. The question now is whether you are to be a hammer—whether you are to give to the world in which you are reared and educated the broadest benefits of that education.

JOHN F. KENNEDY
Address at University of Wisconsin, June 16, 1958;
Ibid., p. 230

30. Education . . . is the mainspring of our economic and social progress. . . . It is the highest expression of achievement in our society, ennobling and enriching human life.

JOHN F. KENNEDY
Message to Congress, Feb. 6, 1962; *Public Papers*
. . . Kennedy, 1962, p. 110

31. The classroom—not the trench—is the frontier of freedom now and forevermore.

LYNDON B. JOHNSON
Address at New York Institute of Technology, Dec. 16, 1958

32. If we, of this generation, are to assure greatness for our nation, survival for our freedoms and honor for ourselves, we must make provision in our land—and in all lands where men are free—for education of the first class on all levels.

LYNDON B. JOHNSON
Address to University of Texas Ex-Students Association,
Apr. 1, 1959

33. Education is mankind's only hope. Education is the imperative of a universal and lasting peace. . . . Education is the key that unlocks progress in the struggle against hunger and want and injustice wherever they may exist on the earth. It is the path which now beckons us toward the planets and the stars. Above all else, it is the well-spring of freedom and peace.

LYNDON B. JOHNSON
Address at University of the Philippines, May 13, 1961;
Story, p. 182–83

34. Education is not a problem. Education is an opportunity.

LYNDON B. JOHNSON
Address at William Jewell College, Nov. 9, 1961; *Ibid.,* p. 182

35. We have entered an age in which education is not just a luxury permitting some men an advantage over others. It has become a necessity without which a person is defenseless in this complex, industrialized society.

Levels of education which were once regarded with awe, have now become commonplace. And jobs which once could be filled by strength and native intelligence now call for a college degree. We have truly entered the Century of the Educated Man. . . .

If we deny a man access to the education to which he is entitled by capacity, we also deny him access to his rightful place in our economy. And, I might add, we also deny ourselves his productive skills.

LYNDON B. JOHNSON
At Tufts University commencement, June 9, 1963;
Vital Speeches, August 15, 1963, p. 644

See also Arts (The) 1, Books, Colleges, Culture, Desegregation 2, Discipline 3, Discrimination 4, 6, Enlightenment, Government 71, 100, Ideals 8, Ignorance, Knowledge, Language 1, Libraries 3, 4, Military Matters 5, Morality 1, Negroes 1, 12, People (The) 8, 11, 13, Preparedness 8, Prosperity 7, Security 5, Suffrage 2, 3, Universities, Women 3

Effort

1. In this life we get nothing save by effort; far better it is to dare mighty things, to win glorious triumphs, even though checkered by failure, than to take rank with those poor spirits who neither enjoy much nor suffer much, because they live in the great twilight that knows neither victory nor defeat.

THEODORE ROOSEVELT
Address in Chicago, Ill., Apr. 10, 1899; *Works, XIII*, 320

2. The only life that is worth living is the life of effort, the life of effort to attain what is worth striving for.

THEODORE ROOSEVELT
At Groton, Mass., May 24, 1904; *Presidential Addresses, III*, 15

See also Achievement 2, 3, Action 1, Greatness 3, 4, 12, Life 6, Revolutions 8

Elections

1. Believing that the restoration of the civil service to the system established by Washington and followed by the early Presidents can be best accomplished by an Executive who is under no temptation to use the patronage of his office to promote his own re-election, I desire to perform what I regard as a duty in now stating my inflexible purpose, if elected, not to be a candidate for election to a second term.

RUTHERFORD B. HAYES
Letter Accepting Nomination for Presidency, July 8, 1876;
Letters and Messages, p. 5

2. You were never more mistaken . . . than to suppose that business men carry elections. A large vote is brought out when all the men in politics are pleased and satisfied and set to work with enthusiasm for the ticket.

CHESTER A. ARTHUR
1878; *Arthur*, p. 211

3. What is the use of being elected or re-elected unless you stand for something?

GROVER CLEVELAND
To a political adviser, 1887; *Man and Statesman, I*, 271

4. If any intelligent and loyal company of American citizens were required to catalogue the essential human conditions of national life, I do

not doubt that with absolute unanimity they would begin with "free and honest elections."

BENJAMIN HARRISON
Second Annual Message to Congress, Dec. 1, 1890;
Messages and Papers, p. 5562

5. If you think too much about being re-elected, it is very difficult to be worth re-electing.

WOODROW WILSON
Address at Philadelphia, Pa., Oct. 25, 1913; *Public Papers, III,* 62

See also Ballots, Democracy 22, Peace 20, Suffrage, Voters

Eloquence

1. Borrowed eloquence, if it contains as good stuff, is as good as own eloquence.

JOHN ADAMS
To Benjamin Rush, Aug. 28, 1811; *Writings,* p. 163

See also Public Speaking 1, Speeches

Emigrants

1. The emigrants . . . although of different political parties and of different religious sects . . . all flew from persecution, in pursuit of liberty, and they inculcated that sentiment on their descendants.

JAMES MONROE

See also Immigration

Enemies

1. Among individuals, the most certain way to make a Man your Enemy, is to tell him you esteem him such; so with public bodies.

GEORGE WASHINGTON
To John Bannister, Apr. 21, 1778; *Writings (Fitzpatrick), XI,* 291

2. My course has always been to put my enemies at defiance, and pursue my own course.

ANDREW JACKSON
To Frank P. Blair, Feb. 20, 1839; *Life (Bassett),* p. 729

3. The foes from whom we should pray to be delivered are our own passions, appetites, and follies; and against these there is always need that we should war.

THEODORE ROOSEVELT
Proclamation, Nov. 2, 1905; *Messages and Papers,* p. 7348

4. No people on earth can be held, as a people, to be an enemy, for

all humanity shares the common hunger for peace and fellowship and justice.

DWIGHT D. EISENHOWER

Address to American Society of Newspaper Editors, Apr. 16, 1953;
Public Papers . . . Eisenhower, 1953, p. 180

See also Friendship 3, 5, 8, 9, Hatred, Peace 2, Preparedness 1, Presidency (The) 30, 50, Public Speaking 1, Success 9, Union 25, United States 6

Energy

1. I am like a taper. When nearly exhausted it will sometimes have the appearance of going out, but will blaze up again for a time.

ANDREW JACKSON

To Amos Kendall, June 18, 1842; *Correspondence, VI,* 160

2. Energy in a nation is like sap in a tree; it rises from the bottom up; it does not come from the top down. . . . When I was a schoolmaster, I used to say that the trouble about the college sophomore was that the sap of manhood was rising in him, but hadn't reached his head.

WOODROW WILSON

Address in Philadelphia, Pa., Oct. 28, 1912; *Crossroads,* p. 489

See also Government 35, 36, Liberty 15, Physical Fitness 4, 5, Power 31, Prosperity 10, Republics 15, Revolutions 8

England

1. Britain and America are staring at each other; and they will probably stare more and more for some time.

JOHN ADAMS

Diary, Jan. 1, 1766; *Works, II,* 170

2. The present conduct of England and America resembles that of the eagle and cat. An eagle scaling over a farmer's yard, espied a creature that he thought a hare; he pounced upon him and took him up in the air; the cat seized him by the neck with her teeth, and round the body with her fore and hind claws. The eagle finding himself scratched and pressed, bids the cat let go and fall down. No, says the cat, I won't let go and fall; you shall stoop and set me down.

JOHN ADAMS

Diary, Nov. 4, 1782; *Ibid., III,* 302

See also Declaration of Independence 4, History 19, Peace 10, War 6

Enlightenment

1. Enlighten the people generally, and tyranny and oppressions of body and mind will vanish like evil spirits at the dawn of day.

THOMAS JEFFERSON

To Du Pont de Nemours, Apr. 24, 1816; *Writings, XIV,* 491

See also Books, Colleges, Education, Errors 5, Knowledge, Libraries, Mankind 6, People 2, 11, Press (The) 10, Universities

Enthusiasm

1. Enthusiasm for a cause sometimes warps judgment.

WILLIAM HOWARD TAFT

See also Progress 2, Youth 2

Equality

1. The foundation on which all our constitutions are built is the natural equality of man. . . .

THOMAS JEFFERSON
To George Washington, Apr. 16, 1784; *Works, I,* 334

2. Distinctions in society will always exist under every just government. Equality of talents, of education, or of wealth can not be produced by human institutions.

ANDREW JACKSON
Veto Message, July 10, 1832; *Messages and Papers,* p. 1153

3. Equality among the States is equity. This equality is the very essence of the Constitution.

JAMES BUCHANAN
Veto Message, Feb. 1, 1860; *Ibid.,* p. 3135

4. As a nation, we began by declaring that *all men are created equal.* We now practically read it, *all men are created equal except Negroes.* When the know-nothings get control, it will read, *all men are created equal* except Negroes and foreigners and Catholics. When it comes to this I shall prefer emigrating to some country where they make no pretense of loving liberty—to Russia, for instance, where despotism can be taken pure, and without the base alloy of hypocrisy.

ABRAHAM LINCOLN
To Joshua Speed, Aug. 24, 1855; *Complete Works, II,* 287

5. I think the authors of that notable instrument [the Declaration of Independence] intended to include *all* men, but they did not intend to declare all men equal *in all respects.* They did not mean to say all were equal in color, size, intellect, moral developments, or social capacity. They defined with tolerable distinctness in what respects they did consider all men created equal—equal with "certain inalienable rights, among which are life, liberty, and the pursuit of happiness." This they said, and this they meant.

ABRAHAM LINCOLN
Speech at Springfield, Ill., June 27, 1857; *Ibid.,* p. 330

6. Let us discard all this quibbling about this man or the other man, this

race and that race, and the other race being inferior and therefore they must be placed in an inferior position—discarding our standard that we have left us! Let us discard all these things and unite as one people throughout this land until we shall once more stand up declaring that all men are created equal. . . . I leave you hoping that the lamp of liberty will burn in your bosoms until there shall no longer be a doubt that all men are created equal.

ABRAHAM LINCOLN
Speech in Chicago, Ill., July 10, 1858; *Ibid., III,* 51

7. Equality—the informing soul of Freedom!

JAMES A. GARFIELD
Maxims, p. 8

8. Our aim is to recognize what Lincoln pointed out: The fact that there are some respects in which men are obviously not equal: but also to insist that there should be an equality of self-respect and of mutual respect, an equality of rights before the law, and at least an approximate equality in the conditions under which each man obtains the chance to show the stuff that is in him when compared to his fellows.

THEODORE ROOSEVELT
Seventh Annual Message to Congress, Dec. 3, 1907;
Messages and Papers, p. 7465

9. There never can be equality of rewards or possessions so long as the human plan contains varied talents and differing degrees of industry and thrift, but ours ought to be a country free from the great blotches of distressed poverty.

WARREN G. HARDING
Inaugural Address, Mar. 4, 1921

10. We believe in equal opportunity for all, but we know that this includes the opportunity to rise to leadership, to be uncommon! The great human advances have not been brought about by mediocre men and women.

HERBERT HOOVER
Remarks, Nov. 11, 1948; *American Road,* p. 171

See also American System, Civil Rights, Declaration of Independence 9, 10, Discrimination, Faith 4, Freedom, Friendship 10, Government 47, 67, Inequality, Nations 4, Negroes 9, 12, Peace 36, Pensions, Republics 8, Rights 2, Security 7, Voters 1

Errors
1. That I have foibles, and perhaps many of them, I shall not deny. I should esteem myself, as the world also would, vain and empty, were I to arrogate perfection.

Knowledge in military matters is to be acquired by practice and experience only; and, if I have erred, great allowance should be made for the want of them; unless my errors should appear to be wilful.

GEORGE WASHINGTON
To Gov. Robert Dinwiddie, Sept. 17, 1757;
Writings (Fitzpatrick), II, 133

2. Why should I expect to be exempt from censure; the unfailing lot of an elevated station? My Heart tells me it has been my unremitted aim to do the best circumstances would permit; yet, I may have been very often mistaken in my judgment of the means, and may, in many instances deserve the imputation of error.

GEORGE WASHINGTON
To Henry Laurens, Jan. 31, 1778; *Ibid., XX,* 411

3. Reason and free inquiry are the only effectual agents against error.

THOMAS JEFFERSON
Notes on Virginia, 1782; *Writings, II,* 221

4. It is error alone which needs the support of government. Truth can stand by itself.

THOMAS JEFFERSON
Notes on Virginia, 1782; *Ibid.,* p. 222

5. Do not be too severe upon the errors of the people, but reclaim them by enlightening them.

THOMAS JEFFERSON
To Edward Carrington, Jan. 16, 1787; *Life and Selected,* p. 412

6. Delay is preferable to error.

THOMAS JEFFERSON
To George Washington, May 16, 1792; *Writings, VIII,* 338

7. I now commend you, fellow-citizens, to the guidance of Almighty God, with a full reliance on His merciful providence for the maintenance of our free institutions, and with an earnest supplication that whatever errors it may be my lot to commit in discharging the arduous duties which have devolved on me will find a remedy in the harmony and wisdom of your counsels.

ANDREW JACKSON
First Annual Message to Congress, Dec. 8, 1829;
Messages and Papers, p. 1025

8. [Inscription over the grave of his horse]: Here lies the body of my good horse, "The General." For twenty years he bore me around the circuit of my practice, and in all that time he never made a blunder. Would that his master could say the same! John Tyler.

JOHN TYLER
Facts, p. 77

9. I shall try to correct errors when shown to be errors, and I shall adopt new views so fast as they shall appear to be true views.

ABRAHAM LINCOLN
To Horace Greeley, Aug. 22, 1862; *Complete Works, VIII*, 16

10. Everything I say, you know, goes into print. If I make a mistake it doesn't merely affect me, or you, but the country. I, therefore, ought at least try not to make mistakes.

ABRAHAM LINCOLN
To a crowd gathered before the White House, Apr. 10, 1865;
Portrait, II, 965

11. History shows that no Administration from the time of Washington to the present has been free from . . . mistakes. But I leave comparisons to history, claiming only that I have acted in every instance from a conscientious desire to do what was right, constitutional, within the law, and for the very best interests of the whole people.

ULYSSES S. GRANT
Annual Message to Congress, Dec. 5, 1876;
Messages and Papers, p. 4354

12. If I have erred, I err in company with Abraham Lincoln.

THEODORE ROOSEVELT
Campaign speech, 1912

13. I wish we might have less condemnation of error and more commendation of right.

WARREN G. HARDING
Address at Arlington National Cemetery, May 30, 1923;
Messages and Papers, p. 9229

14. It would be folly to argue that the people cannot make political mistakes. They can and do make grave mistakes. But compared with the mistakes which have been made by every kind of autocracy they are unimportant.

CALVIN COOLIDGE
Speech at Evanston, Ill., Jan. 21, 1923; *Freedom*, p. 241

15. We may make mistakes—but they must never be mistakes which result from faintness of heart or abandonment of moral principle.

FRANKLIN DELANO ROOSEVELT
Fourth Inaugural Address, Jan. 20, 1945

16. This Administration intends to be candid about its errors; for, as a wise man once said: "An error doesn't become a mistake until you refuse to correct it." We intend to accept full responsibility for our errors.

JOHN F. KENNEDY
Speech in New York, N.Y., Apr. 27, 1961;
Public Papers . . . Kennedy, 1961, p. 153

EXAMPLE 87

17. You can always survive a mistake in domestic affairs but you may get killed by one made in foreign policy.

JOHN F. KENNEDY
1961; *Saturday Review, Mar. 7, 1964*

See also Ignorance 2, League of Nations 3, Opinion 2, People (The) 27, Politics 4, Presidency (The) 31, Press (The) 8, Rights 19

Ethics

1. I have but one system of ethics for men and for nations—to be grateful, to be faithful to all engagements under all circumstances, to be open and generous, promoting in the long run even the interests of both; and I am sure it promotes their happiness.

THOMAS JEFFERSON
Letter to the Duchess d'Auville, Apr. 2, 1790; *Works, III,* 135

Europe

1. It is obvious that all the powers of Europe will be continually manoeuvering with us, to work us into their real or imaginary balances of power. They will all wish to make of us a make-weight candle, when they are weighing out their pounds. Indeed, it is not surprising; for we shall very often, if not always, be able to turn the scale. But I think it ought to be our rule not to meddle; and that of all the powers of Europe, not to desire us, or, perhaps, even to permit us, to interfere, if they can help it.

JOHN ADAMS
Diary, Nov. 18, 1782; *Works, III,* 316

See also Americans 3, Colonialism, Happiness 5, History 19, Kings 1, 3, Mankind 4, Neutrality 4, Power 20, Right 2, Rights 5, Union 1, 4, War 6

Evil

1. The evil that works from a bad centre works both ways.

BENJAMIN HARRISON
As I Knew Them, p. 181

See also Pessimism

2. No man is justified in doing evil on the ground of expediency.

THEODORE ROOSEVELT
Citizen, p. 423

See also Civilization 1, Government 44, 46, Homes 4, Pessimism, Unity 8

Example

1. I have ever deemed it more honorable and more profitable, too, to set a good example than to follow a bad one.

THOMAS JEFFERSON
To Correa de Serra, Dec. 27, 1814; *Writings, XIV,* 222

Exercise

1. The Greeks understood that mind and body must develop in harmonious proportion to produce a creative intelligence. And so did the most brilliant intelligence of our earliest day, Thomas Jefferson, when he said, "Not less than two hours a day should be devoted to exercise." If the man who wrote the Declaration of Independence, was Secretary of State and twice President, could give it two hours, our children can give it ten or fifteen minutes.

> JOHN F. KENNEDY
> Address in New York, N.Y., Dec. 5, 1961;
> *Public Papers . . . Kennedy, 1961*, p. 773

See also Athletics, Health, Physical Fitness

Experience

1. Experience teaches us that it is much easier to prevent an enemy from posting themselves than it is to dislodge them after they have got possession.

> GEORGE WASHINGTON
> To President of Congress, Jan. 11, 1776;
> *Writings (Fitzpatrick)*, *IV*, 230

2. Experience is the surest standard by which to test the real tendency of the existing Constitution of a country.

> GEORGE WASHINGTON
> Farewell Address, Sept. 19, 1796; *Ibid., XXXV*, 225

3. Experience is the oracle of truth; and where its responses are unequivocal, they ought to be conclusive and sacred.

> JAMES MADISON
> "Publius," 1787; *Federalist, No. 20*

See also Errors 1, Foreign Relations 4, History 2, Military Matters 8, Neutrality 4, Politics 3, Power 27, States' Rights 3, Union 12, United Nations 3, Wisdom 5, 6

Expositions

1. Expositions are the timekeepers of progress.

> WILLIAM MCKINLEY
> Last speech, Buffalo, N.Y., Sept. 5, 1901;
> *Messages and Papers*, p. 6618

2. We can not doubt that the great international expositions heretofore held have done much to bring to all mankind a feeling of unity in aspiration and of community in effort.

> WARREN G. HARDING
> Special Message to Congress, Mar. 24, 1922; *Ibid.*, p. 9121

Factions
See Democracy 2, Liberty 14

Failure

1. The probability that we may fail in the struggle ought not to deter us from the support of a cause we believe to be just.

ABRAHAM LINCOLN
Speech at Springfield, Ill., Dec. 10, 1839; *Complete Works, I,* 138

2. It is hard to fail; but it is worse never to have tried to succeed.

THEODORE ROOSEVELT
Address in Chicago, Ill., Apr. 10, 1899; *Works, XIII,* 320

Fair Deal

1. I fear very much that you still have your economic royalist viewpoint and are not particularly interested in the welfare of the vast majority of people. It is my business to see that everybody gets a fair deal and that is exactly what I am trying to do.

HARRY S. TRUMAN
Letter, Apr. 20, 1949; *Mr. President,* p. 57

Faith

1. I am weary of philosophers, theologians, politicians, and historians. They are immense masses of absurdities, vices, and lies. Montesquieu had sense enough to say in jest, that all our knowledge might be comprehended in twelve pages in duodecimo; and I believe him in earnest. I could express my faith in shorter terms.

JOHN ADAMS
To Thomas Jefferson, June 28, 1812; *Works, X,* 19

2. Faith is the great motive power, and no man realizes his full possibilities unless he has the deep conviction that life is eternally important, and that his work, well done, is a part of an unending plan.

CALVIN COOLIDGE
Speech in Washington, D.C., July 25, 1924; *Foundations,* p. 67

3. Faith is a delicate though powerful factor in our economic life.

FRANKLIN DELANO ROOSEVELT
Campaign address at St. Louis, Mo., Oct. 21, 1932;
Public Papers, I, 819

4. The political freedoms we know, the American concept of democracy, certainly include a faith, related to some religion, that man is more than an animal, that he possesses a soul. . . . If we have not that faith, then why should any of us admit that any other is born with equal rights to himself? Each of us instinctively recognizes . . . that an individual,

because he was born, possesses certain rights. And to prove that we must go back and depend upon faith, and faith alone.

> DWIGHT D. EISENHOWER
> Speech at Poughkeepsie, N.Y., June 26, 1948;
> *What Eisenhower Thinks,* p. 50

5. Men grow in stature only as they daily rededicate themselves to a noble faith.

> DWIGHT D. EISENHOWER
> Speech at Valley Forge, Pa., July 4, 1950; *Ibid.,* p. 123

6. At such a time in history, we, who are free, must proclaim anew our faith. This faith is the abiding creed of our fathers. It is our faith in the deathless dignity of man, governed by eternal moral and natural laws.

> DWIGHT D. EISENHOWER
> First Inaugural Address, Jan. 20, 1953

7. Faith is evidently too simple a thing for some to recognize its paramount worth.

> DWIGHT D. EISENHOWER
> Address at Atlantic City, N.J., Oct. 6, 1953; *Peace,* p. 42

8. Faith is our surest strength, our greatest resource.

> DWIGHT D. EISENHOWER
> Radio speech, Feb. 7, 1954; *Index,* p. 38

9. We must proceed by faith, knowing the light of Christmas is eternal, though we cannot always see it.

We must believe that the truth of Christmas is constant; that men can live together in peace as Lincoln said, "with charity for all, with firmness in the right."

> DWIGHT D. EISENHOWER
> Remarks at Washington, D.C., Dec. 20, 1956; *Peace,* p. 139

10. It has always been my faith that eventual triumph of decency and freedom and right in this world is inevitable.

> DWIGHT D. EISENHOWER
> Radio and television address, Nov. 13, 1957;
> *Public Papers . . . Eisenhower, 1957,* p. 816

11. No one who enters upon the office [the Presidency] can fail to recognize how every President of the United States has placed special reliance upon his faith in God. Every President has taken comfort and courage when told . . . that the Lord "will be with thee. He will not fail thee nor forsake thee. Fear not—neither be thou dismayed."

> JOHN F. KENNEDY
> Remarks to Christian Leadership, Inc., Feb. 1, 1961;
> *Public Papers . . . Kennedy, 1961,* p. 76

See also Bible 2, Conduct 1, Democracy 16, Fear 1, 6, Foreign Relations 35, Materialism 2, Peace 68, Religion, Right 6, Virtue 7

Falsehoods
See Press (The) 6, 21

Fame
See Fidelity 3, Monuments 1, Public Affairs 1, Public Speaking 1

Families
See Homes

Farmers
1.   The life of a Husbandman of all others is the most delectable. It is honorable. It is amusing, and, with judicious management, it is profitable.
GEORGE WASHINGTON
To Alexander Spotswood, Feb. 13, 1788;
Writings (Fitzpatrick), XXIX, 414

2.   Corruption of morals in the mass of cultivators is a phenomenon of which no age nor nation has furnished an example.
THOMAS JEFFERSON
Notes on Virginia, 1782; *Writings, II,* 229

3.   Those who labor in the earth are the chosen people of God, if ever He had a chosen people.
THOMAS JEFFERSON
Notes on Virginia, 1782; *Ibid.*

See also Agriculture

Fear
1.   Fear and hope are the two pillars upon which all religious faith is built. But Fear is an instrument of necessity. Hope is the creature of contingency. . . . Fear flies to a refuge. Hope is always attended with doubt, and conscious of its own delusions. Fear is . . . a more efficacious agent than Hope and has far more powerful operation upon religious faith.
JOHN QUINCY ADAMS
Diary, Jan. 7, 1821; *Memoirs, V,* 231

2.   Fear God, in the true sense of the word, means love . . . respect . . . honor God; and all of this can only be done by loving our neighbor, treating him justly and mercifully, and in all ways endeavoring to protect him from injustice and cruelty.
THEODORE ROOSEVELT
1916; *Works, XVIII,* 199

3.   The great malady of public life is cowardice. Most men are not

untrue, but they are afraid. Most of the errors of public life . . . come, not because men are morally bad, but because they are afraid of somebody.

WOODROW WILSON
Address to Princeton University Class of 1879; June 13, 1914;
Typescript in Wilson papers, Library of Congress

4.   The only thing we have to fear is fear itself—nameless, unreasoning, unjustified terror which paralyzes needed efforts to convert retreat into advance.

FRANKLIN DELANO ROOSEVELT
First Inaugural Address, Mar. 4, 1933

5.   The stresses and strains of fear are intensified in our day because everywhere the superstitions of materialism are increasing their holds on the minds of men. . . . Within the Communist orbit . . . the official doctrine makes mankind the helpless pawn of economic forces.

But man's spiritual side is still the dominant one.

DWIGHT D. EISENHOWER
Address at Columbia University, Mar. 23, 1950; *Peace,* p. 20

6.   The men who lack confidence in America are the men who say our people are not up to facing the facts of our missile lag—who say they are not up to bearing the cost of survival.

These are the men who are selling America short—who have substituted fear for faith in our future—who are caught up in their own disbeliefs and doubts about our ability to build a better America.

JOHN F. KENNEDY
Speech at Tulsa, Okla., Sept. 16, 1959; *Strategy,* p. 138

7.   So let us begin anew—remembering on both sides [Russian and American] that civility is not a sign of weakness, and sincerity is always subject to proof. Let us never negotiate out of fear, but let us never fear to negotiate.

JOHN F. KENNEDY
Inaugural Address, Jan. 20, 1961

8.   We have no greater asset than the willingness of a free and determined people, through its elected officials, to face all problems frankly and meet all dangers free from panic or fear.

JOHN F. KENNEDY
State of the Union Message, Jan. 29, 1961; *Tide,* p. 16

See also Foreign Relations 47, Freedom 21, God 11, Government 12, 31, Life 8, Peace 57, 58, 59, 71, Revolutions 8, Security 5

Fidelity

1.   Many free countries have lost their liberty, and ours may lose hers;

but if she shall, be it my proudest plume, not that I was the last to desert, but that I never deserted her.

ABRAHAM LINCOLN
Speech in Springfield, Ill., Dec. 20, 1839; *Complete Works, II,* 137

2. If I were to select a watchword that I would have every young man write above his door and on his heart, it would be that good word "fidelity."

BENJAMIN HARRISON
At Galesburg, Ill., Oct. 8, 1890; *Speeches,* p. 252

3. It is better to be faithful than famous.

THEODORE ROOSEVELT
Citizen, p. 403

See also Government 39, Presidency (The) 3, Public Office 18

Fighting

1. You cannot fight hard unless you think you are fighting to win.

THEODORE ROOSEVELT
Letter to Henry L. Stoddard, July, 1912; *As I Knew Them,* p. 307

2. I want to see you shoot the way you shout.

THEODORE ROOSEVELT
Speech in New York, N.Y., October, 1917

3. The unforgivable crime is soft hitting. Do not hit at all if it can be avoided; but *never* hit softly.

THEODORE ROOSEVELT
Autobiography, p. 85

4. I wish that party battles could be fought with less personal passion and more passion for the common good. I am not interested in fighting persons, but . . . in fighting things.

WOODROW WILSON
Speech at Atlantic City, N.J., Sept. 10, 1912;
Philadelphia Record, Sept. 11, 1912

5. There is such a thing as a man being too proud to fight.

WOODROW WILSON
Speech in Philadelphia, Pa., May 10, 1915;
Messages and Papers (Shaw), I, 117

6. If people want to fight, they'll fight with broomsticks if they can't find anything else.

CALVIN COOLIDGE
1925; *Public Years (Baruch),* p. 192

7. I am fighting, as I have always fought, for the rights of the little man as well as for the big man—for the weak as well as for the strong. . . .

I am fighting to keep this nation prosperous and at peace. I am fighting to keep our people out of foreign wars, and to keep foreign conceptions of government out of our own United States. I am fighting for these great and good causes. I am fighting to defend them against the power and might of those who rise up to challenge them. And I will not stop fighting.

FRANKLIN DELANO ROOSEVELT
At Brooklyn, N.Y., 1940; *As FDR Said*, p. 214

8.   There is nothing I love as much as a good fight.

FRANKLIN DELANO ROOSEVELT
1944; *Ibid.*, p. 204

See also Freedom 22, Peace 30, Treaties 1, War 16

Filibustering

1.   A little group of wilful men [filibustering senators] representing no opinion but their own have rendered the great government of the United States helpless and contemptible.

WOODROW WILSON
Statement to the nation, Mar. 4, 1917; *Public Papers, IV*, 435

Finances

See Banks, Economic Matters, Economy, Money

Flag, The

1.   That [American] flag has waved through three foreign wars . . . cheering the hearts of men . . . wherever its folds have unrolled in the smoke of battle! How many of our countrymen, as they have seen it floating from the masthead in a foreign port, or giving its ample sweep to the breeze over a consular office, have proudly and exultingly exclaimed: "I am an American citizen, and there is the ensign which *commands* for me respect and security, wherever I may choose temporarily to dwell!"

FRANKLIN PIERCE
Letter, Dec. 7, 1859; *Record*, p. 7

2.   I cannot look upon [the flag] without imagining that it consists of alternate stripes of parchment upon which are written the fundamental rights of man, alternating with the streams of blood by which those rights had been vindicated and validated.

WOODROW WILSON
Address in Richmond, Va., Feb. 1, 1912; *Pamphlet, 1912*

3.   The flag has been created by the experience of a great people, and nothing is written upon it that has not been written by their life. It is the embodiment, not of sentiment, but of a history, and no man can rightly

serve under that flag who has not caught some of the meaning of that history.

WOODROW WILSON
Address in Washington, D.C., June 14, 1915;
Public Papers, III, 347

4. This flag which we honor and under which we serve is the emblem of the unity of our power, our thought and purpose as a nation. It has no other character than that which we give it from generation to generation. The choices are ours.

WOODROW WILSON
Address in Washington, D.C., June 14, 1917;
Messages and Papers (Shaw), I, 411

See also Americans 3, Humanity 2, League of Nations 5, Liberty 27, Patriotism 9

Flattery

1. Let those flatter who fear; it is not an American art.

THOMAS JEFFERSON
To Virginia delegates to Congress, August, 1774; *Writings, I,* 209

2. A little flattery will support a man through great fatigue.

JAMES MONROE
To F. A. Vanderkemp, Jan. 24, 1818; *Dictionary,* p. 405

Food

See Peace 63, 69, Poverty, War 56

Force

1. Force cannot give right.

THOMAS JEFFERSON
To Virginia delegates to Congress, August, 1774; *Writings, I,* 209

2. Force is the vital principle and immediate parent of despotism.

THOMAS JEFFERSON
First Inaugural Address, Mar. 4, 1801

3. Neither philosophy, nor religion, nor morality, nor wisdom, nor interest will ever govern nations or parties against their vanity, their pride, their resentment or revenge, or their avarice or ambition. Nothing but force and power and strength can restrain them.

JOHN ADAMS
To Thomas Jefferson, Oct. 9, 1787; *Correspondence I,* 202

4. Force without stint or limit, the righteous triumphant force which shall make right the law of the world and cast every selfish dominion down in the dust.

WOODROW WILSON
Speech at Baltimore, Md., Apr. 6, 1918; *Ibid.,* p. 484

See also Coercion, Diplomacy 2, Foreign Relations 14, 36, Government 58, 82, Laws 28, League of Nations 1, 8, Monroe Doctrine, Peace 57, Public Opinion 12, Religion 16, Revolutions 8, Right 15, Righteousness, Rights 5

Foreign Affairs
See Foreign Relations

Foreign Aid
See Foreign Relations

Foreign Policy
See Errors 17, Foreign Relations

Foreign Relations

1. Observations on the value of peace with other nations are unnecessary. It would be wise, however, by timely provisions to guard against those acts of our own citizens which might tend to disturb it, and put ourselves in a condition to give that satisfaction to foreign nations which we may sometimes have occasion to require from them.

GEORGE WASHINGTON
Fourth Annual Message to Congress, Nov. 6, 1792;
Writings (Fitzpatrick), XII, 31

2. I have always given it as my decided opinion that no nation had a right to intermeddle in the internal concerns of another; that every one had a right to form and adopt whatever government they liked best to live under themselves; and that, if this country could, consistently with its engagements, maintain a strict neutrality and thereby preserve peace, it was bound to do so by motives of policy, interest, and every other considerations.

GEORGE WASHINGTON
To James Monroe, Aug. 25, 1796; *Ibid., XXXV,* 189

3. 'Tis our true policy to steer clear of permanent alliances with any portion of the foreign world.

GEORGE WASHINGTON
Ibid., XII, 234

4. Against the insidious wiles of foreign influence . . . the jealousy of a free people ought to be constantly awake; since history and experience prove that foreign influence is one of the most baneful foes of republican government.

GEORGE WASHINGTON
Farewell Address, Sept. 19, 1796; *Ibid., XXXV,* 233

5. I am for free commerce with all nations; political connection with none; and little or no diplomatic establishment.

THOMAS JEFFERSON
Letter to Elbridge Gerry, Jan. 26, 1799; *Works, IV,* 268

6. Peace, commerce, and honest friendship with all nations—entangling alliances with none.

THOMAS JEFFERSON
First Inaugural Address, Mar. 4, 1801

7. In the intercourse between nations temper is a missionary perhaps more powerful than talent. Nothing was ever lost by kind treatment. Nothing can be gained by sullen repulses and aspiring pretensions.

JOHN QUINCY ADAMS
To the House of Representatives, Mar. 15, 1826;
Messages and Papers, p. 897

8. The foreign policy adopted by our government is to do justice to all, and to submit to wrong by none.

ANDREW JACKSON
Second Inaugural Address, Mar. 4, 1833

9. A faithful observance in the management of our foreign relations of the practice of speaking plainly, dealing justly, and requiring truth and justice in return [are] the best conservatives of the peace of nations.

MARTIN VAN BUREN
Fourth Annual Message to Congress, Dec. 5, 1840;
Messages and Papers, p. 1819

10. The true American policy will be found to consist in the exercise of a spirit of justice, to be manifested in the discharge of all our international obligations to the weakest of the family of nations as well as to the most powerful. . . . The time ought to be regarded as having gone by when a resort to arms is to be esteemed as the only proper arbiter of national differences.

JOHN TYLER
Special Session Message, June 1, 1841; *Ibid.,* p. 1894

11. In the management of our foreign relations it will be my aim to observe a careful respect for the rights of other nations, while our own will be the subject of constant watchfulness. Equal and exact justice should characterize all our intercourse with foreign countries.

JAMES K. POLK
Inaugural Address, Mar. 4, 1845

12. I have no hostility to foreigners. I trust I am their friend.

MILLARD FILLMORE
Speech at Newburgh, N.Y., during the Revolution; *Ovation,* p. 1

13. The great law of morality ought to have a national as well as a personal and individual application. We should act toward other nations as we wish them to act toward us; and justice and conscience should form the rule of conduct between governments instead of mere power, self-interest, and the desire of aggrandizement.

MILLARD FILLMORE
Message, December, 1850; *Chips,* p. 213

14. It has been the uniform policy of this Government, from its foundation to the present day, to abstain from all interference in the domestic affairs of other nations. The consequence has been that while the nations of Europe have been engaged in desolating wars our country has pursued its peaceful course to unexampled prosperity and happiness.

. . . it is said that we ought to interfere between contending sovereigns and their subjects for the purpose of overthrowing the monarchies of Europe and establishing in their place republican institutions . . . that it is consequently our duty to mingle in these contests and aid those who are struggling for liberty.

This is a most seductive but dangerous appeal to the generous sympathies of freemen. . . . Men of the Revolution who drew the sword against the oppressions of the mother country . . . knew that the world is governed less by sympathy than by reason and force; that it was not possible for this nation to become a "propagandist" of free principles without arraying against it the combined powers of Europe, and that the result was more likely to be the overthrow of republican liberty here than its establishment there.

MILLARD FILLMORE
Third Annual Message to Congress, Dec. 6, 1852;
Messages and Papers, p. 2715

15. We ought to cultivate peace, commerce, and friendship with all nations, and this not merely as the best means of promoting our own material interests, but in a spirit of Christian benevolence toward our fellow-men, wherever their lot may be cast. . . . To avoid entangling alliances has been a maxim of our policy ever since the days of Washington, and its wisdom no one will attempt to dispute.

JAMES BUCHANAN
Inaugural Address, Mar. 4, 1857

16. In regard to foreign policy, I would deal with nations as equitable law requires individuals to deal with each other, and I would protect the law-abiding citizen, whether of native or foreign birth, wherever his rights are jeopardized or the flag of our country floats. I would respect the rights of all nations, demanding equal respect for our own.

ULYSSES S. GRANT
First Inaugural Address, Mar. 4, 1869

17. We have for many years maintained with foreign governments the relations of honorable peace, and that such relations may be permanent is desired by every patriotic citizen of the Republic. But if we heed the teachings of history we shall not forget that in the life of every nation emergencies may arise when a resort to arms can alone save it from dishonor.

CHESTER ALAN ARTHUR
First Annual Message to Congress, Dec. 6, 1881;
Messages and Papers, p. 4638

18. I trust that the time is nigh when, with the universal assent of civilized peoples, all international differences shall be determined without resort to arms by the benignant processes of arbitration.

CHESTER ALAN ARTHUR
Second Annual Message to Congress, Dec. 4, 1882;
Ibid., p. 4718

19. We Americans have no commission from God to police the world.

BENJAMIN HARRISON
1888

20. Our relations with foreign powers should be characterized by friendliness and respect. . . . Our Nation is too great, both in material strength and in moral power, to indulge in bluster or to be suspected of timorousness. Vacillation and inconsistency are as incompatible with successful diplomacy as they are with the national dignity.

BENJAMIN HARRISON
At Indianapolis, Ind., Sept. 11, 1888; *Speeches,* p. 114

21. The dealings of this Government with other states have been and should always be marked by frankness and sincerity, our purposes avowed, and our methods free from intrigue. This course has borne rich fruit in the past, and it is our duty as a nation to preserve the heritage of good repute which a century of right dealing with foreign governments has secured to us.

BENJAMIN HARRISON
First Annual Message to Congress, Dec. 3, 1889;
Messages and Papers, p. 5467

22. Will it not be wise to allow the friendship between the nations to rest upon deep and permanent things? . . . Irritations of the cuticle must not be confounded with heart failure.

BENJAMIN HARRISON
North American Review, March, 1901; *Views,* p. 257

23. The United States, in aiming to maintain itself as one of the most enlightened nations, would do its citizens gross injustice if it applied to

its international relations any other than a high standard of honor and morality.

GROVER CLEVELAND
Special Message to Congress, Dec. 18, 1893; *Ibid.,* p. 5903

24. We never have permitted any nation to dictate to us or determine our domestic or foreign policy. We are not and never have been a military people.

WILLIAM MCKINLEY
Speech at Canton, Ohio, May 30, 1891; *Life and Speeches,* p. 175

25. A strong and self-confident nation should be peculiarly careful not only of the rights but of the susceptibilities of its neighbors; and nowadays all the nations of the world are neighbors one to the other. Courtesy, moderation, and self-restraint should mark international, no less than private, intercourse.

THEODORE ROOSEVELT
Directive to government officials, Mar. 10, 1904;
Messages and Papers, p. 7021

26. Ordinarily it is very much wiser and more useful for us to concern ourselves with striving for our own moral and material betterment here at home than to concern ourselves with trying to better the conditions of things in other Nations. We have plenty of sins of our own to war against, and under ordinary circumstances we can do more for the general uplifting of humanity by striving with heart and soul to put a stop to civic corruption, to brutal lawlessness and violent race prejudices here at home than by passing resolutions about wrongdoing elsewhere.

THEODORE ROOSEVELT
Fourth Annual Message to Congress, Dec. 6, 1904;
Works, XV, 258

27. Nine-tenths of wisdom is to be wise in time, and at the right time; and my whole foreign policy was based on the exercise of intelligent forethought and of decisive action sufficiently far in advance of any likely crisis to make it improbable that we would run into serious trouble.

THEODORE ROOSEVELT
On Santa Domingo, 1913, *Ibid., XX,* 496

28. Throughout the seven and a half years that I was President, I pursued without faltering one consistent foreign policy, a policy of genuine international good will and of consideration for the rights of others, and at the same time of steady preparedness.

THEODORE ROOSEVELT
1913; *Autobiography,* p. 538

29. The only safe rule is to promise little, and faithfully to keep every promise; to "speak softly and carry a big stick."

THEODORE ROOSEVELT
Ibid., p. 537

30. The development of the doctrine of international arbitration, considered from the standpoint of its ultimate benefits to the human race, is the most vital movement of our modern times. . . .

The progress already made is a distinct step in the direction of a higher civilization.

WILLIAM HOWARD TAFT
November, 1911; *Dawn*, p. 3

31. It is a very perilous thing to determine the foreign policy of a nation in the terms of material interest.

WOODROW WILSON
Speech at Mobile, Ala., Oct. 27, 1913; *State Papers*, p. 35

32. We cannot form alliances with those who are not going our way.

WOODROW WILSON
Speech in Washington, D.C., May 16, 1914; *Ideals*, p. 71

33. When I have made a promise as a man I try to keep it, and I know of no other rule permissible to a nation.

WOODROW WILSON
Address in Philadelphia, Pa., July 4, 1914; *Public Papers, III*, 145

34. I wish . . . that foreign affairs were as simple as agriculture.

WOODROW WILSON
Address in Washington, D.C., Nov. 14, 1916; *Ibid., IV*, 398

35. If nations may not establish by mutual understanding the rules and principles which are to govern their relationship; if a sovereign and solemn plight of faith by leading nations of the earth is valueless; if nations may not trust one another, then, indeed, there is little on which to hang our faith in advancing civilization or the furtherance of peace. Either we must live and aspire and achieve under a free and common understanding among peoples, with mutual trust, respect, and forbearance, and exercising full sovereignty, or else brutal, armed force will dominate, and the sorrows and burdens of war in this decade will be turned to the chaos and hopelessness of the next. We can no more do without international negotiations and agreements in these modern days than we could maintain orderly neighborliness at home without the prescribed rules of conduct which are more the guaranties of freedom than the restraint thereof.

WARREN G. HARDING
Address to the Senate, Feb. 10, 1922;
Messages and Papers, p. 9072

36. Our country has definitely relinquished the old standard of dealing with other countries by terror and force, and is definitely committed to the new standard of dealing with them through friendship and understanding. . . . I believe . . . this new policy holds a promise of great benefit to humanity. . . . I am especially solicitous that foreign nations should comprehend the candor and sincerity with which we have adopted this position. . . . I want the armed forces of America to be considered by all peoples not as enemies but as friends, as the contribution which is made by this country for the maintenance of the peace and security of the world.

CALVIN COOLIDGE
Second Annual Message to Congress, Dec. 3, 1924;
Messages and Papers, p. 9465

37. The policy of our foreign relations, casting aside any suggestion of force, rests solely on the foundation of peace, good will, and good works.

CALVIN COOLIDGE
Third Annual Message to Congress, Dec. 8, 1925;
Messages and Papers, p. 9519

38. Our foreign policy has one primary object, and that is peace.

HERBERT HOOVER
Speech at Palo Alto, Cal., Aug. 11, 1928; *Policies*, p. 579

39. If our civilization is to be perpetuated, the great causes of world peace, world disarmament and world recovery must prevail. They cannot prevail until a path to their attainment is built upon honest friendship, mutual confidence, and proper co-operation among the nations.

HERBERT HOOVER
Statement to the Press, *re* war debts, Nov. 23, 1932;
State Papers, II, 487

40. In the field of world policy I would dedicate this Nation to the policy of the good neighbor.

FRANKLIN DELANO ROOSEVELT
First Inaugural Address, Mar. 4, 1933

41. To show our faith in democracy, we have made the policy of the good neighbor the corner stone of our foreign relations. No other policy would be consistent with our ideas and our ideals.

FRANKLIN DELANO ROOSEVELT
Message to Tampa Exposition, Feb. 18, 1939;
Public Papers, VIII, 143

42. Our foreign policy is . . . to defend the honor, the freedom, the rights, the interests, and the well-being of the American people.

FRANKLIN DELANO ROOSEVELT
Message to Foreign Policy Association, Oct. 25, 1941; *Ibid., X*, 434

43. Our foreign policy aimed at building up rapidly the combined political, economic, and military strength of the free world.

HARRY S. TRUMAN
1950; *Memoirs, II,* 312

44. I have always advocated for our foreign service personnel—that they should spend one year in every four in their own country. Then they would understand what the home folks were thinking.

HARRY S. TRUMAN
1950; *Ibid.,* p. 363

45. The American approach to world affairs was best demonstrated by the manner in which we treated conquered nations after the first and second world wars. We set up the means to feed and clothe and take care of the physical needs of the people. We rehabilitated the conquered nations instead of attempting to keep them conquered and prostrate. We asked for no reparations.

This was something new in the history of nations.

HARRY S. TRUMAN
1951; *Ibid.,* p. 238

46. In its immediate and long-range effects . . . Point Four [to provide technical assistance so that millions of people in underdeveloped areas could, with a very small capital investment from us, be able to develop their own resources] . . . provided the strongest antidote to Communism that has so far been put into practice. It was created and designed to operate on a continuing basis to point the way to better living for more and more of the world's people—and thus the way to a more lasting peace. Thus it stands as a vitally important development in the search for peace, which lies at the very heart of America's foreign policy.

HARRY S. TRUMAN
1952; *Ibid.,* p. 239

47. The increase of the quality of neighborliness among the nations is as essential to national security as is an adequate military establishment. . . . The barriers to neighborliness are fear and prejudice spawned by ignorance.

DWIGHT D. EISENHOWER
Speech at Lincoln, Neb., Sept. 1, 1946; *Eisenhower Speaks,* p. 123

48. The best foreign policy is to live our daily lives in honesty, decency, and integrity; at home, making our own land a more fitting habitation for free men; and, abroad, joining with those of like mind and heart, to make of the world a place where all men can dwell in peace. Neither palsied by fear nor duped by dreams but strong in the rightness of our purpose, we can then place our case and cause before the bar of world opinion—history's final arbiter between nations.

DWIGHT D. EISENHOWER
Address at Columbia University, Mar. 23, 1950; *Peace,* p. 26

49. Foreign policy must be clear, consistent and confident.

DWIGHT D. EISENHOWER

State of the Union Message, Feb. 2, 1953; *Index*, p. 42

50. A foreign policy is not difficult to state. We are for peace, first, last and always, for very simple reasons. We know that it is only in a peaceful atmosphere, a peace with justice, one in which we can be confident, that America can prosper as we have known prosperity in the past.

DWIGHT D. EISENHOWER

Remarks to League of Women Voters, Washington, D.C., May 1, 1957; *Public Papers . . . Eisenhower, 1957*, p. 315

51. What we call foreign affairs is no longer foreign affairs. It's a local affair. Whatever happens in Indonesia is important to Indiana. . . . We cannot escape each other. . . . We must understand people. As long as any . . . cannot enjoy the blessings of peace with justice, then indeed there is no peace anywhere.

DWIGHT D. EISENHOWER

Speech at Arlington, Va., June 12, 1959; *Public Papers . . . Eisenhower, 1959*, p. 458

52. One of the most serious weaknesses that has hampered the long-range effectiveness of American foreign policy over the past several years . . . is the overemphasis upon our role as "volunteer fire department" for the world. . . . Whenever and wherever fire breaks out . . . our firemen rush in, wheeling up all their heavy equipment, and resorting to every known method of containing and extinguishing the blaze. The crowd gathers—the usually successful efforts of our able volunteers are heartily applauded—and then the firemen rush off to the next conflagration, leaving the grateful but still stunned inhabitants to clean up the rubble, pick up the pieces, and rebuild their homes with whatever resources are available.

The role, to be sure, is a necessary one; but it is not the only role to be played. . . . A volunteer fire department halts, but rarely prevents fires.

JOHN F. KENNEDY

To Conference of Friends of Vietnam, June 1, 1956; *Strategy*, p. 92

53. Every American is now involved in the world. "The tragic events of . . . turmoil through which we have just passed have made us citizens of the world," said Woodrow Wilson. For a time we tried to dodge this new responsibility, but the world depression, World War II, and the Cold War have finally conveyed his message: "There can be no turning back. Our own fortunes as a nation are involved—whether we would have it so or not."

JOHN F. KENNEDY

Address at Madison, Wis., June 16, 1958; *Ibid.*, p. 228

54. Although our aid programs have helped to avoid economic chaos and collapse and assisted many nations to maintain their independence and freedom, nevertheless it is a fact that many of the nations we are helping are not much nearer sustained economic growth than they were when our aid program began. Money spent to meet crisis situations or short-term political objectives, while helping to maintain national integrity and independence, has rarely moved the recipient nation toward greater economic stability.

JOHN F. KENNEDY
Special Message to Congress, Mar. 22, 1961; *Tide*, p. 145

55. There has been a tendency to say that we send food to India because we want to win that nation over to our side . . . that we send technicians to Southeast Asia because we want to halt the spread of communism.

We have been ascribing ignoble motives to noble deeds. And in doing so, we have given the world the impression that we are bidding for friendship as traders bid for a sack of wheat.

Such an impression is an open invitation for those whose friendship we seek to shop around and see what the man on the other side of the street is willing to offer.

I think it is about time for us to change not our policy but our attitudes. I think it is about time for us to start proceeding on the assumption that we do things not because they are expedient but because they are right.

The world wants America to reach out its hand for a handshake, not to leave a tip. That is the kind of America we must be.

LYNDON B. JOHNSON
Address to American Society of Newspaper Editors, Washington, D.C., Apr. 16, 1959; *Vital Speeches, June 1, 1959*, p. 503

56. Any man and any nation that seeks peace—and hates war—and is willing to fight the good fight against hunger, and disease and ignorance and misery will find the United States of America by their side, willing to walk with them—walk with them every step of the way.

LYNDON B. JOHNSON
To the United Nations General Assembly, Dec. 17, 1963; *Ibid., Jan. 1, 1964*, p. 163

France

See Europe, History 19, War 6, 11

Freedom

1. A free people ought not only to be armed, but disciplined; to which end a uniform and well-digested plan is requisite.

GEORGE WASHINGTON

First Annual Message to Congress, Jan. 8, 1790;
Messages and Papers, p. 57

2. Posterity! You will never know how much it cost the present generation to preserve your freedom! I hope you will make good use of it! If you do not, I shall repent it in Heaven that I ever took half the pains to preserve it!

JOHN ADAMS

To Abigail Adams, Apr. 26, 1777; *Familiar Letters*, p. 265

3. When people talk of the freedom of writing, speaking or thinking I cannot choose but laugh. No such thing ever existed. No such thing now exists; but I hope it will exist. But it must be hundreds of years after you and I shall write and speak no more.

JOHN ADAMS

To Thomas Jefferson, July 15, 1818; *Correspondence*, p. 160

4. Our cause is just. Our union is perfect. Our internal resources are great, and, if necessary, foreign assistance is undoubtedly attainable. . . . The arms we have been compelled by our enemies to assume we will, in defiance of every hazard, with unabating firmness and perseverance, employ for the preservation of our liberties; being with one mind resolved to die free men rather than live slaves.

THOMAS JEFFERSON

Declaration of the Causes of Taking Up Arms, July 6, 1775

5. Freedom of religion, freedom of the press, freedom of person under the protection of the habeas corpus; and trial by juries impartially selected, —these principles form the bright constellation which has gone before us.

THOMAS JEFFERSON

First Inaugural Address, Mar. 4, 1801; *Writings, III*, 322

6. I have great hope that some patriotic spirit will, at a favorable moment, call [up the law for religious freedom] and make it the keystone of the arch of our government.

THOMAS JEFFERSON

To John Adams, Oct. 28, 1813; *Ibid., XIII*, 401

7. Since the general civilization of mankind, I believe there are more instances of the abridgment of the freedom of the people by gradual and

silent encroachments of those in power than by violent and sudden usurpations.

JAMES MADISON
Speech in the Virginia Convention, June 5, 1788;
Complete Madison, p. 46

8. In America, a glorious fire has been lighted upon the altar of liberty.
. . . Keep it burning, and let the sparks that continually go up from it fall
on other altars, and light up in distant lands the fire of freedom.

WILLIAM HENRY HARRISON
At Dayton, Ohio, Sept. 10, 1840; *Speech,* p. 8

9. My faith in the proposition that each man should do precisely as he
pleases with all which is exclusively his own lies at the foundation of the
sense of justice there is in me. I extend the principle to communities of
men as well as to individuals. I so extend it because it is politically wise,
as well as naturally just: politically wise in saving us from broils about
matters which do not concern us.

ABRAHAM LINCOLN
Speech at Peoria, Ill., Oct. 16, 1854; *Complete Works, II,* 227

10. A majority held in restraint by constitutional checks and limitations,
and always changing easily with deliberate changes of popular opinions
and sentiments, is the only true sovereign of a free people. Whoever rejects it does, of necessity, fly to anarchy or to despotism.

ABRAHAM LINCOLN
First Inaugural Address, Mar. 4, 1861

11. The free man cannot be long an ignorant man.

WILLIAM McKINLEY
Address at Pittsburgh, Pa., Nov. 3, 1897;
Speeches and Addresses, p. 58

12. Free speech, exercised both individually and through a free press,
is a necessity in any country where the people are themselves free.

THEODORE ROOSEVELT
Kiplinger Washington Letter, Apr. 23, 1918;
Presidents and the Press, p. 597

13. The wisest thing to do with a fool is to encourage him to hire a hall
and discourse to his fellow-citizens. Nothing chills nonsense like exposure
to the air.

WOODROW WILSON
1908; *Constitutional Government,* p. 38

14. The only freedom consists in the people taking care of the government.

WOODROW WILSON
Speech in New York, N.Y., Sept. 4, 1912; *Crossroads,* p. 112

15. There will be no greater burden in our generation than to organize the forces of liberty in our time, in order to make conquest of a new freedom for America.

WOODROW WILSON
Address at Indianapolis, Ind., Oct. 3, 1912; *Crossroads,* p. 325

16. Only free peoples can hold their purpose and their honor steady to a common end, and prefer the interests of mankind to any narrow interest of their own.

WOODROW WILSON
Address to Congress, asking for war, Apr. 2, 1917;
Public Papers, V, 12

17. There is no substitute for a militant freedom.

CALVIN COOLIDGE
Address in Washington, D.C., Apr. 27, 1922; *Freedom,* p. 159

18. Free speech does not live many hours after free industry and free commerce die.

HERBERT HOOVER
Campaign speech in New York, N.Y., Oct. 22, 1928;
Policies, p. 19

19. We believe that the only whole man is a free man.

FRANKLIN DELANO ROOSEVELT
Address at dedication of Great Smoky Mountains National Park,
Sept. 2, 1940; *Public Papers, IX,* 374

20. We have learned that freedom in itself is not enough.
Freedom of speech is of no use to a man who has nothing to say.
Freedom of worship is of no use to a man who has lost his God.

FRANKLIN DELANO ROOSEVELT
Campaign address at Cleveland, Ohio, Nov. 2, 1940; *Ibid.,* p. 547

21. In the future days, which we seek to make secure, we look forward to a world founded upon four essential human freedoms.

The first is freedom of speech and expression—everywhere in the world.

The second is freedom of every person to worship God in his own way —everywhere in the world.

The third is freedom from want—which, translated into world terms, means economic understandings which will secure to every nation a healthy peacetime life for its inhabitants—everywhere in the world.

The fourth is freedom from fear—which, translated into world terms, means a world-wide reduction of armaments to such a point and in such a thorough fashion that no nation will be in a position to commit an act of physical aggression against any neighbor—anywhere in the world.

FRANKLIN DELANO ROOSEVELT
Annual Message to Congress, Jan. 6, 1941; *Ibid.*, p. 672

22. We, too, born to freedom and believing in freedom, are willing to fight to maintain freedom. We, and all others who believe as deeply as we do would rather die on our feet than live on our knees.

FRANKLIN DELANO ROOSEVELT
To Viscount Halifax, June 19, 1941; *Ibid.*, X, 226

23. The winning of freedom is not to be compared to the winning of a game—with the victory recorded forever in history. Freedom has its life in the hearts, the actions, the spirits of men and so it must be daily earned and refreshed—else like a flower cut from its life-giving roots, it will wither and die.

DWIGHT D. EISENHOWER
Speech to the English Speaking Union, London, England, *1944*

24. It is not enough merely to realize how freedom has been won. Essential also is it that we be ever alert to all threats to that freedom. . . . One danger arises from too great a concentration of power in the hands of any individual or group: The power of concentrated finance, the power of selfish pressure groups, the power of any class organized in opposition to the whole—any one of these, when allowed to dominate, is fully capable of destroying individual freedom as is power concentrated in the political head of the state.

DWIGHT D. EISENHOWER
Speech at Columbia University, Oct. 12, 1948;
What Eisenhower Thinks, p. 80

25. The cause of freedom can never be defeated.

DWIGHT D. EISENHOWER
Radio message from Paris, France, Jan. 7, 1951; *Ibid.*, p. 157

26. History does not long entrust the care of freedom to the weak or the timid. We must acquire proficiency in defense and display stamina in purpose.

DWIGHT D. EISENHOWER
First Inaugural Address, Jan. 20, 1953

27. Free men do not lose their patience, their courage, their faith, because the obstacles are mountainous, the path uncharted. Given understanding, they invariably rise to the challenge.

DWIGHT D. EISENHOWER
Speech in New York, N.Y., Apr. 22, 1954; *Peace*, p. 64

28. Freedom has been defined as the opportunity for self-discipline. . . .
Should we persistently fail to discipline ourselves, eventually there will be
increasing pressure on government to redress the failure. By that process
freedom will step by step disappear.

DWIGHT D. EISENHOWER
Fifth Annual Message to Congress, Jan. 10, 1957;
Public Papers . . . Eisenhower, 1957, p. 21

29. In my opinion, you can't take freedom and allow freedom finally to
be pushed back to the shores of the United States and maintain it in the
United States. It can't be done. There's too much interdependence in the
world.

DWIGHT D. EISENHOWER
Remarks in Washington, D.C., May 1, 1957; *Ibid.,* p. 319

30. Freedom bestows on us the priceless gift of opportunity—if we neglect our opportunities we shall certainly lose our freedom.

DWIGHT D. EISENHOWER
Address in New York, N.Y., May 14, 1959; *Public Papers . . .
Eisenhower, 1959,* p. 401

31. The most powerful single force in the world today is neither Communism nor capitalism, neither the H-bomb nor the guided missile—it is
man's eternal desire to be free and independent. The great enemy of that
tremendous force of freedom is called, for want of a more precise term,
imperialism—and today that means Soviet imperialism and, whether we like
it or not, and though they are not to be equated, Western imperialism.

Thus the single most important test of American foreign policy today is
how we meet the challenge of imperialism, what we do to further man's
desire to be free.

JOHN F. KENNEDY
Speech in the Senate, July 2, 1957; *Strategy,* p. 96

32. Freedom and security are but opposite sides of the same coin—and
the free expression of ideas is not more expendable but far more essential
in a period of challenge and crisis. . . . Through the centuries of crises the
American tradition has demonstrated . . . that freedom is the ally of
security—and that liberty is the architecture of abundance.

JOHN F. KENNEDY
Speech in Washington, D.C., Apr. 16, 1959; *Ibid.,* p. 202

33. We stand for freedom. . . . We are not against any man, or any
nation, or any system, except as it is hostile to freedom.

JOHN F. KENNEDY
Special Message to Congress, May 25, 1961; *Tide,* p. 49

34. The cost of freedom is always high, but Americans have always
paid it. . . .

One path we shall never choose, and that is the path of surrender, or submission.

Our goal is not the victory of might, but the vindication of right; not peace at the expense of freedom, but both peace and freedom here in this hemisphere, and, we hope, around the world.

JOHN F. KENNEDY
Radio and television address, Oct. 12, 1962; *Vital Speeches,
Nov. 15, 1962,* p. 68

See also America 18, 23, Censors 5, Democracy 8, Economic Matters 1, Education 6, 12, 26, 31, 33, Equality 7, Foreign Relations 35, Government 64, Greatness 8, Homes 6, Ignorance 5, Justice 15, Knowledge 3, 8, 10, Laws 16, League of Nations 7, Liberalism 1, Liberty 36, 44, Money 12, Negotiations 2, 5, Negroes 10, 12, Peace 38, 71, 82, 88, 90, People (The) 34, Physical Fitness 5, Power 3, 4, Press (The), Religion 31, Republics 13, Revolutions 2, 8, Security 2, 8, Slavery 14, 20, 23, 25, Suffrage 4, Truth 6, 7, Union 12, United States 4, Unity 4, War 51, 68

Free Speech
See Freedom 12, 13, 18, 20, 21, Power 4

Friendship
1.   A slender acquaintance with the world must convince every man that actions, not words, are the true criterion of the attachment to friends; and that the most liberal professions of good-will are very far from being the surest marks of it.

GEORGE WASHINGTON
To John Sullivan, Dec. 15, 1779; *Writings
(Fitzpatrick), XVII,* 266

2.   Be courteous to all, but intimate with few, and let those few be well tried before you give them your confidence. True friendship is a plant of slow growth and must undergo and withstand the shocks of adversity before it is entitled to the appellation.

GEORGE WASHINGTON
To Bushrod Washington, Jan. 15, 1783; *Ibid., XXVI,* 39

3.   An injured friend is the bitterest of foes.

THOMAS JEFFERSON
French Treaties Opinion, Apr. 28, 1793; *Works (Ford), VI,* 225

4.   Friendship is but another name for an alliance with the follies and the misfortunes of others.

THOMAS JEFFERSON
To Maria Cosway, Oct. 12, 1786; *Writings, V,* 440

5. We must do our duty and convince the world that we are just friends and brave enemies.

THOMAS JEFFERSON
To Andrew Jackson, Dec. 3, 1806; *Ibid., XIX, 156*

6. I find friendship to be like wine, raw when new, ripened with age, the true old man's milk and restorative cordial.

THOMAS JEFFERSON
To Benjamin Rush, Aug. 17, 1811; *Ibid., XIII, 77*

7. A long visit to a friend is often a great bore. Never make people twice glad.

JAMES BUCHANAN
To Harriet Lane, Mar. 15, 1853; *Life, II, 96*

8. You have spoken of the consideration which you think I should pay to my friends as contradistinguished from my enemies. I suppose, of course, that you mean by that those who agree or disagree with me in my views of public policy. I recognize no such thing as a political friendship personal to myself.

ABRAHAM LINCOLN
Washington, D.C., 1863; *History, VIII, 217*

9. I do not intend to be bullied by my enemies nor overawed by my friends.

ANDREW JOHNSON
Speech at St. Louis, Mo., Sept. 8, 1866;
Messages and Papers, p. 3915

10. We must prove ourselves . . . friends, and champions upon terms of equality and honor. You can not be friends upon any other terms than upon the terms of equality. You can not be friends at all except upon the terms of honor.

WOODROW WILSON
Address in Philadelphia, Pa., Oct. 25, 1913;
Messages and Papers (Shaw), I, 35

11. There is only one thing that holds nations together, if you exclude force, and that is friendship and good will. . . . Our task . . . is to organize the friendship of the world, to see to it that all the moral forces that make for right and justice and liberty are united.

WOODROW WILSON
Speech in Rome, Italy, Jan. 3, 1919; *Public Papers, V, 363*

See also Appointments 3, Democracy 20, Foreign Relations 6, 36, 39, 55, 56, Gifts 6, Government 45, Loyalty 1, Opinion 5, Peace 28, Politics 3, Presidency (The) 4, 7, 27, 30, 49, 50, Society, Union 25

Frontiers

1. We stand today on the edge of a new frontier, a frontier of unknown opportunities and perils, a frontier of unfulfilled hopes and threats.

JOHN F. KENNEDY
Acceptance of Nomination for Presidency, Los Angeles, Cal.,
July 15, 1960; *Vital Speeches, Aug. 1, 1960*, p. 611

Future, The

1. For mere vengeance I would do nothing. This nation is too great for revenge. But for the security of the future I would do everything.

JAMES A. GARFIELD
Address in New York, N.Y., Apr. 15, 1865

2. If a man is wise, he will gladly do the thing that is next, when the time and the need come together, without asking what the future holds for him. Let the half-god play his part well and manfully, and then be content to draw aside when the god appears.

THEODORE ROOSEVELT
Autobiography, p. 91

3. Ours is a land filled with millions of happy homes, blessed with comfort and opportunity. I have no fear for the future of our country. It is bright with hope.

HERBERT HOOVER
Inaugural Address, Mar. 4, 1929

See also Civilization 8, Health 7, History 2, 18, Hope 2, Past (The) 2, 3, Politics 26, Progress 3, 9, Right 13, Space 1, Voters 5

Gag-Rule
See Gifts 3

Germany
See Europe, Negotiations

Gettysburg

1. We are met on a great battlefield. . . . We have come to dedicate a portion of that field, as a final resting place for those who here gave their lives that that nation might live. It is altogether fitting and proper that we should do this. But, in a larger sense, we cannot dedicate—we cannot consecrate—we cannot hallow—this ground. The brave men, living and dead, who struggled here, have consecrated it, far above our poor power to add or detract. The world will little note, nor long remember what we say here, but it can never forget what they did here. It is for us the living, rather, to be dedicated here to the unfinished work that they who fought here have thus far so nobly advanced. It is rather for us to be here dedicated to the great task remaining before us—that from these honored

dead we take increased devotion to that cause for which they gave the last full measure of devotion. . . .

ABRAHAM LINCOLN
Gettysburg Address, Nov. 19, 1863; *Complete Works, IX,* 209

See also Negroes 11

Gifts

1. The President of the United States presents his Compliments to Mr. C. and with many thanks for his offer of the very elegant figures sent him, begs leave to restore them again to Mr. C. His situation calling for uniformity of conduct in these cases, he relies that Mr. C. will ascribe it in the present instance to its true motives. . . .

GEORGE WASHINGTON
To Giuseppe Ceracchi, May 10, 1792;
Writings (Fitzpatrick), XXXII, 43

2. I had laid it down as a law for my conduct while in office, and hitherto scrupulously observed, to accept of no present beyond a book, a pamphlet, or other curiosity of minor value; as well to avoid imputation on my motives of action, as to shut out a practice susceptible of such abuse.

THOMAS JEFFERSON
To Levett Harris, Apr. 18, 1806; *Writings, XI,* 101

3. There was delivered to me from Julius Pratt & Co., manufacturers . . . a present of a milk-white ivory cane, one yard long, made of one elephant's tooth, tipped with silver and steel, with the American eagle inlaid in gold on its top, and a ring under the pommel, inscribed with my name, and the words, "Justum, et tenacem propositi virum." The letter with it requests that on the day when the gag-rule shall be finally abolished I will insert the date after the inscription on the ring.

After expressing my deep sensibility to this testimonial of kindness and approbation of my public conduct . . . and, alluding to my custom of declining valuable presents from individuals for public service, I accepted the cane as a trust to be returned when the date of the extinction of the gag-rule shall be accomplished.

JOHN QUINCY ADAMS
Mar. 25, 1844; *Memoirs, XI,* 543

4. I am informed that Ahmed Ben Haman had it in charge from your Highness [Imaum of Muscat] to offer for my acceptance, in your name, a munificent present. I look upon this friendly proceeding on your part as a new proof of your Highness's desire to cultivate with us amicable relations; but a fundamental law of the Republic which forbids its servants from accepting presents from foreign States or Princes, precludes me from receiving those your Highness intended for me. I beg your Highness to be assured that, in thus declining your valuable gift, I do but perform a

paramount duty to my country, and that my sense of the kindness which prompted the offer is not thereby in any degree abated.

MARTIN VAN BUREN
To His Highness Seyd Seyd Bin Sultan Bin Ahmed, December, 1839; *Epoch,* p. 451

5. Our laws forbid the President from receiving . . . rich presents as personal treasures. They are therefore accepted . . . as tokens of . . . good will and friendship for the American people. Congress being now in session . . . I have had great pleasure in making known to them this manifestation of your . . . munificence and kind consideration.

ABRAHAM LINCOLN
Letter to the King of Siam, Feb. 3, 1862; *Collected Works, V,* 125

6. Anything that is given me is right out on the record. . . . I need no gifts and I never accept gifts that I believe have any personal motive whatsoever behind them, I mean any selfish motive of any kind. . . . I never have accepted one from a corporation or business firm. I merely try to keep my relations with people on what I think is a friendly, decent basis.

DWIGHT D. EISENHOWER
News conference, Aug. 7, 1957; *Public Papers . . . Eisenhower, 1957,* p. 593

Goals

1. The goal to strive for is a poor government but a rich people.

ANDREW JOHNSON
Ca., 1845; *Not Guilty,* p. 27

2. The goal we seek is peace with justice. . . . The world's hope is that the Soviets will cooperate with all the rest of us in achieving this goal. Our defense effort, large as it is, goes only far enough to deter and defeat attack.

DWIGHT D. EISENHOWER
Radio and television address, Nov. 13, 1957; *Public Papers . . . Eisenhower, 1957,* p. 816

3. For the challenges before us, we need both new ideas and old boldness. But our future lies not in the multiplicity of ideas but in singleness of purpose.

That singleness of purpose must be dedication to the concept that this can be a better and freer world for all the nations.

That is not a goal which can be achieved in one night or by one idea or even by one policy. But it is a goal which is attainable if America assumes not just the political and military but the moral leadership which should be ours.

LYNDON B. JOHNSON
Address to American Society of Newspaper Editors, Washington, D.C., Apr. 16, 1959; *Vital Speeches, June 1, 1959,* p. 504

4. Our ultimate goal is a world without war. A world made safe for diversity, in which all men, goods and ideas can freely move across every border and every boundary.

LYNDON B. JOHNSON
State of the Union Address, Jan. 8, 1964;
Ibid., Jan. 15, 1964, p. 196

See also Convictions, Peace 84, United States 6, Wealth 6

God

1. No people can be bound to acknowledge and adore the Invisible Hand which conducts the affairs of men more than those of the United States. Every step by which they have advanced to the character of an independent nation seems to have been distinguished by some token of providential agency. . . . [Results] can not be compared with the means by which most Governments have been established without some return of pious gratitude, along with an humble anticipation of the future blessings which the past seems to presage.

GEORGE WASHINGTON
First Inaugural Address, Apr. 30, 1789

2. A German ambassador once told me, "he could not bear St. Paul, he was so severe against fornication." On the same principle these philosophers cannot bear a God, because he is just.

JOHN ADAMS
To F. A. Vanderkemp, Mar. 3, 1804; *Works, IX,* 588

3. God has infinite wisdom, goodness, and power; he created the universe; his duration is eternal. . . . His presence is as extensive as space. What is space? An infinite spherical *vacuum.*

JOHN ADAMS
To Thomas Jefferson, Sept. 14, 1813; *Ibid., X,* 67

4. I cannot conceive such a Being could make such a Species as the human, merely to live and die on this earth.

JOHN ADAMS
To Thomas Jefferson, Dec. 8, 1818; *Ibid.,* 363

5. The God who gave us life, gave us liberty at the same time.

THOMAS JEFFERSON
To Virginia delegates to Congress, August, 1774; *Writings, I,* 211

6. It does me no injury for my neighbor to say there are twenty gods, or no God. It neither picks my pocket nor breaks my leg.

THOMAS JEFFERSON
Notes on Virginia, 1782; *Ibid., II,* 221

7.   Indeed, I tremble for my country when I reflect that God is just.

THOMAS JEFFERSON
Notes on Virginia, 1782; *Ibid.*, p. 227

8.   Be constant in your devotions to your God. He is a friend who will never desert you. Men are short-sighted and know not the consequences of their own actions. . . . Ask wisdom and discretion from above.

JAMES BUCHANAN
To Harriet Lane, Nov. 4, 1851; *Life, II*, 19

9.   Fondly do we hope, fervently do we pray, that this mighty scourge of war may speedily pass away. Yet, if God wills that it continue until all the wealth piled up by the bondsman's 250 years of unrequited toil shall be sunk, and until every drop of blood drawn with the lash shall be paid by another drawn with the sword, as was said 3,000 years ago, so still must it be said, "the judgments of the Lord are true and righteous altogether."

ABRAHAM LINCOLN
Second Inaugural Address, Mar. 4, 1865

10.   The Almighty has His own purposes.

ABRAHAM LINCOLN
Second Inaugural Address, Mar. 4, 1865

11.   Fear God; and take your own part!

THEODORE ROOSEVELT
1916; *Works, XVIII*, 199

See also Assassination 6, Conscience 2, 6, 7, Faith, Fear 2, Government 21, 68, Life 3, Presidency (The) 2, 11, Principles 3, Religion 1, 4, 11, 14, 32, 34, Republics 16, Rights 15, 19, Security 1, Standards 1, Success 6, Tyranny 3, War 72

Goodness

1.   I am for those means which will give the greatest good to the greatest number.

ABRAHAM LINCOLN
Speech at Cincinnati, Ohio, Feb. 12, 1861;
Complete Works, VI, 120

2.   I believe in the greatest good to the greatest number.

ULYSSES S. GRANT
Speech at Jersey City, N.J., Oct. 21, 1880; *Gems*, p. 18

3.   If good men don't hold office, bad men will.

CALVIN COOLIDGE

See also America 20, Greatness 7, Reforms 2

Good Sense

1.   The good sense of the people is the strongest army our government can ever have . . . it will not fail them.

THOMAS JEFFERSON

To William Carmichael, Dec. 26, 1786; *Writings, VI,* 31

See also People 7, 14

Good Will

1.   Our policy is not only peace with all, but good will toward all the powers of the earth. While we are just to all, we require that all shall be just to us.

JAMES K. POLK

First Annual Message to Congress, Dec. 2, 1845; *Messages and Papers,* p. 2252

2.   Good will precedes good trade.

WILLIAM McKINLEY

In Philadelphia, Pa., June 2, 1897; *Speeches and Addresses*

See also Justice 10

Government

1.   Influence is no Government.

GEORGE WASHINGTON

To Henry Lee, Oct. 31, 1786; *Writings (Fitzpatrick), XXIX,* 34

2.   When a people shall have become incapable of governing themselves, and fit for a master, it is of little consequence from what quarter he comes.

GEORGE WASHINGTON

To the Marquis de Lafayette, Apr. 28, 1788; *Ibid.,* p. 479

3.   The aggregate happiness of society, which is best promoted by the practice of a virtuous policy, is, or ought to be, the end of all government.

GEORGE WASHINGTON

To Count de Moustier, Nov. 1, 1790; *Ibid., XXXI,* 142

4.   The Unity of Government which constitutes you one people, is also now dear to you. It is justly so; for it is a main Pillar in the edifice of your real independence, the support of your tranquillity at home; your peace abroad; of your safety, of your prosperity; in every shape of that very Liberty which you so highly prize.

GEORGE WASHINGTON

Farewell Address, Sept. 19, 1796; *Ibid., XXXV,* 218

5.   The very idea of the power and the right of the people to establish Government, presupposes the duty of every individual to obey the established Government.

GEORGE WASHINGTON

Farewell Address, Sept. 19, 1796; *Ibid.,* p. 224

6. Toward the preservation of your government and the permanency of your present happy state, it is requisite not only that you steadily discountenance irregular opposition to its acknowledged authority but also that you resist with care the spirit of innovation upon its principles, however specious the pretext.

GEORGE WASHINGTON
Farewell Address, Sept. 19, 1796; *Ibid.*, p. 225

7. [Liberty] is indeed little less than a name, where the Government is too feeble to withstand the enterprises of faction, to confine each member of society within the limits prescribed by the law, and to maintain all in the secure and tranquil enjoyment of the rights of persons and property.

GEORGE WASHINGTON
Farewell Address, Sept. 19, 1796; *Ibid.*, p. 226

8. It is important . . . that the habits of thinking in a free Country should inspire caution, in those intrusted with its administration, to confine themselves within their respective constitutional spheres, avoiding in the exercise of the powers of one department to encroach upon another.

GEORGE WASHINGTON
Farewell Address, Sept. 19, 1796; *Ibid.*, p. 228

9. The most sensible and jealous people are so little attentive to government that there are no instances of resistance until repeated, multiplied oppressions have placed it beyond a doubt that their rulers had formed settled plans to deprive them of their liberties; not to oppress an individual or a few, but to break down the fences of a free constitution, and deprive the people at large of all share in the government, and all the checks by which it is limited.

JOHN ADAMS
"Novanglus," in Boston *Gazette*, Jan. 23, 1774; *Works, IV*, 17

10. As the happiness of the people is the sole end of government, so the consent of the people is the only foundation of it, in reason, morality, and the natural fitness of things.

JOHN ADAMS
Proclamation, Massachusetts Bay Council, 1774; *Ibid., I*, 193

11. A legislative, an executive, and a judicial power comprehend the whole of what is meant and understood by government. It is by balancing each of these powers against the other two, that the efforts in human nature towards tyranny can alone be checked and restrained, and any degree of freedom preserved in the constitution.

JOHN ADAMS
To Richard Henry Lee, Nov. 15, 1775; *Ibid., IV*, 186

12. Fear is the foundation of most governments. . . . The foundation

of every government is some principle or passion in the minds of the people. . . . Honor is a principle which ought to be sacred . . . but at most, is but a part of virtue, and therefore a feeble basis of government. . . .

All sober inquirers after truth, ancient and modern, divines, moralists, and philosophers, have agreed that the happiness of mankind, as well as the real dignity of human nature, consists in virtue; if there is a form of government whose principles and foundation is virtue, will not every wise man acknowledge it more likely to promote the general happiness than any other?

JOHN ADAMS
To John Penn, January, 1776; *Ibid.,* p. 203

13.   The end of the institution, maintenance, and administration of government is to secure the existence of the body politic; to protect it, and to furnish the individuals who compose it with the power of enjoying, in safety and tranquillity, their natural rights and the blessings of life. . . .

JOHN ADAMS
Report of a Constitution . . . for the Commonwealth of Massachusetts; *Ibid.,* p. 219

14.   Mobs will never do to govern states or command armies.

JOHN ADAMS
To Benjamin Hichborn, Jan. 27, 1787; *Works, IX,* 551

15.   You are apprehensive of monarchy; I, of aristocracy. I would therefore have given more power to the President and less to the Senate.

JOHN ADAMS
To Thomas Jefferson, Dec. 6, 1787; *Ibid., VIII,* 464

16.   The declaration that our People are hostile to a government made by themselves, for themselves, and conducted by themselves, is an insult.

JOHN ADAMS
Address in Westmoreland County, Va., July 11, 1789

17.   The essence of a free government consists in an effectual control of rivalries.

JOHN ADAMS
Discourses on Davila, 1789; *Works, VI,* 280

18.   The existence of such a government as ours for any length of time is a full proof of a general dissemination of knowledge and virtue throughout the whole body of the people. . . . If national pride is ever justifiable or excusable it is when it springs, not from power or riches, grandeur or glory, but from conviction of national innocence, information, and benevolence.

JOHN ADAMS
Inaugural Address, Mar. 4, 1797

19. My worthy fellow-citizens! Our form of government, inestimable as it is, exposes us, more than any other, to the insidious intrigues and pestilent influence of foreign nations. Nothing but our inflexible neutrality can preserve us.

JOHN ADAMS
To the Boston *Patriot,* 1809; *Works, IX,* 277

20. While all other sciences have advanced, that of government is at a standstill—little better understood, little better practised now than three or four thousand years ago.

JOHN ADAMS
To Thomas Jefferson, July 9, 1813; *Works of Jefferson, VI,* 159

21. The question before the human race is whether the God of nature shall govern the world by His own laws, or whether priests and kings shall rule it by fictitious miracles.

JOHN ADAMS
To Thomas Jefferson, June 20, 1815; *Ibid., VII,* 423

22. The whole art of government consists in the art of being honest.

THOMAS JEFFERSON
To Virginia delegates to Congress, August, 1774; *Writings, I,* 209

23. Governments [derive] their just powers from the consent of the governed.

THOMAS JEFFERSON
The Declaration of Independence, 1776

24. It is not by consolidation, or concentration of powers, but by their distribution, that good government is effected.

THOMAS JEFFERSON
Autobiography, 1787; *Writings, I,* 122

25. The spirit of resistance to government is so valuable on certain occasions, that I wish it to be always kept alive. It will often be exercised when wrong but better so than not to be exercised at all. I like a little rebellion now and then. It is like a storm in the atmosphere.

THOMAS JEFFERSON
To Abigail Adams, Feb. 22, 1787; *Ibid., V,* 263

26. The earth belongs always to the living generation: they may manage it, then and what proceeds from it, as they please, during their usufruct. They are masters, too, of their own persons, and consequently may govern them as they please. But persons and property make the sum of the objects of government. The constitution and the laws of their predecessors are extinguished then, in their natural course, with those whose will gave them being. This could preserve that being, till it ceased to be itself, and no

longer. Every constitution, then, expires at the end of thirty-four years. If it be enforced longer, it is an act of force, and not of right.

THOMAS JEFFERSON
Letter to James Madison, Sept. 6, 1789; *Works, III,* 106

27.   A wise and frugal Government, which shall restrain men from injuring one another, shall leave them otherwise free to regulate their own pursuits of industry and improvement, and shall not take from the mouth of labor the bread it has earned—this is the sum of good government.

THOMAS JEFFERSON
First Inaugural Address, Mar. 4, 1801

28.   I look with encouragement for that guidance and support which may enable us to steer with safety the vessel in which we are all embarked amidst the conflicting elements of a troubled world. . . .

I deem . . . the preservation of the General Government in its whole constitutional vigor, as the sheet anchor of our peace at home and safety abroad.

THOMAS JEFFERSON
First Inaugural Address, Mar. 4, 1801

29.   That government is the strongest of which every man feels himself a part.

THOMAS JEFFERSON
To Gov. H. D. Tiffin, Feb. 2, 1807; *Works, V,* 38

30.   The care of human life and happiness, and not their destruction, is the first and only legitimate object of good government.

THOMAS JEFFERSON
To Republican Citizens of Maryland, Mar. 31, 1809;
Writings, XVI, 359

31.   No government can be maintained without the principle of fear as well as of duty. Good men will obey the last, but bad ones the former only.

THOMAS JEFFERSON
To John Wayles Eppes, Sept. 9, 1814; *Writings (Ford), IX,* 484

32.   The way to have good and safe government, is not to trust it all to one, but to divide it among the many, distributing to every one exactly the functions he is competent to [perform].

It is by . . . placing under every one what its own eye may superintend, that all will be done for the best.

THOMAS JEFFERSON
Letter to Joseph C. Cabell, Feb. 2, 1816; *Works, VI,* 541

33.   A single good government is a blessing to the whole earth.

THOMAS JEFFERSON
To George Flower, Sept. 12, 1817; *Ibid., VII,* 84

34. The principles and modes of government are too important to be disregarded by an inquisitive mind and I think are well worthy a critical examination by all students that have health and leisure.

JAMES MADISON
To William Bradford, Dec. 1, 1773;
James Madison (*Brant*), *I,* 112

35. Governments destitute of energy, will ever produce anarchy.

JAMES MADISON
Speech to Virginia Convention, June 7, 1788;
Writings (*Hunt*), *V,* 141

36. Energy in government is essential to that security against external and internal danger, and to that prompt and salutary execution of the laws which enter into the very definition of good government. Stability in government is essential to national character and to the advantages annexed to it, as well as to that repose and confidence in the minds of the people, which are among the chief blessings of civil society.

JAMES MADISON
"Publius," 1788; *Federalist, No. 37*

37. In all great changes of established governments, forms ought to give way to substance.

JAMES MADISON
"Publius," 1788; *Ibid., No. 40*

38. But what is government itself, but the greatest of all reflections on human nature? If men were angels, no government would be necessary. If angels were to govern men, neither external nor internal controls on government would be necessary.

JAMES MADISON
"Publius," 1788; *Ibid., No. 51*

39. A good government implies two things: fidelity to the object of government, which is the happiness of the people; secondly, a knowledge of the means by which that object can be best attained.

JAMES MADISON
"Publius," 1788; *Ibid., No. 62*

40. Government is instituted to protect property of every sort; as well that which lies in the various rights of individuals, as that which the term particularly expresses. This being the end of government, that alone is a *just* government, which *impartially* secures to every man, whatever is his *own*.

JAMES MADISON
National Gazette, Mar. 29, 1792; *Writings, VI,* 102

41. We have established a common Government, which, being free in

its principles, being founded in our own choice, being intended as the guardian of our common rights and the patron of our common interests, and wisely containing within itself a provision for its own amendment as experience may point out its errors, seems to promise everything that can be expected from such an institution; and if supported by wise counsels, by virtuous conduct, and by mutual and friendly allowances, must approach as near to perfection as any human work can aspire, and nearer than any which the annals of mankind have recorded.

JAMES MADISON

To George Washington, June 21, 1792; *Ibid.*, p. 116

42. A popular government without popular information or the means of acquiring it is but a prologue to a farce or a tragedy or perhaps both.

JAMES MADISON

Letter to W. T. Barry, Aug. 4, 1822; *Complete Madison*, p. 337

43. Compact is the basis and essence of free government. . . . No right to disregard it belongs to a party till released by causes of which the other parties have an equal right to judge.

JAMES MADISON

To Nicholas P. Trist, Jan. 18, 1833; *Letters, IV*, 268

44. The best frame of government is that which is most likely to prevent the greatest sum of evil.

JAMES MONROE

Observations on the Federal Government, 1789; *Writings, I*, 352

45. I estimate the acts of my friends by the intentions only. Being satisfied on that point I can bear with patience any consequence which may casually result from them. I am aware that under free govt., it is difficult to avoid those of [a] kind . . . for perhaps no important good was ever altogether free from some poison of alloy. I am however equally aware that the evils which are incident to the system . . . even to the individual who suffers by them, are trifling when compared with the great bliss which it imparts.

JAMES MONROE

To Thomas Jefferson, Mar. 22, 1808; *Writings, V*, 34

46. There are no necessary evils in government. Its evils exist only in its abuses.

ANDREW JACKSON

Veto Message, July 10, 1832; *Messages and Papers*, p. 1153

47. It is to be regretted that the rich and powerful too often bend the acts of government to their selfish purposes. . . . In the full enjoyment of the gifts of Heaven and the fruits of superior industry, economy, and virtue, every man is equally entitled to protection by law. But when the laws undertake to add to these natural and just advantages artificial dis-

tinctions, to grant titles, gratuities, and exclusive privileges—to make the rich richer and the potent more powerful—the humble members of society —the farmers, mechanics, and laborers, who have neither the time nor the means of securing like favors to themselves, have a right to complain of the injustice of their government. . . .

If the government would confine itself to equal protection, and, as Heaven does its rains, shower its favors alike on the high and the low, the rich and the poor, it would be an unqualified blessing.

ANDREW JACKSON
Veto Message, July 10, 1832; *Ibid.*

48. The ambition which leads me on is an anxious desire and a fixed determination to restore to the people unimpaired the sacred trust they have confided to my charge; to heal the wounds of the Constitution and to preserve it from further violation; to persuade my countrymen, so far as I may, that it is not in a splendid government supported by powerful monopolies and aristocratical establishments that they will find happiness or their liberties protection, but in a plain system, void of pomp, protecting all and granting favors to none, dispensing its blessings like the dews of heaven, unseen and unfelt save in the freshness and beauty they contribute to produce. It is such a government that the genius of our people requires—such an one only under which our State may remain for ages to come united, prosperous, and free.

ANDREW JACKSON
Protest to the Senate, Apr. 15, 1834; *Messages and Papers*, p. 1311

49. As long as our Government is administered for the good of the people, and is regulated by their will . . . it will be worth defending.

ANDREW JACKSON
First Inaugural Address, Mar. 4, 1829

50. America will present to every friend of mankind the cheering proof that a popular government, wisely formed, is wanting in no element of endurance or strength.

MARTIN VAN BUREN
Inaugural Address, Mar. 4, 1837

51. All communities are apt to look to government too much. . . . The framers of our excellent Constitution . . . wisely judged that the less government interferes with private pursuits the better for the general prosperity.

MARTIN VAN BUREN
Special Session Message, Sept. 4, 1837;
Messages and Papers, p. 1561

52. I believe and I say it is true Democratic feeling, that all the measures

of the Government are directed to the purpose of making the rich richer and the poor poorer.

WILLIAM HENRY HARRISON
Speech, Oct. 1, 1840

53. We admit of no government by divine right . . . the only legitimate right to govern is an express grant of power from the governed.

WILLIAM HENRY HARRISON
Inaugural Address, Mar. 4, 1841

54. A decent and manly examination of the acts of Government should be not only tolerated, but encouraged.

WILLIAM HENRY HARRISON
Inaugural Address, Mar. 4, 1841

55. A government never loses anything by mildness and forbearance to its own citizens, more especially when the consequences of an opposite course may be the shedding of blood.

JOHN TYLER
To Gov. Rufus King of Rhode Island, May 9, 1842; *Messages and Papers*, p. 2147

56. The Government of the United States is one of delegated and limited powers, and it is by a strict adherence to the clearly granted powers and by abstaining from the exercise of doubtful or unauthorized implied powers that we have the only sure guaranty against the recurrence of those unfortunate collisions between the Federal and State authorities which have occasionally so much disturbed the harmony of our system and even threatened the perpetuity of our glorious Union.

JAMES K. POLK
Inaugural Address, Mar. 4, 1845

57. While the people of other countries are struggling to establish free institutions, under which man may govern himself, we are in the actual enjoyment of them—a rich inheritance from our fathers.

JAMES K. POLK

58. Our true mission is not to propagate our opinions upon other countries our form of government by artifice or force, but to teach by example and show by our success, moderation, and justice the blessings of self-government and the advantages of free institutions.

MILLARD FILLMORE
Second Annual Message to Congress, Dec. 2, 1851; *Messages and Papers*, p. 2652

59. The dangers of a concentration of all power in the general government of a confederacy so vast as ours are too obvious to be disregarded.

FRANKLIN PIERCE
Inaugural Address, Mar. 4, 1853

60. The legitimate object of government is to do for a community of people whatever they need to have done, but cannot do at all, or cannot so well do for themselves, in their separate and individual capacities. In all that the people can individually do as well for themselves, government ought not to interfere.

ABRAHAM LINCOLN
In Springfield, Ill., July 1, 1854; *Complete Works, II,* 186

61. Our government rests in public opinion. Whoever can change public opinion can change the government practically just so much.

ABRAHAM LINCOLN
Speech in Chicago, Ill., Dec. 10, 1856; *Ibid.,* p. 310

62. If the minority will not acquiesce, the majority must, or the Government must cease. . . . A majority held in restraint by constitutional checks and limitations, and always changing easily with deliberate changes of popular opinions and sentiments, is the only true sovereign of a free people.

ABRAHAM LINCOLN
First Inaugural Address, Mar. 4, 1861

63. While the people retain their virtue and vigilance no Administration by any extreme of wickedness of folly can very seriously injure the Government in the short space of four years. Perpetuity is implied, if not expressed, in the fundamental law of all national governments. It is safe to assert that no government proper ever had a provision in its organic law for its own termination.

ABRAHAM LINCOLN
First Inaugural Address, Mar. 4, 1861

64. We here highly resolve . . . that this nation, under God, shall have a new birth of freedom, and that government of the people, by the people, for the people, shall not perish from the earth.

ABRAHAM LINCOLN
Gettysburg Address, Nov. 19, 1863;
Complete Works, IX, p. 210

65. It has long been a grave question whether any government, not too strong for the liberties of its people, can be strong enough to maintain its existence in great emergencies.

ABRAHAM LINCOLN
Response to a serenade, Nov. 10, 1864; *Ibid., X,* 263

66. This is the people's Government, they received it as a legacy from Heaven, and they must defend it and preserve it. . . . I am for this government above all earthly possessions and if it perish I do not want to survive it. I am for it though slavery should be struck from existence—I

say, in the face of Heaven, Give me my Government and let the Negro go.

ANDREW JOHNSON
To soldiers in camp, 1862; *Not Guilty,* p. 68

67. The principle of our Government is that of equal laws and freedom of industry.

ANDREW JOHNSON
First Annual Message to Congress, Dec. 4, 1865; *Messages and Papers,* p. 3559

68. We must reason in great matters of government about man as he is; we must conform our actions and our conduct to the example of Him who founded our holy religion.

ANDREW JOHNSON
Speech in Washington, D.C., Feb. 22, 1866; *Document,* p. 4

69. It is the only government suited to our condition; but we have never sought to impose it on others, and we have consistently followed the advice of Washington to recommend it only by its careful preservation.

ANDREW JOHNSON

70. When once a man imbibes the principle that government was instituted to regulate all things, social and domestic, as well as political, it is the most natural error in the world that he should not stop where he began. He wants to apply it to every imaginable case of wrong . . . until there are no personal rights left to the people.

RUTHERFORD B. HAYES
1854; *Rutherford B. Hayes,* p. 170

71. It is vain to hope for the success of a free government without the means of insuring the intelligence of those who are the source of power.

RUTHERFORD B. HAYES

72. Men may die, but the fabrics of our free institutions remain unshaken.

No higher proof could exist of the strength of popular government than the fact that, though the chosen of the people be struck down, his constitutional successor is peacefully installed without shock or strain.

CHESTER A. ARTHUR
Address upon taking the oath of office, Sept. 19, 1881

73. Good government, and especially the government of which every American citizen boasts, has for its objects the protection of every person within its care in the greatest liberty consistent with the good order of society, and his perfect security in the enjoyment of his earnings with the least possible diminution for public needs.

GROVER CLEVELAND
Annual Message to Congress, Dec. 6, 1886; *Messages and Papers,* p. 5094

74. The government is not an almoner of gifts among the people, but an instrumentality by which the people's affairs should be conducted upon business principles, regulated by the public needs.

GROVER CLEVELAND
Message to the House of Representatives, Feb. 26, 1887;
Ibid., p. 5153

75. A government like ours rests upon the intelligence, morality, and patriotism of the people.

WILLIAM MCKINLEY
At Columbia, S.C., Dec. 20, 1898; *Speeches and Addresses,* p. 183

76. Popular government has demonstrated in its one hundred and twenty-four years of trial here its stability and security, and its efficiency as the best instrument of national development and the best safeguard to human rights. . . . The foundation of our Government is liberty; its superstructure peace.

WILLIAM MCKINLEY
Message to Congress, Dec. 3, 1900; *Messages and Papers,*
p. 6416, 6457

77. The government is us; we are the government, you and I.

THEODORE ROOSEVELT
Speech at Asheville, N.C., Sept. 9, 1902; *Dictionary,* p. 486

78. This Government is not and never shall be government by a plutocracy . . .[or] by a mob. It shall continue to be . . . a Government based on the theory that each man, rich or poor, is to be treated simply and solely on his worth as a man, that all his personal and property rights are to be safeguarded, and that he is neither to wrong others nor to suffer wrong from others.

The noblest of all forms of government is self-government; but it is also the most difficult.

THEODORE ROOSEVELT
Fifth Annual Message to Congress, Dec. 5, 1905; *Messages and
Papers,* p. 7366

79. All of us, you and I . . . want to rule ourselves. . . . That is what free government means. If people cannot rule themselves, then they are not fit for free government, and all talk about democracy is a sham.

THEODORE ROOSEVELT
Speech at St. Louis, Mo., Mar. 28, 1912; *Works, XVII,* 173

80. The administration of justice lies at the foundation of government.

WILLIAM HOWARD TAFT
Acceptance of Nomination for Presidency, Chicago, Ill.,
July 28, 1908; *Presidential Addresses, I,* 27

81. Every government is largely what the men are who constitute it.

WOODROW WILSON
1885; *Congressional Government, Chap. 5*

82. The essential characteristic of all government, whatever its form is authority. . . . Government, in its last analysis, is organized force.

The end of government is the facilitation of the objects of society. The rule of governmental action is necessary cooperation; the method of political development is conservative adaptation, shaping old habits into new ones, modifying old means to accomplish new ends.

WOODROW WILSON
1888; *State*, p. 668

83. The wit who described the government of France as despotism tempered by epigram was really formulating one of the approaches to constitutional government.

WOODROW WILSON
1908; *Constitutional Government*, p. 21

84. Government is a matter of insight and of sympathy. If you don't know what the great body of men are up against how are you going to help them?

WOODROW WILSON
Speech at Buffalo, N.Y., Sept. 2, 1912; *Crossroads*, p. 92

85. We used to say that the ideal of government was for every man to be left alone and not interfered with, except when he interfered with somebody else; and that the best government was the government that did as little governing as possible. . . . But we are coming now to realize that life is so complicated that . . . the law has to step in and create new conditions under which we may live, the conditions which will make it tolerable for us to live.

WOODROW WILSON
Address at Fall River, Mass., Sept. 26, 1912; *Ibid.*, p. 275

86. If any part of our people want to be wards, if they want . . . to be taken care of, if they want to be children patronized by the Government, I am sorry, because it will sap the manhood of America. But I don't believe they do. I believe they want to stand on the firm foundations of law and right and take care of themselves.

WOODROW WILSON
1912; *New Freedom (Hale)*, p. 65

87. The firm basis of government is justice, not pity.

WOODROW WILSON
First Inaugural Address, Mar. 4, 1913

88. Government is merely an attempt to express the conscience of every-

body, the average conscience of the nation, in the rules that everybody is commanded to obey. That is all it is. If the government is going faster than the public conscience, it will presently have to pull up; if it is not going as fast as the public conscience, it will presently have to be whipped up.

WOODROW WILSON
Speech in Washington, D.C., Jan. 29, 1915; *Public Papers, III,* 264

89.   No man ever saw a government. I live in the midst of the government of the United States, but I never saw the government of the United States. Its personnel extends through all the nations, and across the seas, and into every corner of the world.

WOODROW WILSON
Speech at Pittsburgh, Pa., Jan. 29, 1916; *Ibid., IV,* 29

90.   The whole art and practice of government consists, not in moving individuals, but in moving masses.

WOODROW WILSON
Speech at Atlantic City, N.J., Sept. 8, 1916; *State Papers,* p. 327

91.   I have the conviction that government ought to be all outside and no inside. I, for my part, believe that there ought to be no place where anything can be done that everybody does not know about.

WOODROW WILSON

92.   I speak as one who believes the highest function of government is to give its citizens the security of peace, the opportunity to achieve, and the pursuit of happiness.

WARREN G. HARDING
Address at Arlington, Va., Nov. 11, 1921;
Messages and Papers, p. 9013

93.   Government is not of supermen, but of normal men, very much like you or me, except that those in authority are, or ought to be, broadened and strengthened in measuring up to great responsibility. . . . Normal men and back to normalcy will steady a civilization which has been fevered by the supreme upheaval of all the world.

Government is a very natural thing and in most instances ought to be a very normal and deliberate proceeding.

WARREN G. HARDING
At Marion, Ohio, July 5, 1920; *Speeches,* p. 19

94.   The Government of the United States is a device for maintaining in perpetuity the rights of the people, with the ultimate extinction of all privileged classes.

CALVIN COOLIDGE
Speech in Philadelphia, Pa., Sept. 25, 1924; *Foundations,* p. 121

95.   Our government rests upon religion. It is from that source that we

derive our reverence for truth and justice, for equality and liberty, and for the rights of mankind. Unless the people believe in these principles they cannot believe in our government.

CALVIN COOLIDGE
Speech in Washington, D.C., Oct. 15, 1924; *Ibid.,* p. 149

96.   The basic tenet of my faith in the American way of life is voluntary co-operation within the community . . . or, self-government outside the government.

HERBERT HOOVER
Oct. 31, 1932; *American Quaker,* p. 161

97.   Constructive government is not conducted on slogans—it is built on sound statesmanship.

HERBERT HOOVER
Speech in Los Angeles, Cal., Oct. 29, 1924; *Policies,* p. 35

98.   We get the fundamental confusion that government, since it can correct much abuse, can also create righteousness.

HERBERT HOOVER
To William O. Thompson, Dec. 30, 1929; *State Papers, I,* 196

99.   As I see it, the object of government is the welfare of the people. . . . It is the purpose of government to see not only that the legitimate interests of the few are protected but that the welfare and rights of the many are conserved. . . . This, I take it, is sound government—not politics.

FRANKLIN DELANO ROOSEVELT
Campaign address at Portland, Ore., Sept. 21, 1932;
Public Papers, I, 727

100.   Government includes the art of formulating a policy, and using the political technique to attain so much of that policy as will receive general support; persuading, leading, sacrificing, teaching always, because the greatest duty of a statesman is to educate.

FRANKLIN DELANO ROOSEVELT
Speech in San Francisco, Cal., Sept. 23, 1932; *Ibid., X,* xvii

101.   It is wholly wrong to call the measures we have taken Government control of farming, industry, and transportation. It is rather a partnership between Government and farming and industry and transportation, not partnership in profits, for the profits still go to the citizens, but rather a partnership in planning, and a partnership to see that the plans are carried out.

FRANKLIN DELANO ROOSEVELT
Fireside Chat, May 3, 1933; *Ibid., II,* 160

102. People require and demand up-to-date Government in place of antiquated Government.

FRANKLIN DELANO ROOSEVELT
Address in New York, N.Y., July 11, 1936; *Ibid., V*, 257

103. That is the spirit with which we are seeking our objective in our national Government—to bring all parts of the country in together so that every part will be prosperous.

FRANKLIN DELANO ROOSEVELT
Remarks at Jacksonville, Ill., Sept. 4, 1936; *Ibid.*, p. 325

104. That Government which thinks in terms of humanity will continue.

FRANKLIN DELANO ROOSEVELT
Campaign address at Rochester, N.Y., Oct. 17, 1936; *Ibid.*, p. 513

105. Government is an instrument of the people, and unless the people want to support measures, and controls necessary for effective and efficient government, representative government will not mean much.

HARRY S. TRUMAN
1947; *Memoirs, II,* 40

106. I don't believe in government for special privilege. Our resources should be used for the benefit of all the people.

HARRY S. TRUMAN
Speech in San Francisco, Cal., Sept. 4, 1951; *Mr. President*, p. 75

107. The problem of government, as I see it today, is to get a new definition almost each day of Lincoln's old exhortation: that government should do for people what they cannot well do for themselves or not do at all, but certainly keep out of those things which people can do for themselves. We will provide the line for the massive single leadership that is necessary and then keep the Federal government out of operations so far as it is possible, whether it be education, the care of the sick, or whatever else we do.

DWIGHT D. EISENHOWER
Remarks to Advertising Council, Washington, D.C., Apr. 2, 1957;
Public Papers . . . Eisenhower, 1957, p. 235

108. In the councils of Government, we must guard against the acquisition of unwarranted influence, whether sought or unsought, by the military-industrial complex.

DWIGHT D. EISENHOWER
Farewell radio and television address, Jan. 17, 1961; *Public Papers
. . . Eisenhower, 1960–61*, p. 1038

109. The business of government is the business of the people.

JOHN F. KENNEDY
Speech on Medicare, in New York, N.Y., May 20, 1962;
Public Papers . . . Kennedy, 1962, p. 420

Gratitude

1. No emotion cools sooner than . . . gratitude . . . but I cannot believe . . . our people would remit the care of disabled veterans.

BENJAMIN HARRISON
Address to Congress, Dec. 6, 1892;
Public Papers and Addresses, p. 151

2. . . . As our power has grown, so has our peril. Today we give our thanks, most of all, for the ideals of honor and faith we inherit from our forefathers—for the decency of purpose, steadfastness of resolve and strength of will, for the courage and the humility, which they possessed and which we must seek every day to emulate as we express our gratitude. We must never forget that the highest appreciation is not to utter words but to live by them.

Let us therefore proclaim our gratitude to Providence for manifold blessings—let us be humbly thankful for inherited ideals—and let us resolve to share those blessings and those ideals with our fellow human beings throughout the world.

JOHN F. KENNEDY
From his undelivered speech, Nov. 22, 1963; *Chicago Daily News,*
Nov. 27, 1963

Greatness

1. It is said that a great life went out here. Great lives such as General Grant's never go out. They go on!

BENJAMIN HARRISON
Speech at Mt. McGregor, N.Y., 1890; *As I Knew Them,* p. 39

2. A great life never dies. Great deeds are imperishable; great names immortal.

WILLIAM MCKINLEY
Address at dedication of Grant's Tomb, New York, N.Y.,
Apr. 27, 1897; *Speeches and Addresses,* p. 17

3. It is only through strife, through hard and dangerous endeavor, that we shall ultimately win the goal of true national greatness.

THEODORE ROOSEVELT
Address at Chicago, Ill., Apr. 10, 1899; *Works, XIII,* 331

4. The great man is always the man of mighty effort, and usually the man whom grinding need has trained to mighty effort.

THEODORE ROOSEVELT
Speech at Galena, Ill., Apr. 27, 1900; *Ibid.,* p. 431

5. The lives of our great men belong to the country. If facts are told showing that they had weaknesses which they overcame, the force of their successful example is greater to lift the youth of the country up to emulate them than if they are painted as perfect without temptation and without weaknesses.

WILLIAM HOWARD TAFT
Speech on Gen. Ulysses S. Grant, New York, N.Y., May 30, 1908;
Problems, p. 61

6. We find every truly great man identified with some special cause. His purposes are steadfastly set in some definite direction.

WOODROW WILSON
University of Virginia magazine, March, 1880; *Story,* p. 13

7. No man is great who thinks himself so, and no man is good who does not strive to secure the happiness and comfort of others.

WOODROW WILSON
Address in New Jersey, 1911

8. America's greatness is built upon freedom—is moral, not material. We have a great ardor for gain; but we have a deep passion for the rights of man. Principles lie back of our action.

WOODROW WILSON
Speech in New York, N.Y., Dec. 6, 1911; *Public Papers, II,* 320

9. Great men are the ambassadors of Providence sent to reveal their unknown selves.

CALVIN COOLIDGE
Address to Women's Roosevelt Memorial Association,
Jan. 23, 1921; *Freedom,* p. 17

10. A people who worship at the shrine of greatness will themselves be truly great.

CALVIN COOLIDGE
Speech at Fredericksburg, Va., July 6, 1922; *Ibid.,* p. 173

11. Great men belong to humanity. They are the incarnation of the truth.

CALVIN COOLIDGE
Speech in Washington, D.C., Oct. 28, 1925; *Foundations,* p. 305

12.   Great men are the product of a great people. They are the result
of many generations of effort, toil, and discipline. They do not stand by
themselves; they are more than an individual. They are the incarnation of
the spirit of a people.

CALVIN COOLIDGE

Speech in Washington, D.C., May 29, 1926; *Ibid.*, p. 416

13.   The way to greatness is the path of self-reliance, independence and
steadfastness in time of trial and stress.

HERBERT HOOVER

Speech at Valley Forge, Pa., May 30, 1931;
Messages and Papers, p. 566

See also America 20, Mothers 1, 5

Growth

See Nations 5, Progress, Religion 28, United Nations 3

Handshaking

1.   The President's mansion was thrown open for the reception of visitors.
. . . I must have shook hands with several thousand persons. Toward the
close of the day some gentlemen asked me if my arm was not sore, and if
I would not suffer from the day's labour. I answered them that judging
from my experience on similar occasions I thought not. I told them that
I had found that there was great art in shaking hands. . . . They were
curious to know what this art was. I told them that if a man surrendered
his arm to be shaken, by some horizontally, by others, perpendicularly,
and by others again with a strong grip, he could not fail to suffer severely
from it, but that if he would shake and not be shaken, grip and not be
gripped, taking care always to squeeze the hand of his adversary as
hard as he squeezed him, that he suffered no inconvenience from it. I
told them also that I could generally anticipate when I was to have a
strong grip, and that when I observed a strong man approaching I generally took advantage of him by being a little quicker than he was and
seizing him by the tip of his fingers, giving him a hearty shake, and thus
preventing him from getting a full grip upon me. They were much
amused at my account of the operation, which I gave to them playfully, but
admitted that there was much philosophy in it. But . . . it is all true.

JAMES K. POLK

Jan. 1, 1849; *Diary (Quaife)*, *IV*, 264

2.   The social routines of the White House were at times a burden. The
nine or ten great annual receptions amounted to a rapidly moving assembly
line of thousands of hand shakes. . . .

President Adams had inaugurated the idea of a New Year's reception at the White House, open to all comers. The report was that 135 people attended the first to wish Mr. and Mrs. Adams a Happy New Year.

On New Year's morning, 1930, I was informed that a long line had been waiting since midnight. . . . Before the day was over I had shaken hands with over 9,000 people. . . . I concluded that that custom might have properly originated with Adams, but that he did not know that the population would increase from 3,000,000 to 130,000,000.

HERBERT HOOVER
1930; *Memoirs, II,* 323

Happiness

1. I am wearied almost to death with the retrograde motion of things, and I solemnly protest, that a pecuniary reward of twenty thousand pounds a year would not induce me to undergo what I do; and after all, perhaps, to lose my character, as it is impossible, under such a variety of distressing circumstances, to conduct matters agreeably to public expectation, or even to the expectation of those who employ me, as they will not make proper allowances for the difficulties their own errors have occasioned. . . .

God grant you all health and happiness. Nothing in this world would contribute so much to mine, as to be once more fixed among you in the peaceable enjoyment of my own "vine and fig-tree." [Micah 4:4]

GEORGE WASHINGTON
To John Augustine Washington, Nov. 19, 1776; *Writings*
(Fitzpatrick), VI, 246

2. It is the peculiar boast of our country, that her happiness is alone dependent on the collective wisdom and virtue of her citizens, and rests not on the exertions of any individual.

GEORGE WASHINGTON
Address to Representatives of South Carolina, May 3, 1791;
Ibid., XII, 196

3. In this enlightened age, there will be no dispute . . . that the happiness of the people, the great end of man, is the end of government; and, therefore, that form of government which will produce the greatest quantity of happiness is the best.

JOHN ADAMS
To John Penn, January, 1776; *Works, IV,* 203

4. Happiness, whether in despotism or democracy, whether in slavery or liberty, can never be found without virtue.

JOHN ADAMS
A Defence of the Constitutions of the Government of the United
States of America, 1787–88; *Ibid., VI,* 219

5. If anybody thinks that kings, nobles, priests are good conservators of the public happiness, send him [to Europe].

THOMAS JEFFERSON
To George Wythe, Aug. 13, 1786; *Writings, V,* 396

6. Of all the cankers of human happiness none corrodes with so silent, yet so baneful an influence, as indolence.

THOMAS JEFFERSON
To Martha Jefferson, Mar. 28, 1787; *Ibid., IV,* 372

7. A mind always employed is always happy. This is the true secret, the grand recipe, for felicity.

THOMAS JEFFERSON
To Martha Jefferson, May 21, 1787; *Ibid., V,* 283

8. I have never been able to conceive how any rational being could propose happiness to himself from the exercise of power over others.

THOMAS JEFFERSON
To A. L. C. Destutt de Tracy, Jan. 26, 1811; *Writings, XIII,* 18

9. He is happiest of whom the world says least, good or bad.

THOMAS JEFFERSON
To John Adams, Aug. 27, 1786; *Works, IV,* 297

10. I have . . . a profound reverence for the Christian religion, and a thorough conviction that sound morals, religious liberty, and a just sense of religious responsibility are essentially connected with all true and lasting happiness.

WILLIAM HENRY HARRISON
Inaugural Address, Mar. 4, 1841

11. It is a fact that so far as our happiness is concerned it matters not much where we are, so that we are satisfied with our situation and whether we will be satisfied or not depends upon ourselves. . . . My doctrine is that almost everything depends upon ourselves. We can be satisfied if we will.

FRANKLIN PIERCE
Letter, June, 1829; *Franklin Pierce,* p. 48

12. Most folks are about as happy as they make up their minds to be.

ABRAHAM LINCOLN

13. Happiness cannot come to any man capable of enjoying true happiness unless it comes as the sequel to duty well and honestly done.

THEODORE ROOSEVELT
Speech at Groton, Mass., May 24, 1904; *Americanism,* p. 71

See also Achievement 3, Equality 5, Ethics, Government 3, 10, 12, 30, 39, 92, Greatness 7, Health 2, 6, History 3, 11, Homes 1, Ignorance 1,

Knowledge 1, 3, 4, Liberty 32, Life 3, People 4, Preparedness 8, Public Office 1, Republics 1, Rights 2, Society 2, 3, 4, States' Rights 9, Travel, Union 2, 12, United States 6, Virtue 5

Hatred

1. Any man who tries to excite class hatred, sectional hate, hate of creeds, any kind of hatred in our community, though he may affect to do it in the interest of the class he is addressing, is in the long run with absolute certainty that class's own worst enemy.

THEODORE ROOSEVELT
Address at Omaha, Neb., Apr. 27, 1903;
Presidential Addresses, I, p. 334

See also Negroes 11, Preparedness 18, Unity 8, War 68

Hawaii

See Brotherhood 3

Health

1. A strong body makes the mind strong.

THOMAS JEFFERSON
To Peter Carr, Aug. 19, 1785; *Writings, V,* 83

2. The most uninformed mind with a healthy body is happier than the wisest valetudinarian.

THOMAS JEFFERSON
To Thomas M. Randolph, Jr., July 6, 1787; *Ibid., VI,* 168

3. Health is the first requisite after morality.

THOMAS JEFFERSON
Letter to Peter Carr, Aug. 10, 1787; *Works, II,* 241

4. The health of our nation is a key to its future—to its economic vitality, to the morale and efficiency of its citizens, to our success in achieving our own goals and demonstrating to others the benefits of a free society. . . . This is a matter of national concern.

JOHN F. KENNEDY
Special Message to Congress, Feb. 9, 1961; *Tide,* p. 135

5. The strength of our democracy and our country is really no greater in the final analysis than the well-being of our citizens. The vigor of our country, its physical vigor and energy, is going to be no more advanced, no more substantial, than the vitality and will of our countrymen.

JOHN F. KENNEDY
Remarks on Youth Fitness program, July 19, 1961; *Public Papers
. . . Kennedy, 1961,* p. 523

6. Good health is a prerequisite to the enjoyment of the "pursuit of hap-

piness." Whenever the miracles of modern medicine are beyond the reach of any group of Americans, for whatever reason—economic, geographic, occupational or other—we must find a way to meet their needs and fulfill their hopes. For one true measure of a nation is its success in fulfilling the promise of a better life for each of its members. Let this be the measure of our nation.

JOHN F. KENNEDY

Special Message to Congress on national health needs, Feb. 27, 1962; *Public Papers . . . Kennedy, 1962*, p. 173

See also Exercise, Physical Fitness, Society 1

History

1. History has informed us that bodies of men as well as individuals are susceptible of the spirit of tyranny.

THOMAS JEFFERSON

To Virginia delegates to Congress, August, 1774; *Writings, II*, 190

2. History, by apprising [men] of the past, will enable them to judge of the future; it will avail them of the experience of other times and other nations.

THOMAS JEFFERSON

Notes on Virginia, 1782; *Ibid.*, p. 207

3. Blest is that Nation whose silent course of happiness furnishes nothing for history to say.

THOMAS JEFFERSON

To M. Le Comte Diodati, Mar. 29, 1807; *Ibid.*, p. 181

4. History, in general, only informs us what bad government is.

THOMAS JEFFERSON

To John Norvel, June 11, 1807; *Ibid.*, p. 223

5. A morsel of genuine history is a thing so rare as to be always valuable.

THOMAS JEFFERSON

To John Adams, Sept. 8, 1817; *Works, VII*, 82

6. Man is fed with fables through life, and leaves it in the belief he knows something of what has been passing, when in truth he has known nothing but what has passed under his own eye.

THOMAS JEFFERSON

To Thomas Cooper, Dec. 11, 1823; *Writings (Ford), X*, 286

7. The public history of all countries, and all ages, is but a sort of mask, richly colored.

JOHN QUINCY ADAMS

Nov. 9, 1822; *Diary*, p. 292

8. Fellow-citizens, *we* cannot escape history.

ABRAHAM LINCOLN
Second Annual Message to Congress, Dec. 1, 1862; *Messages and Papers,* p. 3343

9. The history of the world has been written in vain if it does not teach us that unrestrained authority can never be safely trusted in human hands.

ANDREW JOHNSON
Message to the House of Representatives, Mar. 2, 1867; *Ibid.,* p. 3700

10. The lesson of history is rarely learned by the actors themselves.

JAMES A. GARFIELD
Maxims, p. 7

11. It is a base untruth to say . . . happy is the nation that has no history. Thrice happy is the nation that has a glorious history.

THEODORE ROOSEVELT
Address in Chicago, Ill., Apr. 10, 1899; *Works, XIII,* 321

12. The interest of human history is that it is human. It is a tale that moves and quickens us. . . .

History must be revealed, not recorded, conceived before it is written, and we must all in our several degrees be seers, not clerks. It is a high calling and should not be belittled. Statesmen are guided and formed by what we write, patriots stimulated, tyrants checked. Reform and progress, charity and freedom of belief, the dreams of artists and the fancies of poets, have at once their record and their source with us.

WOODROW WILSON
"The Variety and Unity of History," Sept. 10, 1904; *Congress,* pp. 4, 19

13. History is revelation. It is the manifestation in human affairs of a "power not ourselves that makes for righteousness." Savages have no history. It is the mark of civilization.

CALVIN COOLIDGE
Speech at Springfield, Mass., July 4, 1916; *Faith,* p. 21

14. History is made only by action.

CALVIN COOLIDGE
Speech at Springfield, Mass., July 4, 1916; *Ibid.,* p. 22

15. History cannot be rewritten by wishful thinking.

FRANKLIN DELANO ROOSEVELT

16. Instinctively I sought perspective in the span of history for the de-

cisions I had to make. . . . Most of the problems a President has to face
have their roots in the past.

> HARRY S. TRUMAN
> 1946; *Memoirs, II,* 1

17.   It isn't polls or public opinion alone of the moment that counts. It
is right and wrong, and leadership—men with fortitude, honesty and a belief in the right that make epochs in the history of the world.

> HARRY S. TRUMAN
> Interview, 1946; *Mr. President,* p. 11

18.   There is not really anything new, if you know what has gone before.
What is new to people is what they do not know about their history or the
history of the world. . . .

I'm a great optimist about people and their future. But it's not enough
to know history without doing something about the future.

> HARRY S. TRUMAN
> Interview, *ca.* 1950; *Ibid.,* p. 81

19.   To describe the attitudes of many of us toward the current international scene, I give you the following quotation:

"It is a gloomy moment in history. Not for many years, not in the lifetime of most men . . . has there been so much grave and deep apprehension; never has the future seemed so incalculable as at this time.

"In France the political cauldron seethes and bubbles with uncertainty;
Russia hangs as usual a cloud, dark and silent upon the horizon of Europe;
while all the energies, resources and influences of the British Empire are
sorely tried and are yet to be tried more sorely.

"It is a solemn moment and no man can feel indifference—which happily
no man pretends to feel—in the issue of events.

"Of our own troubles no man can see the end."

That . . . though so vividly descriptive of today, appeared in *Harper's
Weekly,* October 10, 1857. Possibly we are wrong when we fearfully
conclude that for the first time in history the governments regard each
other with fear and suspicion.

> DWIGHT D. EISENHOWER
> Address at Columbia University, Mar. 23, 1950; *Peace,* p. 23

20.   History isn't a guide to the present. In the Archives Building . . .
there is a stone plaque which says, "What is past is prologue." While it
doesn't give us a key to the future, I think it does give us a sense of confidence in the future.

> JOHN F. KENNEDY

See also Flag (The) 3, Foreign Relations 4, 17, Freedom 26, Jews 3,
Majorities 1, Morality 2, Negroes 6, Neutrality 2, Past (The), Patriotism

8, Peace 86, Politics 27, Preparedness 2, Presidency (The) 41, Progress 3, Revolutions 5, Society 5, Success 9, Terror 1, United States 6

Homes

1. The happiness of the domestic fireside is the first boon of heaven; and it is well so, since it is that which is the lot of the mass of mankind.

THOMAS JEFFERSON
To Gen. John Armstrong, Feb. 8, 1813; *Writings, XIII,* 220

2. Without a home there can be no good citizen. With a home there can be no bad one.

ANDREW JOHNSON
May, 1827; *Not Guilty,* p. 10

3. The American home constitutes the strength, security, and integrity of our Government. . . . It is the foundation of a pure national life. The good home makes the good citizen . . . good government necessarily follows.

WILLIAM MCKINLEY
At Cincinnati, Ohio, Sept. 1, 1891; *Life and Speeches,* p. 158

4. When home ties are loosened; when men and women cease to regard a worthy family life, with all its duties fully performed, and all its responsibilities lived up to, as the life best worth living; then evil days for the commonwealth are at hand.

THEODORE ROOSEVELT
Sixth Annual Message to Congress, Dec. 3, 1906; *Messages and Papers,* p. 7428

5. To me the foundation of American life rests upon the home and the family. I read into these great economic forces, these intricate and delicate relations of the government with business and with our political and social life, but one supreme end . . . that we strengthen the security, the happiness, and the independence of every home.

HERBERT HOOVER
Speech at Palo Alto, Cal., Aug. 11, 1928; *Policies,* p. 2

6. There can be no fear for a democracy or self-government or for liberty or freedom from homeowners no matter how humble they may be. . . . To own one's own home is a physical expression of individualism, of enterprise, of independence, and of the freedom of spirit.

HERBERT HOOVER
Speech, Dec. 2, 1931; *Memoirs, II,* 257

See also Future (The) 3, Security 3, 5, War 10

Honesty

1. I hope I shall always possess firmness and virtue enough to maintain

(what I consider the most enviable of all titles) the character of *an honest man*.

GEORGE WASHINGTON
To Alexander Hamilton, Aug. 28, 1788; *Writings
(Fitzpatrick)*, *XXX*, 67

2. Every honest man will suppose honest acts to flow from honest principles, and the rogues may rail without intermission.

THOMAS JEFFERSON
To Benjamin Rush, Dec. 20, 1801; *Writings, X,* p. 304

3. The man who is dishonest as a statesman would be a dishonest man in any station.

THOMAS JEFFERSON
To George Logan, Nov. 12, 1816; *Writings (Ford)*, *X,* 68

4. Honesty is the first chapter in the book of wisdom.

THOMAS JEFFERSON
To Nathaniel Macon, Jan. 12, 1819; *Writings, XV,* 180

5. The *first* of qualities for a *great* statesman is to be honest. . . . I have, and must have, confidence in the *possible* virtue of human nature. . . . To believe all men honest would be folly. To believe none so, is something worse.

JOHN QUINCY ADAMS
To William Eustis, June 22, 1809; *Selected,* p. 267

6. I do not believe that nations any more than individuals can safely violate the rules of honesty and fair dealing.

GROVER CLEVELAND
1886; *Man and Statesman, I,* 240

7. Honesty will cure ten thousand ills of to-day. Honesty of leadership will spare us the popular misconceptions which are ever menacing to democracy. Honesty in statecraft will point the way to impregnable heights. Honesty among nations will dissolve their differences, so that new and lasting friendships may be bound by the ties of fraternity and mutual trust. Honesty in politics will reveal unerring public opinion, and honesty in public service everywhere will diminish public waste and extravagance. Honesty of manhood and womanhood will abolish the sources of discontent which threaten the world's civilization, and will bring us to conviction regarding the fundamentals of the social fabric, without which fundamentals there can be no human progress.

WARREN G. HARDING
Address, May 17, 1923; *Messages and Papers,* p. 9214

See also Class, Government 22, Political Parties 9, Politicians 2, Strife, Wealth 4

Honor

1. Nobody can acquire honor by doing what is wrong.

THOMAS JEFFERSON
To Manchot, War Chief of The Potawatomies, Dec. 21, 1808;
Writings, XVI, 444

2. National honor is national property of the highest value.

JAMES MONROE
First Inaugural Address, Mar. 4, 1817

3. An honorable defeat is better than a dishonorable victory.

MILLARD FILLMORE
Speech at Buffalo, N.Y., Sept. 13, 1844; *Papers, I,* 407

4. It is patriotic sometimes to prefer the honor of the country to its material interest.

WOODROW WILSON
Address in Philadelphia, Pa., July 4, 1914; *Life, IV,* 236

5. No person was ever honored for what he received. Honor has been the reward for what he gave.

CALVIN COOLIDGE
Veto of Salary Increase Bill; *Faith,* p. 173

See also Friendship 10, Labor 8, Peace 35, 37, Prosperity 8, War 22, Wealth 7

Hope

1. We shall nobly save or meanly lose the last best hope of earth.

ABRAHAM LINCOLN
Second Annual Message to Congress, Dec. 1, 1862; *Messages and Papers,* p. 3343

2. Peace requires an international society that is free from vicious provocations to strife among men. These are rooted in inequalities so glaring that, to those who suffer them, they seem to make attractive any alternative. The gamble of war lures the desperate, for even overwhelming defeat can hardly worsen their state; while victory, if it gives the survivors any improvement, will be worth its cost in blood. It is possible, even probable, that hopelessness among a people can be a far more potent cause of war than greed. War in such case is a symptom, not a disease. . . .

Peoples hopeful of their domestic future do not use war as a solution to their problems. Hope spurs humans everywhere to work harder, to endure more now that the future may be better; but despair is the climate of war and death. Even America, without American optimism, can accomplish nothing beyond the needs of each day.

DWIGHT D. EISENHOWER
Address at Columbia University, Mar. 23, 1950; *Peace,* pp. 15, 20

Humanity

1. There have been touches of humanity in this recent [Spanish-American] war that will impress mankind for all time. In the words of the commander of the ship . . . to his crew, "Don't cheer, the poor fellows are dying"; when the commander of that other ship said to his crew, "Don't fire, the flag has gone down"; in the command of the colonel of the Rough Riders, "Don't swear; fight!" we seem to get a glance of the divine spark in the nobility of the men who participated in our war. What we want . . . is that the conclusion of this war . . . shall be a triumph for humanity.

WILLIAM McKINLEY
Speech at Belle Plaine, Ia., Oct. 11, 1898;
Speeches and Addresses, p. 89

2. My dream is . . . that America will come into the full light of the day when all shall know that she puts human rights above all other rights and that her flag is the flag not only of America but of humanity.

WOODROW WILSON
Address in Philadelphia, Pa., July 4, 1914; *Public Papers, III,* 147

3. The interesting and inspiring thought about America . . . is that she asks nothing for herself except what she has a right to ask for humanity itself.

WOODROW WILSON
Speech in New York, N.Y., May 17, 1915; *Ibid.,* p. 330

Human Nature

1. Human nature is more easily wrought upon and governed by promises, and encouragement, and praise, than by punishment, and threatening and blame. . . . Commendation enlivens and stimulates . . . to a noble ardor and emulation.

JOHN ADAMS
Diary, Nov. 21, 1755; *Works, II,* 6

2. Among the dark spots in human nature which in the course of my life I have observed, the devices of rivals to ruin me have been sorry pictures of the heart of man.

JOHN QUINCY ADAMS
1835; *John Quincy Adams (Morse),* p. 297

3. Human nature will not change. In any great national trial, compared with the men of this, we shall have as weak and as strong, as silly and as

wise, as bad and as good. Let us, therefore, study the incidents of this as philosophy to learn wisdom from and none of them as wrongs to be revenged.

ABRAHAM LINCOLN
Response to a serenade, Nov. 10, 1864; *Complete Works, X*, 263

See also Defense 11, Political Parties 12, Politics 3, Rights 1

Human Welfare

1. Human welfare has not increased and does not increase through mere materialism and luxury, but . . . it does progress through integrity, unselfishness, responsibility and justice.

FRANKLIN DELANO ROOSEVELT
Second Annual Message to Congress, Jan. 3, 1934;
Public Papers, III, 8

See also Self-Deception, Poverty

Humility

1. Humility must always be the portion of any man who receives acclaim earned in the blood of his followers and the sacrifices of his friends.

DWIGHT D. EISENHOWER
Speech in London, England, June 12, 1945;
Eisenhower Speaks, p. 15

See also Appointments 2, Military Matters 11, Religion 1

Humor

1. Good humor is one of the preservatives of our peace and tranquility.

THOMAS JEFFERSON
To Thomas Jefferson Randolph, Nov. 24, 1808; *Writings, XII*, 198

2. Above all things, and at all times, practice yourself in good humor.

THOMAS JEFFERSON
To Francis Eppes, May 21, 1816; *Ibid., XIX*, 242

See also Americans 12, Mind 1, Patriotism 7

Hunger
See Loans 1, Peace 63, War 66

Ideals

1. The ideals of yesterday are the truths of to-day.

WILLIAM MCKINLEY
Speech at Cincinnati, Ohio, Sept. 1, 1901;
Life and Speeches, p. 159

2. Sometimes people call me an idealist. Well, that is the way I know I am an American. America is the only idealistic nation in the world.

WOODROW WILSON

Speech at Sioux Falls, S.D., Sept. 8, 1919; *Public Papers, VI,* 52

3. Americans have not fully realized their ideals. There are imperfections. But the ideal is right. It is everlastingly right. What our country needs is the moral power to hold to it.

CALVIN COOLIDGE

Speech at Pittsburgh, Pa., Apr. 28, 1921; *Freedom,* p. 46

4. Ideals and beliefs determine the whole course of society.

CALVIN COOLIDGE

Address at Springfield, Mass., Oct. 11, 1921; *Citizenship,* p. 248

5. The chief ideal of the American is idealism. . . . America is a nation of idealists.

CALVIN COOLIDGE

Address in Washington, D.C., Jan. 17, 1925; *Foundations,* p. 190

6. Governments do not make ideals, but ideals make governments. This is both historically and logically true.

CALVIN COOLIDGE

Speech in Philadelphia, Pa., July 5, 1926; *Foundations,* p. 451

7. America is not and must not be a country without ideals. They are useless if they are only visionary; they are only valuable if they are practical. A nation can not dwell constantly on the mountain tops. It has to be replenished and sustained through the ceaseless toil of the less inspiring valleys. But its face ought always to be turned upward, its vision ought always to be fixed on high.

CALVIN COOLIDGE

Message to Congress, Dec. 7, 1926; *Government pamphlet, 1926*

8. Ideals and aspirations are the touchstones upon which the day-to-day administration and legislative acts of government must be tested. . . . These ideals should be: the preservation of self-government and its full foundations in local government; the perfection of justice whether in economic or in social fields; the maintenance of ordered liberty; the denial of domination by any group or class; the building up and preservation of equality of opportunity; the stimulation of initiative and individuality; absolute integrity in public affairs; the choice of officials for fitness to office; the direction of economic progress toward prosperity and the further lessening of poverty; the freedom of public opinion; the sustaining of education and of the advancement of knowledge; the growth of reli-

gious spirit and the tolerance of all faiths; the strengthening of the home; the advancement of peace.

HERBERT HOOVER
Inaugural Address, Mar. 4, 1929

See also Beliefs, Causes, Convictions, Declaration of Independence 9, Knowledge 6, Laws 34, Legislation 3, Materialism 2, Presidency (The) 57, Principles, Service 3, Strife, War 68, Wealth 7, Women 11

Ideas

1.   He who receives ideas from me, receives instruction himself without lessening mine; as he who lights his taper at mine receives light without darkening me.

THOMAS JEFFERSON
To Isaac McPherson, Aug. 13, 1813; *Writings, XIII,* 334

2.   Ideas are the only thing in this universe that are immortal. . . . Our race has ideas, and because ideas are immortal, if they be true, we build monuments to them.

JAMES A. GARFIELD
Speech at Geneva, Ohio, Aug. 3, 1880; *Gems,* p. 42

3.   Ideas are the great warriors of the world, and a war that has no ideas behind it is simply brutality.

JAMES A. GARFIELD
Maxims, p. 23

See also Knowledge 6, Progress 4, Revolutions 8

Idleness

1.   Idleness begets ennui, ennui the hypochondriac, and that a diseased body. No laborious person was ever yet hysterical.

THOMAS JEFFERSON
To Martha Jefferson, Mar. 28, 1787; *Writings (Ford), IV,* 372

See also Happiness 6

Ignorance

1.   "Ignorance and inconsideration are the two great causes of the ruin of mankind." This . . . with relation to the interest of . . . men in a future and immortal state. But it is of equal truth and importance if applied to the happiness of men in society.

JOHN ADAMS
Dissertation on the Canon and the Feudal Law, August, 1765;
Works, III, 448

2.   Ignorance is preferable to error; and he is less remote from truth who believes nothing, than he who believes what is wrong.

THOMAS JEFFERSON
Notes on Virginia, 1782; *Writings, II,* 43

3. Preach, my dear sir, a crusade against ignorance; establish and improve the law for educating the common people. Let our countrymen know, that the people alone can protect us against these evils [of monarchy], and that the tax which will be paid for this purpose, is not more than a thousandth part of what will be paid to kings, priests, and nobles, who will rise up among us if we keep the people in ignorance.

THOMAS JEFFERSON
To George Wythe, Aug. 13, 1786; *Ibid., V, 397*

4. I think it is Montaigne who has said, that ignorance is the softest pillow on which a man can rest his head. I am sure it is true as to everything political, and shall endeavor to estrange myself to everything of that character.

THOMAS JEFFERSON
To Edmund Randolph, Feb. 3, 1794; *Ibid., VIII, 138*

5. If a nation expects to be ignorant and free, in a state of civilization, it expects what never was and never will be.

THOMAS JEFFERSON
To Col. Charles Yancey, Jan. 6, 1816; *Ibid., X, 4*

6. No nation is permitted to live in ignorance with impunity.

THOMAS JEFFERSON
Report of meeting of visitors to University of Virginia,
Nov. 29, 1821; *Ibid., XIX, 408*

7. I may . . . have exhibited now and then the "exulting stupidity and triumphant ignorance" of which the Senator from Oregon has spoken. Great and magnanimous minds pity ignorance. The Senator . . . rich in intellectual culture, with a mind comprehensive enough to retain the wisdom of ages, and an eloquence to charm a listening Senate, deplores mine; but he should be considerate enough to regard my humility. Unpretending in my ignorance, I am content to gaze at his lofty flights and glorious daring without aspiring to accompany him to regions for which my wings have not been plumed nor my eyes fitted. . . . To me, alas, his heaven appears but as a murky region, dull, opaque, leaden. My pretension has been simply to do my duty to my State and to my country.

ANDREW JOHNSON
To Sen. Joseph Lane in the Senate, Mar. 2, 1861; *Speeches, p. 295*

8. It is in the soil of ignorance that poverty is planted. It is in the soil of ignorance that disease flourishes. It is in the soil of ignorance that racial and religious strife takes root. It is in the soil of ignorance that Communism brings forth the bitter fruit of tyranny.

LYNDON B. JOHNSON
Address at University of the Philippines, May 13, 1961;
Story, p. 182

See also Communism 8, Education, Enlightenment, Foreign Relations 47, Freedom 11, Knowledge, Philanthropy

Immigration

1. My opinion with respect to immigration is that, except of useful mechanics and some particular descriptions of men or professions, there is no need of encouragement, while the policy or advantage of its taking place in a body (I mean the settling of them in a body) may be much questioned; for, by so doing, they retain the language, habits and principles (good or bad) which they bring with them.

GEORGE WASHINGTON
To John Adams, Nov. 15, 1794; *Writings*
(*Fitzpatrick*), *XXXIV,* 23

2. The admitted right of a government to prevent the influx of elements hostile to its internal peace and security may not be questioned, even where there is no treaty stipulation on the subject.

GROVER CLEVELAND
First Annual Message to Congress, Dec. 8, 1885;
Messages and Papers, p. 4914

See also Americans 5, Emigrants, Nationality 2

Imperialism
See Freedom 31, Right 2, Russia 5

Incumbents
See Power 15, Presidency (The) 25

Independence
1. Independence forever!

JOHN ADAMS
Uttered shortly before his death on July 4, 1826; *Family,* p. 199

2. I am of a sect by myself, as far as I know.

THOMAS JEFFERSON
To Ezra Stiles, June 25, 1819; *Writings, XV,* 203

3. That man who, in times of difficulty and danger, shall halt at any course necessary to retain the rights, privileges, and independence of his country, is unsuited to authority.

ANDREW JACKSON
To Samuel Swartwout, Feb. 22, 1824; *Life* (*Parton*), *III,* 76

4. The ability to produce every necessity of life renders us independent in war as well as in peace.

MILLARD FILLMORE

See also Declaration of Independence, Greatness 13, League of Nations 7, Press (The) 2, Slogans, War 12

Individualism

1. Materially we must strive to secure a broader economic opportunity for all men so that each shall have a better chance to show the stuff of which he is made. Spiritually and ethically we must strive to bring about clean living and right thinking. We appreciate that the things of the body are important; but we appreciate also that the things of the soul are immeasurably more important. The foundation stone of national life is and ever must be the high individual character of the individual citizen.

THEODORE ROOSEVELT
Message to Congress; *Public Papers (of F.D.R.)*, II, 493

2. The individual is . . . the first fact of liberty. . . . There can be no such thing as corporate liberty. Liberty belongs to the individual, or it does not exist.

WOODROW WILSON
1908; *Constitutional Government*, p. 16

3. The social force in which I am interested is . . . the sole source of progress; it is American individualism.

HERBERT HOOVER
1922; *Individualism*, p. 9

4. I believe in individualism . . . up to the point where the individualist starts to operate at the expense of society.

FRANKLIN DELANO ROOSEVELT
Campaign address in Chicago, Ill., Oct. 14, 1936;
Public Papers, V, 488

See also Democracy 27, 29, 31, Mobs 1, Nations 11, Prosperity 2, Self-Government 6

Industry
See Freedom 18, Wealth 8

Inequality
1. Inequalities of mind and body are so established by God Almighty, in his constitution of human nature, that no art or policy can ever plane them down to a level.

JOHN ADAMS
To Thomas Jefferson, July 13, 1813; *Works (of Jefferson)*, VI, 162

See also Equality, Negroes 1, 2, Property 1, 3, Rights 7

Infamy
See Japan 4

Inflation

1. We inflated in haste, we must deflate in deliberation. . . . Deflation on the one hand and restoration of the 100-cent dollar on the other ought to have begun on the day after the armistice, but plans were lacking or courage failed. The unpreparedness for peace was little less costly than unpreparedness for war.

WARREN G. HARDING
At Marion, Ohio, July 22, 1920; *Speeches of Warren G. Harding*, p. 30

2. Production is the greatest weapon against inflation.

HARRY S. TRUMAN
Radio address, Jan. 3, 1946; *Public Papers . . . Truman, 1946*, p. 5

3. Inflation is too critical a matter to be left to the politicians.

DWIGHT D. EISENHOWER
Speech at Troy, N.Y., Oct. 22, 1952; *Index*, p. 56

4. Inflation too often follows in the shadow of growth—while price stability is made easy by stagnation or controls. But we mean to maintain both stability and growth in a climate of freedom.

Our first line of defense against inflation is the good sense and public spirit of business and labor—keeping their total increases in wages and profits in step with productivity.

JOHN F. KENNEDY
To Congress, Washington, D.C., Jan. 11, 1962;
Vital Speeches, Feb. 1, 1962, p. 230

See also Debts 11, 12, Depression

Influence

1. If I cannot retain my moral influence over a man except by occasionally knocking him down, if that is the only basis upon which he will respect me, then for the sake of his soul I have got occasionally to knock him down.

WOODROW WILSON
Speech, May 15, 1916; *Public Papers, IV*, 171

See also Government 1

Injury

1. An individual, thinking himself injured, makes more noise than a state.

THOMAS JEFFERSON
To Georgia delegates in Congress, Dec. 22, 1785; *Works, I*, 501

Insult

1. One insult pocketed soon produces another.

THOMAS JEFFERSON
To George Washington, 1790; *Dictionary*, p. 595

See also War 10

Integration

See American System, Civil Rights, Desegregation, Discrimination, Equality, Negroes

Integrity

See Public Office 18

Intelligence

See Preparedness 8, Republics 15

International Organizations

See League of Nations, United Nations

International Relations

See Foreign Relations

Isolationism

1. Isolation is no longer possible or desirable. . . . At the beginning of the nineteenth century there was not a mile of steam railroad on the globe. Now there are enough miles to make its circuit many times. Then there was not a line of electric telegraph; now we have a vast mileage traversing all lands and seas. God and man have linked the nations together. No nation can longer be indifferent to any other. And as we are brought more and more in touch with each other the less occasion there is for misunderstandings and the stronger the disposition, when we have differences, to adjust them in the court of arbitration, which is the noblest forum for the settlement of international disputes.

WILLIAM McKINLEY
Last speech, Buffalo, N.Y., Sept. 5, 1901;
Messages and Papers, p. 6619

2. America can not be an ostrich with its head in the sand. America can not shut itself out from the rest of the world.

WOODROW WILSON
Speech at Des Moines, Ia., Feb. 1, 1916; *Public Papers, IV*, 73

3. We can no longer indulge our traditional provincialism. We are to play a leading part in the world drama whether we wish it or not. We shall lend, not borrow; act for ourselves, not imitate or follow; organize and initiate, not peep about merely to see where we may get in. . . . No

nation stands wholly apart in interest when the life and interests of all
nations are thrown into confusion and peril.

WOODROW WILSON
Address at Long Branch, N.J., Sept. 2, 1916;
Messages and Papers (Shaw), I, 316

4. We are done with provincialism and we have got to have a view now
and a horizon as wide as the world itself. America has a great cause which
is not confined to the American continent. It is the cause of humanity
itself.

WOODROW WILSON
1918; *As I Knew Them, Foreword*

5. The isolation of the United States is at an end, not because we chose
to go into the politics of the world, but because by the sheer genius of this
people and the growth of our power we have become a determining factor
in the history of mankind.

WOODROW WILSON
Speech at Des Moines, Ia., Sept. 6, 1919; *Public Papers, VI*, 18

6. No policy of isolation will satisfy the growing needs and opportunities of America.

WOODROW WILSON
Seventh Annual Message to Congress, Dec. 2, 1919; *Ibid.*, p. 431

7. We are not going to be able to avoid meeting the world and bearing
our part of the burdens of the world. I desire my country to meet them
without evasion and without fear, in an upright, downright, square American way.

CALVIN COOLIDGE
As I Knew Them, Foreword

8. The United States will never survive as a happy and fertile oasis of
liberty surrounded by a cruel desert of dictatorship.

FRANKLIN DELANO ROOSEVELT
Address at Hyde Park, N.Y., July 4, 1941; *Public Papers, X*, 254

9. Isolationism is dead.

HARRY S. TRUMAN
Telegram to Franklin Delano Roosevelt, Nov. 8, 1944;
Memoirs, p. 194

10. One truth must rule all we think and all we do. No people can live
to itself alone. The unity of all who dwell in freedom is their only sure
defense. The economic need of all nations—in mutual dependence—makes
isolation an impossibility; not even America's prosperity could long
survive if other nations did not prosper. No nation can longer be a for-

tress, lone and strong and safe. And any people, seeking such shelter for themselves, can now build only their own prison.

DWIGHT D. EISENHOWER
Second Inaugural Address, Jan. 21, 1957

See also Foreign Relations, Freedom 29, Peace 52, Security 8

Japan

1.   Owing to the peculiar situation of Japan and the anomalous form of its government, the action of that empire in performing treaty stipulations is inconstant and capricious. . . . There is reason also to believe that proceedings have increased rather than diminished the friendship of Japan toward the United States.

ABRAHAM LINCOLN
Fourth Annual Message to Congress, Dec. 6, 1864;
Complete Works, X, 287

2.   Japan attracts increasing attention in this country by her evident desire to cultivate more liberal intercourse with us and to seek our kindly aid in furtherance of her laudable desire for complete autonomy in her domestic affairs and full equality in the family of nations. . . . Our relations with this progressive nation should not be less broad and liberal than those with other powers.

GROVER CLEVELAND
Sixth Annual Message to Congress, Dec. 3, 1894;
Messages and Papers, p. 5959

3.   The Japanese have won in a single generation the right to stand abreast of the foremost and most enlightened peoples of Europe and America. . . . We have as much to learn from Japan as Japan has to learn from us; and no nation is fit to teach unless it is also willing to learn.

THEODORE ROOSEVELT
Sixth Annual Message to Congress, Dec. 3, 1906;
Messages and Papers, p. 7054

4.   On December 7, 1941—a date which will live in infamy—the United States of America was suddenly and deliberately attacked by naval and air forces of the Empire of Japan.

Hostilities exist. There is no blinking the fact that our people, our territories and our interests are in grave danger.

FRANKLIN DELANO ROOSEVELT
Address to Congress, asking for war, Dec. 8, 1941; *Ibid., X,* 514

5.   We have disarmed Japan, and we are promoting reforms which we hope will bring into being a democratic and peaceful nation.

HARRY S. TRUMAN
Address in Chicago, Ill., Apr. 6, 1946; *Public Papers . . .
Truman, 1946,* p. 188

6. It would be a tremendous victory for International Communism if we were to permit [the Communist-inspired riots in Tokyo] to disrupt our economic relationships with that nation; or to weaken the feeling of friendship and understanding which unites the vast majority of the Japanese and American people.

Japan has once again become a great nation. Over the postwar years she has painstakingly created a new image of herself, the image of a responsible, peaceful and cooperative Free World nation, mindful of her obligations and of the rights of others. Japan has made a fine record in the United Nations as well as elsewhere on the international stage.

Since the loss of mainland China to the Communists in 1949, the need to link the other nations of the Far East with the United States more strongly, in their mutual interest, should be apparent to all. We seek, and continue to build and strengthen these links, with Japan as well as with the other countries, by actions of many kinds. . . .

DWIGHT D. EISENHOWER
Radio and television report, June 27, 1960; *Public Papers . . .
Eisenhower, 1960–61,* p. 533

Jews

1. The Hebrews have done more to civilize men than any other nation. If I were an atheist, and believed in blind eternal fate, I should still believe that fate had ordained the Jews to be the most essential instrument for civilizing the nations.

JOHN ADAMS
To F. A. Vanderkemp, Feb. 16, 1809; *Works, IX,* 609

2. I am happy in the restoration, of the Jews, particularly, to their social rights. . . . I have ever felt regret at seeing the sect, the parent and basis of all those of Christendom, singled out by all of them for a persecution and oppression which proved they had profited nothing from the benevolent doctrines of Him whom they profess to make the model of their principle and practice.

THOMAS JEFFERSON
To Jacob De La Motte and Joseph Marx

3. Every inheritance of the Jewish people, every teaching of their secular history and religious experience, draws them powerfully to the side of charity, liberty and progress. . . . Capacity for adaptation in detail, without sacrifice of essentials, has been one of the special lessons which the marvelous history of the Jewish people has taught.

CALVIN COOLIDGE
Address in Washington, D.C., May 3, 1925;
Messages and Papers, p. 9496

4. I have learned of the proposed observance of Brotherhood Day by the National Conference of Jews and Christians and I am deeply interested. . . .

This occasion presents an opportunity for concerted thinking on a vital problem of national welfare; it should help us all in our efforts to rise above ancient and harmful suspicions and prejudices and to work together as citizens of American democracy.

FRANKLIN DELANO ROOSEVELT
Letter to the National Conference, Apr. 18, 1934;
Public Papers, III, 186

5. For the tens of centuries spanned by the history of the Jewish people, members of [the] race have given to mankind almost unbelievable examples of courageous devotion to noble principles—to justice, to liberty, to the right of men to worship according to the inner voice of conscience. Such are the principles which can now give the only sure guide to all men as they seek to establish true peace in the world. . . .

DWIGHT D. EISENHOWER
A statement, Sept. 27, 1954; *Public Papers . . .
Eisenhower, 1954,* p. 884

See also Russia 2

Judgment
See Courage 9, Enthusiasm 1, League of Nations 3, Neutrality 6, People (The) 31, Religion 12, Tolerance 4, Wisdom 5

Jury System
See Freedom 5

Justice
1. The administration of justice is the firmest pillar of Government.

GEORGE WASHINGTON
To Edmund Randolph, Sept. 27, 1789; *Writings
(Fitzpatrick),* II, 432

2. Equal and exact justice to all men of whatever state or persuasion, religious or political. . . .

THOMAS JEFFERSON
First Inaugural Address, Mar. 4, 1801

3. I believe that justice is instinct and innate, that the moral sense is as much a part of our constitution as that of feeling, seeing, or hearing.

THOMAS JEFFERSON
To John Adams, Oct. 14, 1816; *Works, VII,* 39

4. Justice is the end of government. It is the end of society.

JAMES MADISON
"Publius," 1788; *Federalist, No. 51*

5. It is by rendering justice to other nations that we expect it from them.

JAMES MONROE
Seventh Annual Message to Congress, Dec. 2, 1823;
Messages and Papers, p. 777

6. To do justice to all and to submit to wrong from none has been during my Administration its governing maxim.

ANDREW JACKSON
Second Inaugural Address, Mar. 4, 1833

7. We ought to do justice in a kindly spirit to all nations and require justice from them in return.

JAMES BUCHANAN
Inaugural Address, Mar. 4, 1857

8. The severest justice may not always be the best policy.

ABRAHAM LINCOLN
Message to Congress, July 17, 1862; *Complete Works, VII,* 283

9. I have always found that *mercy bears richer fruits than strict justice.*

ABRAHAM LINCOLN
Washington, D.C., 1865; *Everyday Life,* p. 627

10. Justice and good will will outlast passion.

JAMES A. GARFIELD
Letter Accepting Nomination for Presidency, July 12, 1880;
Lives, p. 39

11. It has been the boast of our Government that it seeks to do justice in all things without regard to the strength or weakness of those with whom it deals. I mistake the American people if they favor the odious doctrine that there is no such thing as international morality; that there is one law for a strong nation and another for a weak one, and that even by indirection a strong power may with impunity despoil a weak one of its territory.

GROVER CLEVELAND
Special Message to Congress, Dec. 18, 1893;
Messages and Papers, p. 5902

12. The battlefield as a place of settlement of disputes is gradually yielding to arbitral courts of justice. . . . The spirit of justice governs our relations with other countries, and therefore we are specially qualified to set a pace for the rest of the world.

WILLIAM HOWARD TAFT
November, 1911; *Dawn,* p. 4

13. The firm basis of government is justice, not pity.

WOODROW WILSON
First Inaugural Address, Mar. 4, 1913

14. Fraternities must be just, if they are to survive. . . . Secret fraternity is one thing, secret conspiracy is quite another. . . .

A respect for the rights of others, the very essence of fraternity, is stressed everywhere until the rule of justice is the guarantee of righteous fraternal relationship.

WARREN G. HARDING
Address in Washington, D.C., June 5, 1923;
Messages and Papers, p. 9233

15. Rigid and expeditious justice is the first safeguard of freedom, the basis of all ordered liberty, the vital force of progress.

HERBERT HOOVER
Inaugural Address, Mar. 4, 1929

See also Conduct 1, Duty 4, Education 12, Enemies 4, Failure 1, Foreign Relations 50, 51, Freedom 9, Goals 2, Government 80, 87, Human Welfare, Loyalty 1, Monopolies 4, Nations 7, Negroes 5, 7, 9, 11, Peace 9, 16, 42, 71, 75, People (The) 22, Political Parties 13, Power 21, Preparedness 15, 19, Public Opinion 6, Religion 1, 32, Republics 5, Russia 3, Security 6, 8, United Nations 4, United States 1, 3, 7, Vigilance 2, War 5, 52

Kings

1. A republican government is the best, and, in America, the only one which ought to be adopted or thought of, because the morals of the people, and circumstances of the country, not only can bear it, but require it. But, in several of the great nations of Europe, kings appeared to me to be as necessary as any government at all. Nor had I ever seen any reason to believe that kings were, in general, worse than other men.

JOHN ADAMS
Diary, May 6, 1778; *Works, III,* 154

2. There is no King who, with sufficient force, is not always ready to make himself absolute.

THOMAS JEFFERSON
To George Wythe, 1786; *Dictionary,* p. 633

3. If any of our countrymen wish for a king, give them Aesop's fable of the frogs who asked for a king; if this does not cure them, send them to Europe. They will go back republicans.

THOMAS JEFFERSON
To David Ramsay, Aug. 4, 1787; *Writings, VI,* 226

See also Government 15, Happiness 5, Laws 12, Reason 2, Right 2

Knowledge

1. Knowledge is in every country the surest basis of public happiness.

GEORGE WASHINGTON
First Annual Message to Congress, Jan. 8, 1790;
Messages and Papers, p. 58

2. Let us tenderly and kindly cherish . . . the means of knowledge. Let us dare to read, think, speak and write.

JOHN ADAMS
Dissertation on the Canon and the Feudal Law, August, 1765;
Works, III, 462

3. By far the most important bill in our whole code, is that for the diffusion of knowledge among the people. No other sure foundation can be devised for the preservation of freedom and happiness.

THOMAS JEFFERSON
To George Wythe, Aug. 13, 1786; *Writings, V,* 396

4. . . . knolege is power . . . knolege is safety, and . . . knolege is happiness.

THOMAS JEFFERSON
To George Ticknor, Nov. 25, 1817; *Ibid., X,* 96

5. A diffusion of knowledge is the only guardian of true liberty.

JAMES MADISON
To George Thompson, June 30, 1825; *Complete Madison,* p. 337

6. It is not knowledge that moves the world, but ideals, convictions, the opinions or fancies that have been held or followed.

WOODROW WILSON
Mere Literature, 1896, p. 10

7. I despise the mere accumulation of knowledge. To be a good and useful citizen of this democracy you must have contact with many kinds of men.

WOODROW WILSON
1901

8. Every citizen is entitled to a liberal education. . . . Despotism finds its chief support in ignorance. Knowledge and freedom go hand in hand.

CALVIN COOLIDGE
Proclamation, Sept. 26, 1923; *Messages and Papers,* p. 9325

9. The progress of civilization depends in large degree upon "the increase and diffusion of knowledge among men." We must add to knowledge, both for the intellectual and for the spiritual satisfaction that comes from widening the range of human understanding.

HERBERT HOOVER
Speech, Dec. 28, 1926; *Memoirs, II,* 76

10. Cooperation in the pursuit of knowledge can hopefully lead to cooperation in the pursuit of peace. . . .
The pursuit of knowledge . . . rests everything . . . on the idea of a world based on diversity, self-determination and freedom. . . .
No one can doubt that the wave of the future is not the conquest of

the world by a single dogmatic creed, but the liberation of the diverse energies of free nations and free men. No one can doubt that cooperation in the pursuit of knowledge must lead to freedom of the mind and of the soul. . . .

The specter of thermonuclear war will hang over mankind; and we must heed the advice of Oliver Holmes of "freedom leaning on her spear" until all nations are wise enough to disarm safely and effectively. . . .

In a time of turbulence and change, it is more true than ever that knowledge is power; for only by true understanding and steadfast judgment are we able to master the challenge of history.

If this is so, we must strive to acquire knowledge—and to apply it with wisdom. We must reject oversimplified theories of international life—the theory that the American mission is to remake the world in the American image.

We must seize the vision of a free and diverse world—and shape our policies to speed progress toward a flexible world order. . . .

"Knowledge is the great sun of the firmament," said Daniel Webster. "Life and power are scattered with all its beams."

In its light, we must think and act not only for the moment, but for the century. I am reminded of the story of Marshal Lyautey, who once asked his gardener to plant a tree. The gardener objected that the tree was slow-growing and would not reach maturity for a hundred years. The marshal replied, "In that case, there is no time to lose. Plant it this afternoon."

Today a world of knowledge—a world of cooperation—a just and lasting peace—may well be years away. But we have no time to lose. Let us plant our trees this very afternoon.

JOHN F. KENNEDY
At Berkeley, Cal., Mar. 23, 1962; *Vital Speeches,*
May 15, 1962, p. 450

See also Colleges, Education, Enlightenment, Faith 1, Libraries, Politics 16, Power 3, Success 3, Universities, War 72, Wisdom 5

Labor

1. Melancholy is the condition of that people whose government can be sustained only by a system which periodically transfers large amounts from the labor of the many to the coffers of the few.

JAMES K. POLK
Inaugural Address, Mar. 4, 1845

2. The workingmen are the basis of all governments, for the plain reason that they are the more numerous.

ABRAHAM LINCOLN
Speech at Cincinnati, Ohio, Feb. 12, 1861;
Complete Works, VI, 119

3. Labor is prior to, and independent of, capital. Capital is only the

fruit of labor, and could never have existed if labor had not first existed. Labor is the superior of capital, and deserves much the higher consideration.

ABRAHAM LINCOLN
First Annual Message to Congress, Dec. 3, 1861;
Messages and Papers, p. 3258

4. *Identifying himself with the common man, Johnson harked back to his early days as a tailor:*
I do not forget that I am a mechanic. I am proud to own it. Neither do I forget that Adam was a tailor, sewing fig leaves together for aprons; Tubal Cain was an artificer in brass and iron; Joseph the husband of Mary was a carpenter, and our Saviour probably followed the same trade; the apostle Paul was a tentmaker; Socrates was a sculptor; Archimedes was a mechanic; King Crispin was a shoemaker; and so was Roger Sherman, who helped to form the Constitution.

ANDREW JOHNSON
Ca. 1840; *Not Guilty*, p. 19

5. The laborer is the author of all greatness and wealth. . . . With us, labor is regarded as highly respectable. When it is not so regarded, it is because man dishonors labor. We recognize that labor dishonors no man.

ULYSSES S. GRANT
Speech in London, England, July 3, 1877; *Stories*, p. 155

6. Remember that the genius of success is still the genius of labor. If hard work is not another name for talent, it is the best possible substitute for it. . . . Go forth with brave, true hearts, knowing that fortune dwells in your brain & muscle—& that labor is the only human symbol of Omnipotence.

JAMES A. GARFIELD
Address at Hiram, Ohio, June 14, 1867;
Garfield and Education, p. 22

7. Labor is the capital of our workingmen.

GROVER CLEVELAND
First Annual Message to Congress, Dec. 5, 1885;
Writings and Speeches, p. 67

8. Our labor is honorable in the eyes of every American citizen; and as it lies at the foundation of our development and progress, it is entitled, without affectation or hypocrisy, to the utmost regard. The standard of our laborers' life should not be measured by that of any other country less favored, and they are entitled to their full share of all our advantages.

GROVER CLEVELAND
Third Annual Message to Congress, Dec. 6, 1887;
Messages and Papers, p. 5170

9.   We are a nation of working people. We glory in the fact that in the dignity and elevation of labor we find our greatest distinction among the nations of earth.

WILLIAM MCKINLEY

Speech in Chicago, Ill., July 4, 1895; *Life and Speeches,* p. 158

10.   For labor, a short day is better than a short dollar.

WILLIAM MCKINLEY

To Henry Cabot Lodge, Sept. 8, 1900; *Pamphlet,* p. 5

11.   There is no antidote to worry to be compared with hard labor at important tasks which keep the mind stretched to large views.

WOODROW WILSON

Atlantic Monthly, March, 1897; *Public Papers, I,* 295

12.   The working people of America are, of course, the backbone of the nation.

WOODROW WILSON

Acceptance, at Sea Girt, N.J., of Nomination for Presidency,
Aug. 7, 1912; *Crossroads,* p. 30

13.   Labor is not a commodity. It is a form of cooperation.

WOODROW WILSON

Speech at Long Branch, N.J., Sept. 2, 1916; *Public Papers, IV,* 303

14.   The door of opportunity swings open in our country. Through it, in constant flow, go those who toil. America recognizes no aristocracy save those who work. The badge of service is the sole requirement for admission to the ranks of our nobility.

CALVIN COOLIDGE

Address to labor leaders, Washington, D.C., Sept. 1, 1924;
Foundations, p. 76

See also Education 9, Idleness, Property 7, Slavery 8, 14, 25, 27, Wealth 8, Work

Labor Unions

1.   It is one of the characteristics of a free and democratic nation that it have free and independent labor unions. In country after country in other lands, labor unions have disappeared as the iron hand of the dictator has taken command. Only in free lands have free labor unions survived. When union workers assemble with freedom and independence in a convention . . . it is proof that American democracy has remained unimpaired; it is a symbol of our determination to keep it free.

FRANKLIN DELANO ROOSEVELT

Speech to the Teamsters Union, Washington, D.C., Sept. 11, 1940;
Public Papers, IX, 408

Language

1. I am of opinion, that till the age of about sixteen, we are best employed on languages: Latin, Greek, French, and Spanish. . . . I think Greek the least useful.

THOMAS JEFFERSON
To John Wayles Eppes, July 28, 1787; *Works, II*, 192

2. The new circumstances under which we are placed call for new words, new phrases, and for the transfer of old words to new objects. An American dialect will therefore be formed.

THOMAS JEFFERSON
To John Waldo, Aug. 16, 1813; *Writings, XIII*, 340

Latin America

1. [These Latin American States] lying to the south of us, which have always been our neighbors, will now be drawn closer to us by innumerable ties, and, I hope, chief of all, by the tie of a common understanding of each other. Interest does not tie nations together; it sometimes separates them. But sympathy and understanding does unite them, and I believe that by the new route [the Panama Canal] that is just about to be opened, while we physically cut two continents asunder, we spiritually unite them.

WOODROW WILSON
Speech at Mobile, Ala., Oct. 27, 1913; *State Papers*, p. 32

2. As a result of . . . policies, carried on throughout my administration . . . we established a good will in Latin America not hitherto known for many years, under the specific term "good neighbors."

HERBERT HOOVER
1933; *Memoirs, II*, 334

See also Monroe Doctrine

Laws

1. Laws made by common consent must not be trampled on by individuals.

GEORGE WASHINGTON
To Colonel Vanneter, 1781; *Writings (Fitzpatrick), III*, 24

2. It is not true . . . that any people ever existed who loved the public better than themselves, their private friends, neighbors, etc., and therefore this kind of virtue, this sort of love, is as precarious a foundation for liberty as honor or fear; it is the laws alone that really love the country, the public, the whole better than any part; and that form of government which unites all the virtue, honor, and fear of the citizens, in a reverence and obedience to the laws, is the only one in which liberty can be secure, and

all orders and ranks, and parties, compelled to prefer the public good before their own; that is the government for which we plead.

JOHN ADAMS
A Defence of the Constitutions of the Government of the
United States of America, 1787–88; *Works, VI,* 208

3. Ignorance of the law is no excuse in any country. If it were, the laws
would lose their effect, because it can be always pretended.

THOMAS JEFFERSON
To M. Limozin, Dec. 22, 1787; *Works, II,* 338

4. It is more dangerous that even a guilty person should be punished
without the forms of law than that he should escape.

THOMAS JEFFERSON
To William Carmichael, May 27, 1788; *Ibid.,* 399

5. The execution of the laws is more important than the making them.

THOMAS JEFFERSON
To Abbé Arnond, July 19, 1789; *Ibid., III,* 81

6. A strict observance of the written laws is doubtless *one* of the high
virtues of a good citizen, but it is not the *highest*. The laws of necessity, of
self-preservation, of saving our country when in danger, are of higher
obligation.

THOMAS JEFFERSON
To J. B. Colvin, Sept. 20, 1810; *Writings, XII,* 418

7. Laws are made for men of ordinary understanding, and should therefore be construed by the ordinary rules of common sense. Their meaning
is not to be sought for in metaphysical subtleties, which may make anything mean everything or nothing, at pleasure.

THOMAS JEFFERSON
To Judge William Johnson, June 12, 1823; *Works, VII,* 297

8. The national will is the supreme law of the Republic, and on all subjects within the limits of his constitutional powers should be faithfully
obeyed by the public servant.

MARTIN VAN BUREN
First Annual Message to Congress, Dec. 5, 1837;
Messages and Papers, p. 1597

9. Let every American, every lover of liberty, every well-wisher to his
posterity swear by the blood of the Revolution never to violate in the least
particular the laws of the country, and never to tolerate their violation by
others. . . .

When I so pressingly urge a strict observance of the laws, let me not be
understood as saying there are no bad laws, or that grievances may not

arise for the redress of which no legal provisions have been made. I mean to say no such thing. But I do mean to say that although bad laws, if they exist, should be repealed as soon as possible, still, while they continue in force, for the sake of the example they should be religiously observed.

ABRAHAM LINCOLN
Speech at Springfield, Ill., Jan. 27, 1837; *Complete Works, I,* 42

10. Any serious breach of the organic law, persisted in for a considerable time, can not but create fears for the stability of our institutions. Habitual violation of prescribed rules, which we bind ourselves to observe, must demoralize the people. Our only standard of civil duty being set at naught, the sheet anchor of our political morality is lost, the public conscience swings from its moorings and yields to every impulse of passion and interest.

ANDREW JOHNSON
Third Annual Message to Congress, Dec. 3, 1867;
Messages and Papers, p. 3765

11. I know no method to secure the repeal of bad or obnoxious laws so effective as their stringent execution.

ULYSSES S. GRANT
First Inaugural Address, Mar. 4, 1869

12. To the law we bow with reverence. It is the one king that commands our allegiance. We will change our king when his rule is oppressive.

BENJAMIN HARRISON
At Indianapolis, Ind., July 12, 1888; *Speeches,* p. 46

13. No good cause can be promoted upon the lines of lawlessness. Mobs do not discriminate, and the punishments inflicted by them have no repressive or salutary influence.

BENJAMIN HARRISON
Acceptance of Renomination for Presidency, Sept. 3, 1892;
Public Papers and Addresses, p. 24

14. Those who would use the law as a defense must not deny that use of it to others.

BENJAMIN HARRISON
As I Knew Them, p. 182

15. Law is largely crystallized custom, largely a mass of remedies which have been slowly evolved to meet the wrongs with which humanity has become thoroughly familiar.

THEODORE ROOSEVELT
Annual Message as Governor, Albany, N.Y., Jan. 3, 1900;
Works, XV, 44

16. No nation ever yet retained its freedom for any length of time after

losing its respect for the law, after losing the law-abiding spirit, the spirit that really makes orderly liberty.

THEODORE ROOSEVELT

Speech at Galena, Ill., Apr. 27, 1900; *Ibid., XIII*, 437

17. It is difficult to make our material condition better by the best laws, but it is easy enough to ruin it by bad laws.

THEODORE ROOSEVELT

Speech at Providence, R.I., Aug. 23, 1902;
Presidential Addresses, p. 99

18. No man is above the law and no man is below it; nor do we ask any man's permission when we require him to obey it. Obedience to the law is demanded as a right; not asked as a favor.

THEODORE ROOSEVELT

Third Annual Message to Congress, Dec. 7, 1903; *Works, XV*, 172

19. I give my hearty support in upholding the law, in keeping order, in putting down violence, whether by mob or by an individual. There need not be the slightest apprehension in the heart of the most timid that ever mob spirit will triumph in this country. . . . If ever the need arises *back of the City stands the State and back of the State stands the Nation.*

THEODORE ROOSEVELT

Speech in Chicago, Ill., May 10, 1905;
From McKinley to Harding, p. 142

20. No law is worth anything unless there is the right kind of man behind it.

THEODORE ROOSEVELT

"Nationalism and Progress"; *Works, XVII*, 63

21. We have a right to expect that judges will have their eyes open, even though the law which they administer hasn't awakened. . . .

What this country needs above everything else is a body of laws which will look after the men who are on the make rather than the men who are already made. Because the men who are already made are not going to live indefinitely, and they are not always kind enough to leave sons as able and as honest as they are.

WOODROW WILSON

1912; *New Freedom (Hale)*, pp. 13, 17

22. Law was brought in not to guide the strong, but to protect the weak. . . . Law is meant more for the beginners in every enterprise than for those who have achieved. Law is beckoning on to the future generations, heartening them, cheering them. . . .

WOODROW WILSON

Address at Detroit, Mich., Sept. 19, 1912; *Crossroads*, p. 212

23. The first duty of law is to keep sound the society it serves.

WOODROW WILSON
First Inaugural Address, Mar. 4, 1913

24. There is an old saying that the laws are silent in the presence of war. Alas, yes; not only the civil laws of individual nations but also apparently the law that governs the relation of nations with one another must at times fall silent and look on in dumb impotency.

WOODROW WILSON
Address in Chicago, Ill., Jan. 31, 1916; *State Papers,* p. 182

25. Laws, of course, represent restrictions upon individual liberty, and in these very restrictions make liberty more secure.

WARREN G. HARDING
Speech at Denver, Colo., June 25, 1923;
Messages and Papers, p. 9272

26. Men do not make laws. They do but discover them. Laws must be justified by something more than the will of the majority. They must rest on the eternal foundation of righteousness.

CALVIN COOLIDGE
Address to Massachusetts State Senate, Jan. 7, 1914;
Citizenship, p. 55

27. The observance of the law is the greatest solvent of public ills.

CALVIN COOLIDGE
Acceptance of Nomination for Vice-Presidency, Chicago, Ill.,
July 27, 1920

28. War is the rule of Force. Peace is the reign of Law. Let war and all force end, and peace and all law reign.

CALVIN COOLIDGE
Armistice Day Proclamation, Oct. 21, 1919;
Calvin Coolidge (Hennessy), p. 237

29. A large responsibility rests directly upon our citizens. . . . If citizens do not like a law, their duty is to discourage its violation; their right is openly to work for its repeal.

HERBERT HOOVER
Inaugural Address, Mar. 4, 1929

30. A nation does not fail from its growth of wealth or power. But no nation can for long survive the failure of its citizens to respect and obey the laws which they themselves make.

HERBERT HOOVER
To Wickersham Commission, May 28, 1929; *State Papers, I,* 63

31. If the law is upheld only by government officials, then all law is at an end.

HERBERT HOOVER

Message to Congress, Dec. 3, 1929; *Ibid.*, p. 166

32. Time and again a number of people—I, among them—have argued that you cannot change people's hearts merely by laws. Laws presumably express the conscience of a nation and its determination or will to do something.

DWIGHT D. EISENHOWER

News conference, Sept. 3, 1957;

Public Papers . . . Eisenhower, 1957, p. 640

33. A foundation of our American way of life is our national respect for law.

DWIGHT D. EISENHOWER

Radio and television address, Sept. 24, 1957; *Ibid.*, p. 693

34. We have never stopped sin by passing laws; and in the same way, we are not going to take a great moral ideal and achieve it merely by law.

DWIGHT D. EISENHOWER

News conference, May 13, 1959;

Public Papers . . . Eisenhower, 1959, p. 388

35. Law alone cannot make men see right.

JOHN F. KENNEDY

Radio and television address, June 11, 1963;

Vital Speeches, July 1, 1963, p. 546

See also America 8, Coercion 2, 3, Constitution 4, Corruption 3, Disarmament 3, Discipline 2, Discrimination 1, Government 7, 47, Lawyers, Legislation, Liberty 7, 23, 30, 34, 42, 43, Majorities 11, Negroes 10, Peace 44, 46, 57, People (The) 2, 14, 32, Politics 10, 13, Prohibition 3, Public Office 15, Public Opinion 11, Reforms 6, Religion 29, Republics 1, Rights 16, Security 6, Self-Government 6, Slavery 12, Statesmanship 5, Union 21

Lawyers

1. The study of law is useful in a variety of points of view. It qualifies a man to be useful to himself, to his neighbors and to the public. It is the most certain stepping-stone to preferment in the political line.

THOMAS JEFFERSON

To Thomas M. Randolph, May 30, 1790; *Writings, VIII*, 31

2. Were we to act but in cases where no contrary opinion of a lawyer can be had, we should never act.

THOMAS JEFFERSON

To Albert Gallatin, Sept. 20, 1808; *Ibid., XII*, 169

3. In law it is good policy never to plead what you need not, lest you oblige yourself to prove what you cannot.

ABRAHAM LINCOLN

To U. F. Linder, Feb. 20, 1848; *Complete Works, II*, 3

See also Congress 2, Laws

Leadership

1. In times of peace the people look most to their representatives; but in war, to the executive solely.

THOMAS JEFFERSON

To Caesar A. Rodney, Feb. 10, 1810; *Works, V*, 501

2. A good leader can't get too far ahead of his followers.

FRANKLIN DELANO ROOSEVELT
1940; Public Years (Baruch), p. 279

3. If we falter in our leadership we may endanger the peace of the world, and we shall surely endanger the welfare of the nation.

HARRY S. TRUMAN
Message to Congress, Mar. 12, 1947; Memoirs, II, 106

4. We know—and all the world constantly reminds us—that the future well-being of humanity depends directly upon America's leadership.

I say emphatically that this leadership depends no less directly upon the faith, the courage, the love of freedom, and the capacity for sacrifice of every American citizen, every American home, every American community.

DWIGHT D. EISENHOWER

Address at Atlantic City, N.J., Oct. 6, 1953; *Peace*, p. 42

See also Equality 10, Government 107, History 17, Honesty 7, Opportunity, Political Parties 21, Politics 26, Power 28, Presidency (The) 68, 76, United States 7

League of Nations

1. It would be a master stroke if those great Powers honestly bent on peace would form a league of peace, not only to keep the peace among themselves, but to prevent, by force if necessary, its being broken by others. The man or statesman who should bring about such a condition would have earned his place in history for all time and his title to the gratitude of all mankind.

THEODORE ROOSEVELT

Nobel Prize lecture, May 5, 1910, Christiana, Norway;
Americanism, p. 246

2. The League of Nations was the only hope for mankind. . . . Dare we reject it and break the heart of the world?

WOODROW WILSON
Address to the Senate, July 10, 1919; *Public Papers, V,* 548

3. Is the League an absolute guarantee against war? No, I do not know any absolute guarantee against the errors of human judgment or the violence of human passion, but I tell you this: with a cooling space of nine months for human passion, not much of it will keep hot. . . . Illustrating the great by the small, that is true of the passions of nations. . . . Give them space to cool off. . . . I believe that men will see the truth.

WOODROW WILSON
Speech at Pueblo, Colo., Sept. 25, 1919; *Ibid., VI,* 415

4. The world was led to it by its suffering; it might not have worked just yet; to be a sure success a League of Nations must not come from suffering but from the hearts and spirit of men. We are still in darkness but I am sure it is the darkness that eventually lightens.

WOODROW WILSON
1924; *As I Knew Them,* p. 518

5. I stand for a world association of free nations. I stand against an association of nations in which we will be under the flag of a world supergovernment, and no longer under the American flag. To serve mankind, it is not necessary to subject our country to foreclosure by the sheriff of internationalism.

WARREN G. HARDING
At Marion, Ohio, Oct. 1, 1920;
Speeches of Warren G. Harding, p. 243

6. The conception of the League of Nations was a response to a manifest world hunger. . . . Whether it achieves the great things hoped for, or comes to supercedure, or to failure, the American unwillingness to be a part of it has been expressed.

WARREN G. HARDING
Address to the Senate, Feb. 10, 1922;
Messages and Papers, p. 9072

7. The League exists as a foreign agency. We hope it will be helpful. But the United States sees no reason to limit its own freedom and independence of action by joining it.

CALVIN COOLIDGE
First Annual Message to Congress, Dec. 6, 1923; *Ibid.,* p. 9341

8. From the experience with the League we could have learned something as to the practical results in the use of force to prevent aggression. General commitments of many nations . . . to use force . . . will not

hold against the shifting tides in relations between nations and the changing interest of peoples.

Nor can the use of force be directed by a debating society.

HERBERT HOOVER
1933; *Memoirs, II,* 378

9.   The tragedy of the League was that it was turned into an instrument to protect imperial spoils of war.

HERBERT HOOVER
Address at Emporia, Kan., July 11, 1950; *American Road,* p. 74

10.   The Grand Plan of Henry the Fourth must have given Woodrow Wilson the idea for a League of Nations, because the Grand Plan, or "Great Design," proposed an international union of rulers to keep the peace.

HARRY S. TRUMAN
Interview, *ca.* 1950; *Mr. President,* p. 85

See also United Nations, War 49, 57

Legislation

1.   It is a wise and safe rule to follow in all legislation that whatever the people can do without legislation will be better than by the intervention of the State and Nation.

JAMES A. GARFIELD
Maxims, p. 18

2.   The world is not going to be saved by legislation, and it is not going to be injured by an occasional two years of respite from the panacea and magic that many modern schools of politicians seem to think are to be found in the words: "Be it enacted!"

WILLIAM HOWARD TAFT
Speech at University of Virginia, January, 1915; *Presidency,* p. 10

3.   Necessarily legislation is a matter of compromise. The full ideal is seldom attained.

WARREN G. HARDING
To Congress, Dec. 6, 1921; *Message,* p. 4

4.   Let there be a purpose in all . . . legislation to recognize the right of man to be well born, well nurtured, well educated, well employed and well paid. This is no gospel of ease and selfishness, or class distinction, but a gospel of effort and service, of universal application.

CALVIN COOLIDGE
Speech at Boston, Mass., Jan. 1, 1919; *Coolidge (Hennessy),* p. 91

5. Don't hurry to legislate. Give administration a chance to catch up with legislation.

CALVIN COOLIDGE

To Massachusetts State Senate, Jan. 7, 1914; Citizenship, p. 115

6. Legislative action is always clumsy—it is incapable of adjustment to shifting needs. It often enough produces new economic currents more abusive than those intended to be cured. Government too often becomes the persecutor instead of the regulator.

HERBERT HOOVER

Address, May 7, 1924; Memoirs, II, 171

See also Laws, Reforms 4, States' Rights 13, Veto Power

Leisure

1. We may divide the struggles of the human race into two chapters: first, the fight to get leisure; and second, what to do with our leisure when we have won it. Like all blessings, leisure is a bad thing unless it is well used.

JAMES A. GARFIELD

Address at Chautauqua, N.Y., Aug. 9, 1880; Gems, p. 50

2. The moral and spiritual forces of our country do not lose ground in the hours we are busy on our jobs; their battle is the leisure time. We are organizing the production of leisure. We need better organization of its consumption.

HERBERT HOOVER

1950; Memoirs, II, 166

See also Security 2

Letters

1. The letters of a person, especially of one whose business has been chiefly transacted by letters, form the only full and genuine journal of his life; and few can let them go out of their hand while they live. A life written after these hoards become opened to investigation must supersede any previous one.

THOMAS JEFFERSON

Liberalism

1. True liberalism seeks all legitimate freedom first, in the confident belief that without such freedom the pursuit of other blessings is in vain. Liberalism is a force true of the spirit, proceeding from the deep realization that economic freedom cannot be sacrificed if political freedom is to be preserved.

HERBERT HOOVER

Speech at Colorado Springs, Colo., Mar. 7, 1936; Memoirs, II, 203

2. The most serious threat to our institutions comes from those who refuse to face the need for change. Liberalism becomes the protection for the far-sighted conservative.

FRANKLIN DELANO ROOSEVELT
Address at Syracuse, N.Y., Sept. 29, 1936; *Public Papers, V,* 389

See also Conservatism, Political Philosophy 4, Slogans

Liberty

1. Liberty, when it begins to take root, is a plant of rapid growth.

GEORGE WASHINGTON
To James Madison, Mar. 2, 1788; *Writings*
(*Fitzpatrick*), *XXIX,* 431

2. To the security of a free constitution it contributes . . . to discriminate the spirit of liberty from that of licentiousness. . . .

GEORGE WASHINGTON
First Annual Message to Congress, Jan. 8, 1790;
Messages and Papers, p. 58

3. A constitution of government, once changed from freedom, can never be restored. Liberty, once lost, is lost forever.

JOHN ADAMS
To Abigail Adams, July 7, 1775; *Familiar Letters,* p. 76

4. The decree is gone forth, and it cannot be recalled, that a more equal liberty than has prevailed in other parts of the earth, must be established in America. That exuberance of pride which has produced an insolent domination in a few, a very few, opulent, monopolizing families, will be brought down nearer to the confines of reason and moderation, than they have been used to.

JOHN ADAMS
To Patrick Henry, June 3, 1776; *Works, IX,* 387

5. The way to secure liberty is to place it in the people's hands, that is, to give them the power at all times to defend it in the legislature and in the courts of justice.

JOHN ADAMS
A Defence of the Constitutions of the Government of the
United States of America, 1787–88; *Ibid., VI,* 208

6. Liberty, according to my metaphysics . . . is a self-determining power in an intellectual agent. It implies thought and choice and power.

JOHN ADAMS
To John Taylor, Apr. 15, 1814; *Ibid.,* p. 448

7. I would define liberty to be a power to do as we would be done by.

The definition of liberty to be the power of doing whatever the law permits, meaning the civil laws, does not seem satisfactory.

JOHN ADAMS

To J. H. Tiffany, Mar. 31, 1819; *Ibid., X,* 377

8. It is an axiom in my mind that our liberty can never be safe but in the hands of the people themselves, and that, too, of the people with a certain degree of instruction.

THOMAS JEFFERSON

To George Washington, Jan. 4, 1786; *Writings, XIX,* 24

9. The tree of liberty must be refreshed from time to time with the blood of patriots and tyrants. It is its natural manure.

THOMAS JEFFERSON

To W. S. Smith, Nov. 13, 1787

10. The ground of liberty is to be gained by inches.

THOMAS JEFFERSON

To Rev. Charles Clay, Jan. 27, 1790; *Writings, VI,* 30

11. We are not to expect to be translated from despotism to liberty in a feather bed.

THOMAS JEFFERSON

To Marquis de Lafayette, Apr. 2, 1790; *Ibid., VIII,* 13

12. Timid men who prefer the calm of despotism to the tempestuous sea of liberty.

THOMAS JEFFERSON

To Philip Mazzei, Jan. 1, 1797; *Ibid., VII,* 76

13. The boisterous sea of liberty is never without a wave.

THOMAS JEFFERSON

To Richard Rush, Oct. 20, 1820; *Ibid., XV,* 283

14. Liberty is to faction what air is to fire, an aliment without which it instantly expires. But it could not be less folly to abolish liberty, which is essential to political life, because it nourishes faction, than it would be to wish annihilation of air, which is essential to animal life, because it imparts to fire its destructive agency.

JAMES MADISON

"Publius," 1787; *Federalist, No. 10*

15. Experience has proved that the real danger to America and to liberty lies in the defect of *energy and stability* in the present establishments of the United States.

JAMES MADISON

To Philip Mazzei, Oct. 8, 1788; *Writings (Hunt), V,* 267

16. Liberty and order will never be *perfectly* safe, until a trespass on

the constitutional provisions for either, shall be felt with the same keenness that resents an invasion of the dearest rights, until every citizen shall be an Argus to espy, and an Aegeon to avenge, the unhallowed deed.

JAMES MADISON
Speech to Congress, 1792; *Ibid., VI,* 85

17. The distinction between liberty and licentiousness is . . . a repetition of the Protean doctrine of implication, which is ever ready to work its ends by varying its shape.

JAMES MADISON
Address to General Assembly of Virginia, Jan. 23, 1799;
Complete Madison, p. 295

18. Civil liberty *can* be established on no foundation of human reason which will not at the same time demonstrate the right to religious freedom. . . . The tendency of the spirit of the age is strong toward religious liberty.

JOHN QUINCY ADAMS
To Richard Anderson, May 27, 1823; *Writings (Ford), VII,* 466

19. Liberty is power . . . the nation blessed with the largest portion of liberty must in proportion to its numbers be the most powerful nation upon earth.

JOHN QUINCY ADAMS
First Annual Message to Congress, Dec. 6, 1825;
Messages and Papers, p. 882

20. Eternal vigilance by the people is the price of liberty, and . . . you must pay the price if you wish to secure the blessing.

ANDREW JACKSON
Farewell Address, Mar. 4, 1837; *Ibid.,* p. 1523

21. The spirit of liberty is the sovereign balm for every injury which our institutions may receive. On the contrary, no care that can be used in the construction of our government, no division of powers, no distribution of checks in its several departments, will prove effectual to keep us a free people if this spirit is suffered to decay, and decay it will without constant nurture.

WILLIAM HENRY HARRISON
Inaugural Address, Mar. 4, 1841

22. The blessings of Liberty which our Constitution secures may be enjoyed alike by minorities and majorities.

JAMES K. POLK
Inaugural Address, Mar. 4, 1845

23. Liberty unregulated by law degenerates into anarchy, which soon becomes the most horrid of all despotisms.

MILLARD FILLMORE
Third Annual Message to Congress, Dec. 6, 1852;
Messages and Papers, p. 2716

24. Liberty is Hesperian fruit, and can only be preserved by watchful jealousy.

JAMES BUCHANAN
Speech at Greensburgh, Pa., Oct. 7, 1852; *Life, II,* 48

25. Let us readopt the Declaration of Independence, and with it the practices and policy which harmonize with it. Let North and South—let all Americans—let all lovers of liberty everywhere join in the great and good work. If we do this, we shall not only save the Union, but we shall have so saved it as to make and keep it forever worthy of the saving. We shall have so saved it that the succeeding millions of free, happy people, the world over, shall rise up and call us blessed to the latest generations.

ABRAHAM LINCOLN
Speech at Peoria, Ill., Oct. 16, 1854; *Complete Works, II,* 248

26. The world has never had a good definition of the word liberty, and the American people, just now, are much in want of one. We all declare for liberty; but in using the same *word* we do not mean the same *thing*. With some the word liberty may mean for each man to do as he pleases with himself, and the product of his labor; while with others the same word may mean for some to do as they please with other men, and the product of other men's labor. Here are two, not only different, but incompatible things, called by the same name—liberty. And it follows that each of the things is, by the respective parties, called by two different and incompatible names—liberty and tyranny.

ABRAHAM LINCOLN
Address at Baltimore, Md., Apr. 18, 1864; *Ibid., X,* 77

27. If it were my destiny to die for the cause of liberty I would die upon the tomb of the Union, the American flag as my winding sheet.

ANDREW JOHNSON
To soldiers in camp, 1862; *Not Guilty,* p. 68

28. God gave us Lincoln and Liberty; let us fight for both.

ULYSSES S. GRANT
A toast, Feb. 22, 1863; *Speeches,* p. 7

29. Human liberty, the only true foundation of human government.

ULYSSES S. GRANT
To citizens of Memphis, Tenn., 1863; *Ibid.,* p. 7

30. It should not be forgotten . . . that liberty does not mean lawlessness. Liberty to make our own laws does not give us license to break them. Liberty to make our own laws commands a duty to observe them ourselves and enforce obedience among all others within their jurisdiction. Liberty, my fellow citizens, is responsibility, and responsibility is duty, and that duty is to preserve the exceptional liberty we enjoy within the law and for the law and by the law.

WILLIAM McKINLEY
Address at Cleveland, Ohio, July 4, 1894; *Eloquence, IX,* 853

31. When liberty becomes license, some form of one-man power is not far distant.

THEODORE ROOSEVELT
1887; *Works, VII,* 322

32. Liberty is a means in the pursuit of happiness.

WILLIAM HOWARD TAFT
At Fresno, Cal., Oct. 10, 1909; *Presidential Addresses,* p. 337

33. Liberty cannot live apart from constitutional principle.

WOODROW WILSON
Political Science Quarterly, June, 1887; *Ideals,* p. 34

34. The ideals of liberty cannot be fixed from generation to generation; only its conception can be, the large image of what it is. Liberty fixed in unalterable law would be no liberty at all.

WOODROW WILSON
1908; *Constitutional Government,* p. 4

35. Liberty has never come from the government. Liberty has always come from the subjects of it. The history of liberty is a history of resistance. The history of liberty is a history of limitations of governmental power, not the increase of it.

WOODROW WILSON
Speech at New York Press Club, Sept. 9, 1912; *Crossroads,* p. 130

36. I would rather belong to a poor nation that was free than to a rich nation that had ceased to be in love with liberty. We shall not be poor if we love liberty.

WOODROW WILSON
Speech at Mobile, Ala., Oct. 27, 1913; *State Papers,* p. 36

37. Liberty does not consist . . . in mere general declarations of the rights of man. It consists in the translation of those declarations into definite action.

WOODROW WILSON
Speech in Philadelphia, Pa., July 4, 1914; *Public Papers, III,* 140

38. Liberty is often a fierce and intractable thing, to which no bounds can be set, and to which no bounds of a few men's choosing ought ever to be set.

WOODROW WILSON
Third Annual Message to Congress, Dec. 7, 1915;
State Papers, p. 135

39. We do not profess to be the champions of liberty, and then consent to see liberty destroyed.

WOODROW WILSON
Address at Indianapolis, Ind., Sept. 4, 1919; *Public Papers, V*, 615

40. Liberty is a thing of slow construction. Liberty is a thing of universal co-operation. Liberty is a thing which you must build up by habit. Liberty is a thing which is rooted and grounded in character.

WOODROW WILSON
Address at St. Paul, Minn., Sept. 9, 1919; *Ibid., VI*, 85

41. Liberty is not itself government. In the wrong hands, in hands unpracticed, undisciplined, it is incompatible with government.

WOODROW WILSON
Public Years (Baruch), p. 147

42. Liberty—liberty within the law—and civilization are inseparable . . . and there comes to Americans the profound assurance that our representative government is the highest expression and surest guaranty of both.

WARREN G. HARDING
Inaugural Address, Mar. 4, 1921

43. To support the Constitution, to observe the laws, is to be true to our own higher nature. That is the path, and the only path, towards liberty. . . . Liberty is not collective, it is personal. All liberty is individual liberty.

CALVIN COOLIDGE
Speech in Washington, D.C., Sept. 21, 1924; *Foundations*, p. 108

44. The fundamental precept of liberty is toleration. We cannot permit any inquisition either within or without the law or apply any religious test to the holding of office. The mind of America must be forever free.

CALVIN COOLIDGE
Second Inaugural Address, Mar. 4, 1925

45. True liberty requires that all claims to human power must be subject to live criticism and the common judgment.

HERBERT HOOVER
1934; *Challenge*, p. 30

46.   I believe in the American System of Liberty. . . . It has faults. But it contains the only real ferment of progress.

HERBERT HOOVER
Speech at Colorado Springs, Colo., Mar. 7, 1936; Policies, p. 24

47.   It is all very well to talk of "liberation" or "peaceful evolution." But until we formulate a program of concrete steps as to what this nation can do to help achieve such goals, we are offering those still hopeful partisans of freedom behind the Iron Curtain nothing but empty oratory.

JOHN F. KENNEDY
Speech in the Senate, July 8, 1957; Strategy, p. 115

48.   Let every nation know, whether it wishes us well or ill, that we shall pay any price, bear any burden, meet any hardship, support any friend, oppose any foe in order to assure the survival and the success of liberty.

JOHN F. KENNEDY
Inaugural Address, Jan. 20, 1961

Libraries

1.   Whenever I have completed my library, my end will not be answered. Fame, fortune, power, say some, are the ends intended by a library. The service of God, country, clients, fellow men, say others. Which of these lie dearest to my heart?

JOHN ADAMS
Diary, Jan. 30, 1768; Works, II, 208

2.   Nothing would do more extensive good at small expense than the establishment of a small, circulating library in every county, to consist of a few well-chosen books, to be lent to the people of the county, under such regulations as would secure their safe return in due time.

THOMAS JEFFERSON
To John Wyche, May 19, 1809; Writings, XII, 282

3.   I think Carlyle's saying that the true university is a collection of books is of greater force today than when the Sage of Chelsea uttered it. I have an unshaken conviction that democracy can never be undermined if we maintain our library resources and a national intelligence capable of utilizing them.

FRANKLIN DELANO ROOSEVELT
To Herbert Putnam, 1953; Bookburners

4.   Good libraries are as essential to an educated and informed people as the school system itself. The library is not only the custodian of our cultural heritage but the key to progress and the advancement of knowledge. With increasing leisure its resources can enrich the quality of American life.

Libraries like all other institutions must grow and adapt to changing requirements and conditions. The rate of change in the world today and in our knowledge of it is incredibly fast. We cannot afford to let our libraries slip behind.

JOHN F. KENNEDY
Statement for National Library Week, April, 1963

See also Books

Life

1. The art of life is the avoiding of pain.

THOMAS JEFFERSON
To Maria Cosway, Oct. 12, 1786; *Writings, V,* 439

2. What an ocean is life! And how our barks get separated in beating through it!

THOMAS JEFFERSON
To St. George Tucker, Sept. 10, 1793; *Ibid., VIII,* 41

3. [Advice to a namesake] Adore God; reverence and cherish your parents; love your neighbor as yourself, and your country more than life. Be just; be true; murmur not at the ways of Providence—and the life into which you have entered will be one of eternal and ineffable bliss.

THOMAS JEFFERSON
To Thomas Jefferson Grotjan, Jan. 10, 1824; *Ibid., X,* 287

4. The earth belongs to the living, not the dead.

THOMAS JEFFERSON
To John Wayles Eppes, June 24, 1813; *Ibid., XIII,* 269

5. To carry on the business of life you must have surplus power.

JAMES A. GARFIELD
Speech in Washington, D.C., June 29, 1869; *Lives,* p. 29

6. I wish to preach not the doctrine of ignoble ease but the doctrine of the strenuous life. . . . We admire the man who embodies victorious effort. . . . who has those virile qualities necessary to win in the stern strife of actual life.

THEODORE ROOSEVELT
Address in Chicago, Ill., Apr. 10, 1899; *Works, XIII,* 319

7. Life can mean nothing worth meaning, unless its prime aim is the doing of duty, the achievement of results worth achieving.

THEODORE ROOSEVELT
Address at Oyster Bay, N.Y., Aug. 16, 1903;
Addresses and Papers, p. 166

8. Only those are fit to live who do not fear to die; and none are fit to die who have shrunk from the joy of life and the duty of life.

THEODORE ROOSEVELT
1916; *Works, XVIII,* 199

9. We may well introduce into our lives more courtesy and more politeness—more real, genuine desire to make everybody happy by the little things of life, which after all constitute nearly all there is in life.

WILLIAM HOWARD TAFT
At Salt Lake City, Utah, Sept. 26, 1909;
Presidential Addresses, p. 260

10. The real fruition of life is to do the things we have said we wish to do. There are times when work seems empty and only action seems great. Such a time has come, and in the providence of God America will once more have an opportunity to show the world she was born to serve mankind.

WOODROW WILSON
Speech at Arlington, Va., May 30, 1917; *Foreign Policy,* p. 302

11. It would be folly to ignore that we live in a motor age. . . . It long ago ran down Simple Living, and never halted to inquire about the prostrate figure which fell as its victim.

WARREN G. HARDING
Second Annual Message to Congress, Dec. 8, 1922; *Message,* p. 4

See also Action 2, Death, Effort, Greatness 2, Rights 2, Society 1, Work

Loans

1. Our experience in war shows that foreign governments which are borrowing our money on easy terms cannot expend it with the economy of private individuals and it results in vast waste. Our government cannot higgle in the market to exact the securities and returns appropriate to varied risk that merchants and banks can and will exact. . . . There is no court to which a government can appeal for collection of debt except a battleship. The whole process is involved in inflation, in waste, and in intrigue. The only direct loans of our government should be humane loans to prevent starvation.

HERBERT HOOVER
Speech in Chicago, Ill., Dec. 10, 1920; *Memoirs, II,* 14

2. No nation as a government should borrow or no government lend and nations should discourage their citizens from borrowing or lending unless this money is to be devoted to productive enterprise.

HERBERT HOOVER
Speech to Pan-American Conference, Oct. 8, 1931;
State Papers, II, 7

Loyalty

1. I entirely appreciate loyalty to one's friends, but loyalty to the cause of justice and honor stands above it.

THEODORE ROOSEVELT
To a Senator, May 15, 1905; *His Time, I,* 443

2. Loyalty means nothing unless it has at heart the absolute principle of self-sacrifice.

WOODROW WILSON

Address in Washington, D.C., July 13, 1916; Selections, p. 88

See also Americans 3, Fidelity, Negroes 7

Majorities

1. That the desires of the majority of the people are often for injustice and inhumanity against the minority, is demonstrated by every page of the history of the whole world.

JOHN ADAMS

A Defence of the Constitutions of the Government of the
United States of America, 1787–88; Works, VI, 48

2. Though the will of the majority is in all cases to prevail, that will, to be rightful, must be reasonable. . . . The minority possess their equal rights, which equal laws must protect, and to violate which would be oppression.

THOMAS JEFFERSON

First Inaugural Address, Mar. 4, 1801

3. Great innovations should not be forced on slender majorities.

THOMAS JEFFERSON

To Gen. Thaddeus Kosciusko, May 2, 1808; Works, V, 282

4. There is no maxim, in my opinion, which is more liable to be mis-applied, and which, therefore, more needs elucidation, than the current one, that the interest of the majority is the political standard of right and wrong.

JAMES MADISON

To James Monroe, Oct. 5, 1786; Complete Madison, p. 45

5. On a candid examination of history, we shall find that turbulence, violence, and abuse of power, by the majority, trampling on the rights of the minority, have produced factions and commotions which, in re-publics, have, more frequently than any other cause, produced despotism.

JAMES MADISON

Speech in the Virginia Convention, June 5, 1788; Ibid., p. 46

6. The American people are too well schooled in the duty and practice of submitting to the will of the majority to permit any serious uneasiness on that account.

JAMES MADISON

To Martin Van Buren, July 5, 1830; Letters, IV, 94

7. Desperate courage makes One a majority.

ANDREW JACKSON

Life (Parton), III, title page

8. The bottom principle—sometimes . . . called a cornerstone, sometimes the foundation . . . of our structure of government—is the principle of control by the majority. It is more than the cornerstone or foundation. This structure is a monolith, one from foundation to apex, and that monolith stands for and is this principle of government by majorities, legally ascertained by constitutional methods. Everything else about our government is appendage, it is ornamentation.

BENJAMIN HARRISON
At Detroit, Mich., Feb. 22, 1888; *Speeches*, p. 12

9. The majority voice should be controlling, but it must be after a full, fair, and candid expression.

WILLIAM MCKINLEY
Speech to House of Representatives, May 18, 1888;
Life and Speeches, p. 122

10. You can not have a decent, popular government unless the majority exercise the self-restraint that men with great power ought to exercise.

WILLIAM HOWARD TAFT
At Fresno, Cal., Oct. 10, 1909; *Presidential Addresses*, p. 337

11. One with the law is a majority.

CALVIN COOLIDGE
Acceptance of Nomination for Vice-Presidency, Chicago, Ill.,
July 27, 1920

12. The moment a mere numerical superiority by either states or voters in this country proceeds to ignore the needs and desires of the minority, and for their own selfish purpose or advancement, hamper or oppress that minority, or debar them in any way from equal privileges and equal rights—that moment will mark the failure of our constitutional system.

FRANKLIN DELANO ROOSEVELT
Radio address, Mar. 2, 1930; *New York Times, Mar. 3, 1930*

See also Freedom 10, Government 62, Laws 26, Liberty 22, Minorities, People (The) 27, Republics 11, Suffrage 7

Malice
See Peace 21

Mankind
1. We must . . . make the best of Mankind as they are, since we cannot have them as we wish.

GEORGE WASHINGTON
To Maj.-Gen. Philip Schuyler, Dec. 24, 1775;
Writings (Fitzpatrick), IV, 179

2.   Mankind when left to themselves, are unfit for their own Government.

> GEORGE WASHINGTON
> To Henry Lee, Oct. 31, 1786; *Ibid., XXIX,* 33

3.   What a stupendous, what an incomprehensible machine is man! who can endure toil, famine, stripes, imprisonment, and death itself, in vindication of his own liberty, and the next moment be deaf to all those motives whose power supported him through his trial, and inflict on his fellow men a bondage, one hour of which is fraught with more misery than ages of that which he rose in rebellion to oppose.

> THOMAS JEFFERSON
> Notes, 1785; *Works, IX,* 279

4.   Experience declares that man is the only animal which devours his own kind, for I can apply no milder term to the governments of Europe, and the general prey of the rich on the poor.

> THOMAS JEFFERSON
> To Edward Carrington, Jan. 16, 1787; *Writings, VI,* 58

5.   What a Bedlamite is man!

> THOMAS JEFFERSON
> To John Adams, Jan. 22, 1821; *Ibid., XV,* 309

6.   The generality of mankind have at least sufficient wisdom and patriotism to be reasonably capable of self-government. Through enlightenment and awakening of their nobler instincts they may be made more so.

> JAMES MADISON

7.   Mankind needs a world-wide benediction of understanding. It is needed among individuals, among peoples, among governments, and it will inaugurate an era of good feeling.

> WARREN G. HARDING
> Inaugural Address, Mar. 4, 1921

See also God 4, 8, Ignorance 1, Opinion 8, Peace 39, People (The), Problems, Religion 13, Republics 4, Rights 7

Manners

1.   I would wish my countrymen to adopt just so much of European politeness as to be ready to make all those little sacrifices of self, which really render Europeans amiable, and relieve society from the disagreeable scenes to which rudeness often subjects it.

> THOMAS JEFFERSON
> To Mr. Bellini, Sept. 30, 1785; *Works, I,* 445

See also Life 9, Tolerance 1, Women 2

Martyrs
See Politics 4, Tyranny 1

Materialism

1. I fear we are too much concerned with material things to remember that our real strength lies in spiritual values. I doubt whether there is in this troubled world today, when nations are divided by jealousy and suspicion, a single problem that could not be solved if approached in the spirit of the Sermon on the Mount.

HARRY S. TRUMAN
Address in New York, N.Y., May 11, 1946; *Public Papers*
. . . Truman, 1946, p. 245

2. In the last analysis, our strength does not reside in material things. Our wealth and our arms, our great cities and our mighty buildings will avail us not if we lack spiritual strength to subdue mere objects to the higher purposes of humanity.

One source of spiritual strength is faith—faith in the moral government of the Universe, faith in the reality of ideals, faith which enables man to transcend the vanities of life for the sake of ends beyond himself.

LYNDON B. JOHNSON
Address in Washington, D.C., Dec. 20, 1961; *Story*, p. 189

See also Authors 1, Business 9, Fear 5, Foreign Relations 31, Human Welfare

Maxims

1. In general I esteem it a good maxim, that the best way to preserve the confidence of the people durably is to promote their true interest.

GEORGE WASHINGTON
To Joseph Reed, July 4, 1780; *Writings (Fitzpatrick)*, *VII*, 100

2. Never buy what you do not want because it is cheap; it will be dear to you.

THOMAS JEFFERSON
To Thomas Jefferson Smith, Feb. 21, 1825; *Writings, XVI*, 111

3. Take things always by their smooth handle.

THOMAS JEFFERSON
To Thomas Jefferson Smith, Feb. 21, 1825; *Ibid.*

See also Justice 6, Majorities 4, Navy 7, Political Parties 2, Power 5, Press (The) 13, Veto Power 4

Mercy

See Justice 9, Power 21, Religion 1

Military Matters

1. When we assumed the soldier we did not lay aside the citizen.

GEORGE WASHINGTON
Address to New York Legislature, June 26, 1775; Quotation on the Memorial Amphitheatre in Arlington National Cemetery;
Writings (Fitzpatrick), *III*, 305

2. Discipline and subordination add life and vigor to military movements.
GEORGE WASHINGTON
To Patrick Henry, Oct. 5, 1776; *Ibid., VI,* 167

3. The militia of this country must be considered as the palladium of our security, and the first effectual resort in case of hostility.
GEORGE WASHINGTON
To the Governors, June 8, 1783; *Ibid., XXVI,* 494

4. Overgrown military establishments . . . under any form of government, are inauspicious to liberty and . . . particularly hostile to Republican Liberty.
GEORGE WASHINGTON
Farewell Address, Sept. 19, 1796; *Ibid., XXXV,* 221

5. We must train and classify the whole of our male citizens, and make military instruction a regular part of collegiate education. We can never be safe till this is done.
THOMAS JEFFERSON
To James Monroe, June 18, 1813; *Works, VI,* 131

6. Keep within the requisite limits a standing military force, always remembering that an armed and trained militia is the firmest bulwark of republics—that without standing armies their liberty can never be in danger, nor with large ones safe.
JAMES MADISON
First Inaugural Address, Mar. 4, 1809

7. The safety of these States and everything dear to a free people must depend in an eminent degree on the militia. . . . This arrangement should be formed, too, in time of peace, to be the better prepared for war.
JAMES MONROE
First Inaugural Address, Mar. 4, 1817

8. Considering standing armies as dangerous to free governments in time of peace, I shall not seek to enlarge our present establishment, nor disregard that salutary lesson of political experience which teaches that the military should be held subordinate to the civil power. . . . But the bulwark of our defense is the national militia, which in the present state of our intelligence and population must render us invincible.
ANDREW JACKSON
First Inaugural Address, Mar. 4, 1829

9. The opportunities of observation furnished by my brief experience as a soldier confirmed in my own mind the opinion . . . that the maintenance of large standing armies in our country would be not only dangerous, but unnecessary. . . . The Army as organized must be the nucleus

around which in every time of need the strength of your military power, the sure bulwark of your defense—a national militia—may be readily formed into a well-disciplined and efficient organization.

FRANKLIN PIERCE
Inaugural Address, Mar. 4, 1853

10. Militarism does not consist in the existence of any army. . . . Militarism is a spirit. It is a point of view. It is a system. It is a purpose. The purpose of militarism is to use armies for aggression.

WOODROW WILSON
Speech at West Point, N.Y., June 13, 1916; *Public Papers, IV*, 203

11. I have always believed that the civilian control of the military is one of the strongest foundations of our system of free government. Many of our people are descended from men and women who fled their native countries to escape the oppression of militarism. . . .

One reason that we have been so careful to keep the military within its own preserve is that the very nature of the service hierarchy gives military commanders little if any opportunity to learn the humility that is needed for public service.

HARRY S. TRUMAN
1951; *Memoirs, II*, 444

12. Military pacts provide no long-term solutions.

JOHN F. KENNEDY
Speech in New York, N.Y., Feb. 9, 1959; *Strategy*, p. 156

See also Army, Defense, Discipline, Errors 1, Foreign Relations 24, 36, Freedom 1, Policy 3, Politics 30, 31, Preparedness, Public Opinion 12, Security 8, Veterans, War

Mind

1. I estimate the qualities of the mind: 1, good humor; 2, integrity; 3, industry; 4, science. The preference of the first to the second quality may not at first be acquiesced in; but certainly we had all rather associate with a good humored, light-principled man, than with an ill-tempered rigorist in morality.

THOMAS JEFFERSON
Letter to Benjamin Rush, Jan. 3, 1808; *Works, V*, 226

2. The human mind is our fundamental resource.

JOHN F. KENNEDY
Special Message to the Congress on Education, Feb. 20, 1961;
Tide, p. 129

See also Brains, Health 1, 2, Physical Fitness 3

Minorities

1. Minorities often have been right, but they cease to be right when they use disorderly means.

WOODROW WILSON

Address at Tacoma, Wash., Sept. 13, 1919; *Hope,* p. 143

2. No democracy can long survive which does not accept as fundamental to its very existence the recognition of the rights of its minorities.

FRANKLIN DELANO ROOSEVELT

Speech in Washington, D.C., Jan. 8, 1938; *Public Papers, VII,* 40

See also Government 62, Liberty 22, Majorities, Monopolies 1, 6, Political Parties 21, Republics 11

Mistakes

See Errors

Mobs

1. Progress in the nation is the sum of progress in its individuals. Acts and deeds leading to progress are born out of the womb of the individual mind, not out of the mind of the crowd. The crowd only feels, it has no mind of its own which can plan. The crowd is credulous, it destroys, it hates and it dreams but it never builds. It is one of the most profound of exact psychological truths that man in the mass does not think, but only feels. The mob functions only in a world of emotion.

HERBERT HOOVER

Individualism, p. 24

See also Government 14, 78, Laws 13, 19, Nations 13

Monarchies

See Government 15, Kings, Liberty 1, Public Opinion 10, States' Rights 3, War 7, 30

Money

1. It is not a custom with me to keep money to look at.

GEORGE WASHINGTON

To John P. Custis, Jan. 20, 1780; *Writings (Fitzpatrick), XVII,* 414

2. Those who attend to small expenses are always rich.

JOHN ADAMS

To Abigail Adams, Dec. 18, 1780; *Familiar Letters,* p. 389

3. The glow of one warm thought is to me worth more than money.

THOMAS JEFFERSON

To Charles McPherson, Feb. 25, 1773; *Writings, IV,* 23

4. The purse of the people is the real seat of sensibility. Let it be drawn

upon largely, and they will then listen to truths which could not excite them through any other organ.

THOMAS JEFFERSON
To A. H. Rowan, Sept. 26, 1798; *Ibid., X,* 60

5. Money, and not morality, is the principle of commercial nations.

THOMAS JEFFERSON
To Gov. John Langdon, Mar. 5, 1810; *Works, V,* 513

6. To be liberal with their own money but sparing of that of the Republic was the glory of distinguished public servants among the ancient Romans. When this maxim was reversed, and the public money was employed by artful and ambitious demagogues to secure their own aggrandizement, genuine liberty soon expired. It is true that the forms of the Republic continued for many years; but the animating and inspiring soul had fled forever.

JAMES BUCHANAN
Letter to John Nelson and other citizens of Baltimore, Feb. 3, 1852;
Life, II, 28

7. He mocks the people who proposes that the Government shall protect the rich and that they in turn will care for the laboring poor.

GROVER CLEVELAND
Fourth Annual Message to Congress, Dec. 3, 1888;
Messages and Papers, p. 5361

8. Patriotism is no substitute for a sound currency.

GROVER CLEVELAND
1892; *Man and Statesman, II,* 1

9. There is no dignity quite so impressive, and no independence quite so important as living within your means. . . . Any other course for me would be as the senseless imitation of a fowl which was attempting to light higher than its roost.

CALVIN COOLIDGE
Autobiography, p. 159

10. I believe that . . . the Government itself must be honest fiscally. It must have an honest fiscal policy and it must not indulge in doing anything by deficit spending except in emergency. . . . I believe in the decentralization of power geographically . . . and finally, I believe in preserving the soundness of our money, in the interests of all the people who are going to live on pensions and retired pay.

DWIGHT D. EISENHOWER
News conference, Jan. 30, 1957; *Public Papers . . .
Eisenhower, 1957,* p. 105

11. It is my determined purpose to be a prudent steward of the public funds, to obtain a dollar's worth of results for every dollar we spend.

JOHN F. KENNEDY
Message to Congress, Mar. 24, 1961; *Tide,* p. 100

12. Centuries ago the essayist Burton referred with scorn to those who were "possessed by their money" rather than possessors of it. We . . . do not intend to be mastered by our money or by our monetary problems. We intend to master them, with unity and generosity—and we shall do so in the name of freedom.

JOHN F. KENNEDY
In Washington, D.C., Sept. 20, 1962; *Vital Speeches,*
Oct. 15, 1962, p. 7

See also Avarice, Banks, Debts, Economy, Loans, Maxims 2, Poverty 4, Prosperity, Republics 14, Slogans 1

Monopolies

1. Monopolies . . . are justly classed among the greatest nuisances in Government. . . . Monopolies are sacrifices of the many to the few. Where the power is in the few it is natural for them to sacrifice the many to their own partialities and corruptions. Where the power as with us is in the many not in the few the danger cannot be very great that the few will be thus favored. It is much more to be dreaded that the few will be unnecessarily sacrificed to the many.

JAMES MADISON
To Thomas Jefferson, Oct. 17, 1788; *Writings (Hunt), V,* 275

2. We are debating the . . . difficult problem of how to stop monopoly. . . . Whenever we see monopoly showing its head there is the place for your shillalah.

WOODROW WILSON
Speech in Chicago, Ill., Feb. 12, 1912; *Public Papers, II,* 400

3. The alternative to regulating monopoly is to regulate competition: to say that to go into a community and sell below cost for no other purpose . . . than to squeeze out a competitor shall be an offense against the criminal law of the United States, and anybody who attempts it will have to answer at the bar of a criminal tribunal.

WOODROW WILSON
Speech at Sioux Falls, S.D., Sept. 17, 1912; *Crossroads,* p. 171

4. Monopoly never was conceived in the temper of tolerance. . . . It was conceived with the purpose of special advantage. . . . Justice is what we want, not patronage and condescension and pitiful helpfulness. . . .

WOODROW WILSON
1912; *New Freedom (Hale),* p. 214

5. Monopoly means the atrophy of enterprise.

> WOODROW WILSON
> 1912; *Ibid.,* p. 286

6. With monopolies there can be no industrial democracy. With the control of the few, of whatever kind or class, there can be no democracy of any sort.

> WOODROW WILSON
> Speech at Billings, Mont., Sept. 11, 1919; *Public Papers, VI,* 107

See also Railroads 1, Security 5, Trusts

Monroe Doctrine

1. The Monroe Doctrine should be treated as the cardinal feature of American foreign policy; but it would be worse than idle to assert it unless we intended to back it up, and it can be backed up only by a thoroughly good navy.

> THEODORE ROOSEVELT
> Second Annual Message to Congress, Dec. 2, 1902; p. 6762

2. The Monroe Doctrine is not part of international law. It has never been formally accepted by any international agreement. The Monroe Doctrine merely rests upon the statement of the United States that if certain things happen she will do certain things. So nothing sustains the honor of the United States in respect of these long cherished and long admired promises except her own moral and physical force.

> WOODROW WILSON
> Speech at Topeka, Kan., Feb. 2, 1916; *State Papers,* p. 198

3. I am proposing . . . that the nations should with one accord adopt the doctrine of President Monroe as the doctrine of the world: that no nation should seek to extend its polity over any other nation or people, but that every people should be left free to determine its own polity, its own way of development, unhindered, unthreatened, unafraid, the little along with the great and powerful.

> WOODROW WILSON
> Address to the Senate, Jan. 22, 1917; *Ibid.,* p. 355

See also Colonialism, Conquest, Cuba 1, 2, Defense 4, Foreign Relations 2, 14, Policy 3, Preparedness 12, Territorial Acquisition, Tyranny 4

Monuments

1. A watchful eye must be kept on ourselves, lest while we are building ideal monuments of renown and bliss here, we neglect to have our names enrolled in the annals of Heaven.

> JAMES MADISON
> To William Bradford, Nov. 9, 1772;
> *James Madison (Brant), I,* 104

2. We in America do not build monuments to war. We do not build monuments to conquest. We build monuments to commemorate the spirit of sacrifice in war—reminders of our desire for peace.

FRANKLIN DELANO ROOSEVELT
Address at St. Louis, Mo., Oct. 14, 1936; *Public Papers, V,* 474

See also Ideas 2

Morale
See War 64

Morality

1. Let us with caution indulge the supposition that morality can be maintained without religion. Whatever may be conceded to the influence of refined education on minds of peculiar structure, reason and experience both forbid us to expect that national morality can prevail in exclusion of religious principle.

GEORGE WASHINGTON
Farewell Address, Sept. 19, 1796; *Writings*
(Fitzpatrick), *XXXV*, 232

2. We are firmly convinced, and we act on that conviction, that with nations as with individuals our interests soundly calculated will ever be found inseparable from our moral duties, and history bears witness to the fact that a just nation is trusted on its word when recourse is had to armaments and wars to bridle others.

THOMAS JEFFERSON
Second Inaugural Address, Mar. 4, 1805

3. Reading, reflection and time have convinced me that the interests of society require the observation of those moral precepts only in which all religions agree (for all forbid us to murder, steal, plunder, or bear false witness), and that we should not intermeddle with the particular dogmas in which all religions differ, and which are totally unconnected with morality.

THOMAS JEFFERSON
Letter to James Fishback, Sept. 27, 1809; *Works, V,* 471

4. I never did, or countenanced, in public life, a single act inconsistent with the strictest good faith; having never believed there was one code of morality for a public, and another for a private man.

THOMAS JEFFERSON
To Don Valentine de Feronda, Oct. 4, 1809; *Works, V,* 475

5. Of all the systems of morality, ancient or modern, which have come under my observation, none appear to me so pure as that of Jesus.

THOMAS JEFFERSON
To William Canby, Sept. 18, 1813; *Writings, XIII,* 377

6. Morality is dependent upon the spread of religious conviction to prevail in the government and civilization of this country.

WILLIAM HOWARD TAFT

7. A system of morals is necessary for the welfare of any individual or any nation. The greatest system of morals in the history of the world is that set out in the Sermon on the Mount, which I would advise each one of you to study. . . .

HARRY S. TRUMAN
News conference, Apr. 6, 1946; *Public Papers . . . Truman, 1946,* p. 181

8. To be moral, free nations need not be weak nor pursue the ways of weakness. The highest morality of national leadership is to create and maintain the strength essential to the preservation of our beliefs. It is for the wisdom to use our power wisely that we should pray.

LYNDON B. JOHNSON
Remarks at Presidential Prayer breakfast, Feb. 7, 1963;
Story, p. 188

See also Civilization 5, Conduct 1, Courage, Discrimination 6, Foreign Relations 13, 23, Health 3, Justice 11, Money 5, Peace 30, Prosperity 1, Religion 13, Right 9, Self-Government 6

Mothers

1. Did you ever hear of a great and good man who had not a good mother?

JOHN ADAMS
To Josiah Quincy, Nov. 6, 1821; *Figures,* p. 71

2. Motherhood is the keystone of the arch of matrimonial happiness.

THOMAS JEFFERSON
To Martha Jefferson Randolph, 1791; *Dictionary,* p. 818

3. Under Providence, I attribute any little distinction which I may have acquired in the world to the blessing which He conferred upon me in granting me such a mother.

JAMES BUCHANAN
Autobiography, *ca.* 1814; *Life, I,* 3

4. All I am, all I ever hope to be, I owe to my angel mother.

ABRAHAM LINCOLN
To William H. Herndon; *Herndon's Life,* p. 6

5. Filial love is an attribute of American manhood, a badge which invites our trust and confidence, and an indispensable element of American greatness. A man may compass important enterprises, he may become

famous . . . he may deserve a measure of popular approval, but he is not right at heart, and can never be truly great, if he forgets his mother.

GROVER CLEVELAND
Speech at Ann Arbor, Mich., Feb. 22, 1892;
Writings and Speeches, p. 359

6.   The mother is the one supreme asset of national life; she is more important by far than the successful statesman, or business man, or artist, or scientist.

THEODORE ROOSEVELT
Address in Washington, D.C., Mar. 10, 1908;
Addresses and Papers, p. 433

7.   There can be no proper observation of a birthday which forgets the mother.

CALVIN COOLIDGE
Lincoln Day Proclamation, Jan. 30, 1919; *Faith,* p. 166

Muckrakers

1.   The men with the muckrakes are often indispensable to the well-being of society; but only if they know when to stop raking the muck, and to look upward to the celestial crown above them, to the crown of worthy endeavor. There are beautiful things above and round about them; and if they gradually grow to feel that the whole world is nothing but muck, their power of usefulness is gone.

THEODORE ROOSEVELT
Address in Washington, D.C., Apr. 14, 1906;
Works (Mem. Ed.), XVIII, 574

See also Press (The)

Myths

1.   The great enemy of the truth is very often not the lie—deliberate, contrived and dishonest—but the myth—persistent, persuasive, and un-realistic. . . .

Mythology distracts us everywhere—in government as in business, in politics as in economics, in foreign as in domestic affairs. . . .

Let us take first the question of the size and the shape of Government. The myth is that Government is big, and bad—and steadily getting bigger and worse. . . . The truth about big Government is the truth about any great activity; it is complex. Certainly it is true that size brings dangers, but it is also true that size can bring benefits.

JOHN F. KENNEDY
Speech at Yale University, June 11, 1962; *Public Papers . . .
Kennedy, 1962,* p. 473

Nationality

1. The sentiment of nationality is the sentiment of the Declaration of Independence; it is the sentiment of the fathers; it is the sentiment which carried us through the war of the Revolution, and through the war of the late Rebellion; and it is a sentiment which the people of the United States ought forever to cultivate and cherish.

RUTHERFORD B. HAYES
Speech at Lebanon, Ohio, Aug. 5, 1867; *Life*, p. 168

2. There is here [in America] a great melting pot in which we must compound a precious metal. That metal is the metal of nationality.

WOODROW WILSON
Address in Washington, D.C., Apr. 19, 1915;
Public Papers, III, 299

3. We ask no one to assume responsibility for us; we assume no responsibility which others must bear for themselves, unless nationality is hopelessly swallowed up in internationalism.

WARREN G. HARDING
Second Annual Message to Congress, Dec. 8, 1922;
Messages and Papers, p. 9187

See also Americans 5

Nations

1. The nation which indulges towards another an habitual hatred or an habitual fondness is in some degree a slave . . . to its animosity or to its affection, either of which is sufficient to lead it astray from its duty and its interest.

GEORGE WASHINGTON
Farewell Address, Sept. 19, 1796; *Writings*
(*Fitzpatrick*), *XXXV*, 231

2. There can be no greater error than to expect or calculate upon real favor from nation to nation. It is an illusion which experience must cure, which a just pride ought to discard.

GEORGE WASHINGTON
Farewell Address, Sept. 19, 1796; *Ibid.*, p. 235

3. A nation may be said to consist of its territory, its people and its laws. The territory is the only part which is of certain durability.

ABRAHAM LINCOLN
Message to Congress, Dec. 1, 1862; *Complete Works, VIII*, 110

4. Fourscore and seven years ago, our fathers brought forth upon this continent a new nation, conceived in liberty and dedicated to the proposition that all men are created equal.

ABRAHAM LINCOLN
Gettysburg Address, Nov. 19, 1863; *Ibid., IX*, 209

5. Nations have perished only when their institutions have ceased to be serviceable to the human race. When their faith has become an empty form, and the destruction of the old is indispensable to the growth of the new. Growth is better than permanence; and permanent growth is better than all.

JAMES A. GARFIELD
Address at Hudson College, July 2, 1873; *Future,* p. 5

6. Our nation . . . lives in us—in our hearts and minds and consciences. . . . The land we live in seems to be strong and active. But how fares the land that lives in us?

GROVER CLEVELAND

7. The nation's strength is in the people. The nation's prosperity is in their prosperity. The nation's glory is in the equality of her justice. The nation's perpetuity is in the patriotism of all her people.

GROVER CLEVELAND
First Annual Message to Congress, Dec. 8, 1885;
Messages and Papers, p. 4944

8. It is our duty to remember that a nation has no more right to do injustice to another nation, strong or weak, than an individual has to do injustice to another individual; that the same moral law applies. . . . But we must also remember that it is as much the duty of the Nation to guard its own rights and its own interest as it is the duty of the individual so to do.

THEODORE ROOSEVELT
Fourth Annual Message to Congress, Dec. 6, 1904; *Ibid.,* p. 7052

9. No nation is fit to sit in judgment upon any other nation.

WOODROW WILSON
Address in New York, N.Y., Apr. 20, 1915; *State Papers,* p. 109

10. When people fail in the national viewpoint, and live in the confines of community selfishness or narrowness, the sun of this republic will have passed its meridian, and our larger aspirations will shrivel in the approaching twilight.

WARREN G. HARDING
Address to Congress, Nov. 21, 1922; *Messages and Papers,* p. 9163

11. The nation at its best will not be better than the aggregate of all its citizenship, the national ideal stated in the preamble will be attained by us as a nation in no greater degree than we shall attain it as an aggregate of individuals.

WARREN G. HARDING
Address in Washington, D.C., May 24, 1923; *Ibid.,* p. 9222

12. Lives of Nations are determined not by the count of years, but by the lifetime of the human spirit. The life of a man is threescore years and

ten: a little more, a little less. The life of a Nation is the fullness of the measure of its will to live.

FRANKLIN DELANO ROOSEVELT
Third Inaugural Address, Jan. 20, 1941

13. A tired nation, said Lloyd George, is always a Tory nation. And the United States today cannot afford to be either tired or Tory. For however difficult, however discouraging, however sensitive the issues . . . they must be faced.

In the words of Woodrow Wilson: "We must neither run with the crowd nor deride it—but seek sober counsel for it—and for ourselves."

JOHN F. KENNEDY
Washington, D.C., Apr. 16, 1959; *Strategy*, p. 205

See also Conduct 1, Foreign Relations, Ignorance 6, Liberty 36, Peace 37, 53, 61, 84, Political Philosophy 2, Politics 5, Republics 16, Right 15, Space 2, 4, United Nations 4, Vigilance 2, Virtue 3

Navy

1. A naval power, next to the militia, is a natural defense of the United States.

JOHN ADAMS
Special Session Message, May 16, 1797; *Manual, I,* 110

2. A Navy, well organized, must constitute the natural and efficient defense of this country against all foreign hostility.

JOHN ADAMS
Speech to the House of Representatives, Nov. 27, 1800;
Messages and Papers, p. 302

3. I had always been of opinion . . . that a navy was the most powerful, the safest and the cheapest national defense for this country. . . . That Washington was averse to a navy, I had full proof from his own lips, in many different conversations . . . in which he always insisted that it was only building and arming ships for the English.

JOHN ADAMS
To Thomas Jefferson, Oct. 15, 1822;
Writings (of Jefferson), X, 239

4. I take upon myself, without a moment of hesitancy, all the responsibility of recommending the increase and prompt equipment of that gallant Navy which has lighted up every sea with its victories and spread an imperishable glory over the country.

JOHN TYLER
First Annual Message to Congress, Dec. 7, 1841;
Messages and Papers, p. 1941

5. As the long peace that has lulled us into a sense of fancied security

may at any time be disturbed, it is plain that the policy of strengthening [our Navy] is dictated by considerations of wise economy, of just regard for our future tranquillity, and of true appreciation of the dignity and honor of the Republic.

CHESTER ALAN ARTHUR
Fourth Annual Message to Congress, Dec. 1, 1884; *Ibid.,* p. 4835

6.   A good navy is not a provocative of war. It is the surest guaranty of peace.

THEODORE ROOSEVELT
Second Annual Message to Congress, Dec. 2, 1902; *Ibid.,* p. 6762

7.   It is an accepted naval maxim that a navy can be used to strategic advantage only when acting on the offensive, and it can be free to so operate only after our coast defense is reasonably secure.

THEODORE ROOSEVELT
Special Message to Congress, Mar. 5, 1906; *Ibid.,* p. 7667

8.   The navy of the United States is the right arm of the United States and is emphatically the peacemaker. Woe to our country if we permit that right arm to become palsied or even to become flabby, and inefficient!

THEODORE ROOSEVELT
New York *Times,* Nov. 22, 1914; *Works, XVIII,* 116

9.   A modern navy can not be improvised. It must be built and in existence when the emergency arises.

WILLIAM HOWARD TAFT
Inaugural Address, Mar. 4, 1909

10.   I regard our Navy as a great instrument of peace.

CALVIN COOLIDGE
Speech at Annapolis, Md., June 3, 1925; *Foundations,* p. 241

See also Army, Defense, Discipline 1, Military Matters, Monroe Doctrine 1, Neutrality 2, Peace 31, Preparedness 4, 8, 12, Republics 16

Neglect
See Problems

Negotiations
1.   We cannot negotiate with those who say, "What's mine is mine and what's yours is negotiable." But we are willing to consider any arrangement or treaty in Germany consistent with the maintenance of peace and freedom.

JOHN F. KENNEDY
Report to the Nation, July 25, 1961; *Public Papers . . . Kennedy, 1961,* p. 538

See also Fear 7, Foreign Relations 35, United Nations 3, War 63

Negroes

1. I have supposed the black man, in his present state, might not be in body and mind equal to the white man; but it would be hazardous to affirm that, equally cultivated for a few generations, he would not become so.

THOMAS JEFFERSON
To François Jean de Chastelleux, June 7, 1785; *Works, I,* 341

2. Nothing is more certainly written in the book of fate than that these people are to be free; nor is it less certain that the two races equally free, cannot live in the same government. Nature, habit, opinion have drawn indelible lines of distinction between them.

THOMAS JEFFERSON
Autobiography, 1821; *Ibid.,* 49

3. All I ask for the Negro is that if you do not like him, let him alone. If God gave him but little, that little let him enjoy.

ABRAHAM LINCOLN
Speech at Springfield, Ill., July 17, 1858; *Complete Works, III,* 186

4. The colored men must base their hope on the results of their own industry, self-restraint, thrift and business success, as well as upon the aid and comfort and sympathy which they may receive from their white neighbors. . . . The Negroes are now Americans. . . . We are charged with the sacred duty of making their path as smooth and easy as we can.

WILLIAM HOWARD TAFT
Inaugural Address, Mar. 4, 1909

5. I believe the Negro citizens should be guaranteed the enjoyment of all their rights, that they have earned the full measure of citizenship bestowed, that their sacrifices in blood on the battlefields of the Republic have entitled them to all of freedom and opportunity, all of sympathy and aid that the American spirit of fairness and justice demands.

WARREN G. HARDING
At Marion, Ohio, July 22, 1920; *Speeches of Warren G. Harding,* p. 34

6. The progress of the colored people on this continent is one of the marvels of modern history. We are perhaps even yet too near to this phenomenon to be able fully to appreciate its significance. That can be impressed on us only as we study and contrast the rapid advancement of the colored people in America with the slow and painful upward movement of humanity as a whole throughout the long human story.

CALVIN COOLIDGE
Speech at Howard University, June 6, 1924; *Foundations,* p. 31

7. Nearly one-tenth of our population consists of the Negro race. . . . Our country has no more loyal citizens. But they do still need sympathy,

kindness, and helpfulness. They need reassurance that the requirements of the Government and society to deal out to them even-handed justice will be met. They should be protected from all violence and supported in the peaceable enjoyment of the fruits of their labor.

CALVIN COOLIDGE
Third Annual Message to Congress, Dec. 8, 1925;
Messages and Papers, p. 9536

8. It is truly remarkable, the things which the Negro people have accomplished within living memory—their progress in agriculture and industry, their achievements in the field of education, their contributions to the arts and sciences, and, in general, to good citizenship.

It is my hope and belief that the Negro, inspired by the achievements of the race to date, will go forward to even greater things in the years to come.

FRANKLIN DELANO ROOSEVELT
At Gettysburg, Pa., *As FDR Said,* p. 145

9. I wish to make it clear that I am not appealing for social equality of the Negro. The Negro himself knows better than that, and the highest type of Negro leaders say quite frankly they prefer the society of their own people. Negroes want justice, not social relations.

HARRY S. TRUMAN
To Democratic National Convention, 1940; *Independence,* p. 339

10. One hundred years of delay have passed since President Lincoln freed the slaves, yet their heirs, their grandsons, are not fully free. They are not yet freed from the bonds of injustice; they are not yet freed from social and economic oppression.

And this nation, for all its hopes and all its boasts, will not be fully free until all its citizens are free. . . .

If an American, because his skin is dark, cannot eat lunch in a restaurant open to the public; if he cannot send his children to the best public school available; if he cannot vote for public officials who represent him; if, in short, he cannot enjoy the full and free life which all of us want, then who among us would be content to have the color of his skin changed and stand in his place? Who among us would then be content with counsels of patience and delay?

We have a right to expect that the Negro community will be responsible, will uphold the law. But they have a right to expect the law will be fair, that the Constitution will be color blind. . . .

JOHN F. KENNEDY
Radio and television address, June 11, 1963;
Vital Speeches, July 1, 1963, p. 547

11. One hundred years ago, the slave was freed.

One hundred years later, the Negro remains in bondage to the color of his skin.

The Negro today asks justice.

We do not answer him—we do not answer those who lie beneath this soil—when we reply to the Negro by asking, "Patience."

It is empty to plead that the solution to the dilemmas of the present rests on the hands of the clock. The solution is in our hands. Unless we are willing to yield up our destiny of greatness among the civilizations of history, Americans, white and Negro together, must be about the business of resolving the challenge which confronts us now.

Our nation found its soul in honor on these fields of Gettysburg one hundred years ago. We must not lose that soul in dishonor now on the fields of hate.

LYNDON B. JOHNSON
Address at Gettysburg, Pa., May 30, 1963; *Story,* p. 178

12. To strike the chains of a slave is noble. To leave him the captive of the color of his skin is hypocrisy. While we in America have freed the slave of his chains, we have not freed his heirs of their color. Until justice is blind to color, until education is unaware of race, until opportunity ceases to squint its eyes at pigmentation of human complexions, emancipation will be a proclamation—but it will not be a fact. To the extent that the proclamation of emancipation is not fulfilled in fact, to that extent we shall have fallen short of assuring freedom to the free. . . .

The counsel of delay is not the counsel of courage. A government conceived and dedicated to the purpose that all men are born free and equal cannot pervert its mission by rephrasing the purpose to suggest that men shall be free today—but shall be equal a little later.

LYNDON B. JOHNSON
Address at Wayne State University, Jan. 6, 1963;
Action, pp. 83, 84–85

See also Desegregation, Equality 4, Inequality, Segregation, Self-Government 2, Slavery, Union 26

Neighbors

See Democracy 18, 20, Fear 2, Foreign Relations 25, 35, 40, 41, 47, Latin America, Life, Peace 53, Relief 3

Neutrality

1. Our form of government, inestimable as it is, exposes us, more than any other, to the insidious intrigues and pestilent influence of foreign nations. Nothing but our inflexible neutrality can preserve us.

JOHN ADAMS
To *The Boston Patriot, ca.* 1809; *Works, IX,* 277

2. If a system of universal and permanent peace could be established,

or if in war the belligerent parties would respect the rights of neutral powers, we should have no occasion for a navy or an army. . . . The history of all ages proves that this can not be presumed; on the contrary, that at least one-half of every century, in ancient as well as modern times, has been consumed in wars. . . . Nor is there any cause to infer . . . that we shall in future be exempt from that calamity. . . . And as to the rights of neutral powers . . . little regard will be paid to them whenever they come in conflict with the interest of the powers at war while we rely on the justice of our cause and on argument alone.

> JAMES MONROE
> Speech to the House of Representatives, Jan. 30, 1824;
> *Messages and Papers,* p. 701

3.   In the shock of contending empires it is only by assuming a resolute bearing and clothing themselves with defensive armor that neutral nations can maintain their independent rights.

> MARTIN VAN BUREN
> Fourth Annual Message to Congress, Dec. 5, 1840; *Ibid.,* p. 1820

4.   Long experience has shown that, in general, when the principal powers of Europe are engaged in war the rights of neutral nations are endangered.

> FRANKLIN PIERCE
> Second Annual Message to Congress, Dec. 4, 1854; *Ibid.,* p. 2808

5.   The United States must be neutral in fact as well as in name. We must be impartial in thought as well as in action.

> WOODROW WILSON
> Proclamation, Aug. 19, 1914; *Story,* p. 166

6.   The basis of neutrality . . . is not indifference; it is not self-interest. The basis of neutrality is sympathy for mankind. It is fairness, it is good will, at bottom. It is impartiality of spirit and of judgment.

> WOODROW WILSON
> Address to Associated Press, New York, N.Y., Apr. 20, 1915;
> *State Papers,* p. 110

7.   Neutrality is a negative word. It is a word that does not express what America ought to feel. . . . America has promised the world to stand apart and maintain certain principles of action which are grounded in law and in justice. We are not trying to keep out of trouble; we are trying to preserve the foundations upon which peace can be rebuilt.

> WOODROW WILSON
> Address in Washington, D.C., Oct. 11, 1915; *Ibid.,* p. 124

8.   Armed neutrality is ineffectual enough at best. . . . It is likely only to

produce what it was meant to prevent; it is practically certain to draw us into war without either the rights or the effectiveness of belligerents.

WOODROW WILSON
Address to Congress, asking for war, Apr. 2, 1917; *Ibid.*, p. 375

9. This is not a time to keep the facts from the people—to keep them complacent. To sound the alarm is not to panic but to seek action from an aroused public. For, as Dante once said: "The hottest places in hell are reserved for those who, in a time of great moral crisis, maintain their neutrality."

JOHN F. KENNEDY
Speech at Tulsa, Okla., Sept. 16, 1959; *Strategy,* p. 138

See also Government 19, Preparedness 4

New Deal

1. I pledge you, I pledge myself, to a new deal for the American people.

FRANKLIN DELANO ROOSEVELT
Acceptance of Nomination for Presidency, Chicago, Ill.,
July 2, 1932; *Public Papers, I,* 659

New Frontier
See Frontiers

Newspapers
See Press (The)

Normalcy
See America 17, Government 93

Nullification

1. Nullification means insurrection and war. . . .
Can anyone of common sense believe the absurdity that . . . a state has a right to secede and destroy this union and the liberty of our country with it, or nullify the laws of the Union; then indeed is our constitution a rope of sand; under which I would not live.

ANDREW JACKSON
To Gen. John Coffee, Dec. 14, 1832; *Life (Bassett),* p. 569

See also Secession

Office, Public
See Public Office

Office Seekers

1. I have . . . made public that I will appoint no man who comes to

Washington seeking an office, whilst he remains here, and the effect has been to diminish the number of personal importunities upon me.

ANDREW JACKSON

To James K. Polk, May 22, 1845; *Correspondence*, p. 407

2. There is at present an unusual number of office-seekers . . . who are so patriotic as to desire to serve their country by getting into fat offices. The truth is, I have become greatly disgusted with the passion for office. . . .

JAMES K. POLK

Feb. 27, 1846; *Diary (Quaife)*, *I*, 255

3. Indeed the rage for office is the besetting evil of the times, and does more to weaken the democratic party than all other causes combined.

JAMES K. POLK

Dec. 16, 1847; *Ibid.*, *III*, 249

4. In the midst of the annoyances of the herd of lazy, worthless people who come to Washington for office instead of going to work . . . I am sometimes amused at their applications. . . . One of these office seekers placed his papers of recommendation. . . . No particular office was specified . . . but he answered that he thought he would be a good hand at making Treaties . . . and would like to be a minister abroad. This is about as reasonable as many other applications which are made to me.

JAMES K. POLK

Apr. 10, 1848; *Ibid.*, p. 422

5. These office-seekers are a curse to the country; no sooner was my election certain, than I became the prey of hundreds of hungry, persistent applicants for office, whose highest ambition is to feed at the Government's crib.

ABRAHAM LINCOLN

Washington, D.C., 1861; *Everyday Life*, p. 467

6. This human struggle and scramble for office, for a way to live without work, will finally test the strength of our institutions.

ABRAHAM LINCOLN

Washington, D.C., 1861; *Herndon's Life*, p. 410

7. The truth is, office seeking and office seekers came very near putting a period to my public career.

GROVER CLEVELAND

To Thomas F. Bayard, Sept. 11, 1893; *Letters*, p. 334

See also Appointments, Civilization 4, Congress 4, Debts 2, Patronage, Public Office

Opinion

1. Honesty, sincerity, and openness I esteem essential marks of a good

mind. I am, therefore, of opinion that men ought, (after they have ex-
amined with unbiased judgments every system of religion, and chosen one
system, on their own authority, for themselves), to avow their opinions
and defend them with boldness.

JOHN ADAMS
Diary, Mar. 7, 1756; *Works, II,* 8

2. Subject opinion to coercion: whom will you make your inquisitors?
Fallible men; men governed by bad passions, by private as well as public
reasons. And why subject it to coercion? To produce uniformity. But is
uniformity of opinion desirable? No more than of face and stature. . . .
Is uniformity attainable? Millions of innocent men, women, and children,
since the introduction of Christianity, have been burnt, tortured, fined,
imprisoned; yet we have not advanced an inch toward uniformity. What
has been the effect of coercion? To make one half the world fools, and the
other half hypocrites. To support roguery and error all over the earth.

THOMAS JEFFERSON
Notes on Virginia, 1782; *Writings, II,* 222

3. One had rather have no opinion than a false one.

THOMAS JEFFERSON
Memoranda, June 6, 1787; *Works, IX,* 366

4. Even if we differ in principle . . . I know too well the texture of the
human mind, and the slipperiness of human reason, to consider differences
of opinion otherwise than differences of form or feature. Integrity of
views more than their soundness, is the basis of esteem.

THOMAS JEFFERSON
To Elbridge Gerry, Jan. 26, 1799; *Writings, VII,* 335

5. I never considered a difference of opinion in politics, in religion, in
philosophy, as cause for withdrawing from a friend.

THOMAS JEFFERSON
To William Hamilton, Apr. 22, 1800; *Ibid.,* p. 441

6. Every difference of opinion is not a difference of principle. . . . If
there be any among us who would wish to dissolve this Union or to change
its republican form, let them stand undisturbed as monuments of the safety
with which error of opinion may be tolerated where reason is left free to
combat it.

THOMAS JEFFERSON
First Inaugural Address, Mar. 4, 1801

7. Experience [has] long taught me the reasonableness of mutual sacrifices of opinion among those who are to act together for any common
object, and the expediency of doing what good we can when we cannot
do all we would wish.

THOMAS JEFFERSON
Letter to John Randolph, Dec. 1, 1803; *Works, IV,* 518

8. The good opinion of mankind, like the lever of Archimedes, with the given fulcrum, moves the world.

THOMAS JEFFERSON
To Correa de Serra, Dec. 27, 1814; *Writings, XIV,* 222

9. Opinion is power.

THOMAS JEFFERSON
To John Adams, Jan. 11, 1816; *Ibid.,* p. 396

10. Free and unbiased exercise of political opinion is the only sure foundation and safeguard of republican government.

MARTIN VAN BUREN
First Annual Message to Congress, Dec. 5, 1837;
Messages and Papers, p. 1598

11. I do not care what others say and think about me. But there is one man's opinion which I very much value, and that is the opinion of James Garfield. Others I need not think about. I can get away from them, but I have to be with him all the time. He is with me when I rise up and when I lie down; when I eat and talk; when I go out and come in. It makes a great difference whether he thinks well of me or not.

JAMES A. GARFIELD
Facts, p. 145

See also Controversy, Differences, Knowledge 6, Peace 37, People 6, 17, Preparedness 15, Press (The) 5, Public Opinion, Reason 2, Religion 7, 8, 10, United Nations 4

Opportunity

1. We have developed a cult of the common man. Whoever [he] is, I want him to have all the unique benefits of the American way of life, including a full opportunity to rise to leadership.

HERBERT HOOVER
Remarks, Nov. 11, 1948; *Addresses,* p. 171

See also America 11, American System, Athletics 2, Democracy 31, Education 34, Equality 10, Freedom 30, Government 92, Labor 14, Negroes 5, 12, Peace 38, Slavery 26, Taxation 7, Unity 4, Vigilance 1

Oppression

See Majorities 2, Negroes 10, People 3, Preparedness 18, War 68

Pacifists

1. Professional pacifists should be regarded as traitors to the great cause of justice and humanity.

THEODORE ROOSEVELT
Statement to the press, Sept. 20, 1917; *His Time, II,* 436

2. The parlor pacifist, the white-handed or sissy type of pacifist, represents decadence, represents the rotting out of the virile virtues among people who typify the unlovely, senile side of civilization. The rough-neck pacifist, on the contrary, is a mere belated savage who has not been educated to the virtues of national patriotism.

THEODORE ROOSEVELT
Speech at Minneapolis, Minn., Sept. 28, 1917; *Works, XIX,* 173

See also Peace 27, War 52

Panama Canal

1. I took the Isthmus, started the Canal, and then left Congress—not to debate the Canal, but to debate me. . . . But while the debate goes on the Canal does too.

THEODORE ROOSEVELT
Address at Berkeley, Cal., Mar. 23, 1911; *University of California Chronicle, April, 1911*

See also Latin America 1

Parties, Political
See Political Parties

Past, The

1. The dogmas of the quiet past are inadequate to the stormy present. The occasion is piled high with difficulty, and we must rise—with the occasion. As our case is new, so we must think anew, and act anew. We must disenthrall ourselves, and then we shall save our country.

ABRAHAM LINCOLN
Second Annual Message to Congress, Dec. 1, 1862;
Complete Works, VIII, 131

2. We are not concerned with the past except as it is a guide for the future. . . . We turn our faces to the front. We nail the flag to the mast for a safer and more secure and more peaceful world than ever.

DWIGHT D. EISENHOWER
Remarks in Washington, D.C., Apr. 3, 1957; *Public Papers . . . Eisenhower, 1957,* p. 259

3. Let us not seek the Republican answer or the Democratic answer but the right answer. Let us not seek to fix the blame for the past. Let us accept our own responsibility for the future.

JOHN F. KENNEDY
Speech at Baltimore, Md., Feb. 18, 1958; *Strategy,* p. 212

See also Education 19, History, Progress 9, Time 2

Paternalism

1. The lessons of paternalism ought to be unlearned and the better lesson taught that while the people should patriotically and cheerfully support their Government, its functions do not include the support of the people.

GROVER CLEVELAND
Second Inaugural Address, Mar. 4, 1893

2. Paternalism [the intervention of the government in private initiative] is a method by which we can achieve social reform.

THEODORE ROOSEVELT
1912

3. I am not a paternalist, and yet, I am not a doctrinaire of the *laissez-faire* school. I think a judicious mixture of paternalism where it trains the children of the Government . . . is proper.

WILLIAM HOWARD TAFT
In San Francisco, Cal., Oct. 5, 1909; *Presidential Addresses, I*, 333

4. It is not consonant with the spirit of institutions of the American people that a demand be made upon the public treasury for the solution of every difficulty. . . . Independence and ability of action amongst our own people . . . saves our government from that ultimate paternalism which undermines our whole political system. . . .

HERBERT HOOVER
September, 1921; *Memoirs, II,* 45

See also People (The) 29

Patience

1. Let what will be said or done, preserve your *sang froid* immovably, and to every obstacle oppose patience, perseverance and soothing language.

THOMAS JEFFERSON
To William Short, Mar. 18, 1792; *Writings, VIII,* 316

2. The country is undoubtedly back of me . . . and I feel myself under bonds to it to show patience to the utmost. My chief puzzle is to determine where patience ceases to be a virtue.

WOODROW WILSON
To Edward M. House, Sept. 20, 1915; *Life and Letters, V,* 375

3. It has been my observation in life that, if one will only exercise patience to wait, his wants are likely to be filled.

CALVIN COOLIDGE
Autobiography, p. 50

See also Negroes 10, 11, Politicians 1, Tolerance 5, Virtue 7

Patriotism

1. A great and lasting war can never be supported on patriotism alone. It must be aided by the prospect of interest, or some reward.

GEORGE WASHINGTON
To John Banister, Apr. 21, 1778; *Writings (Fitzpatrick), XI,* 284

2. I would to God we had less professions and more acts of real patriotism.

ANDREW JACKSON
To Maj. William B. Lewis, Feb. 22, 1824; *Life (Parton), III,* 41

3. The approbation I have received from the people everywhere on my return home on the close of my official life, has been a source of much gratification to me. I have been met at every point . . . with a hearty welcome and expressions of "well done thou faithful servant." This is truly the patriot's reward, the summit of my gratification, and will be my solace to the grave.

ANDREW JACKSON
To Martin Van Buren, Mar. 30, 1837; *Life (Bassett),* p. 721

4. Blessed is the country whose defenders are patriots. . . . We cannot exalt patriotism too high; we cannot too much encourage love of country; for, my fellow-citizens, as long as patriotism exists in the hearts of the American people, so long will our matchless institutions be secure and permanent.

WILLIAM MCKINLEY
Speech at Syracuse, N.Y., Aug. 24, 1897;
Speeches and Addresses, p. 37

5. Patriotism should be an integral part of our every feeling at all times, for it is merely another name for those qualities of soul which make a man in peace or in war, by day or by night, think of his duty to his fellows, and of his duty to the nation through which their and his loftiest aspirations must find their fitting expression.

THEODORE ROOSEVELT
1916; *Works, XVIII,* 201

6. The man who loves other countries as much as his own stands on a level with the man who loves other women as much as he loves his own wife.

THEODORE ROOSEVELT
Speech in New York, N.Y., Sept. 6, 1918; *Ibid.,* 551

7. We are a humor-loving people. We dislike shams. Our sense of the ridiculous is very keen, almost too keen, and in the mercantile and material spirit which has been rife, we are prone to make light of exhortations to patriotism, and the forms and symbols through which patriotism

finds expression. I think we have gone too far in this direction. Patriotism is a real virtue, and the forms and symbols which suggest it, and by which we recognize its existence and our respect for it, are proper reminders of a serious duty, and keep us in touch with it as an elevating motive.

WILLIAM HOWARD TAFT
Speech in New York, N.Y., May 30, 1908; *Problems,* p. 63

8.   Patriotism is a principle, not a mere sentiment. No man can be a true patriot who does not feel himself shot through and through with a deep ardor for what his country stands for, what its existence means, what its purpose is declared to be in its history and in its policy.

WOODROW WILSON
Remarks at unveiling of Commodore Perry statue, May 16, 1914;
Public Papers, III, 108

9.   A patriotic American is a man who is not niggardly and selfish in the things that he enjoys that make for human liberty and the rights of man. He wants to share them with the whole world, and he is never so proud of the great flag under which he lives as when it comes to mean to other people as well as to himself a symbol of hope and liberty.

WOODROW WILSON
Address in Philadelphia, Pa., July 4, 1914; *Ibid.,* p. 144

10.   Patriotism is easy to understand in America. It means looking out for yourself by looking out for your country.

CALVIN COOLIDGE
Address at Northampton, Mass., May 30, 1923; *Freedom,* p. 333

See also Americans 3, Citizenship 6, Crisis 1, Defense 8, Duty 3, Honor 4, Liberty 9, Money 8, Nations 7, Pacifists 2, Patronage 2, People 14, Politics 15, Rebellion 2, Union 21, War 31

Patronage

1.   I am confirmed in the truth of the remark which I have long since made, that the patronage of the Government will, from the day any President enters upon his duties, weaken his administration.

JAMES K. POLK
Nov. 13, 1848; *Diary (Quaife), IV,* 194

2.   When you substitute patronage for patriotism, administration breaks down. We need more of the Office Desk and less of the Show Window in politics. Let men in office substitute the midnight oil for the limelight.

CALVIN COOLIDGE
Speech at Hamilton, Mass., September, 1916; *Faith,* p. 46

See also Appointments, Elections 1, Office Seekers, Public Office

Peace

1.   My temper leads me to peace and harmony with all men; and it is

peculiarly my wish to avoid any personal feuds or dissensions with those, who are embarked in the same great national interest with myself, as every difference of this kind must in its consequences be very injurious.

GEORGE WASHINGTON
To Horatio Gates, Feb. 24, 1778; *Writings (Fitzpatrick)*, V, 513

2. A peace establishment ought always to have two objects in view; the one, present security of posts and of stores, and the public tranquillity; the other, to be prepared, if the latter is impracticable, to resist with efficacy the sudden attempts of a foreign or domestic enemy.

GEORGE WASHINGTON
To Baron Friedrich Von Steuben, Mar. 15, 1784; *Ibid.*, IX, 25

3. To be prepared for war is one of the most effective means of preserving peace.

GEORGE WASHINGTON
First Annual Message to Congress, Jan. 8, 1790;
Messages and Papers, p. 57

4. In demonstrating by our conduct that we do not fear war in the necessary protection of our rights and honor we shall give no room to infer that we abandon the desire of peace. An efficient preparation for war can alone insure peace. It is peace that we have uniformly and perseveringly cultivated.

JOHN ADAMS
Second Annual Message to Congress, Dec. 8, 1798; *Ibid.*, p. 262

5. It is unfortunate for our peace, that unmerited abuse wounds, while unmerited praise has not the power to heal.

THOMAS JEFFERSON
To Edward Rutledge, Dec. 27, 1796; *Writings, VII*, 93

6. Peace is our passion.

THOMAS JEFFERSON
To Sir John Sinclair, June 30, 1803; *Ibid., X*, 397

7. We have . . . remained in peace, suffering frequent injuries, but, on the whole, multiplying, improving, prospering, beyond all example. . . . Peace then has been our principle, peace is our interest, and peace has saved to the world this only plant of free and rational government now existing in it.

THOMAS JEFFERSON
To Gen. Thaddeus Kosciusko, Apr. 13, 1811; *Ibid., XIII*, 41

8. A universal and perpetual peace, it is to be feared, is in the catalogue of events, which will never exist but in the imaginations of visionary philosophers, or in the breasts of benevolent enthusiasts. It is still however

true, that war contains so much folly, as well as wickedness, that much is to be hoped from the progress of reason; and if any thing is to be hoped, every thing ought to be tried.

JAMES MADISON
The National Gazette, Feb. 2, 1792; *Writings (Hunt), VI,* 88

9. Indulging no passions which trespass on the rights or the repose of other nations, it has been the true glory of the United States to cultivate peace by observing justice, and to entitle themselves to the respect of the nations at war by fulfilling their neutral obligations with the most scrupulous impartiality.

JAMES MADISON
First Inaugural Address, Mar. 4, 1809

10. I am, against every invitation to war, an advocate of peace. The insults of Spain, Britain, or any others . . . I deem no more worthy of our notice as a nation than those of a lunatic to a man in health,—for I consider them as desperate and raving mad.

JAMES MONROE
To Thomas Jefferson, 1793; *Cocked Hats,* p. 341

11. Peace is the best time for improvement and preparation of every kind; it is in peace that our commerce flourishes most, that taxes are most easily paid, and that the revenue is most productive.

JAMES MONROE
First Inaugural Address, Mar. 4, 1817

12. To preserve peace will no doubt be difficult, but by accomplishing it we can show our wisdom and magnanimity, and secure to our people the enjoyment of a dignified repose by indulging which they will be prosperous and happy.

JAMES MONROE
Letter; *Cocked Hats,* p. 344

13. Our institutions are essentially pacific. Peace and friendly intercourse with all nations are as much the desire of our Government as they are the interest of the people.

ANDREW JACKSON
Sixth Annual Message to Congress, Dec. 1, 1834;
Messages and Papers, p. 1324

14. Peace, above all things, is to be desired, but blood must sometimes be spilled to obtain it on equable and lasting terms.

ANDREW JACKSON

15. Bound by no entangling alliances, yet linked by a common nature and interest with the other nations of mankind, our aspirations are for the

preservation of peace, in whose solid and civilizing triumphs all may participate with a generous emulation.

MARTIN VAN BUREN
Fourth Annual Message to Congress, Dec. 5, 1840;
Messages and Papers, p. 1820

16.   Peace with all the world is the true foundation of our policy, which can only be rendered permanent by the practice of equal and impartial justice to all.

JOHN TYLER
Second Annual Message to Congress, Dec. 6, 1842; *Ibid.*, p. 2050

17.   Adopting the maxim in the conduct of our foreign affairs "to ask nothing that is not right and submit to nothing that is wrong," it has been my anxious desire to preserve peace with all nations, but at the same time to be prepared to resist aggression and maintain all our just rights.

JAMES K. POLK
Inaugural Address, Mar. 4, 1845

18.   One thing is clear. Before lasting peace can be restored, much must be forgiven, if not forgotten.

MILLARD FILLMORE
February, 1864; *Millard Fillmore (Rayback)*, p. 428

19.   The great objects of our pursuit as a people are best to be attained by peace, and are entirely consistent with the tranquillity and interests of the rest of mankind.

FRANKLIN PIERCE
Inaugural Address, Mar. 4, 1833

20.   Such will be a great lesson of peace; teaching men that what they cannot take by an election, neither can they take by a war; teaching all the folly of being the beginners of a war.

ABRAHAM LINCOLN
Message to Congress, July 4, 1861; *Complete Works, VI*, 322

21.   With malice toward none, with charity for all, with firmness in the right, as God gives us to see the right, let us strive on to finish the work we are in . . . to do all which may achieve and cherish a just and lasting peace among ourselves, and with all nations.

ABRAHAM LINCOLN
Second Inaugural Address, Mar. 4, 1865

22.   Peace and universal prosperity—its sequence—with economy of administration, will lighten the burden of taxation while it constantly reduces the national debt. Let us have peace.

ULYSSES S. GRANT
Letter accepting Nomination for Presidency, May 29, 1868;
Meet General Grant, p. 396

23. To maintain peace in the future it is necessary to be prepared for war.

ULYSSES S. GRANT
1885; *Memoirs, II,* 547

24. While it is a grievous thing to contemplate the two great English-speaking peoples of the world as being otherwise than friendly competitors in the onward march of civilization, and strenuous and worthy rivals in all the arts of peace, there is no calamity which a great nation can invite which equals that which follows a supine submission to wrong and injustice and the consequent loss of national self-respect and honor, beneath which are shielded and defended a people's safety and greatness.

GROVER CLEVELAND
Special Message to Congress, Dec. 17, 1895;
Messages and Papers, p. 6090

25. It has been said . . . that the normal condition of nations is war. That is not true of the United States. We never enter upon a war until every effort for peace without it has been exhausted. Ours has never been a military government. Peace, with whose blessings we have been so singularly favored, is the national desire and the goal of every American aspiration.

WILLIAM McKINLEY
Address at Omaha, Neb., Oct. 12, 1898;
Speeches and Addresses, p. 102

26. Let us ever remember that our interest is in concord not in conflict, and that our real eminence as a nation lies in the victories of peace, not those of war.

WILLIAM McKINLEY
Speech in Washington, D.C., 1890; *As I Knew Them,* p. 243

27. We do not admire the man of timid peace.

THEODORE ROOSEVELT
Address in Chicago, Ill., Apr. 10, 1899; *Works, XIII,* 320

28. The true end of every great and free people should be self-respecting peace; and this Nation most earnestly desires sincere and cordial friendship with all others.

THEODORE ROOSEVELT
First Annual Message to Congress, Dec. 3, 1901;
Messages and Papers, p. 6662

29. Generally peace tells for righteousness; but if there is conflict between the two, then our fealty is due first to the cause of righteousness.

Unrighteous wars are common, and unrighteous peace is rare; but both should be shunned.

THEODORE ROOSEVELT
Fourth Annual Message to Congress, Dec. 6, 1904; *Ibid.*, p. 7052

30. As the world is now, only that nation is equipped for peace that knows how to fight, and that will not shrink from fighting if ever the conditions become such that war is demanded in the name of the highest morality.

THEODORE ROOSEVELT
Fifth Annual Message to Congress, Dec. 5, 1905; *Ibid.*, p. 7376

31. In my own judgment the most important service that I rendered to peace was the voyage of the battle fleet round the world.

THEODORE ROOSEVELT
Autobiography, p. 548

32. The example of America must be a special example, not merely of peace because it will not fight, but of peace because peace is the healing and elevating influence of the world and strife is not.

WOODROW WILSON
Address in Philadelphia, Pa., May 10, 1915; *State Papers*, p. 117

33. Peace can be rebuilt only upon the ancient and accepted principles of international law, only upon those things which remind nations of their duty to each other, and, deeper than that, of their duties to mankind.

WOODROW WILSON
Address in Washington, D.C., Oct. 11, 1915; *Ibid.*, p. 124

34. There is a price which is too great to pay for peace, and that price can be put in one word. One cannot pay the price of self-respect.

WOODROW WILSON
Speech at Des Moines, Ia., Feb. 1, 1916; *Ibid.*, p. 190

35. We covet peace, and shall preserve it at any cost but the loss of honor.

WOODROW WILSON
To Sen. William J. Stone, Feb. 24, 1916; *Public Papers, IV,* 123

36. It must be a peace without victory. . . .

There must be, not a balance of power, but a community of power; not organized rivalries, but an organized common peace. . . .

Only a peace between equals can last. Only a peace the very principle of which is equality and a common participation in a common benefit. The right state of mind, the right feeling between nations, is as necessary for a lasting peace as is the just settlement of vexed questions of territory or of racial and national allegiance.

No peace can last, or ought to last, which does not recognize and accept the principle that governments derive all their just powers from the consent of the governed, and that no right anywhere exists to hand peoples about from sovereignty to sovereignty as if they were property.

I am proposing that no nation should seek to extend its polity over any other nation or people, but that every people should be left free to determine its own polity, its own way of developing unhindered, unthreatened, unafraid, the little along with the great and powerful.

WOODROW WILSON
Address to Senate, Jan. 22, 1917, pp. 352, 385

37. A steadfast concert for peace can never be maintained except by a partnership of democratic nations. No autocratic government could be trusted to keep faith within it or observe its covenants. It must be a league of honor, a partnership of opinion.

WOODROW WILSON
Address to Congress, asking for war, Apr. 2, 1917; *Ibid.*, p. 379

38. The American people . . . believe that peace should rest upon the rights of peoples, not the rights of governments—the rights of peoples great or small, weak or powerful . . . to freedom and security and self-government and to a participation upon fair terms in the economic opportunities of the world.

WOODROW WILSON
Reply to the peace proposal of Pope Benedict XV, Aug. 27, 1917;
Selections, p. 152

39. Mankind needs a world-wide benediction of understanding. It is needed among individuals, among peoples, among governments, and it will inaugurate an era of good feeling. . . . In such understanding men will strive confidently for the promotion of their better relationships and nations will promote the comities so essential to peace.

WARREN G. HARDING
Inaugural Address, Mar. 4, 1921

40. I believe it a God-given duty to give of our influence to establish the ways of peace throughout the world.

WARREN G. HARDING
Address at Arlington National Cemetery, May 30, 1923;
Messages and Papers, p. 9231

41. What an object lesson of peace is shown today by our two countries [Canada and the United States] to all the world! No grim-faced fortifications mark our frontier, no huge battleships patrol our dividing waters, no stealthy spies lurk in our tranquil border hamlets. . . .

Our protection is our fraternity; our armour is our faith; the tie that binds more firmly, year by year, is ever increasing acquaintance and comradeship through interchange of citizens; and the compact is not perishable parchment, but of fair and honorable dealing, which, God grant, shall continue for all times.

WARREN G. HARDING
Address at Vancouver, B.C., July 26, 1923;
As I Knew Them, p. 478

42.   The only true and lasting peace [is] based on justice and right.

CALVIN COOLIDGE
Radio broadcast, Dec. 10, 1923; *Messages and Papers,* p. 8922-D

43.   The final establishment of peace, the complete maintenance of good will toward men, will be found only in the righteousness of the people of the earth. . . . Peace will reign when they will that it shall reign.

CALVIN COOLIDGE
Address in New York, N.Y., Apr. 22, 1924; *Ibid.,* p. 9402

44.   The foreign policy of America can be best described by one word— peace. . . .
A peace means fundamentally a reign of law.

CALVIN COOLIDGE
Acceptance of Nomination for Presidency, Cleveland, Ohio,
Aug. 14, 1924; *Ibid.,* p. 9434

45.   Peace must have other guarantees than constitutions and covenants. Laws and treaties may help, but peace and war are attitudes of mind.

CALVIN COOLIDGE
Speech at Baltimore, Md., Sept. 6, 1924; *Foundations,* p. 99

46.   There is another element, more important than all, without which there can not be the slightest hope of a permanent peace. That element lies in the heart of humanity. Unless the desire for peace be cherished there, unless this fundamental and only natural source of brotherly love be cultivated to its highest degree, all artificial efforts will be in vain. Peace will come when there is realization that only under a reign of law, based on righteousness and supported by the religious conviction of the brotherhood of man, can there be any hope of a complete and satisfying life. Parchment will fail, the sword will fail, it is only the spiritual nature of man that can be triumphant.

CALVIN COOLIDGE
Inaugural Address, Mar. 4, 1925

47.   If we are to promote peace on earth, we must have a great deal more than the power of the sword. We must call into action the spiritual and moral forces of mankind.

CALVIN COOLIDGE
Speech at Annapolis, Md., June 3, 1925; *Foundations,* p. 244

48.   We believe that the foundations of peace can be strengthened by

the creation of methods and agencies by which a multitude of incidents may be transferred from the realm of prejudice and force to arbitration and the determination of right and wrong based upon international law.

HERBERT HOOVER
Acceptance of Nomination for Presidency, Chicago, Ill.,
Aug. 11, 1928; *Policies*, p. 579

49. Surely civilization is old enough, surely mankind is mature enough so that we ought in our own lifetime to find a way to permanent peace. . . .

Peace can be contributed to by respect for our ability in defense. Peace can be promoted by the limitation of arms and by the creation of the instrumentalities for peaceful settlement of controversies. But it will become a reality only through self-restraint and active effort in friendliness and helpfulness.

HERBERT HOOVER
Inaugural Address, Mar. 4, 1929

50. One of the primary necessities of the world for the maintenance of peace is the elimination of the frictions which arise from competitive armament and the further necessity to reduce armament is economic relief to the peoples of the world.

HERBERT HOOVER
1929; *Memoirs, II*, 344

51. Real peace in the world requires something more than the documents which we sign to terminate wars. Peace requires unremitting, courageous campaigns, laid with strategy and carried on successfully on a hundred fronts and sustained in the spirit and from the hearts of every individual in every town and village of our country.

HERBERT HOOVER
Speech in Boston, Mass., Oct. 6, 1930; *State Papers, I*, 384

52. The long-view contribution for preserving peace would be for America to stand on moral forces alone in support of law between nations. It [is] not isolationism. It [is] a belief that somewhere, somehow, there must be an abiding place for law and a sanctuary for civilization.

HERBERT HOOVER
1933; *Memoirs, II*, 377

53. The danger to world peace certainly does not come from the United States of America. As a Nation, we are overwhelmingly against engaging in war. As a Nation we are seeking no additional territory at the expense of our neighbors.

FRANKLIN DELANO ROOSEVELT
Radio address, Oct. 13, 1933; *Public Papers, II*, 394

54. It is but an extension of the challenge of Woodrow Wilson for us to propose in this newer generation that from now on war by governments shall be changed to peace by peoples.

FRANKLIN DELANO ROOSEVELT
Address to Woodrow Wilson Foundation, Dec. 28, 1933;
Ibid., p. 549

55. The greatest need of the world today is the assurance of permanent peace—an assurance based on mutual understanding and mutual regard.

FRANKLIN DELANO ROOSEVELT
Address at West Point, June 12, 1935; *Ibid., IV,* 252

56. The continued maintenance and improvement of democracy constitute the most important guarantee of international peace.

FRANKLIN DELANO ROOSEVELT
Address to Pan-American Union, Apr. 14, 1937; *Ibid., VI,* 158

57. It is becoming increasingly clear that peace by fear has no higher or more enduring quality than peace by the sword.

There can be no peace if the reign of law is to be replaced by a recurrent sanctification of sheer force.

There can be no peace if national policy adopts as a deliberate instrument the threat of war.

FRANKLIN DELANO ROOSEVELT
Address to *Herald-Tribune* Forum, Oct. 26, 1938; *Ibid., VII,* 564

58. Today we seek a moral basis for peace. It cannot be a real peace if it fails to recognize brotherhood. It cannot be a lasting peace if the fruit of it is oppression, or starvation, or cruelty, or human life dominated by armed camps. It cannot be a sound peace if small nations must live in fear of powerful neighbors. It cannot be a moral peace if freedom from invasion is sold for tribute. It cannot be an intelligent peace if it denies free passage to that knowledge of those ideals which permit men to find common ground. It cannot be a righteous peace if worship of God is denied.

FRANKLIN DELANO ROOSEVELT
Radio address, Mar. 16, 1940; *Ibid., IX,* 103

59. We can gain no lasting peace if we approach it with suspicion and mistrust or with fear. We can gain it only if we proceed with the understanding, the confidence, and the courage which flows from conviction.

FRANKLIN DELANO ROOSEVELT
Fourth Inaugural Address, Jan. 20, 1945

60. We want to . . . do the things in peace that we have been able to do in war. If we can put this tremendous machine of ours . . . to work

for peace, we can look forward to the greatest age in the history of mankind.

HARRY S. TRUMAN
Remarks in Berlin, Germany, July 20, 1945;
Public Papers . . . Truman, 1945, p. 175

61.   We all have to recognize—no matter how great our strength—that we must deny ourselves the license to do always as we please. No one nation, no regional group, can or should expect any special privilege which harms any other nation. If any nation would keep security for itself, it must be ready and willing to share security with all. That is the price which each nation will have to pay for world peace.

HARRY S. TRUMAN
Address to United Nations Conference, San Francisco, Cal.,
June 26, 1945; *Memoirs, I,* 291

62.   We must keep trying for peace. The false approach of the Russians must not prevent our peace program from going through to a successful conclusion.

HARRY S. TRUMAN
Notes, 1948; *Mr. President,* p. 220

63.   We knew that there could be no lasting peace so long as there were large populations in the world living under primitive conditions and suffering from starvation, disease, and denial of the advantages of modern science and industry.

HARRY S. TRUMAN
1955; *Memoirs, I,* x

64.   We are going to have peace even if we have to fight for it.

DWIGHT D. EISENHOWER
Speech at Frankfort on the Main, Germany, June 10, 1945;
Eisenhower Speaks, p. 14

65.   Progress toward universal and enduring peace, as I see it, lies along three roads—organized international cooperation, mutual international understanding and progressive international disarmament. All must be traveled simultaneously.

DWIGHT D. EISENHOWER
Speech in New York, N.Y., Apr. 25, 1946;
What Eisenhower Thinks, p. 94

66.   Peace is more the product of our day-to-day living than of a spectacular program, intermittently executed.

DWIGHT D. EISENHOWER
Address at Columbia University, Mar. 23, 1950; *Peace,* p. 26

67. Peace is my passion.

Dwight D. Eisenhower
Speech at Cincinnati, Ohio, Sept. 22, 1952; *Index,* p. 80

68. The peace we seek, then, is nothing less than the practice and fulfillment of our whole faith among ourselves and in our dealings with others.
This signifies more than the stilling of guns, easing the sorrow of war.
More than escape from death, it is a way of life. More than a haven for
the weary, it is a hope for the brave.

Dwight D. Eisenhower
First Inaugural Address, Jan. 20, 1953

69. The peace we seek, founded upon decent trust and co-operative
effort among nations, can be fortified, not by weapons of war but by
wheat and by cotton, by milk and by wool, by meat and by timber and by
rice. These are words that translate into every language on earth. These
are needs that challenge this world in arms.

Dwight D. Eisenhower
Address to American Society of Newspaper Editors, Apr. 16,
1953; *Peace,* p. 34

70. The cost of peace is something we must face boldly, fearlessly. Beyond money, it involves changes in attitudes, the renunciation of old
prejudices, even the sacrifice of some seeming self-interest.

Dwight D. Eisenhower
Fifth Annual Message to Congress, Jan. 10, 1957;
Public Papers . . . Eisenhower, 1957, p. 28

71. We seek peace, knowing that peace is the climate of freedom. And
now, as in no other age, we seek it because we have been warned, by the
power of modern weapons, that peace may be the only climate possible
for human life itself.

Yet this peace we seek cannot be born of fear alone: it must be rooted
in the lives of nations. There must be justice, sensed and shared by all
peoples, for, without justice the world can know only a tense and unstable
truce.

Dwight D. Eisenhower
Second Inaugural Address, Jan. 21, 1957

72. You cannot do the things that need to be done, as I call it to wage
the peace, merely with arms. You have got to have the human understanding of human wants, and you have got to make it possible for people to
achieve something in satisfying those wants if we are going to wage peace
successfully.

Dwight D. Eisenhower
News conference, Jan. 23, 1957; *Public Papers . . .
Eisenhower, 1957,* p. 78

73. We are trying to prevent war, not fight one. So, to prevent a war, I should like the nations to know that America is largely one in our readiness to assume burdens and, where necessary, to assume risks to preserve the peace, because this peace is not going to be obtained in any cheap way and it is not going to be maintained in any cheap way.

DWIGHT D. EISENHOWER
News conference, Jan. 23, 1957; *Ibid.*, p. 87

74. You don't promote the cause of peace by talking only to people with whom you agree. That is merely yes-man performance. You have got to meet face to face the people with whom you disagree at times, to determine whether or not there is a way of working out the differences and reaching a better understanding.

DWIGHT D. EISENHOWER
News conference, Jan. 30, 1957; *Ibid.*, p. 98

75. Peace and justice are two sides of the same coin.

DWIGHT D. EISENHOWER
Radio and television address, Feb. 20, 1957; *Ibid.*, p. 152

76. The peace we seek is a creative and dynamic state of flourishing institutions, of prosperous economies, of deeper spiritual insight for all nations and all men.

DWIGHT D. EISENHOWER
Remarks at NATO meeting, Paris, France, Dec. 16, 1957;
Ibid., p. 836

77. People want peace so much that governments had better get out of their way and let them have it.

DWIGHT D. EISENHOWER
London Sunday Times, 1960

78. Let us call a truce to terror. Let us invoke the blessings of peace. And as we build an international capacity to keep peace, let us join in dismantling the national capacity to wage war.

JOHN F. KENNEDY
Address to the United Nations General Assembly, Sept. 25, 1961;
Public Papers . . . Kennedy, 1961, p. 619

79. Every man, woman, and child lives under a nuclear sword of Damocles. . . . All this [a program for world peace] will not be finished in the first 100 days. Nor will it be finished in the first 1,000 days, nor in the life of this administration, nor even perhaps in our lifetime on this planet. But let us begin.

JOHN F. KENNEDY
Address to the United Nations General Assembly, Sept. 25, 1961;
Ibid., p. 620

80. For fifteen years we have sought to make the atom an instrument of peaceful growth rather than of war. But for fifteen years our concessions have been matched by obstruction, our patience by intransigence, and the pleas of mankind for peace have been met with disregard.

JOHN F. KENNEDY
Address to the United Nations General Assembly, Sept. 25, 1961;
Ibid., p. 621

81. Peace is not solely a military or technical problem—it is primarily a problem of politics and people. And unless man can match his strides in weaponry and technology with equal strides in social and political development, our great strength, like that of the dinosaur, will become incapable of proper control—and man, like the dinosaur, will decline and disappear.

JOHN F. KENNEDY
Address to the United Nations General Assembly, Sept. 25, 1961;
Ibid., p. 622

82. Peace and freedom do not come cheap, and we are destined—all of us here today—to live out most if not all of our lives in uncertainty and challenge and peril.

JOHN F. KENNEDY
Address at University of North Carolina, Oct. 12, 1961;
Ibid., p. 668

83. Winning the peace is a lonely battle.

JOHN F. KENNEDY
1962

84. What kind of peace do we seek? Not a Pax Americana enforced on the world by American weapons of war. Not the peace of the grave or the security of the slave. I am talking about the genuine peace—the kind of peace that makes life on earth worth living—and the kind that enables men and nations to grow and to hope and build a better life for their children . . . not merely peace in our time but peace in all time. . . .

There is no single, simple key to this peace—no grand or magic formula to be adopted by one or two powers. Genuine peace must be the product of many nations, the sum of many acts. It must be dynamic, not static, changing to meet the challenge of each new generation. For peace is a process—a way of solving problems. . . .

So let us persevere. Peace need not be impracticable—and war need not be inevitable. By defining our goal more clearly—by making it seem more manageable and less remote—we can help all people to see it, to draw hope from it, and to move irresistibly towards it.

JOHN F. KENNEDY
At American University, Washington, D.C., June 10, 1963;
Vital Speeches, July 1, 1963, p. 558

85. Peace is a daily, a weekly, a monthly process, gradually changing opinions, slowly eroding old barriers, quietly building new structures. And however undramatic the pursuit of peace, that pursuit must go on. . . .

But peace does not rest in the charters and covenant alone. It lies in the hearts and minds of all people. And if it is cast out there, then no act, no pact, no treaty, no organization can hope to preserve it without the support and wholehearted commitment of all people. So let us not rest all our hopes on parchments and on paper—let us strive to build peace, a desire for peace, a willingness to work for peace in the hearts and minds of all of our people.

JOHN F. KENNEDY
To the United Nations General Assembly, Sept. 19, 1963;
Ibid., Oct. 15, 1963, p. 2

86. A pause in the cold war is not a lasting peace, and a detente does not equal disarmament. The United States must continue to seek a relaxation of tensions, but we have no cause to relax our vigilance. . . .

Let us resolve to be the masters, not the victims of our history, controlling our own destiny without giving way to blind suspicions and emotions. Let us distinguish between our hopes and our illusions, always hoping for steady progress towards less critically dangerous relations with the Soviets but never laboring under any illusions about Communist methods or Communist goals.

Let us recognize both the gains we have made down the road to peace and the great distance yet to be covered.

JOHN F. KENNEDY
At the University of Maine, Sept. 28, 1963;
Ibid., Nov. 1, 1963, p. 34

87. We in this country, in this generation, are—by destiny rather than choice—the watchmen on the walls of world freedom. We ask, therefore, that we may be worthy of our power and responsibility—that we may exercise our strength with wisdom and restraint—and that we may achieve in our time and for all time the ancient vision of peace on earth, good will toward men.

JOHN F. KENNEDY
From his undelivered speech, Nov. 22, 1963;
Chicago Daily News, Dec. 29, 1963

88. We keep a vigil of peace around the world.

Until the world knows no aggressors, until the arms of tyranny have been laid down, until freedom has risen up in every land, we shall maintain our vigil to make sure our sons who died on foreign fields shall not have died in vain.

LYNDON B. JOHNSON
Address at Gettysburg, Pa., May 30, 1963; *Story,* p. 177

89. In our 175 years since Washington's first inaugural, we have had frequent occasions to prosecute wars. Until now, we have not had so serious, so hopeful an opportunity to pursue peace—with so full a storehouse of the strengths peace-making requires. . . .

Our agriculture is abundant. Profits are high. Wages and income are at new peaks. We are free of the bitter conflicts that plague the world—between capital and labor, between religions. We are freeing ourselves of the burden of racial discrimination. Our technology leads the world in peaceful and practical uses of space. Our guiding programs nationally are the works of both our parties.

We stand not on a precipice of failure but at the summit of success.

If ever a people were prepared, ready and able to pursue peace, it is we, of this generation of Americans. This is the challenge of our success. We must accept that challenge. We must keep the initiative for peace.

LYNDON B. JOHNSON
To 175th Anniversary dinner at Georgetown University,
Oct. 12, 1963; *Vital Speeches, Nov. 1, 1963*, p. 37

90. We have proved that we are a good and reliable friend to those who seek peace and freedom. We have shown that we can also be a formidable foe to those who reject the path of peace and who seek to impose upon us or our allies the yoke of tyranny. . . . We will be unceasing in the search for peace; resourceful in our pursuit of areas of agreement even with those with whom we differ; and generous and loyal to those who join with us in common cause.

LYNDON B. JOHNSON
Address to Congress, Nov. 27, 1963;
Chicago Daily News, Nov. 27, 1963

91. Peace is a journey of a thousand miles, and it must be taken one step at a time.

LYNDON B. JOHNSON
To the United Nations General Assembly, Dec. 17, 1963;
Vital Speeches, Jan. 1, 1964, p. 163

See also Conduct 1, Conquest, Democracy 12, 27, Disarmament, Economy 4, Education 33, Enemies 4, Foreign Relations 36, 38, 39, 46, 50, 51, Freedom 34, Goals 2, Government 76, 92, Hope 2, Humor 1, Immigration 2, Knowledge 10, Laws 28, League of Nations 1, Navy 6, 8, 10, Negotiations, People (The) 8, Policy 3, Preparedness, Right 16, Security 8, 9, Trade 2, Treaties 3, Union 9, United Nations 3, 4, 5, United States 6, 7, Vigilance 2, War

Peace Corps

1. I recommend to the Congress the establishment of a permanent Peace Corps, *a pool of trained American men and women sent overseas*

*by the U.S. Government or through private organizations and institutions
to help foreign countries meet their urgent needs for skilled manpower.
. . . The initial emphasis of these programs will be on teaching. . . .*

Although this is an American Peace Corps, the problem of world development is not just an American problem. Let us hope that other nations will mobilize the spirit and energies and skill of their people in some form of Peace Corps, making our own effort only one step in a major international effort to increase the welfare of all men and improve understanding among nations.

> JOHN F. KENNEDY
> Message to Congress, Mar. 1, 1961; *Public Papers . . .
> Kennedy, 1961,* p. 143

Penitence
1. Penitence must precede pardon.

> JOHN ADAMS
> *Re* the Sedition Act; *Writings (of Jefferson)*

Pensions
1. The usefulness and the justice of any system for the distribution of pensions depend upon the equality and uniformity of its operation.

> GROVER CLEVELAND
> Second Annual Message to Congress, Dec. 6, 1886;
> *Messages and Papers,* p. 5109

2. I have considered the pension list of the Republic a roll of honor, bearing names inscribed by national gratitude, and not by improvident and indiscriminate almsgiving.

> GROVER CLEVELAND
> Veto of Dougherty Pension Bill, July 5, 1888; *Ibid.,* p. 5269

See also Benevolence, Charity, Philanthropy, Relief

People, The
1. I cannot conceive a rank more honorable, than that which flows from the uncorrupted choice of a brave and free people, the purest source and original fountain of all power.

> GEORGE WASHINGTON
> To Lt.-Gen. Thomas Gage, Aug. 20, 1775;
> *Writings (Fitzpatrick), III,* 66

2. Every valuable end of government is best answered by the enlightened confidence of the people, and by teaching the people themselves to know and to value their own rights . . . to discriminate the spirit of liberty from that of licentiousness—cherishing the first, avoiding the last—and uniting a

speedy but temperate vigilance against encroachment, with an inviolable respect to the laws.

GEORGE WASHINGTON
First Annual Message to Congress, Jan. 8, 1790; *Ibid., XII,* 10

3.   The people are in their nature so gentle, that there never was a government yet in which thousands of mistakes were not overlooked. The most sensible and jealous people are so little attentive to government, that there are no instances of resistance, until repeated, multiplied oppressions have placed it beyond a doubt, that their rulers had formed settled plans to deprive them of their liberties.

JOHN ADAMS
"Novanglus," in Boston *Gazette,* Jan. 23, 1775; *Works, IV,* 17

4.   I am persuaded there is among the mass of our people a fund of wisdom, integrity, and humanity which will preserve their happiness in a tolerable measure.

JOHN ADAMS
To Abigail Adams, June 2, 1777; *Familiar Letters,* p. 279

5.   There is but one element of government, and that is THE PEOPLE. From this element spring all governments. "For a nation to be free, it is only necessary that she will it." For a nation to be slave, it is only necessary that she wills it.

JOHN ADAMS
To John Taylor, 1814; *Works, VI,* 474

6.   The basis of our government [is] the opinion of the people.

THOMAS JEFFERSON
To Edward Carrington, Jan. 16, 1787; *Writings, VI,* 57

7.   The good sense of the people will always be found to be the best army.

THOMAS JEFFERSON
Ibid.

8.   Educate and inform the whole mass of the people. Enable them to see that it is to their interest to preserve peace and order. . . . They are the only sure reliance for the preservation of our liberty.

THOMAS JEFFERSON
To James Madison, Dec. 20, 1787; *Ibid.,* p. 392

9.   The will of the people is the only legitimate foundation of any government.

THOMAS JEFFERSON
To Benjamin Waring, Mar. 23, 1801; *Ibid., X,* 235

10. No government can continue good but under the control of the people.

> THOMAS JEFFERSON
> To John Adams, Dec. 10, 1819; *Ibid., XV*, 234

11. I know no safe depository of the ultimate powers of society but the people themselves; and if we think them not enlightened enough to exercise their control with a wholesome discretion, the remedy is not to take it from them, but to inform their discretion by education.

> THOMAS JEFFERSON
> To W. C. Jarvis, Sept. 28, 1820; *Ibid.,* p. 278

12. The people are the only legitimate fountain of power, and it is from them that the constitutional charter, under which the several branches of government hold their power, is derived. . . .

> JAMES MADISON
> "Publius," 1788; *Federalist, No. 49*

13. It is only when the people become ignorant and corrupt, when they degenerate into a populace, that they are incapable of exercising the sovereignty. . . . The people themselves become the willing instruments of their own debasement and ruin. . . . Let us by all wise and constitutional measures promote intelligence among the people as the best means of preserving our liberties.

> JAMES MONROE
> First Inaugural Address, Mar. 4, 1817

14. Good sense and patriotism, . . . regard for the honor and reputation of their country, . . . respect for the laws which they have themselves enacted for their own government, and the love of order [are qualities] for which the mass of our people have been so long and so justly distinguished.

> MARTIN VAN BUREN
> Second Annual Message to Congress, Dec. 3, 1838;
> *Messages and Papers,* p. 1704

15. The effects of distance have been averted by the inventive genius of our people, developed and fostered by the spirit of our institutions.

> MARTIN VAN BUREN

16. I am too old a soldier to murmur against such high authority as [the American people].

> ZACHARY TAYLOR
> To J. S. Allison, Apr. 12, 1848; *Life,* p. 386

17. While men inhabiting different parts of this vast continent cannot be expected to hold the same opinions . . . they can unite in a common object and sustain common principles.

> FRANKLIN PIERCE

18.   The people know their rights, and they are never slow to assert and maintain them, when they are invaded.

ABRAHAM LINCOLN
Speech at Springfield, Ill., January, 1837; *Complete Works, I,* 26

19.   No man is good enough to govern another man without that other's consent.

ABRAHAM LINCOLN
Speech at Peoria, Ill., Oct. 16, 1854; *Ibid., II,* 227

20.   You can fool some of the people all of the time, and all of the people some of the time, but you cannot fool all of the people all of the time.

ABRAHAM LINCOLN
Attributed to a speech by Lincoln at Clinton, Ill., Sept. 2, 1858;
Ibid., III, 349

21.   The people—the people are the rightful masters of both congresses and courts—not to overthrow the Constitution, but to overthrow the men who pervert it.

ABRAHAM LINCOLN
Notes for speeches in Ohio, Sept. 16, 17, 1859;
Collected Works, III, 435

22.   Why should there not be a patient confidence in the ultimate justice of the people? Is there any better or equal hope in the world? . . . Truth and . . . justice will surely prevail by the judgment of this great tribunal of the American people.

ABRAHAM LINCOLN
First Inaugural Address, Mar. 4, 1861

23.   The people when rightly and fully trusted will return the trust.

ABRAHAM LINCOLN
Washington, D.C., 1865; *War Years, IV,* 217

24.   The people are the safest, the best, and the most reliable lodgment of power. . . . Keep up the middle class; lop off an aristocracy on the one hand, and a rabble on the other; let the middle class . . . have the power, and your Government is always secure.

ANDREW JOHNSON
In the Senate, May 20, 1858; *Speeches,* p. 38

25.   Our Government springs from and was made for the people—not the people for the Government. To them it owes allegiance; from them it must derive its courage, strength, and wisdom.

ANDREW JOHNSON
First Annual Message to Congress, Dec. 4, 1865;
Messages and Papers, p. 3559

26. I shall on all subjects have a policy to recommend, but none to enforce against the will of the people.

ULYSSES S. GRANT
First Inaugural Address, Mar. 4, 1869

27. Let us not fall into the . . . pernicious error that multitude is divine because it is multitude.

JAMES A. GARFIELD
Address at Hudson College, July 2, 1873; *Future,* p. 14

28. All free governments are managed by the combined wisdom and folly of the people.

JAMES A. GARFIELD
Letter, Apr. 21, 1880; *Dictionary,* p. 487

29. Though the people support the Government, the Government should not support the people.

GROVER CLEVELAND
Message to House of Representatives, Feb. 16, 1887;
Messages and Papers, p. 5142

30. I know of no better or safer human tribunal than the people.

WILLIAM McKINLEY
Speech in Boston, Mass., Feb. 16, 1899; *Eloquence, II,* 823

31. Nothing is ever permanently settled, so far as governmental policy is concerned, until it is settled in the consciences of the people, and by their enlightened judgment. . . . It is therefore a great power that the people possess.

WILLIAM McKINLEY
At Wadena, Minn., Oct. 13, 1899; *Speeches and Addresses,* p. 277

32. The biggest corporation, like the humblest private citizen, must be held to strict compliance with the will of the people as expressed in the fundamental law.

THEODORE ROOSEVELT
Speech at Cincinnati, Ohio, 1902; *Outlook (magazine),*
Sept. 27, 1902; p. 206

33. Where the people rule, discussion is necessary.

WILLIAM HOWARD TAFT
At Denver, Colo., Sept. 21, 1909; *Presidential Addresses,* p. 245

34. No selfish interest, no personal ambition, no political campaign can sway the majority will of our people to make America strong—and to keep it free.

FRANKLIN DELANO ROOSEVELT
Address in Washington, D.C., Sept. 11, 1940; *Public Papers,*
IX, 407

35. The whole cornerstone of our democratic edifice was the principle that from the people and the people alone flows the authority of government.

FRANKLIN DELANO ROOSEVELT
Radio address, Feb. 12, 1943; *Ibid., XII,* 78

36. There is no source of strength greater than the people of the United States: courageous, persevering, long-sighted.

JOHN F. KENNEDY
Remarks at Trenton, N.J., Nov. 2, 1961; *Public Papers . . .
Kennedy, 1961,* p. 696

See also Behavior, Censors 1, Constitution 5, Creeds 2, Democracy 2, 8, 10, 11, 22, Education 18, 20, Errors 14, Freedom 14, Goals 1, Government 5, 9, 10, 16, 23, 26, 49, 53, 64, 65, 75, 94, 99, 105, 106, 107, 109, Happiness 3, Isolationism 5, Knowledge 3, Liberty 5, 8, Maxims 1, Nations 7, 10, Paternalism 1, Patriotism 7, Peace 72, 77, 85, Politics 10, 15, Power 5, 9, 21, 22, 25, 30, Presidency (The) 14, 33, Prosperity 8, Republics 10, Right 1, 7, Rulers, Society, Suffrage 1, Truth 4, War 73, Wealth 3

Perfection

1. Perfection falls not to the share of mortals.

GEORGE WASHINGTON
Letter to John Jay, Aug. 1, 1786; *Leaflets, No. 99,* p. 1

See also Errors 1, Government 41

Pessimism

1. How much pain have cost us the evils which have never happened.

THOMAS JEFFERSON
To Thomas Jefferson Smith, Feb. 21, 1825; *Writings, XVI,* 111

Philanthropy

1. Philanthropy, whether governmental or individual, is a curse and not a blessing when marked by a spirit of foolish sentimentality and ignorance.

THEODORE ROOSEVELT
Speech at Jamestown Exposition, Virginia, June 10, 1907;
Works, XVI, 176

See also Charity 1, 2

Philosophy

See Bible 1, Faith 1, God, Political Philosophy, Politics 2

Physical Fitness

1. We received a rude shock when during the [World] War [I] we came to examine physically that "flower of American manhood." In the

first draft of over two and a half million men . . . the percentage of rejections on account of physical unfitness went . . . between twenty-five and thirty-three and a third per cent. . . . It means that one out of every three or four young Americans in their prime—between twenty-one and thirty—are unfit.

WARREN G. HARDING
At Galion, Ohio, Aug. 27, 1920; *Speeches of Warren G. Harding,* p. 80

2. By April 1, 1945, nearly eight and a half million young people who should have been in the prime of health were found to be unfit for military service.

This is a terrible indictment. I believed that the United States should be the healthiest country in the world and lead in finding and developing new ways to improve the health of every citizen. . . . I proposed a national health program. President Roosevelt had set the stage . . . in his "economic bill of rights," which included "the right to adequate medical care and the opportunity to achieve and enjoy good health."

HARRY S. TRUMAN
1945; *Memoirs, II,* 18

3. Our team [in the contest with Russia] is made up of every individual in America. We need to make each one the best player that can be put on the field. This requires fitness in its deepest and broadest sense . . . a healthy body, an alert, disciplined mind. In this meaning, fitness is the individual's maximum development for the nation's good.

DWIGHT D. EISENHOWER
For National Youth Fitness Week, May 3–10, 1959

4. Physical fitness goes with mental fitness. It goes with energy.

JOHN F. KENNEDY
Interview, Jan. 13, 1961; *Public Papers . . . Kennedy, 1961,* p. 30

5. The need for increased attention to physical fitness is clearly established. The Government cannot compel us to act, but freedom demands it. A nation is merely the sum of all its citizens, and its strength, energy and resourcefulness can be no greater than theirs.

JOHN F. KENNEDY

Platforms
See Politics 32

Pleasure
1. Do not bite at the bait of pleasure, till you know there is no hook beneath it. . . . Pleasure is always before us; but misfortune is at our side; while running after that, this arrests us.

THOMAS JEFFERSON
To Maria Cosway, Oct. 12, 1786; *Writings, V,* 439

2. I do not agree that an age of pleasure is no compensation for a moment of pain.

THOMAS JEFFERSON
To John Adams, Aug. 1, 1816; *Ibid., XV*, 57

Point Four
See Foreign Relations 46

Policy

1. Tranquility at home and peaceful relations abroad constitute the true permanent policy of our country.

JAMES K. POLK
Fourth Annual Message to Congress, Dec. 5, 1848;
Messages and Papers, p. 2480

2. We shall not, I believe, be obliged to alter our policy of watchful waiting.

WOODROW WILSON
Seventh Annual Message to Congress, Dec. 2, 1913;
State Papers, p. 39

3. We cannot successfully cope with present world problems or secure a lasting peace without consistent and clearly defined policies and objectives which we are prepared to support and defend. Military strength is no substitute for sound policy.

I give you an example. Over a century ago our country announced the Monroe Doctrine. We never flinched from its support. The world knew what we meant and few have ever tried to breach it. It has contributed to peace throughout all these years.

HERBERT HOOVER
Address in Emporia, Kan., July 11, 1950; *American Road*, p. 77

See also Foreign Relations, Government 100, Justice 8, Patriotism 8, Peace, People (The) 26, 31, Preparedness 8, Presidency (The) 69, Principles 7, Public Opinion 5, Right 2, States' Rights 17, Union 9, United States 1, Unity 2

Political Parties

1. The spirit of party serves always to distract the public councils, and enfeeble the public administration. It agitates the community with ill-founded jealousies and false alarms; kindles the animosity of one part against another; foments occasional riot and insurrection.

GEORGE WASHINGTON
Farewell Address, Sept. 19, 1796;
Writings (Fitzpatrick), XXXV, 237

2. I have always called our Constitution a game of leap-frog. New England is again converted to federalism. The federal administration lasted

twelve years. The republicans then leaped over their heads and shoulders, and have ruled eight years. They may possibly hold out four years more, and then probably the federalists will leap again. But neither party will ever be strong, while they adhere to their austere, exclusive maxims. Neither party will ever be able to pursue the true interest, honor, and dignity of the nation. I lament the narrow, selfish spirit of the leaders of both parties, but can do no good to either. They are incorrigible.

JOHN ADAMS
To Benjamin Rush, Sept. 3, 1808; *Works, IX,* 602

3. I am not a federalist, because I never submitted the whole system of my opinions to the creed of any party of men whatever, in religion, in philosophy, in politics or in anything else, where I was capable of thinking for myself. Such an addiction is the last degradation of a free and moral agent. If I could not go to heaven but with a party, I would not go there at all.

THOMAS JEFFERSON
To Francis Hopkinson, Mar. 13, 1789; *Writings, VII,* 300

4. I am no believer in the amalgamation of parties, nor do I consider it as either desirable or useful for the public; but only that, like religious differences, a difference in politics should never be permitted to enter into social intercourse, or to disturb its friendship, its charities or justice. In that form they are censors of the conduct of each other, and useful watchmen for the public.

THOMAS JEFFERSON
To Henry Lee, Aug. 10, 1824; *Ibid., X,* 317

5. If parties in a republic are necessary to secure a degree of vigilance sufficient to keep the public functionaries within the bounds of law and duty, at that point their usefulness ends.

WILLIAM HENRY HARRISON
Inaugural Address, Mar. 4, 1841

6. We have a country as well as a party to obey.

JAMES K. POLK
Dec. 12, 1848; *Diary (Quaife), IV,* 232

7. I have always believed that what was best for the entire country was going to help both political parties in the end; for we are citizens in common of one great nation.

ULYSSES S. GRANT
Speech at Kansas City, Mo., July 2, 1880

8. He serves his party best who serves the country best.

RUTHERFORD B. HAYES
Inaugural Address, Mar. 5, 1877

9.   Party honesty is party duty, and party courage is party expedience.

GROVER CLEVELAND
Speech in New York, N.Y., Jan 8, 1892;
Writings and Speeches, p. 283

10.   No political party can long pursue advantage at the expense of public honor or by rude and indecent methods without protest and fatal disaffection in its own body.

BENJAMIN HARRISON
Inaugural Address, Mar. 4, 1889

11.   No party can be safely trusted with the interests of the people or the Government without it possesses a fixed, honest, and enlightened purpose.

WILLIAM MCKINLEY
Speech at Bangor, Me., Sept. 8, 1894; *Life and Speeches,* p. 153

12.   Parties are capital epitomes of human nature.

WOODROW WILSON
North American Review, October, 1909; *Ideals,* p. 44

13.   I thank God that we have lived to see a time when men are beginning to reason upon the facts and not upon party tradition. I believe in party tradition, but . . . only as it is founded upon eternal principles of justice.

WOODROW WILSON
Speech at Williams Grove, Pa., Aug. 29, 1912; *Crossroads,* p. 53

14.   The success of a party means little except when the Nation is using that party for a large and definite purpose.

WOODROW WILSON
First Inaugural Address, Mar. 4, 1913

15.   The trouble with the Republican Party is that it has not had a new idea for 30 years. I am not speaking as a politician; I am speaking as an historian.

WOODROW WILSON
Speech at Indianapolis, Ind., Jan. 8, 1915; *State Papers,* p. 81

16.   I love the Democratic Party; but I love America a great deal more. . . . When the Democratic Party thinks that it is an end in itself, then I rise up and dissent.

WOODROW WILSON
Speech at Indianapolis, Ind., Jan. 8, 1915; *Ibid.,* p. 90

17.   What difference does party make when mankind is involved?

WOODROW WILSON
Speech at Richmond, Ind., Sept. 4, 1919; *Public Papers, V,* 606

18.   I believe in political parties. These were the essential agencies of the

popular government which made us what we are. We were never perfect, but under our party system we wrought a development under representative democracy unmatched in all proclaimed liberty and attending human advancement. We achieved under the party system, where parties were committed to policies, and party loyalty was a mark of honor and an inspiration toward accomplishment.

WARREN G. HARDING
Address in New York, N.Y., Apr. 24, 1923;
Messages and Papers, p. 9211

19.   One only serves his party by first serving his country well, and good service to his country ought to be the aspiration of every citizen of our land.

WARREN G. HARDING
Address at St. Louis, Mo., June 21, 1923; *Ibid.*, p. 9238

20.   Let it be . . . the task of our party to break foolish traditions.

FRANKLIN DELANO ROOSEVELT
1932; *As FDR Said*, p. 191

21.   There are two courses open to a minority party. It can indulge in the politics of partisanship, or it can remain true to the politics of responsibility. The first course is tempting to the weak, but ultimately would be rejected by the American people. The second course is difficult but is the road upon which we can offer leadership to the American people that will be accepted.

LYNDON B. JOHNSON
Speech at Jefferson–Jackson Day dinner, New York, N.Y., 1953;
Man and President, p. 49

22.   The Democratic Party at its worst is better for the country than the Republican Party at its best.

LYNDON B. JOHNSON
An address, 1955; *Story*, p. 118

23.   The role of a minority party is to hammer out a program that will solve the problems of America—not just to obstruct the work of the majority party.

All of us are American before we are members of any political organization.

LYNDON B. JOHNSON
Man and President, p. 49

See also Politicians, Politics, Power 22, Presidency (The) 12, Prosperity 13, Republics 2, Union 14

Political Philosophy

1.   Men, chosen as the delegates in Congress are, cannot officially be dangerous. . . .

My political creed, therefore, is, to be wise in the choice of delegates, support them like gentlemen while they are our representatives, give them competent powers for all federal purposes, support them in the due exercise thereof, and, lastly, compel them to close attendance in Congress during their delegation.

GEORGE WASHINGTON
To Benjamin Harrison, Jan. 18, 1784; *Writings (Fitzpatrick)*, *IX*, 12

2. My politics are plain and simple. I think every nation has a right to establish that form of government, under which it conceives it may live most happy; provided it infracts no right, or is not dangerous to others; and that no governments ought to interfere with the internal concerns of another, except for the security of what is due to themselves.

GEORGE WASHINGTON
To the Marquis de Lafayette, Dec. 25, 1789; *Ibid., XXXVIII*, 70

3. Do the day's work. If it be to protect the rights of the weak, whoever objects, do it. If it be to help a powerful corporation better to serve the people, do that. Expect to be called a standpatter, but don't be a standpatter. Expect to be called a demagogue, but don't be a demagogue. Don't hesitate to be as revolutionary as science. Don't hesitate to be as reactionary as the multiplication table. Don't expect to build up the weak by pulling down the strong.

CALVIN COOLIDGE
To Massachusetts State Senate, Jan. 7, 1914; *Citizenship*, p. 115

4. A radical is a man with both feet firmly planted—in the air. A conservative is a man with two perfectly good legs who, however, has never learned to walk forward. A reactionary is a somnambulist walking backwards. A liberal is a man who uses his legs and his hands at the behest . . . of his head.

FRANKLIN DELANO ROOSEVELT
Radio address, Oct. 26, 1939; *Public Papers, VIII*, 556

See also Conservatism, Creeds 2, Liberalism, Standpatism

Politicians

1. Patience. Patience. Patience! the first, the last, and the middle virtue of a politician.

JOHN ADAMS
To Benjamin Rush, Feb. 8, 1778; *Works, IX*, 473

2. Politicians are a set of men who have interests aside from the interests of the people and who, to say the most of them, are, taken as a mass, at least one long step removed from honest men.

ABRAHAM LINCOLN
Speech in Springfield, Ill., January, 1837; *Complete Works, I*, 27

3. I hear our countrymen abroad saying: "You mustn't judge us by our politicians." I always want to interrupt and answer: "You must judge us by our politicians." We pretend to be the masters—we, the people—and if we permit ourselves to be ill served, to be served by corrupt and incompetent and inefficient men, then on our own heads must the blame rest.

THEODORE ROOSEVELT
Speech at Pacific Lutheran Theological Seminary, 1911;
Works, XIII, 653

4. Politicians are to serve the people, not to direct them. And my highest ambition is to be, so far as it is possible to be with the gifts that God has given me, the spokesman, the interpreter, the servant of the people of the United States.

WOODROW WILSON
Address at Pittsburgh, Pa., Oct. 18, 1912; *Crossroads,* p. 467

5. Any good politician with nerve and *a program that is right* can win in the face of the stiffest opposition.

HARRY S. TRUMAN
1948; *Memoirs, II,* 176

6. A professional politician's first duty is to appeal to the forces that unite us, and to channel the forces that divide us into paths where a democratic solution is possible. It is our obligation to resolve issues—not to create them.

LYNDON B. JOHNSON
January, 1963; *Life (magazine), Nov. 29, 1963*

See also Bossism, Faith 1, Inflation 3, Legislation 2, Politics 33, Presidency (The) 64, 68

Politics

1. Politics are the divine science, after all.

JOHN ADAMS
To James Warren, June 12, 1782; *Works, IX,* 512

2. When I was young, and addicted to reading, I had heard about dancing on the points of metaphysical needles; but, by mixing in the world, I found the points of political needles finer and sharper than the metaphysical ones.

JOHN ADAMS
Diary, Nov. 18, 1782; *Ibid., III,* 315

3. I have lived long enough, and had experience enough of the conduct of governments and people, nations and courts, to be convinced that gratitude, friendship, unsuspecting confidence, and all the amiable passions in human nature, are the most dangerous guides in politics.

JOHN ADAMS
To Robert R. Livingston, Jan. 23, 1783; *Ibid., VIII,* 27

4.   Politics, like religion, hold up torches of martyrdom to the reformers of error.

THOMAS JEFFERSON
To James Ogilvie, Aug. 4, 1811; *Writings, XIII,* 69

5.   The nation which reposes on the pillow of political confidence, will sooner or later end its political existence in a deadly lethargy.

JAMES MADISON
Address to General Assembly of Virginia, Jan. 23, 1799;
Complete Madison, p. 295

6.   A man to be a sound politician & in any degree useful to his country must be governed by higher and steadier considerations than those of personal sympathy and private regard.

MARTIN VAN BUREN
To Dr. Graham A. Worth, Apr. 22, 1819; *Epoch,* p. 173

7.   Speak not of the *Tammany men,* they are but a drop in the waters of bitterness.

MARTIN VAN BUREN
To Dr. Graham A. Worth, Apr. 22, 1819; *Ibid.,* p. 174

8.   *Van Buren became noted for his noncommittal stand toward Adams and his program, and many stories were invented to build up an image of his noncommittalism. The word* VANBURENISH *crept into the jargon of the day. One story concerned a wager made by two of his friends that he would not answer any question definitely. Accordingly, one asked Van Buren . . . if he concurred in the general opinion that the sun rose in the East. Van Buren replied:*

I presume the fact is according to the common impression, but as I sleep until after sunrise, I cannot speak from my own knowledge.

MARTIN VAN BUREN
Ca. 1825; *Ibid.,* p. 299

9.   I find that the remark, " 'Tis distance lends enchantment to the view" is no less true of the political than of the natural world.

FRANKLIN PIERCE
Letter, 1832; *Franklin Pierce,* p. 59

10.   *Politics* and law are (or rather, should be)—merely results, merely the expression of what the people wish.

RUTHERFORD B. HAYES
Letter, Nov. 25, 1885; *Diary and Letters, IV,* 177

11.   Men in political life must be ambitious.

RUTHERFORD B. HAYES
To William McKinley, June 27, 1888; *His America,* p. 277

12. We are apt to be deluded into false security by political catch-words, devised to flatter rather than instruct.

JAMES A. GARFIELD
Address at Hudson College, July 2, 1873; *Future*, p. 14

13. When it is remembered that at no period in the country's history has the long political contest which customarily precedes the day of the national election been waged with greater fervor and intensity, it is a subject of general congratulation that after the controversy at the polls is over . . . the public peace suffered no disturbance. . . .

Nothing could more strikingly illustrate the temper of the American citizen, his love of order, and his loyalty to law. Nothing could more signally demonstrate the strength and wisdom of our political institutions.

CHESTER ALAN ARTHUR
Fourth Annual Message to Congress, Dec. 1, 1884;
Messages and Papers, p. 4822

14. Coming suddenly into the higher public life . . . I was warned of one of the worst pitfalls to be found there. Even if it had been possible for me to use the power of a great office for purely partisan or political purposes, the effects of such a policy stood out before me so prominently on the very threshold that I could only have heeded the warning. I encountered a great deal of abuse when President for my refusal to take part in local politics in my own and other States.

GROVER CLEVELAND
1882; *Courage*, p. 106

15. The politics which has no patriotism in it is always defeated before the tribunal of the American People.

WILLIAM MCKINLEY
Speech at Lake Preston, S.D., Oct. 14, 1899;
Speeches and Addresses, p. 291

16. The success of great popular preachers contains a lesson for students of politics who would themselves convert men to a saving doctrine.

The great preacher reaches the heart of his hearers not by knowledge, but by sympathy—by showing himself a brother man to his fellow men.

And this is just the principle which the student of politics must heed.

WOODROW WILSON
The Princeton Review, March, 1887, *Story*, p. 33

17. Politics is not a problem of setting interests off against each other upon such a plan as that one cannot harm the other.

WOODROW WILSON
Speech in New York, N.Y., May 23, 1912; *Public Papers*, *II*, 433

18. The cure for bad politics is the same as the cure for tuberculosis. It is living in the open.

WOODROW WILSON
Speech at Minneapolis, Minn., Sept. 18, 1912; *Crossroads,* p. 189

19. The problem of politics is cooperation.

WOODROW WILSON
Speech in New York, N.Y., May 23, 1912; *Public Papers, II,* 433

20. Publicity is one of the purifying elements of politics. . . . Nothing checks all the bad practices of politics like public exposure. . . . An Irishman, seen digging around the wall of a house, was asked what he was doing. He answered, "Faith, I am letting the dark out of the cellar." Now, that's exactly what we want to do. . . .

WOODROW WILSON
1912; *New Freedom* (*Hale*), p. 115

21. Politics I conceive to be nothing more than the science of the ordered progress of society along the lines of greatest usefulness and convenience to itself.

WOODROW WILSON
Speech in Washington, D.C., Jan. 6, 1916; *Public Papers, III,* 441

22. Politics is not an art, but a means. It is not a product, but a process. It is the art of government.

CALVIN COOLIDGE
On the Nature of Politics; *Faith,* p. 69

23. Politics is the process of action in public affairs. It is personal, it is individual, and nothing more.

CALVIN COOLIDGE
On the Nature of Politics; *Ibid.,* p. 84

24. Our nation was not founded on the pork barrel, and it has not become great by political log-rolling.

HERBERT HOOVER
Press conference, May 27, 1932; *State Papers, II,* 195

25. The science of politics . . . may properly be said to be in large part the science of the adjustment of conflicting group interests.

FRANKLIN DELANO ROOSEVELT
Address at Winter Park, Fla., Mar. 23, 1936; *Public Papers, V,* 148

26. The future lies with those wise political leaders who realize that the great public is interested more in government than in politics.

FRANKLIN DELANO ROOSEVELT
Address at Jackson Day dinner, Jan. 8, 1940; *Ibid., IX,* 25

27. Our American political situation is about the same from generation

to generation. The main difficulty is that the rising generation never knows about the acts of the previous one—most people think it too much trouble to find out.

HARRY S. TRUMAN
Interview, *ca.* 1950; *Mr. President,* p. 94

28. Politics is a fascinating game, because politics is government. It is the art of government.

HARRY S. TRUMAN
Interview, *ca.* 1950; *Ibid.,* p. 198

29. I have always defined politics to mean the science of government, perhaps the most important science, because it involves the art and ability of people to live together.

HARRY S. TRUMAN
1952; *Memoirs, II,* 499

30. The maneuvers in a battle are like the man in politics. In the military they have . . . a five-paragraph order.

In the first paragraph—You make an estimate of the enemy, his condition and what he can do.

In the second . . . —You make an estimate of your condition and what *you* can do.

In the third . . . —You decide what you are *going* to do.

In the fourth . . . —You set up your logistics and supply sources to *carry* out what you are going to do.

In the fifth . . . —You tell *where* you are going to be so that everybody can reach you. That is all there is to politics.

HARRY S. TRUMAN
American Treasury, p. 347

31. The necessary and wise subordination of the military to civil power will be best sustained when life-long professional soldiers abstain from seeking high political office.

DWIGHT D. EISENHOWER
Letter to Truman, January, 1948; *Memoirs (of Truman), II,* 187

32. There may be some cynics who think that a Platform is just a list of platitudes to lure the naive voter—a sort of façade behind which candidates sneak into power and then do as they please. I am not one of those.

DWIGHT D. EISENHOWER
Address in Washington, D.C., June 7, 1957; *Public Papers . . . Eisenhower, 1957,* p. 454

33. Successful politicians, according to Walter Lippmann, are "insecure and intimidated men, who advance politically only as they placate, appease, bribe, seduce, bamboozle, or otherwise manage to manipulate" the

news and votes of the people who elect them. Years ago the humorist Artemus Ward declared: "I am not a politician, and my other habits are good also."

Politics, in short, has become one of our most neglected, our most abused, and our most ignored professions.

JOHN F. KENNEDY
Address at University of Wisconsin, June 16, 1958; *Strategy*, p. 229

34. If you're in politics and you can't tell when you walk into a room who's for you and who's against you, then you're in the wrong line of work.

LYNDON B. JOHNSON
Story, p. 166

See also Government 99, Honesty 7, Lawyers 1, Legislation 2, Political Parties, Political Philosophy 2, Prosperity 12, Rebellion 1, Religion 20, Right 9, Tolerance 3, Women 11

Popularity

1. Popularity, next to virtue and wisdom, ought to be aimed at; for it is the dictate of wisdom, and is necessary to the practice of virtue in most.

JOHN ADAMS
Diary, Jan. 3, 1759; *Works, II,* 57

2. When I was a young man I courted Popularity. I found her but a coy mistress, and I soon deserted her. . . . Our ancestors, the Puritans, were a most unpopular set of men; yet the world owes all the liberty it possesses to them.

JOHN ADAMS
To Josiah Quincy, June 12, 1823; *Figures,* p. 82

See also Presidency (The) 69, Success 6

Population
See Prosperity 4

Posterity

1. Among the sentiments of most powerful operation upon the human heart, and most highly honorable to the human character, are those of veneration for our forefathers and of love for our posterity. They form the connecting links between the selfish and the social passions. . . .

The barbarian chieftain who defended his country against the Roman invasion [made] an appeal to these irresistible feelings—"Think of your forefathers and of your posterity."

As the original founder of the Roman State is said once to have lifted upon his shoulders the fame and fortunes of all his posterity, so let us never forget that the glory and greatness of all our descendants is in our hands.

JOHN QUINCY ADAMS
Oration at Plymouth, Mass., Dec. 22, 1802; *Oration,* pp. 5, 6, 30

2. Few can be induced to labor exclusively for posterity, and none will do it enthusiastically. Posterity has done nothing for us; and, theorize on it as we may, practically we shall do very little for it unless we are made to think we are, at the same time, doing something for ourselves.

ABRAHAM LINCOLN
Speech in Springfield, Ill., Feb. 22, 1842; *Complete Works, I,* 201

See also Freedom 2, Statesmanship 2

Poverty

1. Abolish plutocracy if you would abolish poverty.

RUTHERFORD B. HAYES
Diary, Feb. 16, 1890; *His America,* p. 501

2. To the peoples of half the globe struggling to break the bonds of mass misery we pledge our best efforts to help them help themselves . . . not because the Communists are doing it, not because we seek their votes, but because it is right.

If the free society cannot help the many who are poor, it can never save the many who are rich.

JOHN F. KENNEDY
Inaugural Address, Jan. 20, 1961

3. No nation can long enjoy great affluence when all the other nations are impoverished.

LYNDON B. JOHNSON
May 28, 1961; *Man and President,* p. 107

4. Very often a lack of jobs and money is not the cause of poverty, but the symptom.

The cause may lie deeper in our failure to give our fellow citizens a fair chance to develop their own capacities, in a lack of education and training, in a lack of medical care and housing, in a lack of decent communities in which to live and bring up their children. But whatever the cause, our joint Federal-local effort must pursue poverty, pursue it wherever it exists. . . .

Our aim is not only to relieve the symptom of poverty, but to cure it, and, above all, to prevent it.

LYNDON B. JOHNSON
State of the Union Address, Jan. 8, 1964; *Vital Speeches,
Jan. 15, 1964,* p. 196

See also Communism 1, 8, Dictatorships 3, Economic Matters, Equality 9, Freedom 21, Ignorance 8, Liberty 36, War 66, Wealth

Power

1. No man is a warmer advocate for proper restraints and wholesome checks in every department of government than I am; but I have never yet been able to discover the propriety of placing it absolutely out of the power of men to render essential services, because a possibility remains of their doing ill.

GEORGE WASHINGTON
To Bushrod Washington, Nov. 10, 1787; *Writings*
(*Fitzpatrick*), *XXIX*, 312

2. The spirit of encroachment [on the Constitution] tends to consolidate the powers of all the departments in one, and thus to create, whatever the form of government, a real despotism. A just estimate of that love of power, and proneness to abuse it, which predominates in the human heart, is sufficient to satisfy us of the truth of this position.

GEORGE WASHINGTON
Farewell Address, Sept. 19, 1796; *Ibid.*, *XXXV*, 228

3. That aspiring, noble principle founded in benevolence, and cherished by knowledge; I mean the love of power, which has been so often the cause of slavery, has, whenever freedom has existed, been the cause of freedom.

JOHN ADAMS
Dissertation on the Canon and the Feudal Law, August, 1765;
Works, III, 448

4. The jaws of power are always open to devour, and her arm is always stretched out, if possible, to destroy the freedom of thinking, speaking, and writing.

JOHN ADAMS
Dissertation on the Canon and the Feudal Law, August, 1765;
Ibid., p. 457

5. Nip the shoots of arbitrary power in the bud, is the only maxim which can ever preserve the liberties of any people.

JOHN ADAMS
"Novanglus," in Boston *Gazette,* Feb. 6, 1775; *Ibid.*, *IV*, p. 43

6. Power naturally grows. Why? Because human passions are insatiable.

JOHN ADAMS
Letter to Roger Sherman, July 18, 1789; *Ibid.*, *VI*, 431

7. One precedent in favor of power is stronger than an hundred against it.

THOMAS JEFFERSON
Notes on Virginia, 1782; *Writings, II*, 959

8. To take a single step beyond the boundaries . . . specially drawn

around the powers of Congress, is to take possession of a boundless field of power, no longer susceptible of any definition.

THOMAS JEFFERSON
An opinion, Feb. 15, 1791; *Works, VII,* 556

9. We confide in our strength, without boasting of it; we respect that of others, without fearing it.

THOMAS JEFFERSON
To William Carmichael and William Short, June 30, 1793;
Works, IV, 17

10. In questions of power . . . let no more be heard of confidence in men, but bind him down from mischief by the chains of the Constitution.

THOMAS JEFFERSON
Resolutions, 1803; *Works, IX,* 471

11. Not in our day, but at no distant one, we may shake a rod over the heads of all, which may make the stoutest tremble. But I hope our wisdom will grow with our power, and teach us that the less we use the power the greater it will be.

THOMAS JEFFERSON
Writings, XV, 436

12. The accumulation of all powers, legislative, executive, and judiciary, in the same hands, whether of one, a few, or many . . . may justly be pronounced the very definition of tyranny.

JAMES MADISON
"Publius," 1788; *Federalist,* p. 47

13. What a perversion of the natural order of things! . . . to make power the primary and central object of the social system, and Liberty but its satellite.

JAMES MADISON
National Gazette, Dec. 20, 1792; *Writings (Hunt), VI,* 120

14. The tenure of power by man is, in the moral purposes of his Creator, upon condition that it shall be exercised to ends of beneficence, to improve the condition of himself and his fellow-men.

JOHN QUINCY ADAMS
First Annual Message to Congress, Dec. 6, 1825;
Messages and Papers, p. 882

15. There is a power in public opinion in this country—and I thank God for it; for it is the most honest and best of all powers—which will not tolerate an incompetent or unworthy man to hold in his weak or wicked hands the lives and fortunes of his fellow-citizens. This power operates alike upon the Government and the incumbent. The former dare not disregard it, and the latter can have no adequate wish that they should,

when he once knows the estimation in which he is held. This public ordeal, therefore, is of great value; in my opinion, much more so than what has, with some propriety, been called the scare-crow of the constitution—the power of impeachment.

MARTIN VAN BUREN
1826; *Epoch*, p. 302

16. Irresponsible power of itself excites distrust, and sooner or later causes, on the part of its possessor, an impatience of popular control and, in the sequel, a desire to counteract popular will.

MARTIN VAN BUREN
1854; *Ibid.*, p. 263

17. See to the government. See that the government does not acquire too much power. Keep a check upon your rulers. Do this, and liberty is safe.

WILLIAM HENRY HARRISON
"Log Cabin" campaign meeting at Fort Meigs, 1840;
Quarterly, January, 1908, p. 205

18. Power is insinuating. Few men are satisfied with less power than they are able to procure. . . . No lover is ever satisfied with the first smile of his mistress.

WILLIAM HENRY HARRISON
"Log Cabin" campaign meeting at Fort Meigs, 1840;
Ibid., p. 206

19. Republics can commit no greater error than to adopt or continue any feature in their systems of government which may be calculated to increase the love of power in the bosoms of those to whom necessity obliges them to commit the management of their affairs; and surely nothing is more likely to produce such a state of mind than the long continuance of an office of high trust.

WILLIAM HENRY HARRISON
Inaugural Address, Mar. 4, 1841

20. We have at length reached that stage of our country's career in which the dangers to be encountered and the exertions to be made are the incidents, not of weakness, but of strength. In foreign relations we have to atemper our power to the less happy condition of other Republics in America and to place ourselves in the calmness and conscious dignity of right by the side of the greatest and wealthiest of the Empires of Europe.

FRANKLIN PIERCE
Fourth Annual Message to Congress, Dec. 2, 1856;
Messages and Papers, p. 2950

21. Justice and mercy should hold the reins of power and the upward avenues of hope be free to all the people.

BENJAMIN HARRISON
As I Knew Them, p. 182

22. A government is not by the people when one party fastens its control upon the country and perpetuates its power by cajoling and betraying the people . . . instead of serving them.

GROVER CLEVELAND
Letter Accepting Nomination for Presidency, Aug. 18, 1884;
Writings, p. 10

23. The danger to American democracy lies not in the least in the concentration of administrative power in responsible and accountable hands. It lies in having the power insufficiently concentrated, so that no one can be held responsible to the people for its use. Concentrated power is palpable, visible, responsible, easily reached, quickly held to account.

THEODORE ROOSEVELT
Eighth Annual Message to Congress, Dec. 8, 1908;
Messages and Papers, p. 7585

24. They talk of my power: my power vanishes into thin air the instant that my fellow citizens who are straight and honest cease to believe that I represent them and fight for what is straight and honest; that is all the strength I have.

THEODORE ROOSEVELT
Speech at Binghamton, N.Y., Oct. 24, 1910; *Works, XVII,* 39

25. Whatever of power I at any time had, I obtained from the people. I could exercise it only as long as . . . the people . . . heartily backed me up.

THEODORE ROOSEVELT
Speech in Chicago, Ill., Aug. 6, 1912; *Ibid.,* p. 297

26. I believe in power; but I believe that responsibility should go with power.

THEODORE ROOSEVELT
Time (magazine), Mar. 3, 1958

27. As a matter of fact and experience, the more power is divided the more irresponsible it becomes.

WOODROW WILSON
1885; *Congressional Government,* p. 93

28. Power consists in one's capacity to link his will with the purpose of others, to lead by reason and a gift of cooperation.

WOODROW WILSON
To Mary A. Hulbert, Sept. 21, 1913; *Story,* p. 148

29. While exercising the great powers of the office I hold, I would regret in a crisis . . . to lose the benefit of patriotic and intelligent criticism.

WOODROW WILSON
To Arthur Brisbane, Apr. 25, 1917; *Life, VII,* 36

30. Power cannot be used with concentrated force against free peoples if it is used by free people.

WOODROW WILSON
Speech at Buffalo, N.Y., Nov. 12, 1917; *Public Papers, V,* 119

31. When we resist . . . the concentration of power [we are] resisting the processes of death, because the concentration of power is what always precedes the destruction of human initiative and, therefore, of human energy.

WOODROW WILSON
Address in New York, N.Y., Sept. 14, 1912; *Crossroads,* p. 109

See also Democracy 22, Force, Freedom 7, 24, Government 23, 24, 56, 59, 70, Happiness 8, Isolationism 5, Knowledge 4, 10, Liberty 5, 6, 7, 19, 35, 45, Life 5, Majorities 5, 10, Monopolies 1, Morality 8, Peace 36, 87, People (The) 1, 11, 12, 24, 31, Political Philosophy 1, Politics 31, Precedents 2, Preparedness 19, Religion 34, Republics 10, Revolutions 8, Rights 14, 17, States' Rights 10, 12, 14, 15, Strikes 1, Taxation 9, War 7

Precedents

1. Precedents are dangerous things; let the rein of government then be braced and held with a steady hand.

GEORGE WASHINGTON
To Henry Lee, Oct. 31, 1786; *Writings (Fitzpatrick), XXIX,* 34

2. Precedents once established are so much positive power.

JAMES MADISON
Address to General Assembly of Virginia, Jan. 23, 1799;
Writings (Hunt), VI, 336

3. Mere precedent is a dangerous source of authority.

ANDREW JACKSON
Veto Message to the Senate, July 10, 1832;
Messages and Papers, p. 1144

See also Power 7, Secrecy 1

Predictions
See Government 75, War 49

Prejudice
See Discrimination, Foreign Relations 26, 47, Jews 4, Negroes, United States 1, Virtue 2

Preparedness

1. There is nothing so likely to produce peace as to be well prepared to meet an enemy.

GEORGE WASHINGTON
To Elbridge Gerry, Jan. 29, 1780;
Writings (Fitzpatrick), XVII, 463

2. The United States ought not to indulge a persuasion that, contrary to the order of human events, they will forever keep at a distance those painful appeals to arms with which the history of every nation abounds. There is rank due to the United States among nations, which will be withheld, if not absolutely lost, by the reputation of weakness. If we desire to avoid insult, we must be able to repel it; if we desire to secure peace, one of the most powerful instruments of our rising prosperity, it must be known, that we are, at all times, ready for war.

GEORGE WASHINGTON
Message to Congress, Dec. 3, 1793; *Ibid., XXXIII,* 165

3. Avoiding occasions of expense by cultivating peace, we should remember also that timely disbursements to prepare for danger frequently prevent much greater disbursements to repel it.

GEORGE WASHINGTON
Farewell Address, Sept. 19, 1796; *Ibid., XXXV,* 230

4. The most sincere neutrality is not a sufficient guard against the depredations of nations at war. To secure respect to a neutral flag requires a naval force organized and ready to vindicate it from insult or aggression. . . .

The institution of a military academy is also recommended by cogent reasons. However pacific the general policy of a nation may be, it ought never to be without an adequate stock of military knowledge for emergencies.

GEORGE WASHINGTON
Eighth Annual Message to Congress, Dec. 7, 1796;
Messages and Papers, p. 193

5. Whatever enables us to go to war, secures our peace.

THOMAS JEFFERSON
To James Monroe, July 11, 1790; *Writings (Ford), V,* 198

6. Sound principles will not justify our taxing the industry of our fellow citizens to accumulate treasure for wars to happen we know not when, and which might not perhaps happen but from the temptations offered by that treasure.

THOMAS JEFFERSON
First Annual Message to Congress, Dec. 8, 1801; *Works, VIII,* 9

7. We shall more certainly preserve peace when it is well understood that we are prepared for war.

ANDREW JACKSON
Farewell Address, Mar. 4, 1837; *Principles*, p. 514

8. Prepare for war in time of peace. Not by fortifications, by navies, or by standing armies. But by policies which will add to the happiness and the comfort of all our people and which will tend to the distribution of intelligence and wealth equally among all. Our strength is a contented and intelligent community.

RUTHERFORD B. HAYES
Diary, June 25, 1887; *Diary and Letters, IV,* 329

9. The nation that can not resist aggression is constantly exposed to it. Its foreign policy is of necessity weak and its negotiations are conducted with disadvantage because it is not in condition to enforce the terms dictated by its sense of right and justice.

GROVER CLEVELAND
First Annual Message to Congress, Dec. 8, 1885;
Messages and Papers, p. 4963

10. Preparation for war is the surest guaranty for peace. . . . Again and again we have owed peace to the fact that we were prepared for war.

THEODORE ROOSEVELT
Speech at Naval War College, June 2, 1897; *Works, XIII,* 183

11. The voice of the weakling or the craven counts for nothing when he clamors for peace; but the voice of the just man armed is potent. We need to keep in a condition of preparedness, especially as regards our navy, not because we want war, but because we desire to stand with those whose plea for peace is listened to with respectful attention.

THEODORE ROOSEVELT
Speech in New York, N.Y., Nov. 11, 1902;
Works (Mem. Ed.), XXIII, 265

12. There is a homely adage which runs, "Speak softly and carry a big stick; you will go far." If the American nation will speak softly and yet build and keep at a pitch of the highest training a thoroughly efficient Navy, the Monroe Doctrine will go far.

THEODORE ROOSEVELT
In Chicago, Ill., Apr. 2, 1903; *Presidential Addresses, I,* 266

13. The first step—in the direction of preparation to avert war if possible, and to be fit for war if it should come—is to teach our men to shoot.

THEODORE ROOSEVELT
Special Message to Congress, Dec. 8, 1908;
Messages and Papers, p. 7616

14. America can not be an ostrich with its head in the sand.

WOODROW WILSON
Speech at Des Moines, Ia., Feb. 1, 1916; *State Papers,* p. 191

15. I once believed in armed preparedness. I advocated it. But I have come now to believe there is a better preparedness in a public mind and a world opinion made ready to grant justice precisely as it exacts it. And justice is better served in conferences of peace than in conflicts at arms.

WARREN G. HARDING
Address to Armament Conference, Feb. 6, 1922; *Messages and Papers,* p. 9067

16. One who brandishes a pistol must be prepared to shoot.

HERBERT HOOVER
1931; *Memoirs, II,* 370

17. The primary purpose of our arms is peace, not war. . . . Our arms will never be used to strike the first blow in any attack. This is not a confession of weakness but a statement of strength. It is our national tradition. . . . Our preparation against danger is our hope of safety.

JOHN F. KENNEDY
Special Message to Congress, Mar. 28, 1961; *Tide,* p. 55

18. The United States, as the world knows, will never start a war. We do not want a war. We do not now expect a war. This generation of Americans has already had enough—more than enough—of war and hate and oppression. We shall be prepared if others wish it. We shall be alert to try to stop it. But we shall also do our part to build a world of peace where the weak are safe and the strong are just.

JOHN F. KENNEDY
At American University, Washington, D.C., June 10, 1963;
Vital Speeches, July 1, 1963, p. 560

19. In this age where there can be no losers in peace and no victors in war—we must recognize the obligation to match national strength with national restraint—we must be prepared at one and the same time for both the confrontation of power and the limitation of power—we must be ready to defend the national interest and to negotiate the common interest. . . .

Those who test our courage will find it strong and those who seek our friendship will find it honorable. We will demonstrate anew that the strong can be just in the use of strength—and the just can be strong in the defense of justice.

LYNDON B. JOHNSON
To Congress, Nov. 27, 1963; *Ibid., Dec. 15, 1963,* p. 130

See also Army, Defense, Disarmament, Experience 1, Foreign Relations 28, Freedom 1, Inflation 1, Military Matters, Navy, Peace 2, 3, 23, Policy 3, Providence 4, Republics 16, Security 8, War 39

Presidency, The

1. My movements to the chair of government will be accompanied by feelings not unlike those of a culprit, who is going to the place of his execution; so unwilling am I, in the evening of a life nearly consumed in public cares, to quit a peaceful abode for an ocean of difficulties, without that competency of political skill, abilities, and inclination, which are necessary to manage the helm.

GEORGE WASHINGTON
To Henry Knox, Apr. 1, 1789; *Writings (Fitzpatrick)*, *XXX*, 260

2. Thus supported by a firm trust in the Great Arbiter of the Universe, aided by the collected wisdom of the Union, and imploring the divine benediction on our joint exertions in the service of our country, I readily engage with you in the arduous but pleasing task of attempting to make a nation happy.

GEORGE WASHINGTON
Reply to the Senate, May 18, 1789; *Messages and Papers*, p. 47

3. In executing the duties of my present important station, I can promise nothing but purity of intentions, and, in carrying these into effect, fidelity and diligence.

GEORGE WASHINGTON
Message to Congress, July 9, 1789;
Writings (Fitzpatrick), *XII*, 159

4. No man who ever held the office of President would congratulate a friend on obtaining it. He will make one man ungrateful, and a hundred men his enemies, for every office he can bestow.

JOHN ADAMS
To Josiah Quincy, Feb. 14, 1825; *Figures*, p. 64

5. No man will ever bring out of the Presidency the reputation which carried him into it.

THOMAS JEFFERSON
To Edward Rutledge, Dec. 27, 1796; *Writings, IX*, 353

6. General Washington set the example of voluntary retirement after eight years. I shall follow it. And a few more precedents will oppose the obstacle of habit to any one who after a while shall endeavor to extend his term.

THOMAS JEFFERSON
To John Taylor, Jan. 6, 1805; *Ibid., XI*, 58

7. I am tired of an office where I can do no more good than many others, who would be glad to be employed in it. To myself, personally, it brings nothing but unceasing drudgery and daily loss of friends.

THOMAS JEFFERSON
To John Dickinson, Jan. 13, 1807; *Ibid., IX*, 10

8. I have the consolation of having added nothing to my private fortune during my public service, and of retiring with hands as clean as they are empty.

THOMAS JEFFERSON
To Count Diodati, 1807; *Dictionary*, p. 1087

9. I have the consolation to reflect that during the period of my administration not a drop of the blood of a single fellow citizen was shed by the sword of war or of the law.

THOMAS JEFFERSON
To Count Dugnani, Feb. 14, 1818; *Ibid., XIX*, 256

10. I would take no step to advance or promote pretensions to the Presidency. If that office was to be the prize of cabal and intrigue, of purchasing newspapers, bribing by appointments, or bargaining for foreign missions, I had no ticket in that lottery. Whether I had the qualities necessary for a President of the United States was, to say the least, very doubtful to myself. But that I had no talents for obtaining the office by such means was perfectly clear.

JOHN QUINCY ADAMS
Feb. 25, 1821; *Memoirs, IV*, 298

11. A turbulent time will be the lot of that man who may come in [to the Executive chair] thro any channel save that of preference by the people; and God grant it may always be so.

ANDREW JACKSON
To Maj. Samuel Swartwout, Dec. 14, 1824;
Proceedings, XXXI, 78

12. The chief magistrate of a great and powerful nation should never indulge in party feelings. His conduct should be liberal and disinterested, always bearing in mind that he acts for the whole and not a part of the community. By this course you will exalt the national character, and acquire for yourself a name as imperishable as monumental marble. Consult no party in your choice; pursue the dictates of that unerring judgment which has so long and so often benefitted our country and rendered conspicuous its rulers. These are the . . . feelings of an undissembled patriot.

ANDREW JACKSON
To James Monroe, 1817; *Andrew Jackson*
(*G. W. Johnson*), p. 192

13. If elected, I will:
   1. Confine my service to a single term.
   2. Disclaim all right of control over the public treasury.
   3. Eschew any attempt to influence the elections.
   4. Exercise due regard for laws passed by representatives of the people, and, within specified limitations, limit my exercise of the veto power.

5. Never suffer the influence of my office to be used for partisan purposes.

6. If requested, I will furnish to the Senate my reasons for removals from office.

7. Never suffer the executive "to become the source of legislation" (expunging resolution).

WILLIAM HENRY HARRISON
To Harmar Denny, Dec. 2, 1838; *Tippecanoe,* p. 326

14. It has ever appeared to me, that the office of President of the United States should not be sought after by any individual, but that the people should spontaneously, and with their own free will, accord the distinguishing honor to the man whom they believed would best perform its important duties.

WILLIAM HENRY HARRISON
"Log Cabin" campaign meeting, Fort Meigs, 1840; *Quarterly, January, 1908,* p. 197

15. It is the part of wisdom for a republic to limit the service of that officer at least to whom she has intrusted the management of her foreign relations, the execution of her laws, and the command of her armies and navies to a period so short as to prevent his forgetting that he is the accountable agent not the principal; the servant, not the master.

WILLIAM HENRY HARRISON
Inaugural Address, Mar. 4, 1841

16. No candidate for the Presidency ought ever to remain in the Cabinet. He is an unsafe advisor.

JAMES K. POLK
Feb. 21, 1848; *Diary (Quaife), III,* 350

17. The preservation of the Constitution from infraction is the President's highest duty. . . . The President's power is negative merely, and not affirmative. He can enact no law.

JAMES K. POLK
Fourth Annual Message to Congress, Dec. 5, 1848; *Messages and Papers, IV,* 2512

18. Any attempt to coerce the President to yield his sanction to measures which he cannot approve would be a violation of the spirit of the Constitution, palpable and flagrant; and if successful would break down the independence of the executive department, and make the President . . . the mere instrument of a majority of Congress.

JAMES K. POLK
Message, December, 1848; *Chips,* p. 208

19. I feel exceedingly relieved that I am now free from all public cares. With me it is emphatically true that the Presidency is "no bed of roses." I

am sure I shall be a happier man in my retirement than I have been during the four years I have filled the highest office in the gift of my countrymen.

JAMES K. POLK
Mar. 4, 1849; *Diary (Quaife), IV,* 373

20. The appointive power vested in the President imposes delicate and onerous duties. . . . I shall make honesty, capacity, and fidelity, indispensable prerequisites to the disposal of office, and the absence of [any] of these qualities shall be deemed sufficient cause for removal.

ZACHARY TAYLOR
Inaugural Address, Mar. 5, 1849

21. The Presidency is a distinction far more glorious than the crown of any hereditary monarch in Christendom; but yet it is a crown of thorns.

JAMES BUCHANAN
To Nahum Capen, June 26, 1852; *Life, II,* 42

22. I have no other object of earthly ambition than to leave my country in a peaceful and prosperous condition, and to live in the affections and respect of my countrymen.

JAMES BUCHANAN
Special Message to Congress, Feb. 2, 1858; *Messages,* p. 191

23. I am . . . heartily tired of my position as president. I shall leave it . . . with much greater satisfaction than when entering on the duties of the office.

JAMES BUCHANAN
To Sarah Polk, Sept. 19, 1859; *Works, X,* 332

24. I have had a hard time of it during my administration, but, upon a careful review of all my conduct, I should not change it in a single important measure if this were now in my power.

JAMES BUCHANAN
Letter in the Philadelphia *Times,* Sept. 21, 1861; *Messages,* p. 303

25. I am very grateful for the renewed confidence which has been accorded to me both by the convention and by the National League. . . . The part I am entitled to appropriate as a compliment is only that part which I may lay hold of as being [their] opinion . . . that I am not entirely unworthy to be entrusted with the place which I have occupied for the last three years. But I do not allow myself to suppose . . . that I am either the greatest or best man in America, but rather they have concluded that it is not best to swap horses while crossing the river. . . .

ABRAHAM LINCOLN
Reply to National Union League, June 9, 1864;
Complete Works, X, 122

26. What is the Presidency worth to me if I have no country?

ABRAHAM LINCOLN
Washington, D.C., 1864; *War Years, III,* 282

27. I desire so to conduct the affairs of this administration that if at the end, when I come to lay down the reins of power, I have lost every friend on earth, I shall at least have one friend left, and that friend shall be down inside of me.

ABRAHAM LINCOLN
Reply to Missouri Committee of Seventy, 1864,
Life (Tarbell), II, 175

28. Only events and not a man's exertions in his own behalf, can make a President.

ABRAHAM LINCOLN
Ca. 1859; *Circuit,* p. 153

29. As President, I have no eyes but constitutional eyes; I cannot see you.

ABRAHAM LINCOLN
To a South Carolina commission, *ca.* 1861; *Lincoln Treasury,* p. 55

30. I do not intend to be overawed or controlled by real or pretended friends, nor do I mean to be bullied or driven from my purpose by my enemies.

ANDREW JOHNSON
Speech in Washington, D.C., Feb. 22, 1866; *Document,* p. 5

31. It was my fortune or misfortune to be called to the Chief Magistracy without any prior political training. Under the circumstances it is but reasonable to suppose that errors of judgment must have occurred.

ULYSSES S. GRANT
Message to Congress, December, 1876;
Messages and Papers, p. 400

32. I recommend an amendment to the Constitution prescribing a term of six years for the Presidential office and forbidding a re-election.

RUTHERFORD B. HAYES
Inaugural Address, Mar. 4, 1877

33. I am not liked as a President, by politicians in office, in the press or in Congress. But I am content to abide the judgment—the sober second thought—of the people.

RUTHERFORD B. HAYES
Diary, Mar. 1, 1878; *Diary and Letters, III,* 462

34. Nobody ever left the Presidency with less regret, less disappoint-

ment, fewer heartburnings, or more general content with the result of his term (in his own heart, I mean) than I do.

> RUTHERFORD B. HAYES
> To Guy M. Bryan, Jan. 1, 1881; *Ibid., V,* 632

35. No more public life for me! I will retain the place of the one man who having reached the Presidency would not seek or accept a second term.

> RUTHERFORD B. HAYES
> To Hon. W. H. Smith, Apr. 3, 1888; *Ibid., IV,* 382

36. Presidents in the past have always been better than their adversaries have predicted.

> RUTHERFORD B. HAYES
> Diary, July 26, 1888; *Ibid.,* p. 400

37. Only a few Presidents have had the felicity to see their party stronger at the close of their terms than it was at the beginning. Only a few have left their country more prosperous than they found it. Results determine. The tree is known by its fruit.

> RUTHERFORD B. HAYES
> Diary, Dec. 10, 1891; *Ibid.,* p. 38

38. I look upon the four years next to come as a self-inflicted penance for the good of my country. I see no pleasure in it.

> GROVER CLEVELAND
> To Wilson S. Bissell, Nov. 13, 1884; *Courage,* p. 190

39. Franklin, I wish that you may never become President.

> GROVER CLEVELAND
> Said to Franklin Delano Roosevelt; *Omnibus,* p. 31

40. A President has a great chance; his position is almost that of a king and a prime minister rolled into one; once he has left office he cannot do very much; and he is a fool if he fails to realize it all and to be profoundly thankful for having had the great chance. No President ever enjoyed himself in the Presidency as much as I did; and no President after leaving office took as much joy in life as I am taking.

> THEODORE ROOSEVELT
> To Lady Delamere, Mar. 7, 1911;
> *Theodore Roosevelt (Benson),* p. 223

41. It isn't how long you are President that counts, but what you accomplish as President. I've had my chance; I did fairly well with it. I made some kind of a place in history for myself. Someone else might have done better than I did, but I could not, for I did my best.

> THEODORE ROOSEVELT
> Said to Henry L. Stoddard, 1911; *As I Knew Them,* p. 316

42.   I am strongly inclined to the view that it would have been a wiser provision, as it was at one time voted in the convention, to make the term of Presidency seven years and render him ineligible thereafter.

WILLIAM HOWARD TAFT
Speech at the University of Virginia, January, 1915;
Presidency, p. 4

43.   A President's usefulness is measured, not by efficiency, but by calendar months. It is reckoned that if he be good at all he will be good for four years. A Prime Minister must keep himself in favor of the majority, a President need only keep alive.

WOODROW WILSON
1885; Congressional Government, p. 249

44.   The President is at liberty, both in law and conscience, to be as big a man as he can.

WOODROW WILSON
1908; Constitutional Government, p. 70

45.   A Presidential campaign may easily degenerate into a mere personal contest, and so lose its real dignity. There is no indispensable man.

WOODROW WILSON
Acceptance, at Sea Girt, N.J., of Nomination for Presidency,
Aug. 7, 1912; Crossroads, p. 22

46.   America is safe only because we do not know who the future Presidents of the United States are going to be.

WOODROW WILSON
Address at Scranton, Pa., Sept. 23, 1912; Ibid., p. 240

47.   I never dreamed such loneliness and desolation of heart possible. . . . The very magnitude and fatefulness of the tasks I have every day to face dominates me and holds me steady to my duty. Nothing less great, I imagine, could.

WOODROW WILSON
Letter, Sept. 6, 1914, written after the death of his wife in the
White House; Life and Letters, IV, 460

48.   The presidential office is not a rosewater affair. This is an office in which a man must put on his war paint.

WOODROW WILSON
Life and Letters, IV, 44

49.   I do not think the Presidency ought to deny one the contact with his personal friends or make him insensible to the very agreeable amenities of life.

WARREN G. HARDING
To Bernard Baruch, Jan. 24, 1922;
Public Years (Baruch), p. 189

50. My God, this is a hell of a job! I have no trouble with my enemies. I can take care of them all right. But my damn friends, my God-damn friends, White, they're the ones that keep me walking the floor nights!

WARREN G. HARDING

Told to William Allen White; *Autobiography (of W. A. White)*

51. I do not choose to run.

CALVIN COOLIDGE

Statement, Aug. 2, 1927; *re* his decision about a second term; *Autobiography*, p. 243

52. You have to stand every day three or four hours of visitors [to the White House]. Nine-tenths of them want something they ought not to have. If you keep dead-still they will run down in three or four minutes. If you even cough or smile they will start up all over again.

CALVIN COOLIDGE

To Herbert Hoover, 1928; *Memoirs (of Hoover)*, II, 55

53. The President cannot, with success, constantly appeal to the country. After a time he will get no response.

CALVIN COOLIDGE

Autobiography, p. 224

54. An examination of the records of those Presidents who have served eight years will disclose in most every instance the latter part of their term has shown very little in the way of constructive accomplishment.

CALVIN COOLIDGE

Ibid., p. 242

55. I think the American public wants a solemn ass as a President and I think I'll go along with them.

CALVIN COOLIDGE

To Ethel Barrymore; *Time (magazine)*, *May 16, 1955*

56. The Presidency is more than executive responsibility. It is the inspiring symbol of all that is highest in America's purposes and ideals. . . . The office touches the happiness of every home. It deals with the peace of nations. No man could think of it except in terms of solemn consecration.

HERBERT HOOVER

Message to Republican National Convention, Kansas City, Mo., June 14, 1928; *Memoirs*, II, 196

57. The Presidency is more than an administrative office. It must be the symbol of American ideals. . . . It must be the instrument by which national conscience is livened and it must under the guidance of the Almighty interpret and follow that conscience.

HERBERT HOOVER

1928; *New Day*, p. 44

58.   The original constitutional concept of the President's office [has] certainly become enlarged. He [has] become a broader policymaker in legislation, foreign affairs, economic and social life than the Founding Fathers ever contemplated.

HERBERT HOOVER
1928; *Memoirs, II,* 216

59.   A few hair shirts are part of the mental wardrobe of every man. The President differs only from other men in that he has a more extensive wardrobe.

HERBERT HOOVER
Speech in Washington, D.C., Dec. 14, 1929; *After Dinner,* p. 13

60.   In the end the President has become increasingly the depository of all national ills, especially if things go wrong.

HERBERT HOOVER
1933; *Memoirs, II,* 216

61.   I can do almost anything in the goldfish bowl of the President's life, but I'll be hanged if I can say my prayers in it.

FRANKLIN DELANO ROOSEVELT
1934; *As FDR Said,* p. 146

62.   Theodore Roosevelt said, "Sometimes I wish I could be President and Congress too."

Well, I suppose if the truth were told, he is not the only President that has had that idea.

FRANKLIN DELANO ROOSEVELT
Remarks in Dallas, Tex., June 12, 1936; *Public Papers, V,* 215

63.   My friends, the Presidency is not a prize to be won by mere glittering promises. It is not a commodity to be sold by high-pressure salesmanship and national advertising. The Presidency is a most sacred trust and it ought not to be dealt with on any level other than an appeal to reason and humanity.

FRANKLIN DELANO ROOSEVELT
Campaign speech, Philadelphia, Pa., Oct. 23, 1940; *Ibid., IX,* 488

64.   The first twelve years are the hardest.

FRANKLIN DELANO ROOSEVELT
Press Conference

65.   Decisions that the President has to make often affect the lives of tens of millions of people around the world, but that does not mean that they should take longer to make. Some men can make decisions and some cannot. Some men fret and delay under criticism. I used to have a saying that applies here . . . "If you can't stand the heat get out of the kitchen."

HARRY S. TRUMAN

66. I was very much shocked when I was told of the President's death and the weight of the government had fallen on my shoulders. I did not know what reaction the country would have to the death of a man whom they all practically worshipped. . . . I decided the best thing to do was to go home and get as much rest as possible and face the music. . . . Went to bed, went to sleep, and did not worry any more that day.

HARRY S. TRUMAN
Diary, Apr. 12, 1945; *Mr. President,* p. 110

67. Being a President is like riding a tiger. A man has to keep on riding or be swallowed.

HARRY S. TRUMAN
1945; *Memoirs, II,* 1

68. Jefferson . . . was a master politician, and this helped make him a great leader. A President has to be a politician in order to get the majority to go along with him on his program.

HARRY S. TRUMAN
1948; *Ibid., II,* 192

69. A President cannot always be popular. He has to be able to say *yes* and *no,* and more often *no* to most of the propositions that are put up to him by partisan groups and special interests who are always pulling at the White House for one thing or another. If the President is easily influenced and interested in keeping in line with the press and the polls, he is a complete washout. Every great President in our history had a policy of his own, which eventually won the people's support.

HARRY S. TRUMAN
1948; *Ibid.,* p. 196

70. The official position of the United States . . . is defined by decisions and declarations of the President. There can be only one voice in stating the position of this country in the field of foreign relations. This is of fundamental constitutional significance.

HARRY S. TRUMAN
1950; *Ibid.,* p. 355

71. I am the thirty-second man to be President. If you count the administration of Grover Cleveland twice because another President held office between Cleveland's first and second terms, you might try to justify the designation of me as thirty-third President. But why don't you number all the second terms of other Presidents and the third and fourth terms of President Roosevelt, and where will you be? I am the thirty-second President.

HARRY S. TRUMAN
1951; *Mr. President,* p. 253

72. The man who occupies the high office of President is always aware that he is there only because more people wanted him than wanted the other fellow. But if he is to judge his situation by the people around him, he will hear a hundred voices telling him that he is the greatest man in the world for every one that tells him he is not. A President, if he is to have clear perspective and never get out of touch, must cut through the voices around him, know his history, and make certain of the reliability of the information he gets.

HARRY S. TRUMAN
1952; *Memoirs, II*, 493

73. To be President of the United States is to be lonely, very lonely at times of great decisions.

HARRY S. TRUMAN
1955; *Ibid., I*, ix

74. The President hears a hundred voices telling him that he is the greatest man in the world. He must listen carefully indeed to hear the one voice that tells him he is not.

HARRY S. TRUMAN

75. The duties of the President are essentially endless. No daily schedule of appointments can give a full timetable—or even a faint indication of the President's responsibilities. . . . In Washington, on a weekend absence, indeed even at a ceremonial dinner, the old saying is true: "A President never escapes from his office."

DWIGHT D. EISENHOWER
Radio and television address, Feb. 29, 1956; *Public Papers* . . .
Eisenhower, 1956, p. 48

76. My record of fourteen years supporting public education, supporting complete separation of church and state, and resisting pressures from any source on any issue should be clear by now to everyone. . . .

After Buchanan this nation needed a Lincoln; after Taft, we needed Franklin Roosevelt, and after eight years of drugged and fitful sleep this nation needs strong, creative Democratic leadership in the White House. . . .

We are not here to curse the darkness, but to light the candle that can guide us through that darkness to a safe and sane future. . . .

Courage—not complacency—is our need today. Leadership—not salesmanship.

JOHN F. KENNEDY
Acceptance of Nomination for Presidency, Los Angeles, Cal.,
July 15, 1960; *Vital Speeches, Aug. 1, 1960*, p. 610

77. No President can excuse or pardon the slightest deviation from irreproachable standards of behavior on the part of any member of the

Executive Branch. For his firmness and determination is the ultimate source of public confidence in the government of the United States.

JOHN F. KENNEDY
Special Message to Congress, Apr. 27, 1961; *Public Papers . . . Kennedy, 1961,* p. 334

See also Assassination, Duty 4, Elections 1, Faith 11, Gifts, Government 15, Handshaking, History 16, Office Seekers 5, 6, Politics 14, Press (The) 14, 22, Public Office, Public Opinion 13, Religion 30, Right 3, Soldiers 3, Understanding 2, Veto Power, Vice-Presidency 2

Press, The

1. None of the means of information are more sacred, or have been cherished with more tenderness and care by the settlers of America, than the press. . . . And you, Messieurs printers, whatever the tyrants of the earth may say of your paper, have done important service to your country. . . .

Be not intimidated, therefore, by any terrors, from publishing with the utmost freedom whatever can be warranted by the laws of your country; nor suffer yourselves to be wheedled out of your liberty by any pretenses of politeness, delicacy, or decency. These, as they are often used, are but three different names for hypocrisy, chicanery, and cowardice.

JOHN ADAMS
Dissertation on the Canon and Feudal Law, August, 1765;
Works, III, p. 457

2. The abuses of the press are notorious. . . . License of the press is no proof of liberty. When a people are corrupted, the press may be made an engine to complete their ruin. . . . Liberty can no more exist without virtue and independence, than the body can live and move without a soul.

JOHN ADAMS
"Novanglus," in Boston *Gazette,* Feb. 6, 1775; *Ibid., IV,* 31

3. The freedom of the press is one of the great bulwarks of liberty, and can never be restrained but by despotic governments.

THOMAS JEFFERSON
Article XIV, Virginia Declaration of Rights, 1776; *Writings, I,* 23

4. Our liberty depends on the freedom of the press, and that cannot be hunted without being lost.

THOMAS JEFFERSON
To James Currie, Jan. 18, 1786; *Ibid., IV,* 131

5. The basis of our government being the opinion of the people, the very first object should be to keep that right; and were it left to me to decide whether we should have a government without newspapers, or newspapers without a government, I should not hesitate a moment to pre-

fer the latter. But I should mean that every man should receive those papers, and be capable of reading them.

THOMAS JEFFERSON
To Edward Carrington, Jan. 16, 1787; *Ibid., VI,* 57

6. It is a melancholy truth, that a suppression of the press could not more completely deprive the nation of its benefits than is done by its abandoned prostitution to falsehood.

THOMAS JEFFERSON
To John Norvell, June 11, 1807; *Ibid., XI,* 224

7. Perhaps an editor might . . . divide his paper into four chapters, heading the first, Truths; 2d, Probabilities; 3d, Possibilities; 4, Lies.

THOMAS JEFFERSON
To John Norvell, June 11, 1807; *Ibid.,* p. 225

8. The man who never looks into a newspaper is better informed than he who reads them, inasmuch as he who knows nothing is nearer the truth than he whose mind is filled with falsehoods and errors.

THOMAS JEFFERSON
To John Norvell, June 11, 1807; *Ibid.*

9. Where the press is free, and every man able to read, all is safe.

THOMAS JEFFERSON
To Col. Charles Yancey, Jan. 6, 1816; *Ibid., X,* 4

10. The press is the best instrument for enlightening the mind of man, and improving him as a rational, moral and social being.

THOMAS JEFFERSON
To A. Corey, Oct. 31, 1823; *Ibid., XV,* 489

11. To answer newspaper accusations would be an endless task. The tongue of falsehood can never be silenced, and I have not time to spare from public business to the vindication of myself.

JOHN QUINCY ADAMS
Diary, Dec. 31, 1821; *Memoirs, V,* 469

12. The press is the Palladium of our liberties. . . . It is the object of all who really take an interest in the honor and welfare of our country to elevate the character of the press and make it the vehicle of truth and useful knowledge.

ANDREW JACKSON
To John Randolph, Nov. 11, 1831; *Correspondence, IV,* 371

13. The maxim which our ancestors derived from the mother country that "freedom of the press is the great bulwark of civil and religious liberty" is one of the most precious legacies which they have left us. We have learned, too, from our own as well as the experience of other countries,

that golden shackles, by whomsoever or by whatever pretense imposed, are
as fatal to it as the iron bonds of despotism.

WILLIAM HENRY HARRISON
Inaugural Address, Mar. 4, 1841

14. I must be the head of my own administration, and will not be controlled by any newspaper, or particular individual whom it serves.

JAMES K. POLK
To Andrew Jackson, Mar. 26, 1845; *Correspondence
(of Jackson), VI,* 390

15. With customary newspaper exaggeration of army news we may be
sure that in tomorrow's prints . . . all the little Colt's revolvers will have
grown into horse-pistols.

ABRAHAM LINCOLN
1862; *War Years, II,* 243

16. I would honor the man who would give to his country a good newspaper.

RUTHERFORD B. HAYES
Speech at Baltimore, Md., Feb. 12, 1881;
Presidents and the Press, p. 478

17. The chief danger which threatens the influence and honor of the
press is the tendency of its liberty to degenerate into license. . . .

JAMES A. GARFIELD
Address to the Ohio Editorial Association, July 11, 1878;
Works, II, 580

18. The newspapers must not be taken too seriously.

BENJAMIN HARRISON
"Musings on Current Topics," *North American Review,*
March, 1901

19. We have all of us at times suffered from the liberty of the press, but
we have to take the good and the bad. I think we certainly ought to hesitate very seriously before passing any law that will interfere with the
broadest public utterance. . . . It is a great deal better to err a little bit on
the side of having too much discussion and having too virulent language
used by the press, rather than to err on the side of having them not say
what they ought to say, especially with reference to public men and
measures.

THEODORE ROOSEVELT
Speech in New York Assembly, Mar. 27, 1883; *Works, XIV,* 22

20. The more I see of the Czar, the Kaiser, and the Mikado, the better

I am content with democracy, even if we have to include the American newspapers as one of its assets—liability would be a better term.

THEODORE ROOSEVELT
Letter to Henry Cabot Lodge, June 16, 1905; *His Time, I,* 394

21. I find that it is absolutely useless to try to correct untruths or misrepresentations even of the most flagrant kind in the newspapers.

THEODORE ROOSEVELT
To W. Emlen Roosevelt, Nov. 9, 1907; *Ibid., II,* 52

22. I am going to do what I think is best for the country. The misrepresentations which are made by the muckraking correspondents I cannot neutralize, and I don't intend to. . . .

WILLIAM HOWARD TAFT
To J. H. Cosgrave, Feb. 23, 1910; *Biography, I,* 539

23. I personally find high satisfaction in the knowledge that it is possible in this land of ours for anyone to establish a newspaper or a news service and to enjoy the freedom of operation guaranteed by our fathers. . . . I am glad, too, that our Government never has seen fit to subsidize a newspaper or a news service and I dare make the prediction that it never will.

FRANKLIN DELANO ROOSEVELT
To Joseph V. Connolly, Apr. 13, 1934; *Public Papers, III,* 181

24. Freedom of conscience, of education, of speech, of assembly are among the very fundamentals of democracy and all of them would be nullified should freedom of the press ever be successfully challenged.

FRANKLIN DELANO ROOSEVELT
To W. N. Hardy, Sept. 4, 1940; *Dictionary,* p. 967

25. I . . . will die for the freedom of the press, even for the freedom of newspapers that call me everything that is a good deal less than . . . a gentleman.

DWIGHT D. EISENHOWER
Press conference, Moscow, Russia, Aug. 14, 1945;
Eisenhower Speaks, p. 46

See also Censors, Freedom 5, 12, Muckrakers, Power 4, Supreme Court 2

Pride
See Fighting 5, Public Opinion 7

Principles
1. My fixed principle never to be the tool of any man, nor the partisan of any nation, would forever exclude me from the smiles and favors of courts.

JOHN ADAMS
Diary, Nov. 18, 1782; *Works, III,* 315

2. Every honest man will suppose honest acts to flow from honest principles, and the rogues may rail without intermission.

THOMAS JEFFERSON
To Benjamin Rush, Dec. 20, 1801; *Works, IV,* 426

3. My principle is to do whatever is right, and leave consequences to Him who has the disposal of them.

THOMAS JEFFERSON
To James Martin, Sept. 20, 1813; *Writings, XIII,* 387

4. My principles are convictions.

JAMES BUCHANAN
Speech at Greensburg, Pa., Oct. 7, 1852; *Life, II,* 45

5. Important principles may and must be flexible.

ABRAHAM LINCOLN
Last public address, Washington, D.C., Apr. 11, 1865; *Complete Works, XI,* 92

6. In the support and practice of correct principles we can never reach wrong results.

ANDREW JOHNSON
Speech at Nashville, Tenn., 1864; *Chips,* p. 286

7. Our differences are policies, our agreements principles.

WILLIAM McKINLEY
Speech at Des Moines, Ia., 1901

8. Men and times change—but principles—never.

GROVER CLEVELAND
1904; *Man and Statesman, II,* 321

9. I have gotten over being frightened by being told that I am forgetting the principles of the fathers. The principles of the fathers are maintained by those who maintain them with reason, and according to the fitness of the thing, and not by those who are constantly shaking them before the mass of voters when they have no application.

WILLIAM HOWARD TAFT
In Washington, D.C., May 8, 1909; *Presidential Addresses,* p. 83

10. Principles lie back of our action. America would be unconceivable without them. These principles are not incompatible with great material prosperity. On the contrary . . . they are indispensable to it.

WOODROW WILSON
Address in New York, N.Y., Dec. 6, 1911; *Life, IV,* 55

11. We shall be the more American if we but remain true to the principles in which we have been bred. They are not the principles of a prov-

ince or of a single continent. We have known and boasted all along that they were the principles of a liberated mankind.

WOODROW WILSON
Second Inaugural Address, Mar. 4, 1917

12. We should try to guide ourselves by general principles and not get lost in particulars.

CALVIN COOLIDGE
Autobiography, p. 100

13. The great principles of life do not change; they are permanent and well known. Men are not ignorant of what justice requires. No power can ever be brought into existence which will relieve of obligations. The sole opportunity for progress lies in their faithful discharge.

CALVIN COOLIDGE
Address at Fredericksburg, Va., July 6, 1922; Citizenship, p. 117

14. The basic principles laid down in the Ten Commandments and the Sermon on the Mount are as applicable today as when they were declared, but they require a host of subsidiary clauses. The ten ways to evil in the time of Moses have increased to ten thousand now.

HERBERT HOOVER
Address, May 7, 1924; *Memoirs, II,* 170

15. To stand upon the ramparts and die for our principles is heroic, but to sally forth to battle and win for our principles is something more than heroic.

FRANKLIN DELANO ROOSEVELT
Speech at Houston, Tex., June, 1928

16. A people that values its privileges above its principles soon loses both.

DWIGHT D. EISENHOWER
First Inaugural Address, Jan. 20, 1953

See also Democracy 9, Errors 15, Freedom 5, Greatness 8, Honesty 2, Jews 5, Liberty 33, Neutrality 7, Opinion 6, Patriotism 8, People (The) 17, Politics 16, Preparedness 6, Public Office 21, Reforms 3, Revolutions 1, Right 2, Russia 3, 4, States' Rights 17, Success 8, 9, Tolerance 3, Union 14, Unity 2, Virtue 4, Voters 2, War 32, 44, 46

Privileges

1. Great responsibility must go hand in hand with great privileges.

THEODORE ROOSEVELT
To King Edward VII, Feb. 12, 1908;
Works (Mem. Ed.), XXIV, 318

2. Sound business need have no fear of progressive government. It is only the business that thrives on special privilege that is in danger.

WOODROW WILSON
Speech in Chicago, Ill., Feb. 12, 1912; *Chicago Record Herald,*
Feb. 13, 1912

See also Government 94, 106, Principles 16, Rights 8

Problems

1. Let us not engage in the wrong argument at the wrong time, between the wrong people in the wrong country, while the real problems of our time grow and multiply, fertilized by our neglect.

JOHN F. KENNEDY
Speech at Yale University, June 11, 1962; *Public Papers . . .*
Kennedy, 1962, p. 474

2. Our problems are man-made. Therefore, they can be solved by man. And man can be as big as he wants. No problem of human destiny is beyond human beings. Man's reason and spirit have often solved the seemingly unsolvable—and we believe they can do it again.

JOHN F. KENNEDY
In Washington, D.C., June 10, 1963;
Vital Speeches, July 1, 1963, p. 559

See also Education 19, History 16, Hope 2, Materialism, Peace 84, Policy 3, Women 8

Progress

1. The natural progress of things is for liberty to yield and government to gain ground.

THOMAS JEFFERSON
To Edward Carrington, May 27, 1788; *Works, II,* 404

2. I do not care for these dilettante men who never rise to righteous wrath, for they also never rise to wholesome enthusiasm, and without enthusiasm there is no progress in the world.

WOODROW WILSON

3. The world has to steady down. We have been talking about getting back to normal. That doesn't mean the old order, that doesn't mean looking backward. It is the short and easy way of saying "Again to Stability," "Once More to Regularity." There hasn't been a backward look in America for 300 years, but the man who faces the future with highest assurances is he who has noted the paths which made his progress secure.

WARREN G. HARDING
At Marion, Ohio, Aug. 4, 1920;
Speeches of Warren G. Harding, p. 47

4. Whatever tends to standardize the community, to establish fixed and rigid methods of thought, tends to fossilize society. . . . It is the ferment of ideas, the clash of disagreeing judgments, the privilege of the individual to develop his own thoughts and shape his own character, that makes progress possible.

CALVIN COOLIDGE
Speech at Omaha, Neb., Oct. 6, 1919; *Calvin Coolidge (Hennessy)*, p. 374

5. Today there are almost nine automobiles for each ten families, where seven and one-half years ago only enough automobiles were running to average less than four for each ten families. The slogan of progress is changing from the full dinner pail to the full garage. Our people have more to eat, better things to wear, and better homes. . . . All this progress means far more than increased creature comforts. It finds a thousand interpretations into a greater and fuller life.

HERBERT HOOVER
1928; *New Day*, p. 169

6. Progress is born of cooperation in the community—not from governmental restraints.

HERBERT HOOVER
Inaugural Address, Mar. 4, 1929

7. The word "progress" is a better word than "recovery" because progress means not only a sound business and a sound agriculture, sound from the material point of view, but it means, with equal importance, a sound improvement in American life.

FRANKLIN DELANO ROOSEVELT
Address at Atlanta, Ga., Nov. 29, 1935; *Public Papers, IV*, 478

8. I see one-third of a nation ill-housed, ill-clad, ill-nourished. . . .

The test of our progress is not whether we add more to the abundance of those who have much; it is whether we provide enough for those who have too little. . . .

Government is competent when all who compose it work as trustees for the whole people. It can make constant progress when it keeps abreast of all the facts.

FRANKLIN DELANO ROOSEVELT
Second Inaugural Address, Jan. 20, 1937

9. Our liberty . . . is endangered if we pause for the passing moment, if we rest on our achievements, if we resist the pace of progress. For time and the world do not stand still. Change is the law of life. And those who look only to the past or the present are certain to miss the future.

JOHN F. KENNEDY
At Frankfurt, Germany, June 25, 1963;
Vital Speeches, July 15, 1963, p. 579

Prohibition

1. Constitutional prohibition has been adopted by the Nation. . . . It is the most demoralizing factor in our public life.

WARREN G. HARDING
Second Annual Message to Congress, Dec. 8, 1922; *Message,* p. 9

2. I do not favor the repeal of the Eighteenth Amendment. I stand for the efficient enforcement of the laws enacted thereunder. . . .

Our country has deliberately undertaken a great social and economic experiment, noble in motive and far-reaching in purpose. It must be worked out constructively.

HERBERT HOOVER
Acceptance of Nomination for Presidency, Kansas City, Mo.,
1928; *Memoirs, II,* 201

3. Prohibition cast a cloud over all our problems of law enforcement and was generally a constant worry. I should have been glad to have humanity forget all about strong alcoholic drinks. They are moral, physical and economic curses to the race. But in the present stage of human progress, this vehicle of joy could not be generally suppressed by Federal law.

HERBERT HOOVER
May, 1930; *Ibid.,* p. 275

4. I ask especially that no state shall, by law or otherwise, authorize the return of the saloon, either in its old form or in some modern guise.

FRANKLIN DELANO ROOSEVELT
Proclamation on the repeal of the Eighteenth Amendment,
Dec. 5, 1933; *Public Papers, II,* 512

Promises

See Foreign Relations 33

Property

1. I am conscious that an equal division of property is impracticable. . . . The descent of property . . . to all the children . . . or other relations in equal degree is a politic measure, and a practicable one. . . . Another means of silently lessening the inequality of property is to exempt all from taxation below a certain point, and to tax the higher portions of property in geometrical progression as they rise. Whenever there are in any country, uncultivated lands and unemployed poor, it is clear

that the laws of property have been so far extended as to violate natural rights.

THOMAS JEFFERSON
To James Madison, Oct. 28, 1785; *Writings, XIX,* 18

2. Those who hold and those who are without property have ever formed distinct interests in society. Those who are creditors, and those who are debtors, fall under a like discrimination.

JAMES MADISON
"Publius," 1787; *Federalist, No. 10*

3. The most common and durable source of faction has been the various and unequal distribution of property. . . . Where overmastering self-interests . . . are involved, neither religious nor moral scruples can be depended upon to hold them in check. The establishment of government becomes necessary as the only alternative.

JAMES MADISON
"Publius," 1787; *Ibid.*

4. As a man is said to have a right to his property, he may be equally said to have a property in his rights.

JAMES MADISON
National Gazette, Mar. 29, 1792; *Writings (Hunt),* IV, 101

5. The personal right to acquire property, which is a natural right, gives to property, when acquired, a right to protection, as a social right.

JAMES MADISON
Speech to Virginia State Convention, Dec. 2, 1829; *Letters, IV,* 51

6. The love of property and consciousness of right or wrong have conflicting places in our organization, which often makes a man's course seem crooked, his conduct a riddle.

ABRAHAM LINCOLN
Speech at Hartford, Conn., Mar. 5, 1860;
Complete Works, V, 331

7. Property is the fruit of labor. Property is desirable, is a positive good in the world. Let not him who is houseless pull down the house of another, but let him work diligently and build one for himself, thus by example assuring that his own shall be safe from violence when built.

ABRAHAM LINCOLN
First Annual Message to Congress, Dec. 3, 1861; *Messages and Papers,* p. 3258

8. Property should not be the object of government but the life, liberty and happiness of the people.

ANDREW JOHNSON
Ca. 1845; *Not Guilty,* p. 27

9. The man who wrongly holds that every human right is secondary to his profit must now give way to the advocate of human welfare, who rightly maintains that every man holds his property subject to the general right of the community to regulate its use to whatever degree the public welfare may require it.

THEODORE ROOSEVELT
Speech at Osawatomie, Kan., Aug. 31, 1910; *Works, XVII,* 17

10. We must all recognize that wealth used as capital is the basis of modern civilization, that the right of property is the most valuable right in building up our society, next to the right of personal liberty. The right of property develops in men, and developed in men of the Dark Ages, those virtues of self-restraint and providence upon which we build all the other virtues.

WILLIAM HOWARD TAFT
Speech at Boise, Idaho, Nov. 3, 1906; *Problems,* p. 124

See also Banks 6, Conscience 4, Government 26, 40, Honor 2, Religion 2, Republics 1, Rights 13, Slavery 5, 12, Wealth 2

Prosperity
1. Of all the dispositions and habits which lead to political prosperity, Religion and Morality are indispensable supports.

GEORGE WASHINGTON
Farewell Address, Sept. 19, 1796;
Writings (Fitzpatrick), XXXV, 229

2. Agriculture, manufactures, commerce and navigation, the four pillars of our prosperity, are the most thriving when left most free to individual enterprise.

THOMAS JEFFERSON
First Annual Message to Congress, Dec. 8, 1801; *Writings, III,* 337

3. Canals, railroads, and turnpikes are at once the *criteria* of a wise policy and causes of national prosperity . . . a want of them will be a reproach to our republican system.

JAMES MADISON
To Reynolds Chapman, Jan. 6, 1831; *Letters, IV,* 150

4. Perhaps of all the evidences of a prosperous and happy condition of human society the rapidity of the increase of population is the most unequivocal.

JOHN QUINCY ADAMS
First Annual Message to Congress, Dec. 6, 1825; *Messages and Papers,* p. 880

5. Let it be indelibly engraved on our minds that relief is not to be found

in expedients. Indebtedness can not be lessened by borrowing more money or by changing the form of the debt. . . . Our currency can not be improved by the creation of new banks or more issues from those which now exist. Although these devices sometimes appear to give temporary relief, they almost invariably aggravated the evil in the end. It is only by retrenchment and reform—by curtailing public and private expenditures, by paying our debts, and by reforming our banking system—that we are to expect effectual relief, security for the future, and an enduring prosperity.

MARTIN VAN BUREN
Third Annual Message to Congress, Dec. 2, 1839; *Ibid.*, p. 1771

6.   We shall best promote the prosperity of the new States and Territories by furnishing them with a hardy and independent race of honest and industrious citizens.

JAMES BUCHANAN

7.   At the basis of all prosperity . . . lies the improvement of the intellectual and moral condition of the people.

RUTHERFORD B. HAYES
Inaugural Address, Mar. 5, 1877

8.   A really great people, proud and high-spirited, would face all the disasters of war rather than purchase that base prosperity which is bought at the price of national honor.

THEODORE ROOSEVELT
Address at Naval War College, June 2, 1897; *Works, XIII,* 184

9.   I understand prosperity to be the abundant, intelligent, economic development of resources possessed by the country itself. . . . Prosperity . . . is using the plow, engines, mills, and water powers of this country just as you would use your own intellectual and physical resources.

WOODROW WILSON
Speech in New York, N.Y., Jan. 3, 1912; *Ideals*, p. 53

10.   The originative part of America . . . the class that saves . . . plans . . . spreads its enterprises until they have national scope and character —that middle class is being more and more squeezed out by the processes which we have been taught to call processes of prosperity. Its members are sharing prosperity, no doubt; but what alarms me is that they are not *originating* prosperity. No country can afford to have its prosperity originated by a small controlling class. . . . The treasury of America lies in those ambitions, those energies, that cannot be restricted to a special favored class.

WOODROW WILSON
1912; *New Freedom (Hale)*, p. 17

11.   Prosperity is only an instrument to be used, not a duty to be worshipped.

CALVIN COOLIDGE
American Treasury, p. 188

12.   Prosperity cannot be restored by raids upon the public treasury. . . . Some schemes are ill-considered; some . . . represent the desire of individuals to show that they are more generous . . . than even the leaders of their own parties. They are playing politics at the expense of human misery.

HERBERT HOOVER
Press conference, Dec. 9, 1930; *State Papers, I,* 459

13.   No political party has exclusive patent rights on prosperity.
FRANKLIN DELANO ROOSEVELT
Address at Buffalo, N.Y., Oct. 20, 1930; *Public Papers, I,* 404

14.   While the total production of America is about back to the high point before the depression, only a little over 80 per cent as many human beings are engaged in turning out that production. It does not matter very greatly what the cause of this is. . . .
Some people tell you that even with a completely restored prosperity there will be a vast permanent army of unemployed. I do not accept that. No man who is sensitive to human values dares to accept it. That is why we are not content merely to restore what is sometimes called prosperity. We propose to attack the problem from every conceivable angle.

FRANKLIN DELANO ROOSEVELT
Address at Baltimore, Md., Apr. 13, 1936; *Ibid., V,* 162

15.   I have always felt that the Democratic party stands for a government that encourages a fairer distribution of the nation's prosperity so that every segment of the population will have some access to the good things of life. I was interested always in balancing the figures of the budget . . . but I was even more concerned over the balancing of the human budget in this country.

HARRY S. TRUMAN
1947; *Memoirs, II,* 40

See also Americans 4, Business 3, Discipline 1, Education 9, 51, 103, Nations 7, Peace 22, 76, Principles 10, Security 5, Space 3, Union 5, War 66

Providence

1.   But it is not for man to scan the wisdom of Providence. The best we can do, is to submit to its decrees. Reason, religion, and philosophy

teach us to do this; but it is time alone, that can ameliorate the pangs of humanity and soften its woes.

GEORGE WASHINGTON
To Henry Knox, Mar. 2, 1797; *Writings (Fitzpatrick)*, *XI*, 189

2. Murmur not at the ways of Providence.

THOMAS JEFFERSON
To Thomas Jefferson Smith, Feb. 21, 1825; *Writings*, *XVI*, 111

3. All is wisely ordered by Providence.

JOHN TYLER
June, 1855; *Champion*, p. 435

4. I believe in the Providence of the most men, the largest purse, and the longest cannon.

ABRAHAM LINCOLN
Address at Springfield, Ill., 1865; *Portrait*, *II*, 690

5. I don't want a smug lot of experts to sit down behind closed doors in Washington and play Providence to me. There is a Providence to which I am perfectly willing to submit. But as for other men setting up as Providence . . . I seriously object. I have never met a political savior in the flesh, and I never expect to meet one.

WOODROW WILSON
1912; *New Freedom (Hale)*, p. 60

See also Gratitude 2, Greatness 9, Life 3, Security 1, Wisdom 1

Public Affairs

1. I never engaged in public affairs for my own interest, pleasure, envy, jealousy, avarice or ambition, or even the desire of fame.

JOHN ADAMS
1800; *Family*, p. 115

2. I think that in public affairs stupidity is more dangerous than knavery, because harder to fight and dislodge.

WOODROW WILSON
Fortnightly Review, February, 1913; *New Freedom (Hale)*, p. 74

3. Everyone has an influence on public affairs if he will take the trouble to exert it.

CALVIN COOLIDGE
To Alfred E. Stearns, 1915; *Calvin Coolidge (Hennessy)*, p. 136

See also Public Office

Publicity

1. Public discussion is helping to doom slavery. What kills a skunk is the publicity it gives itself.

ABRAHAM LINCOLN
1860; *Prairie Years*, *II*, 186

2. We have learned that it is pent-up feelings that are dangerous, whispered purposes that are revolutionary, covert follies that warp and poison the mind; that the wisest thing to do with a fool is to encourage him to hire a hall and discourse to his fellow citizens. Nothing chills nonsense like exposure to the air; nothing dispels folly like its publication; nothing so eases the machine as the safety valve.

> WOODROW WILSON
> 1908; *Constitutional Government,* p. 38

3. There is no air so wholesome as the air of utter publicity.

> WOODROW WILSON
> 1912; *New Freedom (Hale),* p. 132

See also Duty 2, Happiness 9

Public Office

1. The happiest moments of my life have been the few which I have past at home in the bosom of my family. Employment any where else is . . . burning the candle of life in perfect waste for the individual himself. . . . Public employment contributes neither to advantage nor happiness.

> THOMAS JEFFERSON
> To Francis Willis, Apr. 13, 1790; *Writings, VI,* 46

2. I have no ambition to govern men. It is a painful and thankless office.

> THOMAS JEFFERSON
> To John Adams, Dec. 28, 1796; *Ibid., IX,* 357

3. When a man assumes a public trust he should consider himself as public property.

> THOMAS JEFFERSON
> To Baron Alexander Von Humboldt, 1807; *Life,* p. 356

4. The ordinary affairs of a nation offer little difficulty to a person of any experience, but the gift of office is the dreadful burthen which oppresses him.

> THOMAS JEFFERSON
> To Gov. James Sullivan, Mar. 3, 1808; *Works, V,* 252

5. Although there is nothing dishonorable or unjust in the pursuit of public office, I . . . consider it as a passion, which requires great moderation, self-management, and control.

> JOHN QUINCY ADAMS
> To John Adams, Aug. 20, 1811; *Writings (Ford), IV,* 183

6. I had been urged . . . from various quarters to sweep away my opponents and provide with their place for my friends. I can justify the refusal to adopt this policy only by the steadiness and consistency of my adhesion to my own. If I depart from this in one instance I shall be called upon by

my friends to do the same in many. An insidious and inquisitorial scrutiny into the personal dispositions of public offices will creep through the whole Union.

JOHN QUINCY ADAMS
To Henry Clay, March, 1826; *John Quincy Adams (Morse)*, p. 181

7.   The man in office greeted with smiles and apparent friendship, his confidence often sought to be betrayed; surrounded thus, where a man must be always guarded, happiness cannot exist.

ANDREW JACKSON
To John Coffee, Oct. 24, 1823; *Correspondence, III*, 213

8.   Every man who has been in office a few years believes he has a life estate in it, a vested right . . . that ought to descend to his children. . . . This is not the principle of our government. It is rotation in office that will perpetuate our liberty.

ANDREW JACKSON
Journal, May–June, 1829; *Life (Bassett)*, p. 447

9.   Offices were not established to give support to particular men at the public expense.

ANDREW JACKSON
First Annual Message to Congress, Dec. 8, 1829; *Principles,* p. 45

10.   Never with my consent shall an officer of the people, compensated for his services out of their pockets, become the pliant instrument of the Executive will.

WILLIAM HENRY HARRISON
Inaugural Address, Mar. 4, 1841

11.   I sincerely wish I had no offices to bestow. I cannot gratify all who apply and it is certain from my experience that the dispensation of the public patronage is a weakening operation.

JAMES K. POLK
July 11, 1846; *Diary (Quaife), II,* 20

12.   It is not the theory of this Government that public offices are the property of those who hold them. They are given merely as a trust for the public benefit.

ANDREW JOHNSON
Third Annual Message to Congress, Dec. 3, 1867;
Messages and Papers, p. 3769

13.   The melancholy thing in our public life is the insane desire to get higher.

RUTHERFORD B. HAYES
Letter to an editor, Apr. 10, 1875; *Life,* p. 144

14.   There are very many characteristics which go to make a model civil

servant. Prominent among them are probity, industry, good sense, good habits, good temper, patience, order, courtesy, tact, self-reliance, manly deference to superior officers, and manly consideration for inferiors. The absence of these traits is not supplied by wide knowledge of books. . . .

I am unwilling, in justice to the present civil servants . . . to dismiss this subject without declaring my dissent from the severe and almost indiscriminate censure with which they have been recently assailed. That they are a class indolent, inefficient, and corrupt is a statement which has been made and widely credited; but when the extent, variety, delicacy, and importance of their duties are considered the great majority of the employees of the Government are, in my judgment, deserving of high commendation.

CHESTER A. ARTHUR
First Annual Message to Congress, Dec. 6, 1881;
Messages and Papers, p. 4648

15.   Public officers are the servants and agents of the people, to execute the laws which the people have made and within the limits of a Constitution which they have established.

GROVER CLEVELAND
Accepting Nomination for Governorship of New York,
Oct. 7, 1882; *Writings and Speeches*, p. 3

16.   It is exceedingly unfortunate that those who in public places battle with the jobbery and treachery fronting them, must constantly feel that malice, uncharitableness, and misrepresentation are treacherously fighting them in the rear.

GROVER CLEVELAND
To Sherman S. Rogers, May 20, 1883; *Courage*, p. 124

17.   As public servants we shall do our duty well if we constantly guard the rectitude of our intentions, maintain unsullied our love of country, and with unselfish purpose strive for the public good.

GROVER CLEVELAND
Fourth Annual Message to Congress, Dec. 3, 1888;
Messages and Papers, p. 5385

18.   The integrity and faithfulness of public servants are not apt to be greater than the public demands.

GROVER CLEVELAND
Speech in Buffalo, N.Y., Oct. 2, 1884;
Writings and Speeches, p. 535

19.   Every public office, small or great, is held in trust for your fellow-citizens.

GROVER CLEVELAND
Address at Ann Arbor, Mich., Feb. 22, 1892;
Writings and Speeches, p. 361

20. A high sense of duty and an ambition to improve the service should characterize all public officers.

BENJAMIN HARRISON
Inaugural Address, Mar. 4, 1889

21. A man should in his public as well as private life strive to conform his conduct to the principles laid down in those two ancient guides to conduct, the Decalogue and the Golden Rule.

THEODORE ROOSEVELT
Campaign speech in New York, N.Y., Oct. 19, 1898;
Works, XIV, 299

22. We must remember not to judge any public servant by any one act, and especially should we be aware of attacking the men who are merely the occasions and not the causes of disaster.

THEODORE ROOSEVELT
Address in Chicago, Ill., Apr. 10, 1899; *Ibid., XIII*, 325

23. The judge who does his full duty well stands higher, and renders a better service to the people, than any other public servant. . . . He must serve the people; but he must serve his own conscience first.

THEODORE ROOSEVELT
Statement to Associated Oil Co., Jan. 31, 1908;
Messages and Papers, p. 7522

24. Of all men in public life, the people hate worst the side-stepper.

WOODROW WILSON
1911; *Outlook (magazine), Aug. 26, 1911,* p. 940

25. Every man who takes office in Washington either grows or swells. . . . When I give a man an office, I watch him carefully to see whether he is swelling or growing. The mischief of it is that when they swell they do not swell enough to burst.

WOODROW WILSON
Speech in Washington, D.C., May 16, 1916;
Public Papers, IV, 174

26. Public officials are not a group apart. They inevitably reflect the moral tone of the society in which they live.

JOHN F. KENNEDY
Special Message to Congress, Apr. 27, 1961;
Public Papers . . . Kennedy, 1961, p. 326

See also Appointments, Civilization 4, Congress 4, Conscience 8, Corruption 4, Criticism 6, Duty 4, Fear 3, Goodness 3, Honesty 7, Office Seekers, Patronage, Politics, Presidency (The), Silence 2, Soldiers 3, Supreme Court 2

Public Opinion

1. We may add to the great honor of science and the arts, that their natural effect is, by illuminating public opinion, to erect it into a censor before which the most exalted tremble for their future as well as present fame.

THOMAS JEFFERSON
To John Adams, Jan. 11, 1816; *Writings, XIV,* 393

2. Public opinion sets bounds to every government, and is the real sovereign in every free one.

JAMES MADISON
National Gazette, Dec. 19, 1791; *Writings (Hunt), VI,* 70

3. Public opinion in this country is all-powerful, and when it reaches a dangerous excess upon any question the good sense of the people will furnish the corrective and bring it back within safe limits.

JAMES BUCHANAN
Third Annual Message to Congress, Dec. 19, 1859;
Messages and Papers, p. 3084

4. Public opinion in this country is everything.

ABRAHAM LINCOLN
Speech at Columbus, Ohio, Sept. 16, 1859;
Complete Works, V, 188

5. No policy that does not rest upon some philosophical public opinion can be permanently maintained.

ABRAHAM LINCOLN
Speech at New Haven, Conn., Mar. 6, 1860;
Collected Works, IV, 17

6. Public opinion, though often formed upon a wrong basis, yet generally has a strong underlying sense of justice.

ABRAHAM LINCOLN
American Treasury, p. 132

7. Public opinion, the fear of losing public confidence, apprehension of censure by the press make all men in power conservative and safe.

RUTHERFORD B. HAYES
Diary, Oct. 22, 1876; *Diary and Letters, III,* 370

8. Public opinion enacted into constitutional statutes . . . which embody the settled public opinion of the people who enacted them and whom they are to govern—can always be enforced.

RUTHERFORD B. HAYES
Diary, Feb. 17, 1882; *Ibid., IV,* 68

9. Lincoln said in his homely way that he wanted "to take a bath in

public opinion." I think I have a right to take a bath before I do much talking.

JAMES A. GARFIELD
To Burke A. Hinsdale, Nov. 17, 1880; *Life and Letters, II,* 1044

10. Public opinion is the most potent monarch this world knows.

BENJAMIN HARRISON
At Detroit, Mich., Feb. 22, 1888; *Speeches,* p. 15

11. There must be public opinion back of the laws or the laws themselves will be of no avail.

THEODORE ROOSEVELT
Seventh Annual Message to Congress, Dec. 3, 1907;
Works, XV, 431

12. The belief that public opinion or international public opinion, unbacked by force, had the slightest effect in restraining a powerful military nation in any course of action . . . has been shown to be a pathetic fallacy.

THEODORE ROOSEVELT
Metropolitan, February, 1916; *Ibid., XVIII,* 242

13. Opinion is the great, indeed the only coordinating force in our system, [and] the only thing that [gives] the President an opportunity to make good his leadership . . . [is] his close and special relation to opinion the nation over.

WOODROW WILSON
1908; *Constitutional Government,* p. 171

14. A Government can be no better than the public opinion which sustains it.

FRANKLIN DELANO ROOSEVELT
Address, Jan. 8, 1936; *Public Papers, V,* 43

15. The whole structure of democracy rests upon public opinion.

FRANKLIN DELANO ROOSEVELT
To Institute of Human Relations, Aug. 20, 1937; *Ibid., VI,* 336

See also Democracy 11, Education 1, 15, Foreign Relations 48, Government 42, 61, History 17, Opinion, People (The) 6, Power 15

Public Speaking

1. Eloquence in public assemblies is not the surest road to fame . . . unless it be used with caution, very rarely, and with great reserve. The examples of Washington, Franklin, and Jefferson, are enough to show that silence and reserve in public, are more efficacious than argumenta-

tion or oratory. A public speaker who inserts himself, or is urged by others . . . to justify his measures, and answer the objections of opponents, makes himself too familiar with the public, and unavoidably makes himself enemies.

JOHN ADAMS
Autobiography, 1776; *Works, II,* 511

2.   When Jefferson came into office he had no facility in public speaking, and he therefore preferred to send written messages, and that had been the practise down to the present administration, when President Wilson has introduced the custom of a personal address to both houses. I think the innovation is a good one.

WILLIAM HOWARD TAFT
Speech at University of Virginia, January, 1915; *Presidency,* p. 35

See also Eloquence, Speeches

Public Works

1.   What we want is the type of public works that will put people to work immediately.

FRANKLIN DELANO ROOSEVELT
Press conference, Apr. 19, 1933; *Public Papers, II,* 141

Purposes

See Causes, Foreign Relations 48, Freedom 26, Goals, Greatness 6, Political Parties 11, 14, Reforms 4, Religion 32, Right 13, Union 21, Unity 8, Voters 4

Quarrels

1.   An association of men who will not quarrel with one another is a thing which never yet existed, from the greatest confederacy of nations down to a town-meeting or a vestry.

THOMAS JEFFERSON
To John Taylor, June 1, 1798; *Writings, X,* 44

See also Controversy, Differences, Progress 4

Races

See Americans 5, Brotherhood 3, Nationality 2

Radicals

See Conservatism, Liberalism, Political Philosophy 3, 4, Standpatism

Railroads

1.   A railroad! It would frighten horses, put the owners of public vehicles out of business, break up inns and taverns, and be a monopoly generally.

ANDREW JOHNSON
Speech in Tennessee Legislature, 1835; *Not Guilty,* p. 18

See also Prosperity 3

Reactionaries

See Conservatism, Liberalism, Political Philosophy 4, Standpatism

Reason

1. Your own reason is the only oracle given you by heaven, and you are answerable for, not the rightness, but the uprightness of the decision.

THOMAS JEFFERSON
Letter to Peter Carr, Aug. 10, 1787; *Works, II,* 240

2. It is comfortable to see the standard of reason at length erected, after so many ages, during which the human mind has been held in vassalage by kings, priests, and nobles; and it is honorable for us, to have provided the first legislature who had the courage to declare, that the reason of man may be trusted with the formation of his own opinions.

THOMAS JEFFERSON
To James Madison, Dec. 16, 1786; *Writings, VI,* 10

See also Differences 1, Errors 3, Peace 8, Power 28, Providence 1, War 55

Rebellion

1. A little rebellion, now and then, is a good thing, and as necessary in the political world as storms in the physical. . . . It is a medicine necessary for the sound health of government.

THOMAS JEFFERSON
To James Madison, Jan. 30, 1787; *Writings, V,* 256

2. What country before ever existed a century and a half without a rebellion? . . . What signify a few lives lost in a century or two? The tree of liberty must be refreshed from time to time with the blood of patriots and tyrants. It is its natural manure.

THOMAS JEFFERSON
To William Stevens Smith, Nov. 13, 1787; *Ibid.,* p. 362

3. Rebellion may delay, but it can never defeat its blessed mission of liberty and humanity.

WILLIAM McKINLEY
Speech at Cliff Haven, N.Y., Aug. 15, 1899;
Speeches and Addresses, p. 210

See also Government 25, Revolutions, Tyranny 3

Red Cross

1. The American Red Cross is the warm heart of a free people.

DWIGHT D. EISENHOWER
In Chicago, Ill., Feb. 28, 1949; *American Speeches, XXI,* 75

Reforms

1. The hole and the patch should be commensurate.

THOMAS JEFFERSON
To James Madison, June 20, 1787; *Works, II,* 152

2. When we reflect how difficult it is to move or deflect the great machine of society, how impossible to advance the notions of a whole people suddenly to ideal right, we see the wisdom of Solon's remark, that no more good must be attempted than the nation can bear.

THOMAS JEFFERSON
To Walter Jones, Mar. 31, 1801; *Writings, X,* 256

3. The people expect reform; they shall not be disappointed; but it must be judiciously done, and upon principle.

ANDREW JACKSON
Memorandum, Mar. 31, 1829; *Proceedings, XVII,* 236

4. Singleness of purpose is necessary to every reform, indispensable to wise administration and legislation.

WILLIAM MCKINLEY
Speech at Bangor, Me., Sept. 8, 1904; *Life and Speeches,* p. 127

5. Standpatism is just as impossible in modern conditions as it is impossible for a thin crust of the earth to keep its place above the force of a volcano. All the blood in this nation is now running into the vital courses of reform, and the men who stand against reform are standing against nature, standing against all the impulses, all the energies, all the hopes, all the ambitions of America.

WOODROW WILSON
Address at Burlington, N.J., Oct. 30, 1912; *Crossroads,* p. 506

6. Laws do not make reforms, reforms make laws.

CALVIN COOLIDGE
On the Nature of Politics; *Citizenship,* p. 97

See also Ballots 4, Change, Politics 4

Relief

1. As a nation we *must* prevent hunger and cold to those of our people who are in honest difficulties.

HERBERT HOOVER
To members of the press, Oct. 17, 1930, after organizing nation-wide program for relief of distress; *Administration,* p. 52

2. The basis of successful relief in national distress is to mobilize and organize the infinite number of agencies of self-help in the community. That has been the American way. . . .

If we break down [the] sense of responsibility of individual generosity

to individual and mutual self-help in the country in times of national difficulty and if we start appropriations of this character we have not only
impaired something infinitely valuable in the life of the American people
but have struck at the roots of self-government.

HERBERT HOOVER
Reply in the press, Feb. 3, 1931, to attacks in the Senate;
State Papers, I, 496

3. May we maintain the spiritual impulses in our people for generous
giving and generous service—in the spirit that each is his brother's keeper.
Personal feeling and personal responsibility of men to their neighbors is
the soul of genuine good will; it is the essential foundation of modern
society. A cold and distant charity which puts out its sympathy only
through the tax collector, yields a very meager dole of unloving and per-
functory relief.

HERBERT HOOVER
To Private Charities organization, Washington, D.C.,
Sept. 15, 1932; *Ibid., II,* 281

4. Continued dependence upon relief induces a spiritual and moral dis-
integration fundamentally destructive to the national fibre. To dole out
relief in this way is to administer a narcotic, a subtle destroyer of the human spirit. . . . The Federal Government must and shall quit this business
of relief.

FRANKLIN DELANO ROOSEVELT
Message to Congress, Jan. 4, 1935; *Public Papers, IV,* 19

See also Benevolence, Charity, Philanthropy, Subsidy, Unemployment

Religion

1. I now make it my earnest prayer that God . . . would graciously be
pleased to dispose us all *to do justice, to love mercy,* and to demean ourselves with charity and humility, and a pacific temper of mind, which were
characteristics of the Divine author of our blessed religion, and without
an humble imitation of Whose example in these things, we can never hope
to be a happy nation.

GEORGE WASHINGTON
Letter to the Governors, June 8, 1783;
Writings (Fitzpatrick), XXVI, 496

2. We should begin by setting conscience free. When all men of all religions consistent with morals and property shall enjoy equal liberty,
property, or rather security of property, and an equal chance for honors
and power, and when government shall be considered as having in it nothing more mysterious or divine than other arts or sciences, we may expect

that improvements will be made in the human character and the state of society. But at what an immense distance is that period.

JOHN ADAMS
To Dr. Price, Apr. 8, 1785; *Works, VIII,* 232

3. The government of the United States of America is not in any sense founded on the Christian Religion,—as it has itself no character of enmity against the law, religion or tranquillity of Musselmen.

JOHN ADAMS
To Benjamin Rush, Aug. 28, 1811; *Ibid., IX,* 636

4. My adoration of the author of the universe is . . . profound and . . . sincere. The love of God and His creation—delight, joy, triumph, exultation in my own existence—though but an atom, a *molécule organique* in the universe—are my religion.

JOHN ADAMS
To Thomas Jefferson, Sept. 14, 1813; *Ibid., X,* 67

5. The Ten Commandments and the Sermon on the Mount contain my religion.

JOHN ADAMS
To Thomas Jefferson, Nov. 4, 1816; *Ibid.,* p. 229

6. Compulsion in religion is distinguished peculiarly from compulsion in every other thing. I may grow rich by an art I am compelled to follow; I may recover health by medicines I am compelled to take against my own judgment: but I cannot be saved by a worship I disbelieve and abhor.

THOMAS JEFFERSON
Notes on Religion, 1776; *Writings (Ford), II,* 102

7. All men shall be free to profess, and by argument to maintain, their opinion in matters of religion; and . . . the same shall in no wise diminish, enlarge, or affect their civil capacities.

THOMAS JEFFERSON
Virginia Statute of Religious Freedom, 1779; *Ibid.,* p. 239

8. Difference of opinion is advantageous in religion. The several sects perform the office of a *censor morum* over each other.

THOMAS JEFFERSON
Notes on Virginia, 1782; *Writings, II,* 223

9. The way to silence religious disputes is to take no notice of them.

THOMAS JEFFERSON
Notes on Virginia, 1782; *Ibid.,* p. 224

10. If thinking men would have the courage to think for themselves,

and to speak what they think, it would be found they do not differ in religious opinions as much as is supposed.

THOMAS JEFFERSON
To John Adams, Aug. 22, 1813; *Ibid., XIII,* 349

11. I must ever believe that religion substantially good which produces an honest life, and we have been authorized by One whom you and I equally respect, to judge of the tree by its fruit.

THOMAS JEFFERSON
To Miles King, Sept. 26, 1814; *Writings, XIV,* 198

12. I never told my own religion nor scrutinized that of another. I never attempted to make a convert, nor wished to change another's creed. I have ever judged of another's religion by their lives . . . for it is in our lives and not from our words, that our religion must be read.

THOMAS JEFFERSON
To Mrs. M. H. Smith, Aug. 6, 1816; *Ibid., XV,* 60

13. On the dogmas of religion as distinguished from moral principles, all mankind, from the beginning of the world to this day, have been quarrelling, fighting, burning and torturing one another, for abstractions unintelligible to themselves and to all others, and absolutely beyond the comprehension of the human mind. Were I to enter on that arena, I should only add an unit to the number of Bedlamites.

THOMAS JEFFERSON
To Mathew Carey, Nov. 11, 1816; *Ibid., X,* 67

14. I rejoice that in this blessed country of free inquiry and belief, which has surrendered its creed and conscience to neither kings nor priests, the genuine doctrine of only one God is reviving, and I trust that there is not a *young man* now living in the United States who will not die a Unitarian.

THOMAS JEFFERSON
To Benjamin Waterhouse, June 26, 1822; *Ibid., XV,* 162

15. Union of religious sentiments begets a surprising confidence.

JAMES MADISON
To William Bradford, Jr., Jan. 24, 1774; *Letters, I,* 11

16. We hold it for a fundamental and inalienable truth that religion and the manner of discharging it can be directed only by reason and conviction, not by force and violence. The religion, then, of every man must be left to the conviction and conscience of every man; and it is the right of every man to exercise it as these may dictate.

JAMES MADISON
Memorial and Remonstrance, 1785; *Complete Madison,* p. 299

17. Religion flourishes in greater purity, without than with the aid of Government.

JAMES MADISON
To Edward Livingston, July 10, 1822; *Ibid.*, p. 309

18. The only importance of religion to my mind consists in its influence upon the conduct of mankind. . . . The question of Trinity or Unity . . . has or ought to have no bearing whatever.

JOHN QUINCY ADAMS
To George Sullivan, Jan. 20, 1821; *Writings (Ford)*, *VII*, 90

19. My god knows whether I have or not always acknowledged a Saviour with a firm belief in the Scriptures, therefore I care not what men may think on this important subject.

ANDREW JACKSON
Manuscript, no date; *Correspondence*, *VI*, 416

20. I am tolerant of all creeds. Yet if any sect suffered itself to be used for political objects I would meet it by political opposition. In my view, Church and State should be separate, not only in form, but fact—religion and politics should not be mingled.

MILLARD FILLMORE
1856; *Millard Fillmore (Rayback)*, p. 407

21. I am not much of a judge of religion, but . . . in my opinion, the religion that sets men to rebel and fight against their government, because, as they think, that government does not sufficiently help some men to eat their bread in the sweat of other men's faces, is not the sort of religion upon which people can get into heaven!

ABRAHAM LINCOLN
Memorandum, Dec. 3, 1864; *Complete Works*, *X*, 280

22. Leave the matter of religion to the family altar, the church, and the private school, supported entirely by private contributions. Keep the church and the State forever separate.

ULYSSES S. GRANT
Speech at Des Moines, Ia., 1875

23. I would rather be defeated than make Capital out of my Religion.

JAMES A. GARFIELD
Remark at Chautauqua, N.Y., Aug. 8, 1880; *Maxims*, p. 11

24. No fellow-citizen of ours is entitled to any peculiar regard because of the way in which he worships his Maker. . . .

THEODORE ROOSEVELT
Fourth Annual Message to Congress, Dec. 6, 1904; *Messages and Papers*, p. 7046

25. There is one test which we have a right to apply to the professors of all creeds—the test of conduct. More and more, people who possess either religious belief or aspiration after religious belief are growing to demand conduct as the ultimate test of the worth of the belief.

THEODORE ROOSEVELT
Speech at Pacific Lutheran Theological Seminary, Spring, 1911;
Works, XIII, 648

26. One verse of Micah . . . I am very fond of—"to do justly and to love mercy and to walk humbly with thy God"—that to me is the essence of religion.

THEODORE ROOSEVELT
1916; *Talks,* p. 65

27. My life would not be worth living if it were not for the driving power of religion, for *faith,* pure and simple. I have seen all my life the arguments against it without ever having been moved by them. . . . There are people who *believe* only so far as they *understand*—that seems to me presumptuous and sets their understanding as the standard of the universe. . . . I am sorry for such people.

WOODROW WILSON
To Mrs. Crawford H. Toy, Jan. 3, 1915;
New Freedom (Hale), p. 64

28. It is only when men begin to worship that they begin to grow.

CALVIN COOLIDGE
Speech at Fredericksburg, Va., July 6, 1922; *Freedom,* p. 173

29. The government of a country never gets ahead of the religion of a country. There is no way by which we can substitute the authority of law for the virtue of man.

CALVIN COOLIDGE
Speech in Washington, D.C., Oct. 15, 1924; *Foundations,* p. 153

30. It would be difficult for me to conceive of anyone being able to administer the duties of a great office like the Presidency without a belief in the guidance of a divine providence. Unless the President is sustained by an abiding faith in a divine power which is working for the good of humanity, I cannot understand how he would have the courage to attempt to meet the various problems that constantly pour in upon him from all parts of the earth.

CALVIN COOLIDGE
To Bruce Barton, Sept. 23, 1926;
Calvin Coolidge (Hennessy), p. 27

31. I come of Quaker stock. My ancestors were persecuted for their be-

liefs. Here they sought and found religious freedom. By blood and conviction I stand for religious tolerance both in act and in spirit.

HERBERT HOOVER
1928; *New Day*, p. 36

32. "Peace on earth, good-will toward men"—democracy must cling to that message. For it is my deep conviction that democracy cannot live without that true religion which gives a nation a sense of justice and of moral purpose.

FRANKLIN DELANO ROOSEVELT
Speech in Chicago, Ill., Oct. 28, 1944; *Wit and Wisdom*, p. 24

33. Religion has always been the most effective process of developing human character strong enough to forget the motivation of selfishness and to act on the larger concept of duty to God, to humanity, and to Country. . . . Religion nurtures men of faith, men of hope, men of love. . . .
   The inner peace of a well integrated life is something that must be continually achieved; the outer peace of a world in which nations live together in a spirit of brotherhood is something that must be continually earned.

DWIGHT D. EISENHOWER
Speech to Chaplains' Association, Washington, D.C., Oct. 23, 1946;
Eisenhower Speaks, p. 144

34. We need to remember that the separation of church and state must never mean the separation of religious values from the lives of public servants. . . . If we who serve free men today are to differ from the tyrants of this age, we must balance the powers in our hands with God in our hearts.

LYNDON B. JOHNSON
Remarks at Presidential Prayer Breakfast, Feb. 1, 1961;
Story, p. 188

See also Civilization 5, Conduct 1, Conscience 6, Creeds, Declaration of Independence 9, Faith, Fear 1, Freedom 5, 6, 20, 21, God, Happiness 10, Liberty 18, Morality 1, 3, 6, Opinion 1, Peace 58, Politics 4, Prosperity 1, Providence 1, Union 5, War 16

Republics

1. Republicanism is not the phantom of a deluded imagination: on the contrary . . . under no form of government, will laws be better supported, liberty and property better secured, or happiness be more effectually dispensed to mankind.

GEORGE WASHINGTON
To Edmund Pendleton, Jan. 22, 1795;
Writings (Fitzpatrick), *XXXIV*, 99

2. When public virtue is gone, when the national spirit is fled, when a

party is substituted for the nation and faction for a party, when venality lurks and sulks in secret, and, much more, when it impudently braves the public censure . . . the republic is lost in essence, though it may still exist in form.

> JOHN ADAMS
> To Benjamin Rush, Sept. 27, 1808; *Works, IX,* 603

3. Of republics, the varieties are infinite, or at least as numerous as the tunes and changes that can be rung upon a complete set of bells. Of all the varieties, a democracy is the most natural, the most ancient, and the most fundamental and essential.

> JOHN ADAMS
> To J. H. Tiffany, Apr. 30, 1819; *Ibid., X,* 378

4. The republican is the only form of government which is not eternally at open or secret war with the rights of mankind.

> THOMAS JEFFERSON
> To William Hunter, Mayor of Alexandria, Va., Mar. 11, 1790;
> *Works, III,* 128

5. I suspect that the doctrine, that small States alone are fitted to be republics, will be exploded by experience, with some other brilliant fallacies. . . . Perhaps it will be found, that to obtain a just republic . . . it must be so extensive as that local egoisms may never reach its greater part. . . . The smaller the societies, the more violent and more convulsive their schisms.

> THOMAS JEFFERSON
> To François d'Ivernois, Feb. 6, 1795; *Writings, IV,* 114

6. The support of State governments in all their rights, as the most competent administration of our domestic concerns, are the surest bulwarks against anti-republican tendencies.

> THOMAS JEFFERSON
> First Inaugural Address, Mar. 4, 1801

7. A republican government is slow to move, yet when once in motion, its momentum becomes irresistible.

> THOMAS JEFFERSON
> To Francis C. Gray, Mar. 4, 1815; *Works, VI,* 438

8. Where then is our republicanism to be found? Not in our constitution certainly, but merely in the spirit of our people. . . . The true foundation of republican government is the equal right of every citizen, in his person and property, and in their management.

> THOMAS JEFFERSON
> To Samuel Kercheval, July 12, 1816; *Ibid., XV,* 39

9. [The mother principle:] Governments are republican only in proportion as they embody the will of the people, and execute it.

THOMAS JEFFERSON

To Samuel Kercheval, July 12, 1816; *Writings, XV*, 33

10. We may define a republic . . . as a government which derives all its powers directly or indirectly from the great body of the people, and is administered by persons holding their offices during pleasure, for a limited period, or during good behavior. It is *essential* to such a government that it be derived from the great body of the society, not from an inconsiderable proportion, or a favoured class of it.

JAMES MADISON

"Publius," 1788; *Federalist, No. 39*

11. In Republics, the great danger is, that the majority may not sufficiently respect the rights of the minority.

JAMES MADISON

Speech to Virginia State Convention, Dec. 2, 1829; *Letters, IV*, 51

12. There is . . . no instance on record of an extensive and well-established republic being changed into an aristocracy.

WILLIAM HENRY HARRISON

Inaugural Address, Mar. 4, 1841; *Messages and Papers*, p. 1873

13. Ours is the great example of a prosperous and free self-governed republic, commanding the admiration and the imitation of all the lovers of freedom throughout the world. How solemn, therefore, is the duty, how impressive the call upon us and upon all parts of the country, to cultivate a patriotic spirit of harmony, of good-fellowship, of compromise and mutual concession, in the administration of the incomparable system of government formed by our fathers in the midst of almost insuperable difficulties, and transmitted to us with the injunction that we should enjoy its blessings and hand it down unimpaired to those who may come after us.

JAMES K. POLK

Fourth Annual Message to Congress, Dec. 5, 1848; *Ibid.*, p. 2489

14. Public virtue is the vital spirit of republics; and history shows that when this has decayed, and the love of money has usurped its place, although the forms of free government may remain for a season, the substance has departed forever.

JAMES BUCHANAN

Inaugural Address, Mar. 4, 1857

15. The life of a republic lies certainly in the energy, virtue, and intelligence of its citizens; but it is equally true that a good revenue system is the life of an organized government.

ANDREW JOHNSON

First Annual Message to Congress, Dec. 4, 1865; *Messages and Papers*, p. 3562

16. It is my firm conviction that the civilized world is tending toward republicanism, or government by the people through their chosen representatives, and that our own great Republic is destined to be the guiding star to all others. . . .

I do not share in the apprehension held by many as to the danger of governments becoming weakened and destroyed by reason of their extension of territory. . . . Rather do I believe that our Great Maker is preparing the world, in His own good time, to become one nation, speaking one language, and when armies and navies will be no longer required.

ULYSSES S. GRANT
Second Inaugural Address, Mar. 4, 1873

17. Americans ought ever be asking themselves about their concept of the ideal republic.

WARREN G. HARDING
Speech at Kansas City, Mo., June 22, 1923; *Ibid.*, p. 9260

See also Democracy, Kings 1, 3, Military Matters 4, 6, Opinion 10, Power 19, Presidency (The) 15, War 30, Women 2

Reputation

1. Associate yourself with men of good quality if you esteem your own reputation; for 'tis better to be alone than in bad company.

GEORGE WASHINGTON
Early copybook, 1746; *Writings (Sparks)*, II, 413

2. If you would preserve your reputation, or that of [your] state, you must take a straight forward determined course, regardless of the applause or censure of the populace, and of the forebodings of [those] who may be expected to clamor continually in your ears.

ANDREW JACKSON
To Gov. William Blount, 1813; *Life (Bassett)*, p. 110

See also Presidency (The) 5, Slander

Resources
See Freedom 4

Responsibility

1. Responsibility is a tremendous engine in a free government.

THOMAS JEFFERSON
Letter to Archibald Stuart, Dec. 23, 1791; *Works, III*, 315

2. This civilization and this great complex, which we call American life, is builded and can alone survive upon the translation into individual action of that fundamental philosophy announced by the Savior nineteen centuries ago. Part of our national suffering today is from failure to observe these primary yet inexorable laws of human relationship. Modern society cannot survive with the defense of Cain, "Am I my brother's keeper?"

No governmental action, no economic doctrine, no economic plan or project can replace that God-imposed responsibility of the individual man and woman to their neighbors.

HERBERT HOOVER
Radio address, Fortress Monroe, Va., Oct. 18, 1931;
State Papers, II, 12

See also Desegregation 3, Disarmament 5, Duty, Errors 16, Homes 4, Human Welfare, Laws 29, Liberty 30, Peace 87, Political Parties 21, Power 1, 26, 27, Presidency (The) 56, Privileges 1, Relief 2, 3, Self-Government 6, States' Rights 11, Success 9, Work 6

Revenge
See Future (The) 1

Revenue
1. The delicate duty of devising schemes of revenue should be left where the Constitution has placed it—with the immediate representatives of the people.

WILLIAM HENRY HARRISON
Inaugural Address, Mar. 4, 1841

See also Republics 15, Tariff, Taxation

Revolutions
1. It is an observation of one of the profoundest inquirers into human affairs that a revolution of government, successfully conducted and compleated, is the strongest proof that can be given, by a people of their virtue and good sense. An enterprise of so much difficulty can never be planned and carried on without abilities, and a people without principle cannot have confidence enough in each other.

JOHN ADAMS
Diary, July 16, 1786; *Works, III,* 399

2. Let us remember that revolutions do not always establish freedom. Our own free institutions were not the offspring of our Revolution. They existed before.

MILLARD FILLMORE
Third Annual Message to Congress, Dec. 5, 1852; *Messages and Papers,* p. 2716

3. Any people anywhere being inclined and having the power have the right to rise up and shake off the existing government, and form a new one that suits them better. This is a most valuable, a most sacred right—a right which we hope and believe is to liberate the world. . . . It is a quality of revolutions not to go by old ideas or old laws; but to break up both, and make new ones.

ABRAHAM LINCOLN
Speech to Congress, Jan. 12, 1848; *Complete Works, I,* 338

4. Be not deceived. Revolutions do not go backward.

ABRAHAM LINCOLN
Speech at Bloomington, Ill., May 29, 1856;
Writings (Lapsley), II, 253

5. It is a fact attested in history that sometimes revolutions most disastrous to freedom are effected without the shedding of blood. The substance of your Government may be taken away, while the form and the shadow remain to you.

ANDREW JOHNSON
Speech in Washington, D.C., Feb. 22, 1866; *Document,* p. 4

6. The seed of revolution is repression.

WOODROW WILSON
Seventh Annual Message to Congress, Dec. 2, 1919;
Public Papers, VI, 437

7. Here in America we are descended in blood and spirit from revolutionists and rebels—men and women who dare to dissent from accepted doctrine. As their heirs, we may never confuse honest dissent with disloyal subversion.

DWIGHT D. EISENHOWER
Address at Columbia University, May 31, 1954; *Public Papers
. . . Eisenhower, 1954,* p. 128

8. Let us once again transform the American continent into a vast crucible of revolutionary ideas and efforts—a tribute to the power of the creative energies of free men and women—an example to all the world that liberty and progress walk hand in hand. Let us once again awaken our American revolution until it guides the struggle of people everywhere—not with an imperialism of force or fear—but the rule of courage and freedom and hope for the future of man.

JOHN F. KENNEDY
Address at a White House reception, Mar. 13, 1961; *Public Papers
. . . Kennedy, 1961,* p. 175

See also American Revolution, Rebellion

Right

1. We shall keep the people on our side by keeping ourselves in the right.

THOMAS JEFFERSON
To James Madison, Aug. 11, 1793; *Jefferson and Madison,* p. 143

2. The policy of all European nations towards South America has been founded upon selfish principles of interest incongruously combined with erroneous principles of government. . . . Emperors and kings have assumed as the foundation of human society the doctrine of unalienable allegiance. Our doctrine is founded upon the principle of unalienable right.

JOHN QUINCY ADAMS

To Richard Anderson, May 27, 1823; *Writings (Ford)*, *VII*, 440

3.   In the language of the lamented but immortal [Henry] Clay: "I had rather be right than be President!"

MILLARD FILLMORE

Speech at Albany, N.Y.; *Ovation*, p. 5

4.   It is better only sometimes to be right than at all times wrong.

ABRAHAM LINCOLN

Speech at New Salem, Ill., Mar. 9, 1832; *Complete Works*, *I*, 8

5.   Stand with anybody that stands right, stand with him while he is right and part with him when he goes wrong.

ABRAHAM LINCOLN

Speech at Peoria, Ill., Oct. 16, 1854; *Ibid.*, *II*, 243

6.   Let us have faith that right makes might, and in that faith let us to the end dare to do our duty as we understand it.

ABRAHAM LINCOLN

Address in New York, N.Y., Feb. 27, 1860; *Ibid.*, *V*, 328

7.   My good fortune . . . is in doing right and being for the people.

ANDREW JOHNSON

Speech in Washington, D.C., Feb. 22, 1866; *Document*, p. 8

8.   I intend to do what's right, as nearly as I can get at it, and I won't shirk the consequences.

ANDREW JOHNSON

Conversation, July 21, 1867; *Presidents and the Press*, p. 417

9.   Every step made in advance toward the standard of the right has . . . always proved a safe and wise step . . . in politics, in morals, in public and private life, the right is always expedient.

RUTHERFORD B. HAYES

Speech at Lebanon, Ohio, Sept. 4, 1867; *Life*, p. 222

10.   I would rather be beaten in Right than succeed in Wrong.

JAMES A. GARFIELD
Maxims, p. 1

11.   It is no credit to me to do right. I am never under any temptation to do wrong!

GROVER CLEVELAND
Courage, p. 765

12. I have tried so hard to do right.

GROVER CLEVELAND
Last words, June 24, 1908; *Man and Statesman,* p. 385

13. Right action follows right purpose. We may not at all times be able to divine the future . . . but if our aims are high and unselfish, somehow and in some way the right end will be reached.

WILLIAM MCKINLEY
Speech at Omaha, Neb., Oct. 12, 1898; *Speeches and Addresses,* p. 106

14. If I can be right 75 per cent of the time I shall come up to the fullest measure of my hopes.

THEODORE ROOSEVELT
To Franklin Delano Roosevelt, *ca.* 1905; *Public Papers (of F.D.R.), II,* 165

15. There is such a thing as a nation being so right that it does not need to convince others by force that it is right.

WOODROW WILSON
Speech in Philadelphia, Pa., May 10, 1915; *State Papers,* p. 117

16. The right is more precious than peace.

WOODROW WILSON
Address to Congress, asking for war, Apr. 2, 1917; *Ibid.,* p. 382

17. May we pursue the right—without self-righteousness.

DWIGHT D. EISENHOWER
Second Inaugural Address, Jan. 21, 1957

See also Errors 13, 17, Faith 10, Force 1, History 17, Laws 35, Minorities 1, Peace 42, Principles 3, Righteousness, Russia 3, Square Deal 2, United States 3, Wrong 3

Righteousness

1. A milk-and-water righteousness unbacked by force is to the full as wicked as and even more mischievous than force divorced from right.

THEODORE ROOSEVELT
To Hugo Münsterberg, Oct. 3, 1914; *Letters, VIII,* 825

See also Government 98, Laws 26, Peace 29, 43, 46, Strife, War 50

Rights

1. Human nature itself, from indolence, modesty, humanity, or fear, has always too much reluctance to a manly assertion of its rights. Hence, perhaps, it has happened, that nine-tenths of the species are groaning and gasping in misery and servitude.

JOHN ADAMS
Dissertation on the Canon and the Feudal Law, August, 1765; *Works, III,* 459

2. We hold these truths to be self-evident: that all men are created equal; that they are endowed by their creator with *inherent* and inalienable rights; that among these are life, liberty, and the pursuit of happiness.

THOMAS JEFFERSON
Declaration of Independence, 1776; *Writings, I,* 35

3. A bill of rights is what the people are entitled to against every government on earth, general or particular, and what no just government should refuse, or rest on inferences.

THOMAS JEFFERSON
To James Madison, Dec. 20, 1787; *Ibid., V,* 371

4. If we cannot secure all our rights, let us secure what we can.

THOMAS JEFFERSON
To James Madison, Mar. 15, 1789; *Works, III,* 4

5. Circumstances sometimes require that rights the most unquestionable should be advanced with delicacy. . . . With respect to America, Europeans in general have been too long in the habit of confounding force with right.

THOMAS JEFFERSON
Letter to William Short, July 28, 1791; *Ibid.,* 276

6. Nothing then is unchangeable but the inherent and unalienable rights of man.

THOMAS JEFFERSON
1824; *American Treasury,* p. 147

7. All eyes are opened or opening to the rights of man. The general spread of the lights of science has already opened to every view the palpable truth, that the mass of mankind has not been born with saddles on their backs, nor a favored few booted and spurred, ready to ride them legitimately, by the grace of God.

THOMAS JEFFERSON
To R. C. Weightman, June 24, 1826; *Writings, XVI,* 182

8. Equal rights for all, special privileges for none.

THOMAS JEFFERSON

9. The rights of man as the foundation of just Government had been long understood; but the superstructures projected had been sadly defective.

JAMES MADISON
To Nicholas P. Trist, February 15, 1830; *Letters, IV,* 58

10. We must support our rights or lose our character, and with it, perhaps, our liberties.

JAMES MONROE
First Inaugural Address, Mar. 4, 1817

11. A manly assertion by each of his individual rights, and a manly concession of equal right to every other man, is the boast and the law of good citizenship.

BENJAMIN HARRISON
At Indianapolis, Ind., July 19, 1888; *Speeches,* p. 53

12. There is no security for the personal or political rights of any man in a community where any man is deprived of his personal or political rights.

BENJAMIN HARRISON
Acceptance of Renomination for Presidency, Minneapolis, Minn.,
Sept. 3, 1892; *Public Papers and Addresses,* p. 20

13. What I am interested in is having the government of the United States more concerned about human rights than about property rights. Property is an instrument of humanity; humanity isn't an instrument of property.

WOODROW WILSON
Speech at Minneapolis, Minn., Sept. 18, 1912; *Crossroads,* p. 190

14. I am willing to get anything for an American that money and enterprise can obtain except the suppression of the rights of other men. I will not help any man buy a power which he ought not to exercise over his fellow beings.

WOODROW WILSON
Speech in Philadelphia, Pa., July 4, 1914; *Ideals,* p. 8

15. Inherent rights are of God, and the tragedies of the world originate in their attempted denial.

WARREN G. HARDING
Address to Armament Conference, Washington, D.C.,
Nov. 12, 1921; *Messages and Papers,* p. 9042

16. Men speak of natural rights, but I challenge any one to show where in nature any rights existed or were recognized until there was established for their declaration and protection a duly promulgated body of corresponding laws.

CALVIN COOLIDGE
Acceptance of Nomination for Presidency, July 27, 1920;
Dictionary, p. 1044

17. The individual has rights but only the citizen has the power to protect rights. And the protection of rights is righteous.

CALVIN COOLIDGE
Address at Carnegie Institute of Technology, Pittsburgh, Pa.,
Apr. 28, 1921; *Freedom,* p. 46

18. The fundamental basis of this nation's law was given to Moses on the Mount. The fundamental basis of our Bill of Rights comes from the

teachings which we get from Exodus and St. Matthew, from Isaiah and St. Paul. I don't think we emphasize that enough these days.

If we don't have the proper fundamental moral background, we will finally wind up with a totalitarian government which does not believe in rights for anybody except the state.

HARRY S. TRUMAN
Address to Attorney General's Conference on Law Enforcement, Washington, D.C., Feb. 15, 1950; *Mr. President,* p. 72

19. Today we proudly assert that the government of the United States is still committed to the concept [that every individual is endowed with certain inalienable rights]. . . .

The purpose is Divine; the implementation is human.

Our country and its government have made mistakes—human mistakes. They have been of the head—not of the heart. And it is still true that the great concept of the dignity of all men, alike created in the image of the Almighty, has been the compass by which we have tried and are trying to steer our course.

DWIGHT D. EISENHOWER
Fifth Annual Message to Congress, Jan. 10, 1957; *Public Papers . . . Eisenhower, 1957,* p. 30

See also American System, Civil Rights, Defense 4, 13, Flag (The) 2, Foreign Relations 25, Freedom, Government 7, 94, Greatness 8, Independence, Justice 14, Legislation 4, Liberty, Majorities 2, Minorities 2, Negroes 5, Neutrality 2, 3, 4, Peace 9, 17, 38, People (The) 18, Political Philosophy 2, 3, Property 1, 4, Republics 4, 5, Revolutions 3, Russia 4, Security 5, States' Rights, Strikes 1, 2, Union 3, War 32

Rulers

1. There has never been any organized society without rulers. . . . Democracy is obedience to the rule of the people.

CALVIN COOLIDGE
Address at Wellesley Hills, Mass., Aug. 2, 1922; *Citizenship,* p. 60

See also Kings

Russia

1. Russia and the United States being in character and practice essentially pacific, a common interest in the rights of peaceable nations gives us a common cause in their maintenance.

THOMAS JEFFERSON
To André de Dashkoff, Aug. 12, 1809; *Writings, XII,* 303

2. Our long-established friendliness with Russia has remained unshaken. It has prompted me to proffer the earnest counsels of this Government that measures be adopted for suppressing the proscription which the Hebrew race in that country has lately suffered. . . . There is reason to

believe that the time is not far distant when Russia will be able to secure toleration to all faiths within her borders.

CHESTER A. ARTHUR
Second Annual Message to Congress, Dec. 4, 1882; *Messages and Papers*, p. 4714

3. For the people of Russia the people of the United States have ever entertained friendly feelings, which have now been greatly deepened by the knowledge that, actuated by the same lofty motives, the two Governments and peoples are co-operating to bring to a successful termination the conflict now raging for human liberty and a universal acknowledgment of those principles of right and justice which should direct all Governments.

WOODROW WILSON
Address in Washington, D.C., July 5, 1917; *Selections*, p. 148

4. Russia presents notable difficulties. We have every desire to see that great people, who are our traditional friends, restored to their position among the nations of the earth. We have relieved their pitiable destitution with an enormous charity. Our Government offers no objection to the carrying on of commerce by our citizens with the people of Russia. Our Government does not propose, however, to enter into relations with another regime which refuses to recognize the sanctity of international obligations. I do not propose to barter away for the privilege of trade any of the cherished rights of humanity. I do not propose to make merchandise of any American principles. These rights and principles must go wherever the sanctions of our Government go.

CALVIN COOLIDGE
First Annual Message to Congress, Dec. 6, 1923; *Messages and Papers*, p. 9342

5. When you try to conquer other people or extend yourself over vast areas you cannot win in the long run. . . .
The Russians today foolishly think that we are imperialistic and want to conquer their land. The very opposite is true. They are the imperialists. We are not imperialists. We do not want any more territory. We do not want to conquer any people. We want to help people because helping them means helping ourselves.

HARRY S. TRUMAN
Interview, *ca.* 1950; *Mr. President*, p. 82

6. The Soviet government's decision to resume nuclear weapons testing presents a hazard to every human being throughout the world. . . . It indicates the complete hypocrisy of its professions.

JOHN F. KENNEDY
White House statement, Aug. 30, 1961; *Public Papers . . . Kennedy, 1961*, p. 580

7. They have offered to trade us an apple for an orchard. We don't do that in this country.

JOHN F. KENNEDY
Remark after meeting Andrei Gromyko, Oct. 6, 1961;
New York Times, Oct. 8, 1961

See also Communism, Cuba 2, Disarmament 3, Freedom 31, Goals 2, History 19, Peace 62, 86, Physical Fitness 3

Sacrifice
See Bravery 1, Self-Sacrifice

Safety
See Preparedness 17

Satisfaction
See Achievement 2, Happiness 11

Schools
See Colleges, Education, Universities

Science
See Public Opinion 1, Rights 7

Secession
1. If one State may secede, so may another; and when all shall have seceded none is left to pay the debts. Is this quite just to creditors?

ABRAHAM LINCOLN
Special Session Message, July 4, 1861; *Messages and Papers,*
p. 3229

See also Nullification

Secrecy
1. The nature of foreign negotiations requires caution, and their success must often depend on secrecy; and even when brought to a conclusion a full disclosure of all the measures, demands . . . would be extremely impolitic; . . . The necessity of such caution and secrecy was one cogent reason for vesting the power of making treaties in the President, with the advice and consent of the Senate. . . . To admit, then, a right in the House of Representatives to demand and to have . . . all the papers respecting a negotiation with a foreign power would be to establish a dangerous precedent.

GEORGE WASHINGTON
Message to House of Representatives, Mar. 30, 1796; *Messages and Papers,* p. 2416

2. It has been a subject of serious deliberation with me whether I could, consistently with my constitutional duty and my sense of the public in-

terests involved . . . violate an important principle, always heretofore held sacred by my predecessors [in this case, to divulge instructions and orders issued to the minister plenipotentiary of the United States to Mexico].

JAMES K. POLK
Message to House of Representatives, Jan. 12, 1848; *Ibid.*

See also Wrong 2

Security

1.   But let not the foundation of our hope rest upon man's wisdom. . . . It must be felt that there is no national security but in the nation's humble, acknowledged dependence upon God and His overruling providence.

FRANKLIN PIERCE
Inaugural Address, Mar. 4, 1853

2.   The first of social securities is freedom—freedom of men to worship, to think, to speak, to direct their energies, to develop their own talents, and to be rewarded for their effort. . . .

The second of social securities is the capacity to produce a plenty of goods and services with which to give economic security to the whole of us. . . .

Universal social security cannot be had by sudden inspiration of panaceas. There are no short cuts. Permanent social growth cannot be had by hothouse methods. . . .

Social security must be builded upon a cult of work, not a cult of leisure.

HERBERT HOOVER
Speech, June 16, 1935; *Policies,* p. 48

3.   These three great objectives—the security of the home, the security of livelihood, and the security of social insurance—are, it seems to me, a minimum of the promise that we can offer to the American people.

FRANKLIN DELANO ROOSEVELT
Message to Congress, June 8, 1934; *Public Papers, III,* 292

4.   Because it has become increasingly difficult for individuals to build their own security single-handed, government must now step in and help them lay the foundation stones, just as government in the past has helped lay the foundation of business and industry.

FRANKLIN DELANO ROOSEVELT
Radio address, Aug. 15, 1938; *Ibid., VII,* 479

5.   We have accepted . . . a second Bill of Rights under which a new basis of security and prosperity can be established for all—regardless of station, race or creed. Among these are: The right of a useful and remunerative job in the industries or shops or farms or mines of the Nation:

The right to earn enough to provide adequate food and clothing and recreation;

The right of every farmer to raise and sell his products at a return which will give him and his family a decent living;

The right of every businessman, large and small, to trade in an atmosphere of freedom from unfair competition and domination by monopolies at home or abroad;

The right of every family to a decent home;

The right to adequate medical care and the opportunity to achieve and enjoy good health;

The right to adequate protection from the economic fears of old age, sickness, accident, and unemployment;

The right to a good education.

All of these spell security.

FRANKLIN DELANO ROOSEVELT
Twelfth Annual Message to Congress, Jan. 11, 1944; *Ibid., XIII,* 41

6. Real security will be found only in law and justice.

HARRY S. TRUMAN
American Speeches, 1944–45, p. 160

7. If all that Americans want is security, then they can go to prison. They'll have enough to eat, a bed and a roof over their heads. But if an American wants to preserve his dignity and his equality as a human being, he must not bow his neck to any dictatorial government. . . .

DWIGHT D. EISENHOWER
Speech in Galveston, Tex., December, 1949

8. America alone and isolated cannot assure even its own security. We must be joined by the capability and resolution of nations that have proved themselves dependable defenders of freedom. Isolation from them invites war. Our security is also enhanced by the immeasurable interest that joins us with all peoples who believe that peace with justice must be preserved, that wars of aggression are crimes against humanity.

. . . Our Nation has made great strides in assuring a modern defense, so armed in new weapons, so deployed, so equipped, that today our security force is the most powerful in our peacetime history. . . . It is a major deterrent to war. . . .

National security requires far more than military power. Economic and moral factors play indispensable roles. Any program that endangers our economy could defeat us. Any weakening of our national will and resolution, any diminution of the vigor and initiative of our individual citizens, would strike a blow at the heart of our defenses.

DWIGHT D. EISENHOWER
Fifth Annual Message to Congress, Jan. 10, 1957; *Public Papers . . . Eisenhower, 1957,* p. 25

9. In today's world, a nation's security does not always increase as its arms increase, when its adversary is doing the same. And unlimited com-

petition in the testing and development of new types of destructive nuclear weapons will not make the world safer for either side. . . .

If we are to open new doorways to peace, if we are to seize this rare opportunity for progress, if we are to be as bold and farsighted in our control of weapons as we have been in their invention, then let us show all the world . . . that a strong America also stands for peace.

> JOHN F. KENNEDY
> Radio and television address, July 26, 1963; *Vital Speeches,*
> *Aug. 15, 1963,* p. 646

See also Aggression 2, Communism 5, 7, Freedom 32, Government 36, Immigration 2, Military Matters 3, Peace 38, 61, Political Philosophy 2, Politics 12, Prosperity 5, Religion 2, Rights 12, Slogans, War 1

Segregation

1. Segregation has been abolished in the Armed Forces, in Veterans' Hospitals, in all Federal employment, and throughout the District of Columbia—administratively accomplished progress in this field that is unmatched in America's recent history.

This pioneering work in civil rights must go on. Not only because discrimination is morally wrong, but also because its impact is more than national—it is world-wide.

> DWIGHT D. EISENHOWER
> Annual Message to Congress, Jan. 12, 1961; *Public Papers*
> . . . *Eisenhower, 1960–61,* p. 927

2. Racial segregation and violence which badly distort our image abroad while weakening us here at home constitute only a small part of the American scene.

> JOHN F. KENNEDY
> Speech in New York, N.Y., June 28, 1959; *Strategy,* p. 165

See also Civil Rights, Desegregation, Discrimination, Equality, Negroes

Self-Control

1. Nothing gives one person so much advantage over another as to remain always cool and unruffled under all circumstances.

> THOMAS JEFFERSON
> To Francis Eppes, May 21, 1816; *Writings, XIX,* 241

See also Self-Government 5

Self-Deception

1. There is nothing in the science of human nature more curious, or that deserves a critical attention from every order of men so much, as that principle which moral writers have distinguished by the name of self-deceit. This principle is the spurious offspring of self-love; and is, perhaps,

the source of far the greatest and worst part of the vices and calamities among mankind.

JOHN ADAMS
"Novanglus," in Boston *Gazette*, Aug. 29, 1763; *Works, III,* 433

Self-Government

1. The qualifications of self-government in society are not innate. They are the result of habit and long training, and for these they will require time and probably much suffering.

THOMAS JEFFERSON
To Edward Everett, Mar. 27, 1824; *Writings, XVI,* 22

2. The doctrine of self-government has . . . application depending upon whether a Negro is not or is a man. If he is not a man, in that case he who is a man may as a matter of self-government do just what he pleases with him. But if the Negro is a man, is it not to that extent a total destruction of self-government to say that he, too, shall not govern himself? . . .

Allow all the governed an equal voice in the government, and that, and that only, is self-government.

ABRAHAM LINCOLN
Speech at Peoria, Ill., Oct. 16, 1854; *Complete Works, II,* 227, 229

3. It must not be forgotten that only a local government which recognizes and maintains inviolate the rights of all is a true self-government.

RUTHERFORD B. HAYES
Inaugural Address, Mar. 4, 1877

4. Only peoples capable, not merely of mastering others, but of mastering themselves, can achieve real liberty, can achieve real self-government.

THEODORE ROOSEVELT
In Washington, D.C., Apr. 7, 1904; *Presidential Addresses, III,* 5

5. Self-government is not a thing that can be "given" to any people, because it is a form of character and not a form of constitution. No people can be "given" the self-control of maturity.

WOODROW WILSON
1908; *Constitutional Government,* p. 53

6. Our country was conceived in the theory of local self-government. . . . It makes the largest promise to the freedom and development of the individual. . . . It cannot be denied that the present tendency is not in harmony with this spirit. The individual, instead of working out his own salvation and securing his own freedom by establishing his own economic and moral independence by his own industry and his own self-mastery, tends to throw himself on some vague influence which he denominates society and to hold that in some way responsible for the sufficiency of his support and the morality of his actions. . . . We cannot maintain the

western standard of civilization on that theory. . . . It will have to be supported on the principle of individual responsibility.

If we are too weak to take charge of our own morality, we shall not be strong enough to take charge of our own liberty. If we cannot govern ourselves, if we cannot observe the law, nothing remains but to have someone else govern us, to have the law enforced against us, and to step down from the honorable abiding place of freedom to the ignominious abode of servitude.

CALVIN COOLIDGE
Address at Arlington, Va., May 30, 1925; *Messages and Papers*, p. 9504

See also Democracy 27, Despotism, Government 50, 78, 79, 96, Mankind 6, Peace 38, Relief 2, Republics 13, States' Rights

Selfishness

1. I emphatically believe in unselfishness, but I also believe that it is a mistake to let other people grow selfish.

THEODORE ROOSEVELT
Autobiography, p. 166

Self-Reliance

1. Sirens still sing the song of the easy way for the moment of difficulty . . . but the truth which echoes upward from this soil of blood and tears, the way to the nation's greatness is the path of self-reliance, independence, and steadfastness in times of trial and stress.

HERBERT HOOVER
Speech at Valley Forge, Pa., May 30, 1931; *State Papers, I*, 566

See also Brotherhood 2, Character 3, Negroes 4, Relief 2, 4, Self-Government 6

Self-Respect

See American Revolution 2, Peace 34, War 15

Self-Sacrifice

1. Our life is but a little plan. One generation follows another very quickly. If a man with red blood in him had his choice, knowing that he must die, he would rather die to vindicate some right, unselfish to himself, than die in his bed. We are all touched with the love of the glory which is real glory, and the only glory comes from utter self-forgetfulness and self-sacrifice. We never erect a statue to a man who has merely succeeded. We erect statues to men who have forgotten themselves and been glorified by the memory of others. This is the standard that America holds up to mankind in all sincerity and in all earnestness.

WOODROW WILSON
Speech at Kansas City, Mo., Feb. 2, 1916; *Messages and Papers (Shaw)*, p. 204

See also Bravery 1, Loyalty 2

Sensibility

1. Sensibility of mind is indeed the parent of every virtue, but it is the parent of much misery, too.

THOMAS JEFFERSON
To Countess Barziza, July 8, 1788; *Writings, XIX,* 46

Service

1. I have no private purposes to accomplish, no party projects to build up, no enemies to punish—nothing to serve but my country.

ZACHARY TAYLOR
To J. S. Allison, Apr. 12, 1848; *Life,* p. 383

2. Service is the supreme commitment of life. I would rejoice to acclaim the era of the Golden Rule and crown it with the autocracy of service.

WARREN G. HARDING
Inaugural Address, Mar. 4, 1921

3. Service is both the inspiration and the accomplishment of quite everything worth while which impels us onward and upward. With service which the Nazarene would approve are associated all our ideals and our finer aspirations.

WARREN G. HARDING
Speech at Denver, Colo., June 25, 1923;
Messages and Papers, p. 9278

Silence

1. We often repent of what we have said, but never, never, of that which we have not.

THOMAS JEFFERSON
To Gideon Granger, Mar. 9, 1814; *Writings, XIV,* 117

2. The time comes upon every public man when it is best for him to keep his lips closed.

ABRAHAM LINCOLN
1860; *Life (Tarbell), I,* 376

3. *Re the comment, "Everybody says you never talk":*
   Well, many times I only say "yes" or "no" [to people], and even that winds *them* up for twenty minutes more.

CALVIN COOLIDGE
Said to Bernard Baruch, 1924; *Public Years (Baruch),* p. 191

See also Criticism 1, Presidency (The) 52, Public Speaking 1, Slander 2

Slander

1. Defamation is becoming a necessity of life; inasmuch as a dish of tea in the morning or evening cannot be digested without this stimulant.

THOMAS JEFFERSON
To John Norvell, June 11, 1807; *Writings, XI,* 226

2. I have been twelve years submitting in silence to the foulest and basest aspersions. Is the time arriving for me to speak? Or must I go down to the grave and leave posterity to do justice to my father and to me.

JOHN QUINCY ADAMS
August, 1840; *John Quincy Adams (Morse)*, p. 299

3. Unless some mode is adopted to frown down by society the slanderer, who is worse than the murderer, all attempts to put down duelling will be in vain. The murderer only takes the life of the parent and leaves his character as a goodly heritage to his children, whilst the slanderer takes away his good reputation and leaves him a living monument to his children's disgrace.

ANDREW JACKSON
Note, August, 1837; *Life (Bassett)*, p. 729

See also Criticism, Truth 3

Slavery

1. I can only say that there is not a man living who wishes more sincerely than I do to see a plan adopted for the abolition of slavery.

GEORGE WASHINGTON
To Robert Morris, Apr. 12, 1786;
Writings (Fitzpatrick), XXVIII, 408

2. I never mean (unless some particular circumstances should compel me to it) to possess another slave by purchase; it being among my first wishes to see some plan adopted, by which slavery in this country may be abolished by slow, sure, and imperceptible degrees.

GEORGE WASHINGTON
To John Francis Mercer, Sept. 9, 1786; *Ibid., XXIX,* 5

3. Consenting to slavery is a sacrilegious breach of trust, as offensive in the sight of God as it is derogatory from our own honor or interest or happiness.

JOHN ADAMS
Dissertation on the Canon and the Feudal Law, August, 1765;
Works, III, 463

4. Although I have never sought popularity by any animated speeches or inflammatory publications against the slavery of the blacks, my opinion against it has always been known, and my practice has been so conformable to my sentiments that I have always employed freemen, both as domestics and laborers, and never in my life did I own a slave. The abolition of slavery must be gradual, and accomplished with much caution and circumspection.

JOHN ADAMS
To George Churchman and Jacob Lindley, Jan. 24, 1801;
Works, IX, 92

5. It is wrong to admit into the Constitution the idea that there can be property in man.

> JOHN ADAMS
> *Chips,* p. 126

6. This abomination must have an end. And there is a superior bench reserved in Heaven for those who hasten it.

> THOMAS JEFFERSON
> To Edward Rutledge, July 14, 1787; *Writings, VI,* 173

7. No defender of slavery, I concede that it has its benevolent aspects in lifting the Negro from savagery and helping prepare him for that eventual freedom which is surely written in the Book of Fate.

> THOMAS JEFFERSON
> *Cocked Hats,* p. 364

8. Another of my wishes is to depend as little as possible on the labour of slaves.

> JAMES MADISON
> To Edmund Randolph, July 26, 1785; *Letters, I,* 161

9. Our opinions agree as to the evil, moral, political, and economical, of slavery.

> JAMES MADISON
> To Francis Corbin, Nov. 26, 1820; *Writings, XI,* 40

10. We have found that this evil has preyed upon the very vitals of the Union, and has been prejudicial to all the States in which it has existed.

> JAMES MONROE
> *Epoch,* p. 511

11. Oh, if but one man could arise with a genius capable of comprehending, and an utterance capable of communicating those eternal truths that belong to this question, to lay bare in all its nakedness that outrage upon the goodness of God, human slavery!

> JOHN QUINCY ADAMS
> 1820; *Mr. and Mrs. John Quincy Adams,* p. 198

12. Holders of slaves often delude themselves, by assuming that the test of property is human law. The soul of one man cannot by human law be made the property of another. The owner of a slave is the owner of a living corpse; but he is not the owner of the man.

> JOHN QUINCY ADAMS
> Speech at Bangor, Me., July 4, 1843; *Selected,* p. 408

13. If slavery must go by blood and war, let war come.

> JOHN QUINCY ADAMS
> Speech to House of Representatives, Feb. 4, 1843

14. It is only perverted sentiment—mistaking labor for slavery and dominion for freedom. In the abstract they admit that slavery is an evil; but when
probed to the quick they show at the bottom of their souls pride and vain-
glory in their condition of masterdom. They fancy themselves more generous and noble-hearted than the plain freemen who labor for subsistence.
They look down upon the simplicity of a Yankee's manners because he
has no habits of overbearing like theirs and cannot treat Negroes like dogs.

JOHN QUINCY ADAMS
Diary; *Cocked Hats*, p. 363

15. I deprecated the agitation of the slavery question in congress, and
though a southwestern man and from a slave-holding State as well . . .
I did not desire . . . to give occasion for the agitation of a question which
might sever and endanger the Union itself. . . . The question of slavery
would probably never be a practical one if we acquired New Mexico and
California, because there would be but a narrow ribbon of territory south
of the Missouri Compromise line of 36° 30', and in it slavery would
probably never exist.

JAMES K. POLK
Jan. 23, 1847; *Diary (Quaife)*, *II*, 350

16. The agitation of the slavery question is mischievous & wicked, and
proceeds from no patriotic motive by its authors. It is a mere political
question on which demagogues & ambitious politicians hope to promote
their own prospects for political promotion. And this they seem willing to
do even at the hazard of disturbing the harmony if not dissolving the
Union itself.

JAMES K. POLK
Diary, Dec. 22, 1848; *Ibid.*, *IV*, 251

17. God knows that I detest slavery, but it is an existing evil, for which
we are not responsible, and we must endure it, and give it such protection
as is guaranteed by the Constitution, till we can get rid of it without destroying the last hope of free government in the world.

MILLARD FILLMORE
To Daniel Webster, Oct. 28, 1850; *Millard Fillmore*
(Rayback), p. 271

18. We have just as little right to interfere with slavery in the South as
we have to touch the right of petition.

JAMES BUCHANAN
1836; *Works*, *III*, 10

19. How easy would it be for the American people to settle the slavery
question forever, and to restore peace and harmony to this distracted
country! They, and they alone, can do it. All that is necessary to accomplish the object and all for which the slave States have ever contended, is

to be let alone and permitted to manage their domestic institutions in their own way. As sovereign States, they and they alone are responsible before God for the slavery existing among them.

JAMES BUCHANAN
Fourth Annual Message to Congress, Dec. 3, 1860; *Messages,*
p. 136

20.   This is a world of compensation; and he who would be no slave must consent to have no slave. Those who deny freedom to others deserve it not for themselves; and, under a just God, cannot long retain it.

ABRAHAM LINCOLN
To H. L. Pierce, Apr. 6, 1859; *Ibid.,* V, 126

21.   I have no purpose directly or indirectly to interfere with the institution of slavery in the States where it exists. I believe I have no lawful right to do so, and I have no inclination to do so.

ABRAHAM LINCOLN
First Inaugural Address, Mar. 4, 1861

22.   Although volume upon volume is written to prove slavery a very good thing, we never hear of the man who wishes to take the good of it by being a slave himself.

ABRAHAM LINCOLN
July 1, 1854; *Complete Works, II,* 183

23.   In giving freedom to the slave we assure freedom to the free,—honorable alike in what we give and what we preserve.

ABRAHAM LINCOLN
Second Annual Message to Congress, Dec. 1, 1862; *Messages
and Papers,* p. 3343

24.   It may seem strange that any men should dare to ask a just God's assistance in wringing their bread from the sweat of other men's faces.

ABRAHAM LINCOLN
Second Inaugural Address, Mar. 4, 1865

25.   Away with slavery, the breeder of Aristocrats. Up with the Stars and Stripes, symbol of free labor and free men.

ANDREW JOHNSON
1861; *Not Guilty,* p. 54

26.   Slavery is dead, and you must pardon me if I do not mourn over its dead body; you can bury it out of sight. . . . I desire that all men shall have a fair start and an equal chance in the race of life, and let him succeed who has the most merit. I am for emancipation, for two reasons: first, because it is right in itself; and second, because in the emancipation

of the slaves we break down an odious and dangerous aristocracy. I think that we are freeing more whites than blacks in Tennessee.

ANDREW JOHNSON
Speech at Nashville, Tenn., 1864; *Chips,* p. 286

27. Now that slavery is at an end, or near its end, the greatness of its evil in the point of view of public economy becomes more and more apparent. Slavery was essentially a monopoly of labor, and as such locked the States where it prevailed against the incoming of free industry.

ANDREW JOHNSON
First Annual Message to Congress, Dec. 4, 1865; *Messages and Papers,* p. 3559

28. We shall never know why slavery dies so hard in this Republic . . . till we know why sin is long-lived and Satan is immortal.

JAMES A. GARFIELD
Speech in Congress, 1864; *Public Services,* p. 175

29. I will not be a party to any treaty that makes anybody a slave; now that is all there is to it.

DWIGHT D. EISENHOWER
Press conference, June 30, 1954;
Public Papers . . . Eisenhower, 1954, p. 604

See also Democracy 3, Despotism 1, Freedom 4, Government 65, Liberty 26, Mankind 3, Negroes, People (The) 5, Power 3, Publicity 1, Rights 7, States' Rights 13, Union 13, 17, 24, 26

Slogans

1. A device of the advocates of gigantic spending is the manipulation of words, phrases, and slogans to convey new meanings different from those we have long understood. These malignant distortions drug thinking. They drown it in emotion.

For instance, we see government borrowing and spending transformed into the soft phrase "deficit spending." The slogan of a "welfare state" has emerged as a disguise for a collectivist state by the route of spending. The Founding Fathers would not recognize this distortion of the simple word "welfare" in the Constitution. Certainly Jefferson's idea of the meaning of welfare lies in his statement "To preserve our independence. . . . We must make a choice between economy and liberty or profusion and servitude. . . . If we can prevent government from wresting the labors of the people under the pretence of caring for them we shall be happy."

Another of these distortions is by those who support such a state and call themselves "liberals." . . .

Out of these slogans and phrases and new meanings of words come vague promises and misty mirages, such as "security from the cradle to the grave." In action that will frustrate those basic human impulses to production which alone make a dynamic nation.

HERBERT HOOVER
Address at Stanford University, Aug. 10, 1949;
American Road, p. 19

See also Americans 9, Clichés, Government 97, Taxation 14

Socialism
See Communism 2

Socialized Medicine
1.   The term . . . "socialized medicine" was constantly used by [my] opposition in an attempt to confuse the provisions of the national health insurance program.

HARRY S. TRUMAN
1945; *Memoirs, II,* 481

See also Health 6, Physical Fitness 2

Society
1.   Life is of no value but as it brings us gratifications. Among the most valuable of these is rational society. It informs the mind, sweetens the temper, cheers our spirits, and promotes health.

THOMAS JEFFERSON
To James Madison, Feb. 20, 1784; *Papers, VI,* 550

2.   Agreeable society is the first essential in constituting the happiness and of course the value of our existence.

THOMAS JEFFERSON
To James Madison, Dec. 8, 1784; *Ibid., VII,* 559

3.   Without society, and a society to our taste, men are never contented.

THOMAS JEFFERSON
To Colonel James Monroe, Dec. 18, 1786; *Writings, VI,* 17

4.   The transcendent law of nature and of nature's God . . . declares that the safety and happiness of society are the objects at which all political institutions aim, and to which all institutions must be sacrificed.

JAMES MADISON
"Publius," 1788; *Federalist*

5.   The complacent, the self-indulgent, the soft societies are about to be swept away with the debris of history.

JOHN F. KENNEDY
Address to newspaper editors, Apr. 20, 1961; *Tide,* p. 47

See also Friendship, Reforms 2, Soldiers 1

Soldiers

1. I am rather badly off here [in Kentucky] on the score of society, but a soldier ought not to repine at that circumstance for when he enters the army he ought to give up society entirely.

ZACHARY TAYLOR
To Richard Taylor, Nov. 24, 1808; *Soldier,* p. 35

2. Better to have a practical, than a theoretical soldier, if they are to possess but one qualification, but when a soldier can combine both, it gives him every advantage. . . . Such unfortunately is the passion in our country for making roads, fortifications, and building barracks . . . with soldiers . . . that a man who would make a good overseer, or Negro driver, is better qualified for our service, than one who had received a first rate military education. . . . The ax, pick, saw and trowel, has become more the implement of the American soldier, than the cannon, musket or sword.

ZACHARY TAYLOR
To Thomas S. Jesup, Sept. 18, 1820; *Ibid.,* p. 67

3. From Caesar to Cromwell, and from Cromwell to Napoleon . . . history presents the same solemn warning—beware of elevating to the highest civil trust the commander of your victorious armies.

JAMES BUCHANAN
Speech at Greensburg, Pa., Oct. 7, 1852; *Life, II,* 46

See also Army, Military Matters 1, Navy, War 20

South America
See Right 2

Sovereignty
See Freedom 10, States' Rights 15

Soviet Union
See Disarmament 3, 5, Goals 2, Russia

Space

1. Now it is time to take longer strides—time for a great new American enterprise—time for this nation to take a clearly leading role in space achievement, which in many ways may hold the key to our future on earth. . . . This is not merely a race. Space is open to us now; and our eagerness to share its meaning is not governed by the efforts of others. We go into space because whatever mankind must undertake, free men must fully share. . . . This nation will move forward, with the full speed of freedom, in the exciting adventure of space.

JOHN F. KENNEDY
Special Message to Congress, May 25, 1961; *Public Papers* . . .
Kennedy, 1961, p. 404

2. We of the United States do not acknowledge that there are landlords of outer space who can presume to bargain with the nations of the earth on the price of access to this new domain.

We must not—and need not—corrupt this great opportunity by bringing to it the very antagonisms which we may, by courage, overcome and leave behind forever through a joint adventure into this new realm. . . .

Men who have worked together to reach the stars are not likely to descend together into the depths of war and desolation.

LYNDON B. JOHNSON
Address to the First Committee on Outer Space, United Nations,
Nov. 17, 1958; *Action*, pp. 63, 64

3. I confidently believe that the developments of the Space Age will bring the beginning of the longest and greatest boom of abundance and prosperity in the history of man.

LYNDON B. JOHNSON
Address at Southwest Texas State Teachers College, May 28, 1961

4. We cannot wishfully and unrealistically assume that no nation will extend its objectives of world domination by means of space weapons. To reach for the moon is a risk, but it is a risk we must take. Keep in mind that failure to go into space is even riskier.

LYNDON B. JOHNSON
Address in Dallas, Tex., Apr. 23, 1963; *Story*, p. 184

5. We must assure our pre-eminence in the peaceful exploration of outer space, focusing on an expedition to the moon in this decade, in cooperation with other powers, if possible, alone, if necessary.

LYNDON B. JOHNSON
State of the Union Address, Jan. 8, 1964; *Vital Speeches*,
Jan. 15, 1964, p. 196

Speeches
1. Amplification is the vice of the modern orator. Speeches measured by the hour die by the hour.

THOMAS JEFFERSON
To David Harding, Apr. 20, 1824; *Writings, XVI*, 30

2. No one knows how I hate making speeches.

CALVIN COOLIDGE
To Everett Sanders, Sept. 21, 1932; *Meet Calvin Coolidge*, p. 202

See also Eloquence, Preparedness 11, 12, Public Speaking

Spiritual Values
See Fear 5, Materialism, War 68

Spoils System
See Patronage

Square Deal

1. A man who is good enough to shed his blood for his country is good enough to be given a square deal afterward. More than that no man is entitled to, and less than that no man shall have.

THEODORE ROOSEVELT
Speech at Springfield, Ill., June 4, 1904;
Addresses and Papers, p. 446

2. We demand that big business give the people a square deal; in return we must insist that when any one engaged in big business honestly endeavors to do right he shall himself be given a square deal; and the first, and most elementary, kind of square deal is to give him in advance full information as to just what he can, and what he cannot, legally and properly do.

THEODORE ROOSEVELT
1911; *Autobiography,* p. 569

Standards

1. Let us raise a standard to which the wise and honest can repair; the rest is in the hands of God.

GEORGE WASHINGTON
To the Constitutional Convention, 1787

See also Self-Sacrifice

Standpatism

1. Nothing else in the world is standing still except the Standpatters.

WOODROW WILSON
Wit and Wisdom, p. 58

See also Reforms 5

Statesmanship

1. Statesmanship consists rather in removing causes than in punishing or evading results.

JAMES A. GARFIELD
Speech on the Ninth Census; *Chips,* p. 451

2. Statesmanship must be wise as well as fearless—not the statesmanship which will command the applause of the hour, but the approving judgment of posterity.

WILLIAM MCKINLEY
Speech in Chicago, Ill., Oct. 19, 1898; *Eloquence, II,* 815

3. The first requisite in the statesmanship that shall benefit mankind

. . . is that that statesmanship shall be thoroughly American. . . . The man who lifts America higher, by just so much makes higher the civilization of all mankind.

THEODORE ROOSEVELT
Speech in New York, N.Y., Feb. 17, 1899; *Works, XI,* 266

4. Statesmanship consists, not in the cultivation and practice of the arts of intrigue . . . but in the life-long endeavor to lead first the attention and then the will of the people to the acceptance of truth in its applications to the problems of government.

WOODROW WILSON
University of Virginia magazine, March, 1880; *Story,* p. 14

5. The whole process of statesmanship consists in bringing facts to light, and shaping law to suit, or, if need be, mould them.

WOODROW WILSON
The Making of the Nation, July, 1897; *Life, IV,* 1

See also Defense 2, Government 97, 100, Honesty 3, 5, Mothers 6, War 71

States' Rights

1. Were not this great country divided into states, that division must be made, that each might do for itself what concerns itself directly, and what it can so much better do than a distant authority. . . . Were we directed from Washington when to sow, and when to reap, we should soon want bread.

THOMAS JEFFERSON
Autobiography, 1787; *Writings, I,* 122

2. The States should be left to do whatever acts they can do as well as the general government.

THOMAS JEFFERSON
To John Harvie, July 25, 1790; *Writings (Ford) V,* 214

3. I wish to preserve the line drawn by the federal constitution between the general and particular governments . . . and to take every prudent means of preventing either from stepping over it. . . . It is easy to foresee, that the encroachments of the State governments will tend to an excess of liberty which will correct itself . . . while those of the general government will tend to monarchy, which will fortify itself from day to day, instead of working its own cure, as all experience shows. I would rather be exposed to the inconvenience attending to too much liberty, than those attending too small a degree of it. . . . It is important to strengthen the State governments.

THOMAS JEFFERSON
Letter to Archibald Stuart, Dec. 23, 1791; *Works, III,* 314

4. I dare say that in time all the State governments as well as their central government, like the planets revolving round their common sun, acting and acted upon according to their respective weights and distances, will produce that beautiful equilibrium on which our Constitution is founded, and which I believe it will exhibit to the world in a degree of perfection, unexampled but in the planetary system itself.

THOMAS JEFFERSON
To Peregrine Fitzhugh, Feb. 23, 1798; *Writings, VII,* 210

5. Our country is too large to have all its affairs directed by a single government. . . . The true theory of our Constitution is surely the wisest and best, that the states are independent as to everything within themselves, and united as to everything respecting foreign nations.

THOMAS JEFFERSON
To Gideon Granger, Aug. 13, 1800; *Ibid.,* p. 451

6. But the true barriers of our liberty in this country are our State governments. . . .

THOMAS JEFFERSON
To Comte Antoine Destutt de Tracy, Jan. 26, 1811; *Ibid., XIII,* 18

7. To respect the rights of the State governments is the inviolable duty of that of the Union; the government of every State will feel its own obligation to respect and preserve the rights of the whole.

JOHN QUINCY ADAMS
Inaugural Address, Mar. 4, 1825

8. Our government is [not] to be maintained or our Union preserved by invasions of the rights and powers of the several States. . . . Its true strength consists in leaving individuals and States as much as possible to themselves . . . in binding the States more closely to the center, but in leaving each to move unobstructed in its proper orbit.

ANDREW JACKSON
Veto Message, July 10, 1832; *Messages and Papers,* p. 1153

9. The right of the people of a single State to absolve themselves at will and without the consent of the other States from their most solemn obligations, and hazard the liberties and happiness of the millions composing this Union, can not be acknowledged.

ANDREW JACKSON
Message to Congress, Jan. 16, 1833; *Ibid.,* p. 1184

10. The destruction of our State governments or the annihilation of their controls over the local concerns of the people would lead directly to revolution and anarchy, and finally to despotism and military domination. In proportion, therefore, as the General Government encroaches upon the

rights of the States, in the same proportion does it impair its own power and detract from its ability to fulfill the purposes of its creation.

ANDREW JACKSON
Second Inaugural Address, Mar. 4, 1833

11.   The government was created by the States, is amenable to the States, is preserved by the States, and may be destroyed by the States. . . . I owe no responsibility, politically speaking, elsewhere than to my State. . . .

JOHN TYLER
Speech in the Senate, Feb. 6, 1833; *Register*, p. 360

12.   While the General Government should abstain from the exercise of authority not clearly delegated to it, the States should be equally careful that in the maintenance of their rights they do not overstep the limits of powers reserved to them.

JAMES K. POLK
Inaugural Address, Mar. 4, 1845

13.   No enactment of Congress could restrain the people of any of the sovereign States of the Union, old or new, North or South, slaveholding or nonslaveholding, from determining the character of their own domestic institutions as they may deem wise and proper.

JAMES K. POLK
Fourth Annual Message to Congress, Dec. 5, 1848; *Messages and Papers*, p. 2491

14.   If the Federal Government will confine itself to the exercise of powers clearly granted by the Constitution, it can hardly happen that its action upon any question should endanger the institutions of the States or interfere with their right to manage matters strictly domestic according to the will of their own people.

FRANKLIN PIERCE
Inaugural Address, Mar. 4, 1853

15.   I cannot find any authority in the Constitution for making the Federal Government the great almoner of public charity throughout the United States. . . . Indeed, to suppose it susceptible . . . would be . . . to clothe the Federal Government with authority over the sovereign states, by which they would be dwarfed into provinces or departments, and all sovereignty vested in an absolute, consolidated central power against which the spirit of liberty has so often and in so many countries struggled in vain.

FRANKLIN PIERCE
Veto Message to Congress, May 3, 1854; *Messages and Papers*, p. 2782

16.   State's rights should be preserved when they mean the people's rights, but not when they mean the people's wrongs; not, for instance, when

they are invoked to prevent the abolition of child labor, or to break the force of the laws which prohibit the importance of contract labor to this country.

THEODORE ROOSEVELT
Address before the Harvard Union, Cambridge, Mass.,
Feb. 23, 1907; *Works, XIII,* 567

17.   What America needs is to hold to its ancient and well-charted course.
Our country was conceived in the theory of local self-government. It has been dedicated by long practice to that wise and benevolent policy. It is the foundation principle of our system of liberty.

CALVIN COOLIDGE
Address at Arlington Cemetery, May 30, 1925; *Messages and Papers,* p. 9504

See also Government 24, Nullification, Republics 6, Slavery 18, 19, 21, Union 3

Stick, Big
See Foreign Relations 29

Strength
See People (The) 25, 36, Power 8, 19, Preparedness 8, 18, 19, States' Rights 8, Understanding 1, Unity 8

Strife
1.   Let us boldly face the life of strife, resolute to do our duty well and manfully, resolute to uphold righteousness by deed, by word; resolute to be both honest and brave, to serve high ideals, yet to use practical methods. Above all, let us shrink from no strife, moral or physical, within or without the nation, provided we are certain that the strife is justified.

THEODORE ROOSEVELT
Speech in Chicago, Ill., Apr. 10, 1899; *Works, XIII,* 331

See also Greatness 3, Union 23

Strikes
1.   The right of individuals to strike is inviolate and ought not to be interfered with by any process of government, but there is a predominant right and that is the right of the Government to protect all of its people and to assert its power and majesty against the challenge of any class.

WOODROW WILSON
Address to Congress, Dec. 2, 1919; *Selections,* p. 113

2.   There is no right to strike against the public safety by anybody, anywhere, any time.

CALVIN COOLIDGE
Telegram to Samuel Gompers, Sept. 14, 1919; *Faith,* p. 223

Subsidy

1. I know full well the hostility in the popular mind to the word "subsidy." It is stressed by the opposition and associated with "special privilege" by those who are unfailing advocates of Government aid whenever vast numbers are directly concerned. "Government aid" would be a fairer term than "subsidy" in defining what we are seeking to do . . . and the interests are those of all the people, even though the aid goes to the few who serve.

WARREN G. HARDING
Address to Congress, Nov. 21, 1922; *Messages and Papers*, p. 9161

See also Education 10

Success

1. The thinking part of mankind do not form their judgment from events; and their equity will ever attach equal glory to those actions, which deserve success, and those which have been crowned with it. It is in the trying circumstances . . . that the virtues of a great mind are displayed in their brightest lustre, and that a general's character is better known, than in the moment of victory.

GEORGE WASHINGTON
To Comte d'Estaing, Sept. 11, 1778;
Writings (Fitzpatrick), *VI*, 57

2. We can succeed only by concert. It is not, "Can any of us imagine better?" but, "Can we all do better?"

ABRAHAM LINCOLN
Second Annual Message to Congress, Dec. 1, 1862;
Complete Works, VIII, 130

3. To have any success in life, or any worthy success, you must resolve to carry into your work a fulness of knowledge—not merely a sufficiency, but more than a sufficiency.

JAMES A. GARFIELD
Speech in Washington, D.C., June 29, 1869; *Lives*, p. 29

4. Poets may be born, but success is made.

JAMES A. GARFIELD
Speech in Washington, D.C., June 29, 1869; *Ibid.*, p. 31

5. Real success consists in doing one's duty well in the path where one's life is led.

THEODORE ROOSEVELT
Speech at Upper Divide Creek, Colo., Apr. 30, 1905;
Presidential Addresses, III, 347

6. I am . . . interested when I see gentlemen supposing that popularity is the way to success in America. The way to success in this great country,

with its fair judgments, is to show that you are not afraid of anybody except God and His final verdict. If I did not believe that, I would not believe in democracy.

WOODROW WILSON
Address in Philadelphia, Pa., July 4, 1914; *Public Papers, III,* 146

7. I have no expectation of making a hit every time I come to bat.
FRANKLIN DELANO ROOSEVELT
Fireside Chat, May 7, 1933; *Public Papers, II,* 165

8. Any man who has come up through the process of political selection, as it functions in our country, knows that success is a mixture of principles steadfastly maintained and adjustments made at the proper time and place—adjustments to conditions, not adjustment of principles.

HARRY S. TRUMAN
1951; *Memoirs, II,* 445

9. Of those to whom much is given, much is required. And when at some future date the high court of history sits in judgment on each of us, recording whether in our brief span of service we fulfilled our responsibilities to the state, our success or failure, in whatever office we hold, will be measured by the answers to four questions:

First, were we truly men of courage, with the courage to stand up to one's enemies, and the courage to stand up, when necessary, to one's associates, the courage to resist public pressure as well as private greed?

Second, were we truly men of judgment, with perceptive judgment of the future as well as the past, of our own mistakes as well as the mistakes of others, with enough wisdom to know what we did not know, and enough candor to admit it?

Third, were we truly men of integrity, men who never ran out on either the principles in which we believed or the people who believed in us, men whom neither financial gain nor political ambition could ever divert from the fulfillment of our sacred trust?

Finally, were we truly men of dedication, with an honor mortgaged to no single individual or group, and compromised by no private obligation or aim, but devoted solely to serving the public good and the national interest?

Courage, judgment, integrity, dedication—these are the historic qualities . . . which, with God's help . . . will characterize our government's conduct in the . . . stormy years that lie ahead.

JOHN F. KENNEDY
Speech to Massachusetts State Legislature, Jan. 9, 1961; *Tide,* p. 5

See also Americans 10, Chance 2, Failure 2, Labor 6, Right 10, Unity 4

Suffrage

1. The exercise of the elective franchise is the highest attribute of an

American citizen, and when guided by virtue, intelligence, patriotism, and a proper appreciation of our institutions constitutes the true basis of a democratic form of government, in which the sovereign power is lodged in the body of the people.

ANDREW JOHNSON
Veto Message, Jan. 5, 1867; *Messages and Papers*, p. 3676

2.   Universal suffrage should rest upon universal education.

RUTHERFORD B. HAYES
Inaugural Address, Mar. 4, 1877

3.   Liberty can be safe only when Suffrage is illuminated by Education.

JAMES A. GARFIELD
September, 1880; *Maxims*, p. 8

4.   Bad local government is certainly a great evil, which ought to be prevented; but to violate the freedom and sanctities of the suffrage is more than an evil. It is a crime which, if persisted in, will destroy the Government itself.

JAMES A. GARFIELD
Inaugural Address, Mar. 4, 1881

5.   There can be no permanent disfranchised peasantry in the United States.

JAMES A. GARFIELD
Inaugural Address, Mar. 4, 1881

6.   How shall those who practice election frauds recover that respect for the sanctity of the ballot which is the first condition and obligation of good citizenship? The man who has come to regard the ballot box as a juggler's hat has renounced his allegiance.

BENJAMIN HARRISON
Inaugural Address, Mar. 4, 1889

7.   Our chief national danger lies . . . in the overthrow of majority control by the suppression or perversion of the popular suffrage.

BENJAMIN HARRISON
Third Annual Message to Congress, Dec. 9, 1891; *Messages and Papers*, p. 5645

See also Ballots, Elections, Voters, Women 7, 9, 10

Supreme Court
1.   It is a very dangerous doctrine to consider the judges as the ultimate arbiters of all constitutional questions. It is one which would place us under the despotism of an oligarchy.

THOMAS JEFFERSON
To W. C. Jarvis, Sept. 28, 1820; *Writings (Ford)*, X, 160

2. A sentiment, I had almost said, of idolatry, for the Supreme Court, has grown up, which claims for its members an almost entire exemption from the fallibilities of our nature, and arraigns with unsparing bitterness the motives of all who have the temerity to look with inquisitive eyes into this consecrated sanctuary of the law. So powerful has this sentiment become, such strong hold has it taken of the press of this country, that it requires not a little share of firmness in a public man, however imperious may be his duty, to express sentiments that conflict with it.

MARTIN VAN BUREN
1826; *Epoch*, p. 303

Tariff

1. A careful Tariff is much wanted to pay our national debt, to afford us the means of that defense within ourselves on which the safety and liberty of our country depend . . . and to give a proper distribution to our labor, which must prove beneficial to the happiness, independence and wealth of the community.

ANDREW JACKSON
To Dr. L. H. Colman, Apr. 26, 1814; *Life (Parton), III*, 36

2. A high tariff can never be permanent. It will cause dissatisfaction and will be changed. It excludes competition, and thereby invites the investment of capital in manufactures to such excess that when changed it brings distress, bankruptcy, and ruin upon all who have been misled by its faithless protection. . . . But to make a tariff uniform and permanent it is not only necessary that the laws should not be altered, but that the duty should not fluctuate.

MILLARD FILLMORE
First Annual Message to Congress, Dec. 2, 1850; *Messages and Papers, IV*, 2620

3. The tariff question, as dealt with in our time . . . has not been business. It has been politics. Tariff schedules have been made up for the purpose of keeping a large number . . . of the rich and influential manufacturers of the country in good humor.

WOODROW WILSON
Acceptance, at Sea Girt, N.J., of Nomination for Presidency,
Aug. 7, 1912; *Crossroads*, p. 22

See also Revenue

Taxation

1. Another means of silently lessening the inequality of property is to exempt all from taxation below a certain point, and to tax the higher portions of property in geometric progression as they rise.

THOMAS JEFFERSON
To James Madison, Oct. 28, 1785; *Writings, XIX*, 18

2. The wisdom of man never yet contrived a system of taxation that would operate with perfect equality.

ANDREW JACKSON
Proclamation, Dec. 10, 1832; *Messages and Papers,* p. 1207

3. In exercising a sound discretion in levying discriminating duties . . . care should be taken that it be done in a manner not to benefit the wealthy few at the expense of the toiling millions by taxing *lowest* the luxuries of life, or articles of superior quality and high price, which can only be consumed by the wealthy, and *highest* the necessaries of life, or articles of coarse quality and low price, which the poor and great mass of our people must consume.

JAMES K. POLK
Inaugural Address, Mar. 4, 1845

4. No favored class should demand freedom from assessment, and the taxes should be so distributed as not to fall unduly on the poor, but rather on the accumulated wealth of the country.

ANDREW JOHNSON
First Annual Message to Congress, Dec. 4, 1865; *Messages and Papers,* p. 3564

5. When more of the people's sustenance is exacted through the form of taxation than is necessary to meet the just obligations of Government and expenses of its economical administration, such exaction becomes ruthless extortion and a violation of the fundamental principles of a free Government.

GROVER CLEVELAND
Second Annual Message to Congress, Dec. 6, 1886; *Ibid.,* p. 5094

6. There should be a certainty and stability about the enforcement of taxation which should teach the citizen that the Government will only use the power to tax in cases where its necessity and justice are not doubtful. . . .

A government is not only kind, but performs its highest duty when it restores to the citizen taxes unlawfully or oppressively extorted by its agents or officers; but . . . the people should not be familiarized with the spectacle of their Government repenting the collection of taxes and restoring them.

GROVER CLEVELAND
Message to the Senate, Mar. 2, 1889; *Ibid.,* p. 5425

7. A heavy progressive tax upon a very large fortune is in no way such a tax upon thrift or industry as a like tax would be on a small fortune. . . . As an incident to its function of revenue raising, such a tax would help to

preserve a measurable equality of opportunity for the people of the generations growing to manhood.

> THEODORE ROOSEVELT
> Message to Congress, Dec. 4, 1907; *Addresses and Papers,* p. 410

8. I believe in a graduated income tax on big fortunes, and in another tax which is far more easily collected and far more effective—a graduated inheritance tax on big fortunes, properly safeguarded against evasion and increasing rapidly in amount with the size of the estate.

> THEODORE ROOSEVELT
> Speech at Osawatomie, Kan., Aug. 31, 1910;
> *Works (Mem. Ed.), XVII,* 14

9. The power to tax is the power to destroy. . . . A government which lays taxes on the people not required by urgent public necessity and sound public policy is not a protector of liberty, but an instrument of tyranny.

> CALVIN COOLIDGE
> Speech in Washington, D.C., June 30, 1924; *Foundations,* p. 40

10. The collection of any taxes which are not absolutely required, which do not . . . contribute to the public welfare, is only a species of legalized larceny.

> CALVIN COOLIDGE
> Inaugural Address, Mar. 4, 1925

11. Creative enterprise is not stimulated by vast inheritances. . . . A tax upon inherited economic power is a tax upon static wealth, not upon that dynamic wealth which makes for the healthy diffusion of economic good.

> FRANKLIN DELANO ROOSEVELT
> Message to Congress *re* tax revision, June 19, 1935;
> *Public Papers, IV,* 272

12. Taxes have grown up like Topsy in this country.

> FRANKLIN DELANO ROOSEVELT
> Remarks at a conference of mayors, Nov. 19, 1935; *Ibid.,* p. 467

13. In 1776 the fight was for democracy in taxation. In 1936 that is still the fight. . . . One sure way to determine the social conscience of a government is to examine the way taxes are collected and how they are spent. And one sure way to determine the social conscience of an individual is to get his tax-reaction.

Taxes, after all, are the dues that we pay for the privileges of membership in an organized society. . . .

Here is my principle: Taxes shall be levied according to ability to pay. That is the only American principle.

> Franklin Delano Roosevelt
> Campaign address at Worcester, Mass., Oct. 21, 1936; *Ibid.*, V, 523, 525

14. Expense-account living has become a byword in the American scene. The slogan—"It's deductible"—should pass from our scene.

> John F. Kennedy
> Message to Congress, Apr. 20, 1961; *Public Papers . . . Kennedy, 1961*, p. 299

15. The most damaging thing you can do to any businessman in America is to keep him in doubt, and to keep him guessing, on what our tax policy is.

> Lyndon B. Johnson
> State of the Union Address, Jan. 8, 1964; *Vital Speeches, Jan. 15, 1964*, p. 195

See also Economy 6, Education 4, Government 73, Ignorance 3, Labor 1, Money 4, 6, Preparedness 6, Property 1, Revenue

Territorial Acquisition

1. Although with difficulty, [Bonaparte] will consent to our receiving Cuba into our Union, to prevent our aid to Mexico and the other provinces. That would be a price, and I would immediately erect a column on the southernmost limit of Cuba, and inscribe on it a *ne plus ultra* as to us in that direction. . . . It will be objected to our receiving Cuba, that no limit can then be drawn to our future acquisitions. Cuba can be defended by us without a navy, and this develops the principle which ought to limit our views. Nothing should ever be accepted which would require a navy to defend it.

> Thomas Jefferson
> Letter to James Madison, Apr. 27, 1809; *Works*, V, 444

See also Colonialism, Conquest, Foreign Relations, Monroe Doctrine, Peace 53, Republics 16, Tyranny 4

Territory

1. A nation may be said to consist of its territory, its people, and its laws. The territory is the only part which is of certain durability. "One generation passeth away and another generation cometh, but the earth abideth forever." It is of the first importance to duly consider and estimate this ever-enduring part. That portion of the earth's surface which is owned and inhabited by the people of the United States is well adapted to

be the home of one national family, and it is not well adapted for two or more.

ABRAHAM LINCOLN
Second Annual Message to Congress, Dec. 1, 1862; *Messages and Papers,* p. 3334

See also Republics 16, Russia 5, United States 6, War 30

Terror

1.   Terror is not a new weapon. Throughout history it has been used by those who could not prevail either by persuasion or by example. But inevitably they failed—either because men are not afraid to die for a life worth living, or because the terrorists themselves came to realize that free men cannot be frightened by threats and that aggression will meet its own response.

JOHN F. KENNEDY
Address to United Nations General Assembly, Sept. 25, 1961; *Public Papers . . . Kennedy, 1961,* p. 625

See also Peace 78

Theories

1.   The moment a person forms a theory, his imagination sees in every object only the traits which favor that theory.

THOMAS JEFFERSON
To Charles Thompson, Sept. 20, 1787; *Writings, VI,* 312

Thought

1.   People always used to say of me that I was an astonishingly good politician and divined what the people were going to think. This really was not an accurate way of stating the case. I did not "divine" how the people were going to think; I simply made up my mind what they *ought* to think, and then did my best to get them to think it. Sometimes I failed, and then my critics said that "my ambition had overleaped itself." Sometimes I succeeded, and then they said that I was an uncommonly astute creature to have detected what the people were going to think and to pose as their leader in thinking it.

THEODORE ROOSEVELT
To Mr. Van Valkenberg, Sept. 5, 1916; *Works (Mem. Ed.), XXIV,* 487

See also Authors 1, Money 3, Opinion 6

Time

1.   No person will have occasion to complain of the want of time who

never loses any. It is wonderful how much may be done if we are always doing.

THOMAS JEFFERSON
To Maria Jefferson, May 5, 1787; *Writings (Ford), IV,* 388

2. While the present is bright with promise and the future full of demand and inducement for the exercise of active intelligence, the past can never be without useful lessons of admonition and instruction. If its dangers serve not as beacons, they will evidently fail to fulfill the object of a wise design.

FRANKLIN PIERCE
First Annual Message to Congress, Dec. 5, 1853; *Messages and Papers,* p. 2755

3. Time is a great conservative power.

JAMES BUCHANAN
Message to Congress, Jan. 2, 1861; *Ibid.,* p. 3188

4. We must use time as a tool, not as a couch. We must carve our own destiny.

JOHN F. KENNEDY
Speech in New York, N.Y., Dec. 6, 1961; *Public Papers . . . Kennedy, 1961,* p. 497

Tolerance

1. The manners of every nation are standards of orthodoxy within itself. But these standards being arbitrary, reasonable people in all allow free toleration for the manners, as for the religion, of others.

THOMAS JEFFERSON
To Jean Baptiste Say, 1815; *Works, VI,* 433

2. I would be tolerant to men of all creeds, but would exact from all faithful allegiance to our republican institutions.

MILLARD FILLMORE
Speech at Newburgh, N.Y., June 26, 1856; *Papers, II,* 16

3. Tolerance is an admirable intellectual gift; but it is of little worth in politics. Politics is a war of *causes;* a joust of principles.

WOODROW WILSON
University of Virginia magazine, March, 1880; *Story,* p. 13

4. We need to learn and exemplify the principle of toleration. We are a nation of many races and of many beliefs. The freedom of the human mind does not mean the mere privilege of agreeing with others, it means the right of individual judgment.

CALVIN COOLIDGE
Speech at Evanston, Ill., Jan. 21, 1923; *Citizenship,* p. 84

5. As we make gains in mutual understanding, there will inevitably follow greater mutual tolerance. . . . It is important to remember that we can be firm without being offensive in support of principles that are sacred to us. We must realize that good humor, patience and tolerance are as important internationally as they are individually.

Dwight D. Eisenhower
Speech in New York, N.Y., April, 1946;
What Eisenhower Thinks, p. 95

See also Defense 13, Education 23, Liberty 44, Monopolies 4, Virtue 7

Trade

1. Experience has shown that the trade of the East is the key to national wealth and influence. The opening of China to the commerce of the whole world has benefited no section more than the States of our own Pacific Coast.

Chester A. Arthur
Veto Message, Apr. 4, 1882; *Messages and Papers,* p. 4704

2. International commerce is beneficial to the community of nations and conducive to the establishment of a just and lasting peace in the world. Our national trade policy, which seeks to promote the continued growth of mutually profitable world trade, is thus doubly in the self-interest of the United States.

Dwight D. Eisenhower
Message to Congress, Feb. 11, 1957; *Public Papers . . .
Eisenhower, 1957,* p. 142

See also Good Will 2

Traditions
See Political Parties 20

Tranquility

1. Tranquility is the old man's milk.

Thomas Jefferson
To Edward Rutledge, June 24, 1797; *Writings, VIII,* 319

2. The *summum bonum* with me is now truly epicurean, ease of body and tranquillity of mind; and to these I wish to consign my remaining days.

Thomas Jefferson
To John Adams, June 27, 1813; *Correspondence,* p. 59

See also Humor 1, War 5

Travel

1. Travelling makes men wiser, but less happy.

Thomas Jefferson
To Peter Carr, Aug. 10, 1787; *Works, II,* 241

Treason

See Pacifists 1, Tyranny 1

Treaties

1. Can aliens make treaties easier than friends can make laws? Can treaties be more faithfully enforced between aliens than laws can among friends? Suppose you go to war, you can not fight always; and when, after much loss on both sides and no gain on either, you cease fighting, the identical old questions, as to terms of intercourse, are again upon you.

ABRAHAM LINCOLN
First Inaugural Address, Mar. 4, 1861

2. A nation is justified in repudiating its treaty obligations only when they are in conflict with great paramount interests.

CHESTER A. ARTHUR
Veto Message, Apr. 4, 1882; *Messages and Papers*, p. 4699

3. Open covenants of peace, openly arrived at.

WOODROW WILSON
Address to Congress, Jan. 8, 1918;
Messages and Papers (Shaw), p. 468

4. Treaties are too often scraps of paper; in our age the signal for two World Wars was the callous repudiation of pacts and pledged word. There must be a universal urge of decency.

DWIGHT D. EISENHOWER
Address at Columbia University, Mar. 23, 1950; *Peace*, p. 15

See also Secrecy 1, Slavery 29

Trusts

1. The trusts and combinations—the communism of pelf . . .

GROVER CLEVELAND
To Representative T. C. Catchings, Aug. 1, 1894; *Courage*, p. 586

2. The great corporations which we have grown to speak of rather loosely as trusts are the creatures of the state, and the state not only has the right to control them, but it is in duty bound to control them whenever the need of such control is shown.

THEODORE ROOSEVELT
At Providence, R.I., Aug. 23, 1902; *Addresses and Presidential Messages*, p. 15

3. A trust does not bring efficiency to the aid of business; it *buys efficiency out of business*.

WOODROW WILSON
1912; *New Freedom (Hale)*, p. 180

See also Monopolies

Truth

1. Truth will ultimately prevail where there is pains to bring it to light.

GEORGE WASHINGTON
To Charles M. Thruston, Aug. 10, 1794;
Writings (Fitzpatrick), XXXIII, 465

2. There is not a truth existing which I fear, or would wish unknown to the whole world.

THOMAS JEFFERSON
To Henry Lee, May 15, 1826; *Works, VII,* 448

3. Truth is generally the best vindication against slander.

ABRAHAM LINCOLN
To Secretary of War Edwin Stanton, July 14, 1864; *Complete Works, X,* 158

4. I have faith in the people. . . . The danger is, in their being misled. Let them know the truth and the country is safe.

ABRAHAM LINCOLN
Ca. 1865; *War Years, III,* 223

5. It is possible to sift truth.

WOODROW WILSON
Speech to Associated Press, New York, N.Y., Apr. 20, 1915;
Messages and Papers (Shaw), I, 112

6. The only thing that ever set any man free, the only thing that ever set any nation free, is the truth. A man that is afraid of the truth is afraid of the law of life. A man who does not love the truth is in the way of decay and of failure.

WOODROW WILSON
Speech in Philadelphia, Pa., June 29, 1916; *Public Papers, IV,* 215

7. The truth is found when men are free to pursue it.

FRANKLIN DELANO ROOSEVELT
Address in Philadelphia, Pa., Feb. 22, 1936; *Public Papers, V,* 84

8. Eternal truths will be neither true nor eternal unless they have fresh meaning for every new social situation.

FRANKLIN DELANO ROOSEVELT
Address at University of Pennsylvania, Sept. 20, 1940;
Ibid., IX, 435

See also Errors 4, Experience 3, Greatness 11, Ignorance 2, Myths, Press (The) 8, Statesmanship 4

Tyranny

1. The unsuccessful strugglers against tyranny have been the chief martyrs of treason laws in all countries.

THOMAS JEFFERSON
To William Carmichael and William Short, Apr. 24, 1792;
Writings, VIII, 332

2. I have sworn on the Altar of God eternal hostility against every form of tyranny over the mind of man.

THOMAS JEFFERSON
To Dr. Benjamin Rush, Sept. 23, 1800; *Ibid., X*, 175

3. Rebellion to tyrants is obedience to God.

THOMAS JEFFERSON
Motto on Jefferson's seal; *Ibid., XVII*, i

4. To those new states whom we welcome to the ranks of the free, we pledge our word that one form of colonial control shall not have passed away merely to be replaced by a far more iron tyranny. . . .

And let every power know that this hemisphere intends to remain the master of its own house.

JOHN F. KENNEDY
Inaugural Address, Jan. 20, 1961

See also Corruption 1, Enlightenment, Government 11, History 1, Ignorance 8, Liberty 9, Peace 88, 90, Power 12, Rebellion 2, Religion 34, Taxation 9, Veto Power 2

Understanding

1. The only strength that any man can boast of and be proud of is that great bodies of his fellow citizens trust him and are ready to follow him. It is not only a belief in his character, but . . . an agreement with his opinions. That is the reason that gentlemen have to go around as I am . . . and expose themselves to the public gaze. Not because it is a particular indulgence of taste to look at them, because personal beauty is not necessarily their strong point. . . . To repeat a limerick . . . :

> For beauty I am not a star;
> There are others more handsome by far
> But my face, I don't mind it,
> Because I'm behind it;
> It's the people in front that I jar.

But what . . . you should be interested in is not the binding of the book but the table of contents: what is inside of it, what kind of purpose, what kind of understanding of your interests.

WOODROW WILSON
Speech at Minneapolis, Minn., Sept. 18, 1912; *Crossroads*, p. 187

2. If I may be credited with one desire more than another it is to act as an apostle of understanding. I have been trying to preach understanding ever since I came to the Presidency, for I believe that understanding is the remedy for nearly all our ills. . . . If the nations of the world could have a complete and ample understanding each with the other, there never would be war.

WARREN G. HARDING
Speech at Wrangell, Alaska, July 9, 1923;
Speeches and Addresses, p. 304

3. Our understanding of how to live—live with one another—is still far behind our knowledge of how to destroy one another.

LYNDON B. JOHNSON
To the United Nations General Assembly, Dec. 17, 1963;
Vital Speeches, Jan. 1, 1964, p. 163

See also Differences, Foreign Relations 35, Freedom 27, Knowledge 10, Latin America 1, Mankind 7, Peace 39, 55, 59, 65, 72, 74, Peace Corps, Tolerance 5, Unity 4

Unemployment

1. There are those who think that the only approach to unemployment should be the approach of charity. There are others who even toy with the idea that a certain amount of unemployment is "healthy" and "normal." A healthy, normal, stable country is one that makes fullest use of the productive capacity of its citizens. A stable and prosperous country is one in which working men and women are on payrolls—not on relief rolls.

LYNDON B. JOHNSON
Address to AFL–CIO Unemployment Congress, Washington, D.C.,
1959; *Story*, p. 152

See also Dictatorships 3, Poverty 4, Prosperity 14, Public Works, Security 5, Work 5

Uniformity
See Opinion 2

Union

1. It remains only for the States to be wise, and to establish their independence on the basis of an inviolable, efficacious union, and a firm confederation, which may prevent their being made the sport of European policy.

GEORGE WASHINGTON
To Gen. Nathanael Greene, Mar. 31, 1783; *Writings*
(*Fitzpatrick*), *VIII*, 410

2. It is of infinite moment that you should properly estimate the immense value of your national union to your collective and individual happiness; that you should cherish a cordial, habitual, and immovable

attachment to it; accustoming yourselves to think and speak of it as of the palladium of your political safety and prosperity; watching for its preservation with jealous anxiety; discountenancing whatever may suggest even a suspicion that it can in any event be abandoned, and indignantly frowning upon the first dawning of every attempt to alienate any portion of our country from the rest or to enfeeble the sacred ties which now link together the various parts.

GEORGE WASHINGTON
Farewell Address, Sept. 19, 1796; *Ibid., XXXV,* 219

3. When any one State in the American Union refuses obedience to the Confederation by which they have bound themselves, the rest have a natural right to compel them to obedience.

THOMAS JEFFERSON
To M. de Meusnier, Jan. 24, 1786; *Writings, XVII,* 121

4. Whatever follies we may be led into as to foreign nations, we shall never give up our Union, the last anchor of hope, and that alone which is to prevent this heavenly country from becoming an arena of gladiators. Much as I abhor war, and view it as the greatest scourge of mankind, and anxiously as I wish to keep out of the broils of Europe, I would yet go with my brethren into these, rather than separate from them.

THOMAS JEFFERSON
To Elbridge Gerry, May 13, 1797; *Ibid., VII,* 122

5. To preserve the peace of our fellow citizens, promote their prosperity and happiness, reunite opinion, cultivate a spirit of candor, moderation, charity, and forbearance towards one another, are objects calling for the efforts and sacrifices of every good man and patriot. Our religion enjoins it; our happiness demands it; and no sacrifice is requisite but of passions hostile to both.

It is a momentous truth, and happily of universal impression on the public mind, that our safety rests on the preservation of our Union.

THOMAS JEFFERSON
Letter to the General Assembly of Rhode Island and Providence Plantations, May 26, 1801; *Works, V,* 397

6. The cement of this Union is the heart blood of every American.

THOMAS JEFFERSON
To Marquis de Lafayette, Feb. 14, 1815; *Ibid., XIV,* 252

7. The advice nearest to my heart and deepest in my convictions, is that the Union of the States be cherished and perpetuated. Let the open enemy to it be regarded as a Pandora with her box opened, and the disguised one as the serpent creeping with deadly wiles into Paradise.

JAMES MADISON
Found among his papers after his death;
Writings (Hunt), IX, 610

8. Our Union is not held together by standing armies, or by any ties, other than the positive interests and powerful attractions of its parts toward each other.

> James Monroe
> Message to Congress, May 4, 1822; *Manual, II*, 531

9. The policy of our country is peace and the ark of our salvation union.

> John Quincy Adams
> Inaugural Address, Mar. 4, 1825

10. Before I would see one State of this Union severed from the rest, I would die in the last ditch.

> Andrew Jackson
> To Aaron Burr, 1806; *Life (of Hayes)*, p. 211

11. The absurdity of the Virginia doctrine is too plain to need much comment. . . . A State cannot come into the Union without the consent of Congress, but it can go out when it pleases. Such a union as this would be like a bag of sand with both ends open—the least pressure and it runs out at both ends. It is an insult to the understanding of the sages who formed it, to believe that such a union was ever intended. It could not last a month.

> Andrew Jackson
> To Martin Van Buren, Dec. 25, 1832; *Life (Bassett)*, p. 579

12. Experience, the unerring test of all human undertakings, has shown the wisdom and foresight of those who formed the Constitution, and has proved that in the union of these States there is a sure foundation for the brightest hopes of freedom and for the happiness of the people. At every hazard and by every sacrifice this Union must be preserved.

> Andrew Jackson
> Farewell Address, Mar. 4, 1837; *Messages and Papers*, p. 1513

13. That union should so long have been preserved in a confederacy which contains an element of discord of such magnitude and so disturbing a nature as that of slavery, is a wonder—more surprising than its dissolution would be.

> Martin Van Buren
> To Moses Tilden, 1858; *Epoch*, p. 534

14. It is union that we want, not of a party for the sake of that party, but a union of the whole country for the sake of the whole country, for the defense of its interests and its honor against foreign aggression, for the defense of those principles for which our ancestors so gloriously contended.

> William Henry Harrison
> Inaugural Address, Mar. 4, 1841

15. Of all the great interests that appertain to our country, that of Union

. . . is by far the most important, since it is the only true and sure guaranty of all others.

WILLIAM HENRY HARRISON

16.   We should never forget that this Union of confederated States was established and cemented by kindred blood and by the common toils, sufferings, dangers, and triumphs of all its parts, and has been the ever-augmenting source of our national greatness and of all our blessings.

By its preservation we have been rapidly advanced as a nation to a height of strength, power, and happiness without parallel in the history of the world.

JAMES K. POLK
Message to Congress, July 6, 1848; *Messages and Papers,* p. 2440

17.   I feared there were a few Southern men who had become so excited that they were indifferent to the preservation of the Union. . . . I put my face alike against Southern agitators and Northern fanatics and [did] everything in my power to allay excitement by adjusting the question of slavery and preserving the Union.

JAMES K. POLK
Jan. 20, 1849; *Diary (Quaife), IV,* 299

18.   In my judgment, its dissolution would be the greatest of calamities, and to avert that should be the study of every American. Upon its preservation must depend our own happiness and that of countless generations to come.

ZACHARY TAYLOR
Message to Congress, Dec. 27, 1849; *Chips,* p. 211

19.   The Union—no North—no South—no East—no West—but a sacred maintenance of the common bond, and true devotion to the common brotherhood.

FRANKLIN PIERCE
1851; *Record, flyleaf*

20.   We have . . . to cherish with loyal fealty and devoted affection this Union, as the only sure foundation on which the hopes of civil liberty rest.

FRANKLIN PIERCE
Second Annual Message to Congress, Dec. 4, 1854;
Franklin Pierce, p. xi

21.   We may all have regarded with too much indifference the swelling tide of reckless fanaticism, but we are not too late to breast it now. If honest men, who really think the Union worth preserving, will stand forth in the majesty and strength of patriotism and law, and with united purpose and becoming energy, they can and will roll that tide back, to the dismay

and discomfiture of all conspirators against the public peace, and the integrity of the sacred bond which holds us a united people.

FRANKLIN PIERCE
Letter, Dec. 7, 1859; *Record*, p. 7

22. Our Union is the star of the West, whose genial and steadily increasing influence will at last, should we remain an united people, dispel the gloom of despotism from the ancient nations of the world. Its moral power will prove to be more potent than millions of armed mercenaries.

JAMES BUCHANAN
To a public meeting, Nov. 19, 1850; *Life, II,* 11

23. Our Union is a stake of such inestimable value as to demand our constant and watchful vigilance for its preservation. In this view, let me implore my countrymen, North and South, to cultivate the ancient feelings of mutual forbearance and good will toward each other and strive to allay the demon spirit of sectional hatred and strife now alive in the land.

JAMES BUCHANAN
Third Annual Message to Congress, Dec. 19, 1859; *Messages and Papers,* p. 3084

24. If we could first know where we are, and whither we are tending, we could better judge what to do, and how to do it. . . . "A house divided against itself cannot stand." [Mark 3:25] I believe this government cannot endure permanently half slave and half free. I do not expect the Union to be dissolved—I do not expect the house to fall—but I do expect it will cease to be divided. It will become all one thing, or all the other.

ABRAHAM LINCOLN
Speech at Springfield, Ill., June 16, 1858; *Complete Works, III,* 2

25. We are not enemies, but friends. We must not be enemies. Though passion may have strained, it must not break our bonds of affection. The mystic chords of memory, stretching from every battlefield, and patriot grave, to every living heart and hearthstone, all over this broad land, will yet swell the chorus of the Union, when again touched, as surely they will be, by the better angels of our nature.

ABRAHAM LINCOLN
First Inaugural Address, Mar. 4, 1861

26. I would save the Union. I would save it the shortest way under the Constitution. . . . If I could save the Union without freeing any slave, I would do it; and if I could save it by freeing all the slaves, I would do it. . . . What I do about slavery and the colored race, I do because I believe it helps to save the Union; and what I forbear, I forbear because I do not believe it helps to save the Union.

ABRAHAM LINCOLN
To Horace Greeley, Aug. 22, 1862; *Complete Works, VIII,* 15

27. I am still for the preservation of the Union. I am still in favor of this great Government of ours going on and on, and filling out its destiny.

ANDREW JOHNSON
Speech in Washington, D.C., Feb. 22, 1866; *Document,* p. 5

28. The Civil War created in this country what had never existed before—a national consciousness. It was not the salvation of the Union; it was the rebirth of the Union.

WOODROW WILSON
Address at Arlington, Va., May 31, 1915; *Public Papers, III,* 336

See also Coercion 2, Liberty 25, 27, Nullification, Opinion 6, Presidency (The) 2, Secession, Slavery 10, 15, 16, States' Rights 7, 8, United Nations 3, United States 1

Unions
See Labor Unions

United Nations
1. The tragedy of the United Nations was that it turned into an instrument to protect Red imperialism.

HERBERT HOOVER
Address at Emporia, Kan., July 11, 1950; *American Road,* p. 74

2. I am not in favor of special conferences [between nations] because I want to see the United Nations do its job. The League of Nations was ruined by a lot of special conferences.

HARRY S. TRUMAN
News conference, Nov. 29, 1945;
Public Papers . . . Truman, 1945, p. 511

3. The aim of the United Nations is to substitute peaceful negotiations for war. We must make the United Nations grow in legal and moral strength as an instrument of world peace and order, remembering our experience and difficulties and growth as a federal union.

HARRY S. TRUMAN
Interview, *ca.* 1950; *Mr. President,* p. 246

4. We voluntarily joined an association which is to further international law and to secure peace with justice. As long as we can operate through that organism, we should do so; and in spite of all its failures, and in spite of its admitted weaknesses, I think that it would be well for all of us at times to look on some of the things it has accomplished. After all, it does mobilize world opinion, and nations are still very sensitive to world opinion.

DWIGHT D. EISENHOWER
News conference, Mar. 7, 1957;
Public Papers . . . Eisenhower, 1957, p. 184

5. Our strength and our hope [for peace] is the United Nations, and I see little merit in the impatience of those who would abandon this imperfect world instrument because they dislike our imperfect world.

JOHN F. KENNEDY
State of the Union Address, Jan. 29, 1961

See also League of Nations, Unity 4, War 57, 74

United States

1. There are four things, which, I humbly conceive, are essential to the well-being, I may even venture to say, to the existence of the United States. . . .

1st. An indissoluble Union of the States under one Federal Head.
2nd. A sacred regard to Public Justice.
3rd. The adoption of a proper Peace Establishment, and
4th. The prevalence of that pacific and friendly Disposition, among the people of the United States, which will induce them to forget their local prejudices and policies, to make those mutual concessions which are requisite to the general prosperity, and in some instances, to sacrifice their individual advantages to the interest of the Community.

These are the Pillars on which the glorious Fabrick of our independency and National Character must be supported. . . .

GEORGE WASHINGTON
Circular to the Governors, June 8, 1783;
Writings (Fitzpatrick), *XXVI*, 487

2. Talleyrand once said to the first Napoleon that "the United States is a giant without bones." Since that time our gristle has been rapidly hardening.

JAMES A. GARFIELD
Address at Hudson College, July 2, 1873; *Future*, p. 17

3. The mission of the United States is one of benevolent assimilation, substituting the mild sway of justice and right for arbitrary rule.

WILLIAM McKINLEY
Letter, 1898; *American Treasury*, p. 15

4. The power of the United States is a menace to no nation or people.
. . . It springs out of freedom and is for the service of freedom.

WOODROW WILSON
Message to Congress, Feb. 11, 1918;
Messages and Papers (Shaw), p. 479

5. War made us a creditor Nation. We did not seek an excess possession of the world's gold. . . . We do not seek to become an international dictator because of its power.

WARREN G. HARDING
Second Annual Message to Congress, Dec. 8, 1922; *Message*, p. 8

6. We had won the war. . . . The United States . . . wanted no territory, no reparations. Peace and happiness for all countries were the goals toward which we would work and for which we had fought. No nation in the history of the world had taken such a position in complete victory. No nation with the military power of the United States of America had been so generous to its enemies and so helpful to its friends. Maybe the teachings of the Sermon on the Mount could be put into effect.

HARRY S. TRUMAN
August 14, 1945; *Memoirs, I,* 437

7. I want to make an observation—a sort of truism from my old military life . . . that went something like this: in war you can do nothing positive except as you do it from a firm base. . . .

The firm base for the problem of leading the world toward the achievement of human aspirations—toward peace with justice in freedom—must be the United States.

DWIGHT D. EISENHOWER
Address in Philadelphia, Pa., Sept. 26, 1960; *Public Papers . . .
Eisenhower, 1960–61,* p. 722

See also America, Disarmament 5, Isolationism 5, 8, Nations 1, Neutrality 5, Peace 9, 25, 53, 86, Preparedness 2, 18, Presidency (The) 70, Religion 3, Rights 13, 19, Russia 1, 3, Unity 8, War 15, 41

Unity

1. The supreme test of the nation has come. We must all speak, act and serve together.

WOODROW WILSON
Message to the American people, Apr. 15, 1917;
First Year of War, p. 39

2. There is a proper urge in all Americans for unity in troubled times. But unless unity is based on right principles and right action it is a vain and dangerous thing.

Honest difference of views and honest debate are not disunity. They are the vital process of policy among free men.

HERBERT HOOVER
Address in New York, N.Y., Dec. 20, 1950; *American Road,* p. 209

3. These words—"national unity"—must not be allowed to become merely a high-sounding phrase, a vague generality, a pious hope, to which everyone can give lip-service. . . .

For national unity is, in a very real and a very deep sense, the fundamental safeguard of all democracy.

FRANKLIN DELANO ROOSEVELT
Eighth Annual Message to Congress, Jan. 3, 1940;
Public Papers, IX, 8

4. The possibility of total destruction, terrible though it is, could be a blessing as all nations, great and small, for the first time in human history, are confronted by an inescapable physical proof of their common lot. Franklin's "If we don't hang together, we shall each hang separately," has its international application today. There is no prod so effective as a common dread; there is no binder so unifying.

And we know the formula of success: First, justice, freedom, and opportunity for all men; Second, international understanding; Third, disarmament; Fourth, a respected United Nations.

DWIGHT D. EISENHOWER
Address at Columbia University, Mar. 23, 1950; *Peace*, p. 18

5. May we know unity—without conformity.

DWIGHT D. EISENHOWER
Second Inaugural Address, Jan. 21, 1957

6. One truth must rule all we think and all we do. No people can live to itself alone. The unity of all who dwell in freedom is their only sure defense.

DWIGHT D. EISENHOWER
Second Inaugural Address, Jan. 21, 1957

7. Eighteen years ago . . . Ernie Pyle, describing those tens of thousands of young men who crossed the "ageless and indifferent sea" of the English Channel, searched in vain for a word to describe what they were fighting for—and finally he concluded that they were at least fighting "for each other."

You and I leave here today to meet our separate responsibilities, to protect our nation's interests—by peaceful means if possible, by resolute action if necessary, and we go forth confident of support and success because we know that we are working and fighting "for each other," and for all those men and women, all over the globe, who are determined to be free.

JOHN F. KENNEDY
At United States Military Academy, June 6, 1962; *Vital Speeches, July 1, 1962;* p. 546

8. The time has come for Americans of all races and creeds and political beliefs to understand and respect one another.

Let us put an end to the teaching and preaching of hate and evil and violence. Let us turn away from the fanatics of the far left and the far right, from the apostles of bitterness and bigotry, from those defiant of law, and those who pour venom into our nation's bloodstream. . . .

These are the United States—a united people with unity of purpose.

Our American unity does not depend upon unanimity. We have differences; but now, as in the past, we can derive from those differences strength, not weakness, wisdom, not despair. Both as a people and as a government we can unite upon a program which is wise and just, enlightened and constructive.

LYNDON B. JOHNSON
Address to Congress, Nov. 27, 1963; *Chicago Daily News,
Nov. 27, 1963*

See also America 15, 16, Flag (The) 4, Goals 3, Government 4, 103, Isolationism 10, Religion 15, War 65

Universities

1. That a national university in this country is a thing to be desired, has always been my decided opinion.

GEORGE WASHINGTON
To John Adams, Nov. 22, 1794; *Writings (Fitzpatrick), XI,* 1

2. I congratulate you, and Madison and Monroe, on your noble employment in founding a university [University of Virginia]. From such a noble triumvirate, the world will expect something very great and very new, but if it contains anything quite original, and very excellent, I fear the prejudices are too deeply rooted to suffer it to last long, though it may be accepted at first. It will not always have three such colossal reputations to support it.

JOHN ADAMS
To Thomas Jefferson, May 26, 1817; *Writings
(of Jefferson), XV,* 123

3. I have always thought the chief object of education was to awaken the spirit, and that—inasmuch as a literature whenever it has touched its great and higher notes was an expression of the spirit of mankind—the best induction into education was to feel the pulses of humanity which had beaten from age to age through the universities of men who had penetrated to the secrets of the human spirit.

WOODROW WILSON
Address in Paris, France, Dec. 21, 1918; *Selections,* p. 178

4. Everyone is familiar with the assertion of President Garfield that Mark Hopkins, sitting on one end of a log with a student on the other, would constitute a university. He did not particularize about the student, but he was careful to provide that the head of the institution was to be Doctor Hopkins. Only a trained and tried educator could fill the requirements for the head of a seat of learning that was to be dignified by the name of a university.

CALVIN COOLIDGE
Speech at Reynoldsville, Pa., Dec. 21, 1922; *Freedom,* p. 211

See also Colleges, Education, Knowledge, Libraries 3

Valor

1. Valor is self-respecting. Valor is circumspect. Valor strikes only when it is right to strike.

WOODROW WILSON
Address at a gridiron dinner, Feb. 26, 1916; *Life, VI,* 118

See also Bravery

Vanity

1. Vanity, I am sensible, is my cardinal vice and cardinal folly; and I am in continual danger, when in company, of being led an *ignis fatuus* chase by it.

JOHN ADAMS
Diary, May 3, 1756; *Works, II,* 16

2. They say I am vain. Thank God I am so. Vanity is the cordial drop which makes the bitter cup of life go down. . . . What is not vanity is sure to be vexation.

JOHN ADAMS
1822; *Figures,* p. 68

3. Upon each recurrence of my birthday I am solemnly impressed with the vanity & emptiness of worldly honors and worldly enjoyments, and of the wisdom of preparing for a future estate.

JAMES K. POLK
Nov. 1, 1848; *Diary (Quaife), IV,* 177

Veterans

1. The nation which forgets its defenders will be itself forgotten.

CALVIN COOLIDGE
Acceptance of Nomination for Presidency, Cleveland, Ohio,
July 27, 1920

See also Gettysburg, Gratitude 1, Square Deal 1, War 47

Veto Power

1. The power of the Executive veto was exercised by five of my predecessors . . . in the administration of the Government, and it is believed in no instance prejudicially to the public interests.

JAMES K. POLK
Fourth Annual Message to Congress, Dec. 5, 1848;
Messages and Papers, p. 2519

2. The veto power . . . was established to enable the people to resist and repel encroachments on their rights. It had its origin in old Rome . . . and before Christ 497 . . . which would make, since its origin, 2345 years. . . .

Washington and Jefferson (who never exercised the power while President) . . . were in favor of the veto-power, as established in the Constitution.

James Madison . . . "the great Apostle of Liberty," exercised . . . this power six times during his eight years' administration.

Mr. Monroe . . . a war-hating and peace-loving man . . . ventured to exercise this power once.

By Andrew Jackson . . . it was exercised nine times, and the people said, "Well done, thou good and faithful servant."

John Tyler exercised this power four times . . . and his is the only instance in which a law was passed over a veto. . . .

Since Mr. Polk came into power it has been exercised three times.

Thus it will be seen, that from the origin of the government . . . the veto, as exercised by the Executives, is conservative. . . . If it is tyranny to exercise this power . . . I am willing to abide by it.

ANDREW JOHNSON
To House of Representatives, Aug. 2, 1848; *Speeches*, p. 2

3.   The unpleasant incidents which accompany the use of the veto power would tempt its avoidance if such a course did not involve an abandonment of constitutional duty and an assent to legislation for which the Executive is not willing to share the responsibility.

GROVER CLEVELAND
To the Senate, June 1, 1896; *Messages and Papers*, p. 6114

4.   There were only four Presidents . . . who did not exercise the veto power—Washington, the first Adams, Jefferson, and the second Adams. They were fortunate enough to have friendly Congresses. It is an old maxim that there are other ways of killing a cat than by choking it with butter, and it is a great deal easier . . . to use one's influence with the legislators to prevent objectionable bills passing than it is to wait until they do pass and then veto them.

WILLIAM HOWARD TAFT
Speech at the University of Virginia, January, 1915;
Presidency, p. 14

5.   I found it necessary to veto more major bills than any other President, with the possible exception of Grover Cleveland.

HARRY S. TRUMAN
1952; *Memoirs, II*, 479

Vice-Presidency

1.   My country has, in its wisdom, contrived for me the most insignificant office (the Vice-Presidency) that ever the invention of man contrived or his imagination conceived.

JOHN ADAMS
Letter to Abigail Adams, Dec. 19, 1789; *Letters to Wife, II*, 133

2. The second office of the government is honorable and easy, the first is but a splendid misery.

THOMAS JEFFERSON
To Elbridge Gerry, May 13, 1797; *Writings, IX,* 381

Victory

1. Victory and defeat are each of the same price.

THOMAS JEFFERSON

See also Honor 3, Hope 2, Peace 36, War 1, 67, 74

Vigilance

1. Eternal vigilance is the price of opportunity for honest business.

FRANKLIN DELANO ROOSEVELT
Address in Washington, D.C., July 12, 1937;
Public Papers, VI, 300

2. As we maintain the vigil of peace, we must remember that justice is a vigil, too. . . . In this hour it is not our respective races which are at stake—it is our nation.

LYNDON B. JOHNSON
1963; *Life (magazine), Nov. 29, 1963*

See also Foreign Relations 11, Liberty 16, 20, 24, Peace 87, 88, People (The) 2, Policy 2, Political Parties 4, 5

Virtue

1. Few men have virtue to withstand the highest bidder.

GEORGE WASHINGTON
To Robert Howe, Aug. 17, 1779; *Writings (Fitzpatrick), XVI,* 116

2. Virtue is not always amiable. Integrity is sometimes ruined by prejudices and by passions. . . .
   The wisdom of Solomon, the meekness of Moses, and the patience of Job, all united in one character, would not be sufficient to qualify a man to act in the situation in which I am at present (as minister plenipotentiary to France); and I have scarcely a spice of either of these virtues.

JOHN ADAMS
Diary, Feb. 9, 1779; *Works, III,* 188

3. Virtue is the master of all things. Therefore a nation that should never do wrong must necessarily govern the world.

JOHN ADAMS
Diary, Aug. 4, 1796; *Ibid.,* p. 423

4. Everything is useful which contributes to fix the principles and practices of virtue.

THOMAS JEFFERSON
To Robert Skipwith, Aug. 3, 1771; *Writings, IV,* 237

5. And if the Wise be the happy man . . . he must be virtuous, too, for, without virtue, happiness cannot be.

THOMAS JEFFERSON
To Amos J. Cook, Jan. 21, 1816; *Ibid., XIV*, 405

6. My desire was to achieve results, and not merely to issue manifestoes of virtue. It is very easy to be efficient if the efficiency is based on unscrupulousness, and it is still easier to be virtuous if one is content with the purely negative virtue which consists in not doing anything wrong, but being wholly unable to accomplish anything positive for good.

THEODORE ROOSEVELT
Autobiography, p. 287

7. Patience, forbearance, faith and Christian tolerance. Those are rare virtues, too seldom found among the men who have the strength to rise to high places. They are the virtues that men need to seek and cultivate in these years of stress in the world. They point the way to salvation for men, for nations, for humanity itself.

CALVIN COOLIDGE
Radio address, Dec. 10, 1923; *Messages and Papers*, p. 8922-D

See also Government 12, Happiness 4, Patience 2, Popularity 1, Press (The) 2, Religion 29, Republics 2, 14, 15, War 17, Wealth 1

Voters

1. It is dangerous to open so fruitful a source of controversy and altercation as would be opened by attempting to alter the qualification of voters; there will be no end of it. . . . Women will demand a vote; lads from twelve to twenty-one will think their rights not enough attended to; and every man who has not a farthing, will demand an equal voice with any other, in all acts of state. It tends to confound and destroy all distinctions, and prostrate all ranks to one common level.

JOHN ADAMS
To James Sullivan, May 26, 1776; *Works, IX*, 378

2. Always vote for a principle, though you vote alone, and you may cherish the sweet reflection that your vote is never lost.

JOHN QUINCY ADAMS
1821

3. Your every voter, as surely as your chief magistrate, exercises a public trust.

GROVER CLEVELAND
First Inaugural Address, Mar. 4, 1885

4. Every voter ought not merely to vote, but to vote under the inspiration of a high purpose to serve a nation.

CALVIN COOLIDGE
Address in Washington, D.C., 1924; *Citizenship*, p. 241

5. The future of this republic is in the hands of the American voter.

DWIGHT D. EISENHOWER
Address, 1949

See also Ballots, Elections, Suffrage, Women 7, 9, 10

Want
See Freedom 21

War

1. The satisfaction I have in any success that attend us, even in the alleviation of misfortunes, is always allayed by a fear that it will lull us into security. Supineness and a disposition to flatter ourselves seem to make parts of our national character. When we receive a check, and are not quite undone, we are apt to fancy we have gained a victory; and, when we do gain any little advantage, we imagine it decisive and expect the war immediately at an end. The history of the war is a history of false hopes and temporary expedients. Would to God they were to end here!

GEORGE WASHINGTON
To James Duane in Congress, Oct. 4, 1780; *Writings*
(*Fitzpatrick*), *VII*, 227

2. It is my most ardent desire, not only to soften the inevitable calamities of war, but even to introduce on every occasion as great a share of tenderness and humanity, as can possibly be exercised in a state of hostility.

GEORGE WASHINGTON
To Lt.-Gen. James Robertson, May 4, 1782; *Ibid., VIII*, 282

3. My first wish is to see this plague of mankind banished from the earth, and the sons and daughters of this world employed in more pleasing and innocent amusements, than in preparing implements and exercising them for the destruction of mankind.

GEORGE WASHINGTON
To David Humphreys, July 25, 1785; *Ibid., IX*, 113

4. The power of making war often prevents it, and in our case would give efficacy to our desire of peace.

GEORGE WASHINGTON
1788; *Writings (Ford), V*, 57

5. Nothing short of self-respect and that justice which is essential to a national character ought to involve us in war; for sure I am, if this country is preserved in tranquillity twenty years longer, it may bid defiance, in a just cause, to any power whatever; such, in that time, will be its population, wealth, and resources.

GEORGE WASHINGTON
To Gouverneur Morris, Dec. 22, 1795; *Writings*
(*Fitzpatrick*), *XI*, 102

6.   For my own part, I thought America had been long enough involved in the wars of Europe. She had been a foot-ball between contending nations from the beginning, and it was easy to foresee that France and England both would endeavor to involve us in their future wars. I thought it our interest and duty . . . to be completely independent, and have nothing to do, but in commerce, with either of them.

JOHN ADAMS
Diary, Nov. 11, 1782; *Works, III,* 308

7.   War is not the most favorable moment for divesting the monarchy of power. On the contrary, it is the moment when the energy of a single hand shows itself in the most seducing form.

THOMAS JEFFERSON
To St. John de Crèvecoeur, 1788; *Dictionary,* p. 1264

8.   We are sincerely anxious that war may be avoided; but not at the expense either of our faith or honor. . . . As to myself, I love peace, and I am anxious that we should give the world still another useful lesson, by showing to them other modes of punishing injuries than by war, which is as much punishment to the punisher as to the sufferer.

THOMAS JEFFERSON
To Tench Coxe, May 1, 1794; *Writings, VIII,* 147

9.   I have seen enough of one war never to wish to see another.

THOMAS JEFFERSON
To John Adams, 1794; *Works, IV,* 104

10.   Establish the eternal truth that acquiescence under insult is not the way to escape war.

THOMAS JEFFERSON
To H. Tazewell, Sept. 13, 1795; *Writings, IX,* 308

11.   France has sincerely wished peace, and their seducers have wished war, as well for the loaves and fishes which arise out of war expenses, as for the chance of changing the Constitution.

THOMAS JEFFERSON
To Thomas Lomax, Mar. 12, 1799; *Ibid., X,* 124

12.   If ever there was a holy war, it was that which saved our liberties and gave us independence.

THOMAS JEFFERSON
To John Wayles Eppes, Nov. 6, 1813; *Works, VI,* 246

13.   My views and feeling [are] in favor of the abolition of war . . . and I hope it is practicable, by improving the mind and morals of society, to lessen the disposition to war; but of its abolition I despair.

THOMAS JEFFERSON
To Noah Worchester, Nov. 26, 1817; *Writings, XVIII,* 298

14. Each generation should be made to bear the burden of its own wars, instead of carrying them on, at the expense of other generations.

JAMES MADISON
National Gazette, Feb. 2, 1792; *Writings*, *VI*, 90

15. Great calamities make appeals to the benevolence of mankind, which ought not to be resisted. Good offices in such emergencies exalt the character of the party rendering them. By exciting grateful feelings, they soften the intercourse between nations, and tend to prevent war.

Surely if the United States have a right to make war, they have a right to prevent it.

JAMES MONROE
Message to Congress, May 4, 1822; *Statesman's Manual*, *II*, 520

16. Since war is *not* biologically impelled, it is comparatively easy to stay men's primordial motive for fighting by satisfying the biological necessities such as eating and reproducing; but these imperatives having been met, it becomes paramount—as men embroider on the basic pattern and add to the initial drives of their being with religion, art and the skills, and so find it necessary to defend their civilizations by wars culturally induced—to erect cultural as well as economic and military barriers against the institution of war.

JAMES MONROE
Cocked Hats, p. 346

17. I consider an unjust war as the greatest of all human atrocities; but I esteem a just one as the highest of all human virtues. War calls into exercise the highest feelings and powers of man.

JOHN QUINCY ADAMS
1820; *Figures*, p. 66

18. With regard to war . . . considered in the abstract . . . I held it in utter abhorrence, as much so as the Roman mothers in the days of Horace and of Augustus Caesar; but . . . there are, and always have been as long as the race of men has existed, times and occasions of dire necessity for war; and, philosophically speaking, I believed that war was not a corrupter, but rather a purifier, of the moral character of man; that peace was the period of corruption to the human race.

JOHN QUINCY ADAMS
Mar. 25, 1846; *Memoirs*, *XII*, 254

19. War is a blessing compared with national degradation.

ANDREW JACKSON
To James K. Polk, May 2, 1845; *Diary* (*of Polk*), p. 4

20. We can never be too tardy to begin the work of blood. . . . But it

is a bad mode of settling disputes to make soldiers your ambassadors, and to point to the halter and the gallows as your ultimatum.

JOHN TYLER

To his children, Aug. 24, 1841; *Champion*, p. 389

21. The war will continue to be prosecuted with vigor, as the best means of securing peace.

JAMES K. POLK

Second Annual Message to Congress, Dec. 8, 1846;
Messages and Papers, p. 2364

22. My life has been devoted to arms, yet I look upon war, at all times . . . as a national calamity, to be avoided if compatible with the national honor.

ZACHARY TAYLOR

To J. S. Allison, Apr. 12, 1848; *Life*, p. 385

23. Civil War has been inaugurated, and we must meet it. . . . It is no time now to inquire by whose fault or folly this state of things has been produced. . . . Rather, let every man stand to his post, and . . . let posterity . . . find our skeleton and armor on the spot where duty required us to stand.

MILLARD FILLMORE

Speech at Buffalo, N.Y., Apr. 16, 1861;
Millard Fillmore (Rayback), p. 424

24. Self-preservation is the first instinct of nature, and therefore any state of society in which the sword is all the time suspended over the heads of the people must at last become intolerable.

JAMES BUCHANAN

Third Annual Message to Congress, Dec. 19, 1859;
Messages and Papers, p. 3085

25. Our strife pertains to ourselves—to the passing generations of men; and it can without convulsion be hushed forever with the passing of one generation.

ABRAHAM LINCOLN

Message to Congress, Dec. 1, 1862; *Complete Works, VIII*, 116

26. No terms other than unconditional and immediate surrender can be accepted. I propose to move immediately upon your works.

ULYSSES S. GRANT

Dispatch to Gen. Simon Bolivar Buckner, Fort Donelson,
Feb. 14, 1862; *Speeches*, p. 5

27. I propose to fight it out on this line, if it takes all summer.

ULYSSES S. GRANT

Dispatch from Spottsylvania Court House, Va., May 11, 1864;
Sayings, p. 149

28. Wars of extermination, engaged in by people pursuing commerce and all industrial pursuits, are expensive even against the weakest people, and are demoralizing and wicked.

ULYSSES S. GRANT
Second Inaugural Address, Mar. 4, 1873

29. [Our republic] has shown itself capable of dealing with one of the greatest wars that was ever made, and our people have proven themselves to be the most formidable in war of any nationality.

But this [Civil] War was a fearful lesson, and should teach us the necessity of avoiding wars in the future.

ULYSSES S. GRANT
1885; *Memoirs, II,* 544

30. I regard the Mexican War as one of the most unjust ever waged by a stronger against a weaker nation. It was an instance of a republic following the bad example of European monarchies, in not considering justice in their desire to acquire additional territory.

ULYSSES S. GRANT
1885; *Ibid.,* p. 544

31. There are good points about all . . . wars. People forget self. The virtues of magnanimity, courage, patriotism, etc., are called into life. People are more generous, more sympathetic, better, than when engaged in the more selfish pursuits of peace.

RUTHERFORD B. HAYES
To S. Birchard, May 8, 1861; *Diary and Letters, II,* 15

32. War with us has always been a means of conquering an honorable peace, and has never been resorted to until everything else short of surrender of principle and essential rights failed to bring peace.

WILLIAM McKINLEY
Speech at Canton, Ohio, May 30, 1891; *Life and Speeches,* p. 175

33. We want no wars of conquest. . . . War should never be entered upon until every agency of peace has failed.

Arbitration is the true method of settlement of international as well as local or individual differences.

WILLIAM McKINLEY
Inaugural Address, Mar. 4, 1897

34. Half-heartedness never won a battle.

WILLIAM McKINLEY
In New York, N.Y., Jan. 27, 1898; *Speeches and Addresses,* p. 64

35. We accepted war for humanity. We can accept no terms of peace which shall not be in the interest of humanity.

WILLIAM McKINLEY
At Cedar Rapids, Ia., Oct. 11, 1898; *Ibid.,* p. 87

36.   War is not merely justifiable, but imperative, upon honorable men, upon an honorable nation, where peace can only be obtained by the sacrifice of conscientious conviction or of national welfare.

THEODORE ROOSEVELT
Sixth Annual Message to Congress, Dec. 3, 1906;
Works (Mem. Ed.), XVII, 472

37.   War is a dreadful thing, and unjust war is a crime against humanity. But it is such a crime because it is unjust, not because it is war.

THEODORE ROOSEVELT
Speech at the Sorbonne, Paris, France, Apr. 23, 1910;
Ibid., XV, 357

38.   [Wars] are the birth-pangs of a new and vigorous people. . . . The wrongs done and suffered cannot be blinked. Neither can they be allowed to hide the results to mankind of what has been achieved.

THEODORE ROOSEVELT
The Winning of the West; *Works, IX,* 156

39.   I abhor violence and bloodshed. I believe that war should never be resorted to when, or so long as, it is honorably possible to avoid it. I respect all men and women who from high motives and with sanity and self-respect do all they can to avert war. I advocate preparation for war in order to avert war; and I should never advocate war unless it were the only alternative to dishonor.

THEODORE ROOSEVELT
Autobiography, p. 206

40.   It is said that there is one word that is never allowed to creep into the diplomatic correspondence between nations, however hostile, and that word is "war." But I am not a diplomat and am not bound by diplomatic usage. I can talk of war. I am not one of those who hold that war is so frightful that nothing justifies a resort to it. We have not yet reached the millenium, and there are international grievances that can be redressed and just international purposes that can be accomplished in no other way. But, as one of our great generals has said, "War is hell," and nothing but a great and unavoidable cause can justify it.

WILLIAM HOWARD TAFT
Speech in Tokyo, Japan, Sept. 30, 1907; *Problems,* p. 55

41.   Why should the United States wish war? War would change her in a year or more into a military nation and her great resources would be wasted in a vast equipment that would serve no good purpose but to tempt her into warlike policies. . . . Why should she risk war in which all the evils of society flourish and all the vultures fatten?

WILLIAM HOWARD TAFT
Speech in Tokyo, Japan, Sept. 30, 1907; *Ibid.,* p. 57

42. Civil War discovered the foundations of our government to be in fact unwritten; set deep in a sentiment which constitutions can neither originate nor limit. The law of the Constitution reigned until war came.

What gave the war its passion, its hot energy as of a tragedy from end to end, was that in it sentiment met sentiment, conviction conviction.

WOODROW WILSON
Atlantic Monthly, January, 1901; *Public Papers, I,* 388

43. War is only a sort of dramatic representation, a sort of dramatic symbol of a thousand forms of duty.

WOODROW WILSON
Speech at Brooklyn, N.Y., May 11, 1914; *Ibid., III,* 105

44. Great democracies are not belligerent. They do not seek or desire war. . . . Conquest and dominion are not in our reckoning, or agreeable to our principles. . . .

War has never been a mere matter of men and guns. It is a thing of disciplined might. . . .

We regard war merely as a means of asserting the rights of a people against aggression. . . . We will not maintain a standing army except for uses . . . as necessary in times of peace as in times of war.

WOODROW WILSON
Third Annual Message to Congress, Dec. 7, 1915;
State Messages and Papers (Shaw), p. 138

45. Do you remember the experience of the Spanish-American War? . . . It did not last very long. You remember the satirical verse:
"War is rude and impolite, it quite upsets a nation;
   It's made of several weeks of fight and years of conver-
      sation."

A war which was parodied in verse and yet what happened? You sent thousands of men to their death because they were ignorant . . . sent to their death by miserable diseases. . . . Our loss in that war by disease in camp was greater than the percentage of the loss of the Japanese by disease and battle in their war with Russia. It is a very mortifying thing. . . . We poured crude, ignorant, untrained boys into the ranks of those armies and they died before they got sight of an enemy. Do you want to repeat that?

WOODROW WILSON
Speech at Kansas City, Mo., Feb. 2, 1916; *Ibid.,* p. 204

46. To such a task we dedicate our lives, our fortunes, everything that we are and everything that we have, with the pride of those who know that the day has come when America is privileged to spend her blood and her might for the principles that gave her birth and happiness and the peace which she has treasured. God helping her, she can do no other.

WOODROW WILSON
Address to Congress, asking for war, Apr. 2, 1917; *Ibid.,* p. 388

47.   If the League of Nations . . . should ever . . . be impaired, I would . . . get the boys who went . . . to fight together . . . and say, "Boys, I told you . . . this was a war against wars, and I did my best to fulfill the promise; but I am obliged to come to you in mortification and shame and say I have not been able to fulfill the promise. You are betrayed. You fought for something you did not get."

WOODROW WILSON
Address to veterans, St. Louis, Mo., Sept. 5, 1919;
Public Papers, V, 633

48.   Is there any man . . . who does not know that the seed of war in the modern world is industrial and commercial rivalry?

WOODROW WILSON
Address to veterans, St. Louis, Mo., Sept. 5, 1919; *Ibid.*

49.   I can predict with absolute certainty that within another generation there will be another world war if the nations of the world do not concert the method by which to prevent it.

WOODROW WILSON
Speech at Omaha, Neb., Sept. 8, 1919; *Ibid., VI, 36*

50.   We want to do our part in making offensive warfare so hateful that Governments and peoples who resort to it must prove the righteousness of their cause or stand as outlaws before the bar of civilization.

WARREN G. HARDING
Inaugural Address, Mar. 4, 1921

51.   When the Governments of the earth shall have established a freedom like our own and shall have sanctioned the pursuit of peace as we have practiced it, I believe the last sorrow and the final sacrifice of international warfare will have been written.

WARREN G. HARDING
Inaugural Address, Mar. 4, 1921

52.   I speak not as a pacifist who fears war, but as one who loves justice and hates war.

WARREN G. HARDING
Address at Arlington, Va., Nov. 11, 1921;
Messages and Papers, p. 9013

53.   Viewed in retrospect we see more clearly than ever the sordid side of war. . . . If war must come again—God grant that it shall not!—then we must draft all of the nation. . . . It is not enough to draft the young manhood. It is not enough to accept the voluntary service of both women and men whose patriotic devotion impels their enlistment. It will be righteous and just, it will be more effective in war and marked by less regret in the aftermath, if we draft all of capital, all of industry, all of agriculture, all of commerce, all of talent and capacity and energy . . . to make the

supreme and united and unselfish fight for the national triumph. When we do that there will be less of war.

. . . If we are committed to universal service . . . without compensation except the consciousness of service and the exaltations in victory, we will be slower to make war and more swift in bringing it to a triumphant close.

WARREN G. HARDING
Speech at Helena, Mont., June 29, 1923; *Ibid.,* p. 9292

54. We are against war because it is destructive. We are for peace because it is constructive.

CALVIN COOLIDGE
Address to Associated Press, Apr. 22, 1924; *Citizenship,* p. 222

55. Removing the burden of expense and jealousy, which must always accrue from a keen rivalry, is one of the most effective methods of diminishing that unreasonable hysteria and misunderstanding which are the most potent means of fomenting war.

. . . a display of reason rather than a threat of force should be the determining factor in the intercourse among nations.

CALVIN COOLIDGE
Inaugural Address, Mar. 4, 1925

56. Food will win the war.

HERBERT HOOVER
1917; *American Quaker,* p. 93

57. I suggest to you a fundamental truism. War is justified only as an instrument for a specific consequence. That consequence for America was lasting peace. In four directions we strayed from that major objective.

First. Both [world] wars proved that we cannot change ideas in the minds of men and races with machine guns or battleships. . . . Such wars have no ending and no victory. The way of life of a people must come from within; it cannot be compelled from without.

Second. Our second departure . . . was concentration on winning military battles. Winning battles which do not drive to the major purpose of lasting peace are battles lost.

Third. In our political settlements after both wars, we departed from our true path and left many nations in such a plight as to become the prey of others. We yielded to the spirits of greedy imperialism in other nations and of vindictiveness and revenge. We sowed the dragon's teeth of another war.

Fourth. Truly, in both wars we realized that lasting peace could come only from suppression of aggression and from disarmament. The League of Nations and the United Nations were set up in that hope.

HERBERT HOOVER
Speech at Emporia, Kan., July 11, 1950; *American Road,* p. 73

58. I have seen war. . . . I hate war.

> FRANKLIN DELANO ROOSEVELT
> Address at Chautauqua, N.Y., Aug. 14, 1936;
> *Public Papers, V,* 289

59. War is a contagion.

> FRANKLIN DELANO ROOSEVELT
> Address in Chicago, Ill., Oct. 5, 1937; *Ibid., VI,* 411

60. We cannot accept the doctrine that war must be forever a part of man's destiny.

> FRANKLIN DELANO ROOSEVELT
> Campaign address at Cleveland, Ohio, Nov. 2, 1940; *Ibid., IX,* 546

61. I hate war. War destroys individuals and whole generations. It throws civilization into the dark ages. But there is only one kind of war the American people have any stomach for and that is war against hunger and pestilence and disease.

> HARRY S. TRUMAN
> Interview, *ca.* 1950; *Mr. President,* p. 242

62. I have always been opposed even to the thought of fighting a "preventive war." There is nothing more foolish than to think that war can be stopped by war. You don't "prevent" anything by war except peace.

> HARRY S. TRUMAN
> 1952; *Memoirs, II,* 383

63. Warfare, no matter what weapons it employs, is a means to an end, and if that end can be achieved by negotiated settlements of conditional surrender, there is no need for war.

> HARRY S. TRUMAN
> 1955; *Ibid., I,* 210

64. Morale is the greatest single factor in successful wars.

> DWIGHT D. EISENHOWER
> June 23, 1945

65. There is one thing you have in war that you do not have in peace. You have unification, compelled by a very threatening danger. In other words, Franklin's old saying, "If we don't hang together, we'll hang separately," applies in war more definitely than it does in peace.

> DWIGHT D. EISENHOWER
> Press Conference, Paris, France, June 16, 1945;
> *Eisenhower Speaks,* p. 23

66. Prosperous nations are not war-hungry, but a hungry nation will always seek war if it has to in desperation.

> DWIGHT D. EISENHOWER
> Speech in New York, N.Y., June 19, 1945; *Ibid.,* p. 44

67. I hate war as only a soldier who has lived it can, only as one who

has seen its brutality, its futility, its *stupidity*. Yet there is one thing to say on its credit side—victory required a mighty manifestation of the most ennobling of the virtues of man—faith, courage, fortitude, sacrifice!

DWIGHT D. EISENHOWER
Address in Ottawa, Canada, Jan. 10, 1946; *Ibid.*, p. 64

68. In discussing war and peace, we incline to paint one all black and the other all white. We like to repeat "there never was a good war, or a bad peace." But war often has provided the setting for comradeship and understanding and greatness of spirit—among nations, as well as men—beyond anything in quiet days; while peace may be marked by . . . chicanery, treachery, and the temporary triumph of expediency over all spiritual values.

The pact of Munich was a greater blow to humanity than the atomic bomb at Hiroshima. Suffocation of human freedom among a once free people, however quietly and peacefully accomplished, is more far-reaching in its implications and its effects on their future than the destruction of their homes, industrial centers, and transportation facilities. Out of rubble heaps, willing hands can rebuild a better city; but out of freedom lost can stem only generations of hate and bitter struggle and brutal oppression. . . .

Without the ideals, the hopes and aspirations of humanity; those things of the soul and spirit which great men of history have valued far above peace and material wealth and even life itself . . . peace is an inhuman existence.

DWIGHT D. EISENHOWER
Address at Columbia University, Mar. 23, 1950; *Peace*, p. 12

69. The war maker is first of all a propagandist. . . .

Until war is eliminated from international relations, unpreparedness for it is well nigh as criminal as war itself. . . .

It is shocking . . . that, though many millions have been voluntarily donated for research in cancer of the individual body, nothing similar has been done with respect to the most malignant cancer of the world body—war.

DWIGHT D. EISENHOWER
Address at Columbia University, Mar. 23, 1950; *Ibid.*, pp. 14, 19

70. Possibly my hatred of war blinds me so that I cannot comprehend the arguments that its advocates adduce. But, in my opinion, there is no such thing as a preventive war. Although this suggestion is repeatedly made, no one has yet explained how war prevents war. Nor has anyone been able to explain away the fact that war begets conditions that beget further war.

DWIGHT D. EISENHOWER
Address at Pittsburgh, Pa., October, 1950;
What Eisenhower Thinks, p. 91

71.   Abhorring war as a chosen way to balk the purpose of those who threaten us, we hold it to be the first task of statesmanship to develop the strength that will deter the forces of aggression and promote the conditions of peace. For, as it must be the supreme purpose of all free men, so it must be the dedication of their leaders, to save humanity from preying upon itself.

> DWIGHT D. EISENHOWER
> First Inaugural Address, Jan. 20, 1953

72.   The hope of the world is that wisdom can arrest conflict between brothers. I believe that war is the deadly harvest of arrogant and unreasoning minds. And I find grounds for this belief in the wisdom literature of Proverbs. It says . . . panic strikes like a storm and calamity comes like a whirlwind to those who hate knowledge and ignore their God.

> DWIGHT D. EISENHOWER
> Address to National Education Association, Apr. 4, 1957;
> *Public Papers . . . Eisenhower, 1957,* p. 264

73.   We know we are peaceful . . . Government only with the consent of the governed does not start wars, because it is the people that have to fight them that make the decision.

> DWIGHT D. EISENHOWER
> Remarks to League of Women Voters, Washington, D.C.,
> May 1, 1957; *Ibid.,* p. 317

74.   In the development of this organization (the United Nations) rests the only true alternative to war—and war appeals no longer as a rational alternative. Unconditional war can no longer lead to unconditional victory. It can no longer serve to settle disputes. It can no longer be of concern to great powers alone. For a nuclear disaster, spread by winds and waters and fear, could well engulf the great and the small, the rich and the poor, the committed and the uncommitted alike.

Mankind must put an end to war—or war will put an end to mankind.

> JOHN F. KENNEDY
> Address to the United Nations General Assembly, Sept. 25, 1961;
> *Public Papers . . . Kennedy, 1961,* p. 619

75.   Aggressive conduct, if allowed to go unchecked and unchallenged, ultimately leads to war.

This nation is opposed to war. We are also true to our word.

> JOHN F. KENNEDY
> Radio and television address, Oct. 22, 1962;
> *Vital Speeches, Nov. 15, 1962,* p. 67

See also Army, Conquest, Defense, Democracy 11, Disarmament 1, Foreign Relations 35, Goals 4, God 9, Hope 2, Humanity 1, Ideas 3, Laws 25, 28, Leadership 1, League of Nations 3, Navy, Neutrality, Pacifists,

Weakness

See Preparedness 2

Wealth

1.   Birth and wealth together have prevailed over virtue and talent in all ages.

JOHN ADAMS
To Thomas Jefferson, July 9, 1813; *Works, X,* 52

2.   Measures should be enacted which, without violating the rights of property, would reduce extreme wealth towards a state of mediocrity, and raise extreme indigence towards a state of comfort.

JAMES MADISON
Writings (Hunt), VI, 86

3.   He mocks the people who proposes that the Government shall protect the rich and that they in turn will care for the laboring poor.

GROVER CLEVELAND
Fourth Annual Message to Congress, Dec. 3, 1888;
Messages and Papers, p. 5361

4.   Every manifestation of hostility toward honest men who acquire wealth by honest means should be crushed.

THEODORE ROOSEVELT
Speech to New York Legislature, May 22, 1899;
Works, XXIII, 143

5.   We are a rich Nation, and undefended wealth invites aggression.

THEODORE ROOSEVELT
Special Message to Congress, Apr. 14, 1908;
Messages and Papers, p. 7528

6.   Common welfare is the goal of our national endeavor. Wealth is not inimical to welfare; it ought to be its friendliest agency.

WARREN G. HARDING
Inaugural Address, Mar. 4, 1921

7.   We want wealth, but there are many other things we want very much more. Among them are peace, honor, charity and idealism.

CALVIN COOLIDGE
Address in Washington, D.C., Jan. 17, 1924;
Autobiography, p. 358

8.   Wealth comes from industry and from the hard experience of human toil. To dissipate it in waste and extravagance is disloyalty to humanity.

This is by no means a doctrine of parsimony. . . . Both men and nations should live in accordance with their means.

CALVIN COOLIDGE
Ibid., p. 182

See also Liberty 36, Mankind 4, Money, Preparedness 8

Welfare
See Wealth 6

West, The
1. Nearly a century ago, one of those rare minds to whom it is given to discern future greatness . . . pronounced . . . "Westward the star of empire takes its way." Let us unite in ardent supplications . . . that what was then prophecy may continue unfolding into history.

JOHN QUINCY ADAMS
Oration at Plymouth, Mass., Dec. 22, 1802; *Oration*, p. 31

White House
1. I pray Heaven to bestow the best of blessings on this House and all that shall hereafter inhabit it. May none but honest and wise men ever rule under this roof.

JOHN ADAMS
To Abigail Adams, Nov. 2, 1800; *Letters to Wife, II*, 267

2. If you are as happy, my dear sir, on entering this house as I am in leaving it and returning home, you are the happiest man in this country.

JAMES BUCHANAN
To Abraham Lincoln at the White House, Mar. 4, 1861;
Works, XI, 161

3. You don't live there [in the White House]. You are only Exhibit A to the country.

THEODORE ROOSEVELT
Ca. 1908; *As I Knew Them*, p. 537

4. I never forget that I live in a house owned by all the American people and that I have been given their trust.

FRANKLIN DELANO ROOSEVELT
Fireside Chat, April, 1938; *As FDR Said*, p. 224

5. The finest prison in the world.

HARRY S. TRUMAN
American Treasury, p. 332

Wisdom
1. There is no such thing as human wisdom; all is the providence of God.

JOHN ADAMS
Diary, Feb. 13, 1779; *Works, III*, 191

2. The wise know too well their weakness to assume infallibility; and he who knows most, knows best how little he knows.

THOMAS JEFFERSON
The Batture of New Orleans, 1810; *Writings, XVIII*, 130

3. The wisdom of our fathers, foreseeing even the most dire possibilities, made sure that the government should never be imperiled because of the uncertainty of human life. Men may die, but the fabric of our free institutions remains unshaken.

CHESTER A. ARTHUR
Inaugural Address, Mar. 4, 1881

4. Nine-tenths of wisdom is being wise in time.

THEODORE ROOSEVELT
Kansas City Star, Nov. 1, 1917; *Works, XIX*, 183

5. Knowledge comes, but wisdom lingers. It may not be difficult to store up in the mind a vast quantity of facts within a comparatively short time, but the ability to form judgments requires the severe discipline of hard work, and the tempering heat of experience and maturity.

CALVIN COOLIDGE

6. We must not be misled by the claim that the source of all wisdom is in the Government. Wisdom is born out of experience, and most of all out of precisely such experience as is brought to us by the darkest moments. It is in the meeting of such moments that are born new insights, new sympathies, new powers, new skills.

HERBERT HOOVER
Speech at Valley Forge, Pa., May 30, 1931;
Messages and Papers, p. 566

See also Foreign Relations 27, Honesty 4, Popularity 1, Power 10, Security 1, Unity 8

Women

1. I never did, nor do I believe I ever shall, give advice to a woman, who is setting out on a matrimonial voyage; first, because I never could advise one to marry without her own consent; and, secondly, because I know it is to no purpose to advise her to refrain, when she has obtained it. A woman very rarely asks an opinion or requires advice on such an occasion, till her resolution is formed; and then it is with the hope and expectation of obtaining a sanction, not that she means to be governed by your disapprobation. . . .

GEORGE WASHINGTON
To Lund Washington, Sept. 20, 1783;
Writings (Fitzpatrick), VIII, 486

2. The manners of women are the surest criterion by which to determine whether a republican government is practicable in a nation or not.

JOHN ADAMS
Diary, June 2, 1778; *Works, III*, 171

3. The capacity of the female mind for studies of the highest order cannot be doubted, having been sufficiently illustrated by its works of genius, of erudition, and of science. . . . It merits an improved system of education.

JAMES MADISON
To Albert Picket, *et al.*, September, 1821;
Complete Madison, p. 315

4. Female character never should be introduced or touched by my friends, unless a continuation of attack should continue to be made against Mrs. J. and then only, by way of *Just retaliation* upon the known guilty. . . . *I never war against females* and it is only the base and cowardly that do. . . .

ANDREW JACKSON
To Duff Green, Aug. 13, 1827; *Correspondence, III*, 376

5. A woman is the only thing I am afraid of that I know will not hurt me.

ABRAHAM LINCOLN
Ca. 1829; *Prairie Years, II*, 266

6. Put it aside as a jest if we will . . . still, the woman question is rising in our horizon larger than the size of a man's hand; and some solution ere long, that question find . . . this nation must open up new avenues of work and usefulness to the women of this country, so that everywhere they may have something to do.

JAMES A. GARFIELD
Speech at Washington, D.C., June 29, 1869; *Lives*, p. 29

7. I am not in favor of suffrage for women until I can be convinced that all the women desire it; and when they desire it I am in favor of giving it to them.

WILLIAM HOWARD TAFT
Address at Columbus, Miss., Nov. 2, 1909;
Presidential Addresses, 397

8. It is vital to the right solution of the great problems which we must settle . . . when the war is over. We shall need them in our vision of affairs, as we have never needed them before, the sympathy and insight and clear moral instinct of the women of the world. We shall need their moral sense to preserve what is right and fine and worthy in our system

of life, as well as to discover just what it is that ought to be purified and reformed. Without their counselings, we shall be only half wise.

WOODROW WILSON
Address to the Senate, on woman suffrage, Sept. 30, 1918;
Guarantees, p. 76

9. Let us not share the apprehension of many . . . as to the danger of this momentous extension of the franchise. Women have never been without influence in our political life. Enfranchisement will bring to the polls . . . women educated in our schools, trained in our customs and habits of thought, and sharers of our problems. It will bring the alert mind, the awakened conscience, the sure intuition, the abhorrence of tyranny or oppression, the wide and tender sympathy that distinguish the women of America. Surely there can be no danger there.

WARREN G. HARDING
At Marion, Ohio, July 22, 1920; *Speeches of
Warren G. Harding,* p. 36

10. I know that the influence of womanhood will guard the home, which is the citadel of the nation. I know it will be the protector of childhood. I know it will be on the side of humanity. I welcome it as a great instrument of mercy and a mighty agency of peace. I want every woman to vote.

CALVIN COOLIDGE
Acceptance of Nomination for Presidency, Aug. 14, 1924;
Messages and Papers, p. 9441

11. I believe women bring to politics the enthusiasm and the idealism which men often forget. I think perhaps it is their concern for their children, the raising of good children in a proper atmosphere, the thinking of a good life ahead for them. Women comprehend spiritual, intellectual and material development. That is the reason they bring idealism—and I may say, this country needs it.

DWIGHT D. EISENHOWER
Remarks at Republican Women's National Conference,
Washington, D.C., Apr. 3, 1957; *Public Papers . . .
Eisenhower, 1957,* p. 258

See also Mothers, Voters 1

Words

See Action 3, Authors, Democracy 7, Fighting 2, Foreign Relations 29, Friendship 1, Gratitude 2, Humanity 1, Liberty 47, Religion 12, Slogans

Work

1. In the long run, the chief difference in men will be found in the amount of work they do. Do not trust to what lazy men call the spur of

the occasion. If you wish to wear spurs in the tournament of life, you must buckle them to your own heels before you enter the lists.

JAMES A. GARFIELD
Address at Hiram, Ohio, June 14, 1867; *Works, I,* 283

2. The law of worthy work well done is the law of successful American life.

THEODORE ROOSEVELT
At Chattanooga, Tenn., Sept. 8, 1902; *Addresses and Presidential Messages,* p. 53

3. No man needs sympathy because he has to work. . . . Far and away the best prize that life offers is the chance to work hard at work worth doing.

THEODORE ROOSEVELT
Address at Syracuse, N.Y., Sept. 7, 1903; *Addresses and Papers,* p. 166

4. Work is not a curse, it is the prerogative of intelligence, the only means to manhood, and the measure of civilization. Savages do not work.

CALVIN COOLIDGE
Speech at Boston, Mass., Feb. 4, 1916; *Faith,* p. 13

5. When more and more people are thrown out of work unemployment results.

CALVIN COOLIDGE
News report

6. We can repay the debt which we owe to our God, to our dead, and to our children only by work—by ceaseless devotion to the responsibilities which lie ahead of us. If I could give you a single watchword for the coming months, that word is—work, work, and more work.

HARRY S. TRUMAN
Radio address, May 8, 1945;
Public Papers . . . Truman, 1945, p. 48

See also Common Sense, Greatness 3, 12, Idleness, Labor, Security 2, Unemployment, Wealth 8, Wisdom 5

World Policies
See Foreign Relations

Worship
1. Reverence is the measure not of others but of ourselves. . . . What men worship that will they become.

CALVIN COOLIDGE
Speech to the Roxbury Historical Society, June 17, 1918;
Faith, p. 109

See also Religion 28

Writers

See Authors

Wrong

1. It is more honorable to repair a wrong than to persist in it.

THOMAS JEFFERSON
To the Cherokee Chiefs, Jan. 10, 1806; *Writings, XIX,* 147

2. Never suffer a thought to be harbored in your mind which you would not avow openly. When tempted to do anything in secret, ask yourself if you would do it in public. If you would not, be sure it is wrong.

THOMAS JEFFERSON
To Francis Eppes, May 21, 1816; *Ibid.,* p. 241

3. I am one of those who believe that a man may sin and do wrong, and after that may do right. If all of us who have sinned were put to death . . . there would not be many of us left.

ANDREW JOHNSON
Speech in New York, N.Y., August, 1866;
President on Trial, p. 197

4. I am not afraid of a knave. I am not afraid of a rascal. I am afraid of a strong man who is wrong, and whose wrong thinking can be impressed upon other persons by his own force of character and force of speech.

WOODROW WILSON
1912; *New Freedom (Hale),* p. 220

See also Errors, Foreign Relations, Honor 1, Ignorance 2, Laws 15, Peace 17, 24, Problems, Right, States' Rights 16, Virtue 6, War 38

Youth

1. The fortune of our lives . . . depends on employing well the short period of youth.

THOMAS JEFFERSON
To Martha Washington, Mar. 28, 1787; *Writings (Ford), IV,* 372

2. A boy is a complete self-starter, and therefore wisdom in dealing with him consists most in what to do with him next.

The priceless treasure of boyhood is his endless enthusiasm, his high store of idealism, his affection and his hopes. When we preserve these, we have made men. We have made citizens, and we have made Americans.

HERBERT HOOVER

3. I have used the words "the qualities of youth." Be wise enough, be tolerant enough, you who are young in years, to remember that millions of older people have kept and propose to keep these qualities of youth. You ought to thank God tonight if, regardless of your years, you are

young enough in spirit to dream dreams and see visions—dreams and visions about a greater and finer America that is to be. . . . Hold fast to your dream. America needs it.

FRANKLIN DELANO ROOSEVELT
Speech at Baltimore, Md., Apr. 13, 1936; *Public Papers, V*, 166

See also Greatness 5

Zeal

1. A single zealot may commence prosecutor, and better men be his victims.

THOMAS JEFFERSON
Notes on Virginia, 1782; *Writings, II*, 225

2. I have never yet seen unpretending, but honest zeal and practical efforts to be useful, go without their ultimate reward.

MARTIN VAN BUREN
Speech at Albany, N.Y., July, 1827; *Life*, p. 314

Bibliography

Adams, John

ADAMS, CHARLES FRANCIS (ed.). *Familiar Letters of John Adams and His Wife Abigail, During the Revolution*. Boston: Houghton Mifflin Co., 1875.

———. *Letters of John Adams Addressed to His Wife*. 2 vols. Boston: Charles C. Little & James Brown, 1841.

———. *The Works of John Adams*. 10 vols. Boston: Little, Brown & Co., 1856.

ADAMS, JAMES TRUSLOW. *The Adams Family*. Boston: Little, Brown & Co., 1930.

KOCH, ADRIENNE, AND WILLIAM PEDEN (eds.). *Selected Writings of John and John Quincy Adams*. New York: Alfred A. Knopf, 1946.

WILSTACH, PAUL (ed.). *The Correspondence of John Adams and Thomas Jefferson (1812–1826)*. Indianapolis: Bobbs-Merrill Co., Inc., 1925.

Adams, John Quincy

ADAMS, CHARLES FRANCIS (ed.). *Memoirs of John Quincy Adams*. 12 vols. Philadelphia: (no publisher listed) 1874–77.

ADAMS, JOHN QUINCY. *An Address at the City of Washington, July 4, 1821*. Cambridge, Mass.: Hilliard and Metcalf, 1821.

———. *An Oration at Plymouth, Dec. 22, 1802*. Boston: Russell & Cutler, 1802.

BOBBE, DOROTHIE. *Mr. and Mrs. John Quincy Adams*. New York: Minton, Balch & Co., 1930.

FORD, WORTHINGTON CHAUNCEY (ed.). *Writings of John Quincy Adams*. 7 vols. New York: Macmillan Co., 1917.

KOCH. *Selected Writings of John and John Quincy Adams*. See John Adams bibliography.

MORSE, JOHN T., JR. *John Quincy Adams*. Boston: Houghton Mifflin Co., 1910.

NEVINS, ALLAN (ed.). *The Diary of John Quincy Adams* (1794–1845). New York: Longman's, Green & Co., 1928.

STYRON. *The Last of the Cocked Hats.* See Monroe bibliography.

Arthur, Chester Alan

HOWE, GEORGE FREDERICK. *Chester A. Arthur.* New York: Frederick Unger Publishing Co., 1935.

Buchanan, James

CURTIS, GEORGE TICKNOR. *The Life of James Buchanan.* 2 vols. New York: Harper & Bros., 1883.

——. *James Buchanan, His Doctrines and Policy.* Privately printed, n.d.

HENRY, J. BUCHANAN (ed.). *Messages of President Buchanan.* New York: Private printing, n.d.

KLEIN, PHILIP SHRIVER. *President James Buchanan.* University Park, Pa.: Pennsylvania State University Press, 1962.

MOORE, JOHN BASSETT (ed.). *The Works of James Buchanan.* 4 vols. Philadelphia: J. B. Lippincott Co., 1908–11.

Cleveland, Grover

MCELROY, ROBERT. *Grover Cleveland, the Man and the Statesman.* New York: Harper & Bros., 1923.

NEVINS, ALLAN (ed.). *The Letters of Grover Cleveland.* Boston: Houghton Mifflin Co., 1933.

——. *A Study in Courage.* New York: Dodd, Mead & Co., 1938.

PARKER, GEORGE F. (ed.). *Writings and Speeches of Grover Cleveland.* New York: Cassell Publishing Co., 1892.

Coolidge, Calvin

COOLIDGE, CALVIN. *Autobiography.* New York: Cosmopolitan Book Corp., 1929.

——. *Foundations of the Republic.* New York: Charles Scribner's Sons, 1926.

——. *The Price of Freedom.* New York: Charles Scribner's Sons, 1924.

——. *Have Faith in Massachusetts.* Boston: Houghton Mifflin Co., 1919.

——. *Message to Congress,* Dec. 6, 1923. Washington, D.C.: Government Printing Office, 1923.

——. *Message to Congress,* Dec. 7, 1923. Washington, D.C.: Government Printing Office, 1926.

FUESS, CLAUDE M. *The Man from Vermont.* Boston: Little, Brown & Co., 1940.

HENNESSY, M. E. *Calvin Coolidge.* New York: G. P. Putnam's Sons, 1924.

LATHEM, EDWARD C. *Meet Calvin Coolidge.* Brattleboro, Vt.; Stephen Greene Press, 1961.

WHITING, EDWARD ELWELL. *Calvin Coolidge: His Ideals of Citizenship.* Boston: W. A. Wilde Co., 1924.

Eisenhower, Dwight D.

EISENHOWER, DWIGHT D. *Mandate for Change.* Garden City, N.Y.: Doubleday & Co., 1963.

———. *Peace with Justice.* New York: Popular Library, 1961.

Public Papers of the Presidents of the United States, Dwight D. Eisenhower, 1953–1961. 8 vols. Washington, D.C.: National Archives & Records Service, 1954–1961.

SHOEMAKER, RALPH J. (ed.). *The President's Words: An Index.* Louisville, Ky.: Elsie DeGraff Shoemaker and Ralph J. Shoemaker, 1954.

TAYLOR, ALLAN. *What Eisenhower Thinks.* New York: Thomas Y. Crowell, 1952.

TRUENFELS, RUDOLPH L. (ed.). *Eisenhower Speaks.* New York: Farrar, Straus & Co., 1948.

Fillmore, Millard

RAYBACK, ROBERT J. *Millard Fillmore.* Buffalo, N.Y.: Henry Stewart, Inc., 1959.

———. *The Ovation to Mr. Fillmore.* New York: J. & E. Brooks, n.d.

SEVERANCE, FRANK H. (ed.). *The Papers of Millard Fillmore.* 2 vols. Buffalo, N.Y.: Buffalo Historical Society, 1907.

Garfield, James A.

BALCH, WILLIAM RALSTON. *Maxims of James Abram Garfield.* Pamphlet, no publisher listed, 1880.

DOYLE, BURTON T., AND HOMER H. SWANEY. *The Lives of James A. Garfield and Chester A. Arthur.* Washington, D.C.: Rufus H. Darby, 1881.

GARFIELD, JAMES A. "Address at Hiram, Ohio, June 14, 1867." Cleveland: Fairbanks, Benedict & Co., 1867.

———. *College Education.* Cleveland: Fairbanks, Benedict & Co., 1867.

———. "The Future of the Republic: Its Dangers and Its Hopes." Address, 1873. Cleveland: Nevins Bros., 1873.

———. *President Garfield and Education.* Boston: James R. Osgood & Co., 1882.

———. *Gems of the Campaign of 1880, of General Grant and Garfield.* See Ulysses S. Grant bibliography.

General Garfield as a Statesman and Orator. New York: National Republican Committee, 1880.

McCabe, James D. *The Life and Public Services of Gen. James A. Garfield.* Dayton, Ohio: Alvin Peabody, 1881.

Hinsdale, Burke A. *President Garfield and Education.* Boston: James R. Osgood & Co., 1882.

——. *The Works of James Abram Garfield* (ed.). 2 vols. Boston: James R. Osgood & Co., 1882–83.

Smith, Theodore C. *The Life and Letters of James A. Garfield.* 4 vols. New Haven: Yale University Press, 1925.

Grant, Ulysses S.

Grant, Ulysses S. *Gems of the Campaign of 1880, of General Grant and Garfield.* Jersey City: Lincoln Assoc., 1880.

——. *The Personal Memoirs of Ulysses S. Grant.* 2 vols. New York: Charles L. Webster & Co., 1886.

McClure, J. B. *Stories, Sketches and Speeches of General Grant.* Chicago: Rhodes and McClure, 1880.

The Speeches of Ulysses S. Grant. Washington, D.C.: Union Republican Congressional Executive Committee, 1868.

Woodward, W. E. *Meet General Grant.* New York: Horace Liveright, 1923.

Harding, Warren G.

Harding, Warren G. Message to Congress, Dec. 8, 1922. Washington: Government Printing Office, 1922.

——. Speeches of Warren G. Harding. Privately printed, 1923.

Murphy, James W. *Speeches and Addresses of Warren G. Harding.* Privately printed, 1923.

White, William Allen. *Autobiography.* New York: Macmillan Co., 1946.

Harrison, Benjamin

Harrison, Mary Lord (ed.). *Views of an Ex-President.* Indianapolis: Bowen-Merrill Co., 1901.

Hedges, Charles (ed.). *Speeches of Benjamin Harrison.* New York: U.S. Book Co., 1892.

Public Papers and Addresses of Benjamin Harrison. Washington, D.C.: Government Printing Office, 1893.

Harrison, William Henry

Cleaves, Freeman. *Old Tippecanoe.* New York: Charles Scribner's Sons, 1939.

Harrison, William Henry. "Harrison's Great Speech," *Ohio Archaeological and Historical Quarterly,* January, 1909.

General Harrison's Speech at the Dayton Convention. Boston: The Whig Republican Association, 1840.

Hayes, Rutherford B.

BARNARD, HARRY. *Rutherford B. Hayes and His America.* Indianapolis: Bobbs-Merrill Co., Inc., 1954.

HOWARD, J. Q. *The Life, Public Services and Select Speeches of Rutherford B. Hayes.* Cincinnati: Robert Clarke & Co., 1876.

Letters and Messages of Rutherford B. Hayes. Washington, D.C.: Privately printed, 1881.

WILLIAMS, CHARLES RICHARD (ed.). *Diary and Letters of Rutherford B. Hayes.* 5 vols. Columbus, Ohio: Ohio State Archaeological and Historical Society, 1922.

Hoover, Herbert

HINSHAW, DAVID. *Herbert C. Hoover: American Quaker.* New York: Farrar, Straus & Co., 1950.

HOOVER, HERBERT. *Addresses Upon the American Road, 1948–1950.* Stanford, Cal.: Stanford University Press, 1951.

———. *American Individualism.* New York: Doubleday, Page Co., 1922.

———. *Challenge to Liberty.* New York: Charles Scribner's Sons, 1934.

———. *The Memoirs of Herbert Hoover.* 3 vols. New York: Macmillan Co., 1952.

———. *The New Day.* Stanford, Cal.: Stanford University Press, 1928.

JOSLIN, THEODORE G. *Hoover After Dinner.* New York: Charles Scribner's Sons, 1933.

MYERS, WILLIAM STARR (ed.). *State Papers and Other Writings of Herbert C. Hoover.* 2 vols. New York: Doubleday, Doran & Co., 1934.

———, AND WALTER H. NEWTON. *The Hoover Administration.* New York: Charles Scribner's Sons, 1936.

WILBUR, RAY LYMAN, AND ARTHUR MASTICK HYDE. *The Hoover Policies.* New York: Charles Scribner's Sons, 1934.

Jackson, Andrew

BASSETT, JOHN SPENCER (ed.). *Correspondence of Andrew Jackson.* 6 vols. Washington, D.C.: Carnegie Institution of Washington, 1933.

———. *The Life of Andrew Jackson.* New York: Macmillan Co., 1928

———. *Letters and Papers of Andrew Jackson.* Bulletin, 1900.

JOHNSON, GERALD WHITE. *Andrew Jackson.* New York: Minton, Balch & Co., 1927.

PARTON, JAMES. *The Life of Andrew Jackson.* 3 vols. Boston: Houghton Mifflin Co., 1888.

"Some Letters of Andrew Jackson," *Proceedings of the American Antiquarian Society,* XVII and XXXI, 1922.

THORP, FRANCIS NEWTON. *Principles of American Statesmanship.* New York: Tandy-Thomas Co., 1909.

Jefferson, Thomas

BOYD, JULIAN P. (ed.). *The Papers of Thomas Jefferson.* 15 vols. Princeton, N.J.: Princeton University Press, 1950.

BOYKIN, EDWARD. *The Wisdom of Thomas Jefferson.* New York: Doubleday, Doran & Co., Inc., 1941.

FORD, PAUL LEICESTER (ed.). *The Writings of Thomas Jefferson* (Federal ed.). 12 vols. New York: G. P. Putnam's Sons, 1904.

KOCH, ADRIENNE. *Jefferson and Madison.* New York: Alfred A. Knopf, 1950.

——, AND WILLIAM PEDEN. *Life and Selected Writings of Thomas Jefferson.* New York: Modern Library, 1944.

LIPSCOMB, ANDREW A., AND ALBERT ELLERY BERGH (eds.). *The Writings of Thomas Jefferson* (Monticello ed.). 20 vols. Washington, D.C.: Thomas Jefferson Memorial Assoc., 1904.

RAYNER, B. L. *Life of Thomas Jefferson.* Boston: Lilly, Wait, Colman & Holden, 1834.

STYRON. *The Last of the Cocked Hats.* See Monroe bibliography.

WASHINGTON, H. A. (ed.). *The Works of Thomas Jefferson.* 9 vols. New York: Townsend MacCoun, 1884.

WILSTACH. *The Correspondence of John Adams and Thomas Jefferson.* See John Adams bibliography.

Johnson, Andrew

LOMASK, MILTON. *Andrew Johnson, President on Trial.* New York: Farrar, Straus & Cudahy, 1960.

MOORE, FRANK. *Speeches of Andrew Johnson.* Boston: Little, Brown & Co., 1866.

——. *Document No. 2.* Washington, D.C.: National Johnson Club, 1866.

TAPPAN, GEORGE L. *Andrew Johnson, Not Guilty.* New York: Comet Press Books, 1955.

WINSTON, ROBERT W. *Andrew Johnson* (*Plebeian and Patriot*). New York: Henry Holt & Co., 1928.

Johnson, Lyndon B.

JOHNSON, LYNDON B. *A Time for Action.* New York: Atheneum Publishers, 1964.

MOONEY, BOOTH. *The Lyndon Johnson Story.* New York: Farrar, Straus & Co., 1964.

ZEIGER, HENRY A. *Lyndon B. Johnson: Man and President.* New York: Popular Library, Inc., 1963.

Kennedy, John F.

GARDNER, JOHN W. *To Turn the Tide.* New York: Harper & Bros., 1962.

KENNEDY, JOHN F. *Profiles in Courage.* New York: Pocket Books, Inc., 1957.

NEVINS, ALLAN. *The Strategy of Peace.* New York: Popular Library, 1960.

Public Papers of the Presidents of the United States—John F. Kennedy, 1961, 1962. Washington, D.C.: National Archives and Record Service.

Lincoln, Abraham

BASLER, ROY A. (ed.). *Abraham Lincoln: His Speeches and Writings.* Cleveland: World Publishing Co., 1946.

——. *The Collected Works of Abraham Lincoln.* 8 vols. and Index. New Brunswick, N.J.: Rutgers University Press, 1953.

BROWNE, FRANCIS F. *The Everyday Life of Abraham Lincoln.* New York: G. P. Putnam's Sons, 1915.

HARNSBERGER, CAROLINE THOMAS. *The Lincoln Treasury.* Chicago: Follett Publishing Co., 1950.

HERNDON, WILLIAM H., AND JESSE WEIK. *Herndon's Life of Lincoln.* Cleveland: World Publishing Co., 1949.

HERTZ, EMANUEL. *Abraham Lincoln, a New Portrait.* 2 vols. New York: Horace Liveright, Inc., 1931.

LAPSLEY, ARTHUR B. (ed.). *The Writings of Abraham Lincoln* (Constitutional ed.). 8 vols. New York: G. P. Putnam's Sons, 1888, 1905.

MORSE, JOHN T. *Abraham Lincoln.* 2 vols. Boston: Houghton Mifflin Co., 1893.

NICOLAY, JOHN G., AND JOHN HAY. *Abraham Lincoln: a History.* 10 vols. New York: The Century Co., 1890.

——. *Complete Works of Abraham Lincoln.* 2 vols. (Lincoln Memorial Library ed., 1894). New York: The Century Co., 1894.

——. *Complete Works of Abraham Lincoln.* 12 vols. New York: Francis D. Tandy Co., 1905. (Known as Tandy ed.)

SANDBURG, CARL. *Abraham Lincoln: The Prairie Years* (2 vols.) and *Abraham Lincoln: The War Years* (4 vols.). New York: Harcourt, Brace & Co., 1939.

SCOTT, TEMPLE. *The Wisdom of Abraham Lincoln.* New York: Brentano's, 1909.

TARBELL, IDA M. *The Life of Abraham Lincoln.* (2 vols.). New York: McClure, Phillips Co., 1900.

TOWNSEND, GEORGE ALFRED. *Real Life of Abraham Lincoln*. New York: Bible House, 1867.

WHITNEY, HENRY CLAY. *Life on the Circuit with Lincoln*. Caldwell, Idaho: Caxton Printers, Ltd., 1940.

McKinley, William

McKINLEY, WILLIAM. "Letter to Henry Cabot Lodge," Sept. 8, 1900. Washington, D.C.: Government Printing Office, 1900.

——. *Speeches and Addresses of William McKinley*. New York: Doubleday & McClure Co., 1900.

OGILVIE, J. S. *The Life and Speeches of William McKinley*. New York: J. J. Ogilvie Publishing Co., 1896.

Madison, James

BRANT, IRVING. *James Madison*. 3 vols. Indianapolis: Bobbs-Merrill Co., 1950.

——. *The James Madison Letters and Other Writings*. 4 vols. Philadelphia: J. B. Lippincott & Co., 1865.

HUNT, GAILLARD (ed.). *The Writings of James Madison*. 9 vols. New York: G. P. Putnam's Sons, 1904.

LODGE, HENRY CABOT. *The Federalist*. New York: G. P. Putnam's Sons, 1888.

PADOVER, SAUL K. (ed.). *The Complete Madison—His Basic Writings*. New York: Harper & Bros., 1953.

Monroe, James

Bulletin of the New York Public Library, vol. IX. New York: New York Public Library, 1900.

HAMILTON, STANISLAUS MURRAY (ed.). *The Writings of James Monroe*. 7 vols. New York: G. P. Putnam's Sons, 1898.

STYRON, ARTHUR. *The Last of the Cocked Hats*. Norman, Okla.: University of Oklahoma, 1945.

Pierce, Franklin

NICHOLS, ROY FRANKLIN. *Franklin Pierce: Young Hickory of the Granite Hills*. Philadelphia: University of Pennsylvania Press, 1931.

PIERCE, FRANKLIN. *The Record of a Month* (letters, Dec. 7, 1859–Jan. 6, 1860). No place, no publisher specified.

Polk, James K.

QUAIFE, MILO M. (ed.). The Diary of James K. Polk. 4 vols. Chicago: A. C. McClurg & Co., 1910.

Presidents

AGAR, HERBERT. *The People's Choice*. Boston: Houghton Mifflin Co., 1933.

BARUCH, BERNARD M. *The Public Years.* New York: Holt, Rinehart & Winston, 1960.

CHAPLIN, JEREMIAH. *Chips from the White House.* Boston: Lothrop, 1881.

FADIMAN, CLIFTON. *The American Treasury.* New York: Harper & Bros., 1955.

Inaugural Addresses of the Presidents of the United States (House Document No. 218). Washington, D.C.: Government Printing Office, 1961.

ISLEY, BLISS. *The Presidents—Men of Faith.* New York: W. A. Wilde Co., 1953.

KANE, JOSEPH NATHAN. *Facts About the Presidents.* New York: H. W. Wilson, 1959.

MENCKEN, H. L. *A New Dictionary of Quotations on Historical Principles.* New York: Alfred A. Knopf, 1942.

POLLARD, JAMES E. *The Presidents and the Press.* New York: Macmillan Co., 1947.

Public Papers of the Presidents of the United States. See Dwight D. Eisenhower, John F. Kennedy and Harry S. Truman bibliographies. Washington, D.C.: National Archives & Records Service, 1953–1963.

QUINCY, JOSIAH. *Figures of the Past.* Boston: Roberts Bros., 1883.

REED, THOMAS B. *Modern Eloquence.* 10 vols. Philadelphia: John D. Morris & Co., 1900.

Representative American Speeches. Annual series of Reference Shelf, 1937–New York: H. W. Wilson Co., 1937.

RICHARDSON, JAMES D. *Messages and Papers of the Presidents, 1789–1897* (10 vols.) with supplement (to 1924) (2 vols.). New York: Bureau of National Literature and Art, 1897 and 1924.

——. *Messages and Papers of the Presidents.* New York: Bureau of National Literature and Art, 1900.

SMITH, DON. *Peculiarities of the Presidents.* Van Wert, Ohio: Wilkinson Printing Co., 1938.

STODDARD, HENRY L. *As I Knew Them.* New York: Harper & Bros., 1927.

VINMONT, R. B. *Presidents at a Glance.* New York: Grosset & Dunlap, 1933.

Vital Speeches of the Day, 1962–February, 1964. Pelham, N.Y.: City News Publishing Co.

WALKER, EDWARD (ed.). *Addresses and Messages of the Presidents of the United States.* 1 vol. New York: Edward Walker, 1841.

WILLIAMS, EDWIN. *Statesman's Manual.* 4 vols. New York: Edwin Walker, 1849.

WOODS, HENRY F. *American Sayings.* New York: Duell, Sloan & Pearce, 1949.

382 BIBLIOGRAPHY

Roosevelt, Franklin Delano

"Don't Join the Bookburners" (pamphlet). Dartmouth Broadside ed., 1953.

KINGDON, FRANK (ed.). *As FDR Said*. New York: Duell, Sloan and Pearce, 1950.

MYERSON, MAXWELL. *The Wit and Wisdom of Franklin Roosevelt*. Boston: Beacon Press, 1950.

The Public Papers and Addresses of Franklin D. Roosevelt. 13 vols. New York: Random House, 1938.

WHARTON, DON (ed.). *The Roosevelt Omnibus*. New York: Alfred A. Knopf, 1934.

Roosevelt, Theodore

Addresses and Presidential Messages (1902–04). New York: G. P. Putnam's Sons, 1904.

BENSON, GODFREY RATHBONE (Lord Charnwood). *Theodore Roosevelt*. Boston: Little, Brown & Co., 1923.

BISHOP, JOSEPH B. *Theodore Roosevelt and His Time*. 2 vols. New York: Charles Scribner's Sons, 1920.

DOUGLAS, GEORGE WILLIAM. *The Many-Sided Roosevelt*. New York: Dodd, Mead & Co., 1907.

HAGEDORN, HERMANN. *The Americanism of Theodore Roosevelt*. Boston: Houghton Mifflin Co., 1923.

———. *Roosevelt in the Bad Lands*. Boston: Houghton Mifflin Co., 1921.

HART, ALBERT BUSHNELL AND HERBERT RONALD FERLEGER (eds.). *Theodore Roosevelt Cyclopedia*. New York: Roosevelt Memorial Association, 1941.

JOHNSON, WILLIS FLETCHER (ed.). *Addresses and Papers of Theodore Roosevelt*. New York: Unit Book Publishing Co., 1909.

KOHLSAAT, H. H. *From McKinley to Harding*. New York: Charles Scribner's Sons, 1923.

MORISON, ELTING E. (ed.). *Letters of Theodore Roosevelt*. 8 vols. Cambridge, Mass.: Harvard University Press, 1951–54.

Presidential Addresses and State Papers: European Addresses (Homeward Bound ed.). 8 vols. New York: Review of Reviews Co., 1910.

PRINGLE, HENRY F. *Theodore Roosevelt: A Biography*. 1 vol. New York: Harcourt, Brace & Co., 1931.

RIIS, JACOB A. *Theodore Roosevelt, the Citizen*. New York: Macmillan Co., 1918.

ROOSEVELT, THEODORE. *Autobiography*. New York: Charles Scribner's Sons, 1926.

——. *A Charter of Democracy*. Washington, D.C.: Government Printing Office, 1912.

The Works of Theodore Roosevelt (Mem. ed.). 24 vols. New York: Charles Scribner's Sons, 1926.

The Works of Theodore Roosevelt (Natl. ed.). 20 vols. New York: Charles Scribner's Sons, 1926.

Taft, William Howard

Presidential Addresses and State Papers. New York: Doubleday, Page & Co., 1910.

PRINGLE. *Theodore Roosevelt: A Biography*. See Theodore Roosevelt bibliography.

TAFT, WILLIAM HOWARD. *The Dawn of World Peace*. New York: American Association for International Conciliation, 1911.

——. *Present Day Problems*. New York: Dodd, Mead & Co., 1908.

——. *The Presidency: Its Duties, Its Powers, Its Opportunities, Its Limitations*. New York: Charles Scribner's Sons, 1916.

Taylor, Zachary

HAMILTON, HOLMAN. *Zachary Taylor—Soldier of the Republic*. Indianapolis: Bobbs-Merrill Co., 1941.

MONTGOMERY, H. *The Life of Major-General Zachary Taylor*. Auburn, N.Y.: Derby, Miller & Co., 1849.

Truman, Harry S.

DANIELS, JONATHAN. *The Man of Independence*. New York: J. B. Lippincott Company, 1950.

HILLMAN, WILLIAM. *Mr. President*. New York: Straus & Young, 1952.

TRUMAN, HARRY S. *Memoirs*. 2 vols. Garden City, N.Y.: Doubleday & Co., Inc., 1955.

Public Papers of the Presidents of the United States, Harry S. Truman, 1945, 1946. Wash., D.C.: National Archives & Records Service, 1946, 1947.

Tyler, John

CHITWOOD, OLIVER PERRY. *John Tyler: Champion of the South*. New York: D. Appleton–Century Co., 1939.

Register of Debates. Washington, D.C.; Twenty-second Congress, Second Session.

Van Buren, Martin

HOLLAND, WILLIAM M. *The Life and Political Opinion of Martin Van Buren*. Hartford: Belknap & Hamersley, 1836.

LYNCH, DENIS TILDEN. *An Epoch and a Man*. New York: Horace Liveright, 1929.

SHEPARD, EDWARD MOORE. *Martin Van Buren*. Boston: Houghton Mifflin Co., 1916.

Washington, George

FITZPATRICK, JOHN C. (ed.). *The Writings of George Washington*. 39 vols. Washington, D.C.: U.S. George Washington Bicentennial Commission, 1931–44.

FORD, WORTHINGTON CHAUNCEY (ed.). *The Writings of George Washington*. 14 vols. New York: G. P. Putnam's Sons, 1892.

Old South Leaflets, #99.

SCHROEDER, JOHN FREDERICK (ed.). *Maxims of Washington*. Mt. Vernon, Va.: Mount Vernon Ladies Association, 1942.

SPARKS, JARED (ed.). *The Writings of George Washington*. 12 vols. Boston: Little, Brown & Co., 1855.

Wilson, Woodrow

Addresses of President Wilson. Document No. 803. Washington, D.C.: Government Printing Office, 1916.

BAKER, RAY STANNARD. *Woodrow Wilson: Life and Letters*. 8 vols. New York: Doubleday & Co., Inc., 1927.

——, AND WILLIAM E. DODD. *The Public Papers of Woodrow Wilson*. (1875–1924). 6 vols.

——. *Selected Literary and Political Papers and Addresses*. 3 vols. New York: Grosset & Dunlap, 1893, 1925, 1927.

DAVIDSON, JOHN WELLS. *A Crossroads of Freedom*. New Haven: Yale University Press, 1956.

DAY, DONALD. *Woodrow Wilson's Own Story*. Boston: Little, Brown & Co., 1952.

HALE, WILLIAM B. *The New Freedom*. New York: Doubleday, Page & Co., 1913.

HOOVER, HERBERT AND HUGH GIBSON. *The Problems of Lasting Peace*. New York: Doubleday, Doran and Company, 1943.

LATHAM, EARL. *The Philosophy and Policies of Woodrow Wilson*. Chicago: University of Chicago Press, 1958.

LINK, ARTHUR S. *Wilson: The New Freedom*. Princeton, N.J.: Princeton University Press, 1956.

LINTHICUM, RICHARD (ed.). *Wit and Wisdom of Woodrow Wilson*. Garden City, L.I.: Doubleday, Page & Co., 1916.

PADOVER, SAUL K. *Wilson's Ideals*. Washington, D.C.: American Council on Public Affairs, 1942.

President Wilson's Great Speeches and Other History Making Documents. Chicago: Stanton & Van Vliet Co., 1917.

RODGERS, HOWARD J. (ed.). *Congress of Arts and Science*, Boston: Houghton, Mifflin Co., 1906.

SCOTT, JAMES BROWN. *President Wilson's Foreign Policy*. New York: Oxford University Press, 1918.

TOURTELLOT, ARTHUR BERNON (ed.). *Selections for Today*. New York: Duell, Sloan & Pearce, 1945.

WILSON, WOODROW. *Mere Literature and Other Essays*. Boston: Houghton, Mifflin Co., 1896.

——. *The State*. Boston: D. C. Heath & Co., 1918.

——. *In Our First Year of War*. New York: Harper & Bros., 1919.

——. *Guarantee of Peace*. New York: Harper & Bros., 1919.

——. *The Hope of the World*. New York: Harper & Bros., 1920.

——. *Congressional Government, A Study in American Politics*. Boston: Houghton, Mifflin Co., 1925.

——. *Constitutional Government in the United States*. New York: Columbia University Press, 1927.

Index by Authorship

Adams, John
America 4
Americans 1
Anxiety 1
Army 2
Arts, The, 1
Bible 1
Declaration of Independence 1, 2
Defense 2
Democracy 1
Discipline 1, 2
Education 2, 3
Eloquence 1
England 1, 2
Europe 1
Faith 1
Force 2
Freedom 2, 3
God 2, 3, 4
Government 9, 10, 11, 12, 13, 14, 15, 16, 17, 18, 19, 20, 21
Happiness 3, 4
Human Nature 1
Ignorance 1
Independence 1
Inequality 1
Jews 1
Kings 1
Knowledge 2
Laws 2
Liberty 3, 4, 5, 6, 7
Libraries 1
Majorities 1
Money 2
Mothers 1
Navy 1, 2, 3
Neutrality 1
Opinion 1
Peace 4
Penitence 1
People, The, 3, 4, 5
Political Parties 2
Politicians 1

Adams, John (*cont.*)
Politics 1, 2, 3
Popularity 1, 2
Power 3, 4, 5, 6
Presidency, The, 4
Press, The, 1, 2
Principles 1
Public Affairs 1
Public Speaking 1
Religion 2, 3, 4, 5
Republics 2, 3
Revolutions 1
Rights 1
Self-Deception 1
Slavery 3, 4, 5
Universities 2
Vanity 1, 2
Vice-Presidency 1
Virtue 2, 3
Voters 1
War 6
Wealth 1
White House 1
Wisdom 1
Women 2

Adams, John Quincy
America 6
Confederation 1
Congress 3
Constitution 5
Creeds 2
Defense 5
Destiny 1
Fear 1
Foreign Relations 7
Gifts 3
History 7
Honesty 5
Human Nature 2
Liberty 18, 19
Posterity 1
Power 14
Presidency, The, 10
Press, The, 11

Adams, John Quincy (*cont.*)
Prosperity 4
Public Office 5, 6
Religion 18
Right 2
Slander 2
Slavery 11, 12, 13, 14
States' Rights 7
Union 9
Voters 2
War 17, 18
West, The, 1

Arthur, Chester A.
Elections 2
Foreign Relations 17, 18
Government 72
Navy 5
Politics 13
Public Office 14
Russia 2
Trade 1
Treaties 2
Wisdom 3

Buchanan, James
Ballots 1
Constitution 11, 12
Corruption 2
Economy 1
Equality 3
Foreign Relations 15
Friendship 7
God 8
Justice 7
Liberty 24
Money 6
Mothers 3
Presidency, The, 21, 22, 23, 24
Principles 4
Prosperity 6
Public Opinion 3
Republics 14
Slavery 18, 19

Subject-Concept Index

All words in capitals are subjects or concepts on which quotations are given in the text. Those in bold-face capitals are the actual subject headings under which the quotations are given.

410   SUBJECT-CONCEPT INDEX